MONOPOLIES AND MERGERS COMMISSION

# The supply of residential mortgage valuations

A report on the supply in the UK of residential mortgage valuations

**Presented to Parliament by the Secretary of State for Trade and Industry by Command of Her Majesty April 1994**

Cm 2542        LONDON: HMSO        £20.00 net

## Members of the Monopolies and Mergers Commission as at 4 February 1994

Mr G D W Odgers  *(Chairman)*
Mr P H Dean CBE  *(Deputy Chairman)*
Mr D G Goyder[1]  *(Deputy Chairman)*
Mr H H Liesner CB  *(Deputy Chairman)*
Mr A G Armstrong
Mr I S Barter
Professor M E Beesley CBE
Mrs C M Blight[1]
Mr P Brenan
Mr J S Bridgeman
Mr R O Davies[1]
Professor S Eilon
Mr J Evans
Mr A Ferry MBE
Mr N H Finney OBE
Sir Archibald Forster
Sir Ronald Halstead CBE
Ms P A Hodgson
Mr M R Hoffman
Mr D J Jenkins MBE
Mr A L Kingshott
Mr G C S Mather
Mr N F Matthews
Professor J S Metcalfe CBE
Professor A P L Minford
Mr J D Montgomery
Dr D J Morris[1]
Professor J F Pickering
Mr L Priestley
Mr M R Prosser
Dr A Robinson[1]
Mr J K Roe
Dr L M Rouse
Mr D P Thomson
Mrs C Tritton QC
Professor G Whittington

Mr A J Nieduszynski  *(Secretary)*

---

[1]These members formed the group which was responsible for this report under the chairmanship of Mr D G Goyder.

iii

## Note by the Department of Trade and Industry

In accordance with section 83(3) and (3A) of the Fair Trading Act 1973, the Secretary of State has excluded from the copies of the report, as laid before Parliament and as published, certain matters, publication of which appears to the Secretary of State to be against the public interest, or which he considers would not be in the public interest to disclose and which, in his opinion, would seriously and prejudicially affect certain interests. The omission is indicated by a note in the text.

# Contents

# 1 Summary

1.1. On 6 May 1992 we were asked to examine the arrangements for residential mortgage valuations. Our terms of reference (see Appendix 1.1) direct us to investigate and report on the possible existence of a monopoly situation in the supply of residential mortgage lending. We were, however, limited to examining agreements and practices relating to the making or procuring of mortgage valuations and the making of charges, including administration charges, in connection with these valuations.

1.2. There are more than 150 residential mortgage lenders in the UK. Since the 1980s the long-established building societies have been joined as lenders by banks and centralized lenders; building societies themselves have been allowed to widen their activities under the Building Societies Act 1986, for example into estate agency, insurance and pensions, and are able to compete more freely for mortgage business. The structure of the industry is competitive and home buyers who need a mortgage can choose from a wide variety of mortgage packages.

1.3. Prudential responsibilities mean that virtually all lenders require a valuation when lending on residential property. Building societies are required by law to have one in writing, made by a competent valuer, in their possession before making an advance. Such valuations are required not only for the initial purchase of a property but for remortgages and for further advances.

1.4. Valuations traditionally were commissioned by lenders from independent professional valuers, and most building societies operate panels of external valuers approved by them as competent in terms of qualifications, local knowledge and professional indemnity insurance cover. Most banks and centralized lenders also operate panels but appear to have been more flexible than building societies in accepting valuations from non-panel valuers. In recent years, larger building societies have increasingly used valuers employed in-house or in subsidiary firms. The sharp fall in house prices in the last three years has put residential mortgage valuations under particular scrutiny by lenders and brought to light cases of fraud or negligence by valuers. All lenders have reviewed, and in many cases tightened, their procedures for selecting and monitoring valuers, as a result both of their own experiences of fraud and negligence and of pressure from the Building Societies Commission (BSC), the police, and insurers.

1.5. We estimate that the total number of residential mortgage valuations carried out has fallen from a peak of about 2.4 million in 1988 to 1.4 million in 1992. The fall in total numbers of valuations required, the increasing reliance by some lenders on valuers employed in-house or through subsidiaries, and moves generally to limit the size of panels of approved valuers, have all led to a substantial fall in the number of instructions to independent valuers; single practitioners have found it particularly difficult to secure work from lenders. Most of the complaints about lenders' practices which gave rise to this inquiry came from such independent valuers.

1

1.6. We have established the existence of a complex monopoly situation, ie that at least a quarter of all residential mortgage lending is by lenders engaging in one or more of the following practices:

— refusing to accept valuations by any competent valuer;

— requiring a prospective borrower to pay a set fee for the valuation based on a national scale;

— paying external valuers a set fee based on a national scale established by the lender; and

— requiring borrowers to pay fees which do not separately identify the fee for the valuation from any administrative charges levied at the same time.

1.7. Lenders argued that, in order to satisfy their prudential responsibilities to establish that security for the proposed loan was adequate, it was necessary for them to control the selection of valuer and to be satisfied of his competence. They emphasized that the valuation was their property, commissioned by them for their own purposes, and it was for them, not the borrower, to make what arrangements they saw fit to obtain it.

1.8. However, borrowers are required to pay a fee to cover the cost of the valuation and in recent years it has become standard practice for them to see the report. Over the last decade a series of judgments have also established that in many circumstances the valuer owes a duty of care to the borrower. Many borrowers seem to rely on the report as a general guide to the acceptability of the property although some commission their own structural survey or a homebuyers report (which is similar but less detailed). We consider that these features taken together establish a recognizable borrower's interest in the arrangements for carrying out the mortgage valuation.

1.9. We accept that lenders' prudential responsibilities require them to be satisfied on the competence of a valuer, ie his professional training, local knowledge and possession of adequate professional indemnity insurance. In the absence at present of any authority able and willing to certify competence it is not unreasonable for lenders to operate panels and to contain costs by limiting numbers on these panels. We found no evidence that, as at present operated, restriction of panels leads to poorer quality of valuations, that the use of in-house valuers or valuers in subsidiary companies leads to lower standards of service to borrowers, or that their use significantly increased the risk of conflicts of interest arising. We consider that a lender should be free to employ such valuers as he sees fit.

1.10. We looked at the effect of lenders' selection procedures and set fee scales on levels of valuation charges to borrowers. Although it is difficult to disaggregate this sector of lenders' business, the information we obtained suggests that the largest lenders are making modest margins overall on valuations. We are not satisfied that, if lenders' fee scales for borrowers and valuers were abolished or if borrowers were free to negotiate their own charges with lenders or valuers, the general level of fees would fall. Nor do we see any better way of setting charges than the present fee scales linked to property prices.

1.11. We consider therefore that the borrowers' interests generally would not be assisted by reducing the lenders' control of valuation arrangements. We recognize, however, that this situation disadvantages the minority of borrowers who have selected their own surveyor before making their mortgage application. If their chosen valuer is not on the lenders' panel they are likely either to have to abandon their choice or to pay the lender separately for the valuation and thus incur additional expense. We consider that the benefits that lenders' control of valuations provide for depositors, borrowers and the public generally in safeguarding loans and maintaining valuation standards outweigh these disadvantages. But for those borrowers affected the disadvantages are serious. We therefore considered carefully whether some way could be found to introduce changes to lenders' present arrangements which would remove or lessen these disadvantages while retaining lenders' responsibility for control over selection. We considered a number of suggestions but all have themselves major disadvantages and could not in practice be combined with lenders' ultimate responsibility for the valuation. We consider the best guarantee that lenders will take a reasonable approach to borrowers' requests lies in the continuation of active competition between them and the borrower's ability to shop around between lenders. We therefore conclude that lenders' practices in the selection of valuers and the setting of fee scales for borrowers and valuers do not operate and may not be expected to operate against the public interest.

1.12. We bore in mind throughout our consideration the different legal framework for house purchase in Scotland and the different procedures operating there for providing mortgages and mortgage valuations. None of these differences affected our findings, which apply to the whole UK.

1.13. Finally, we examined the practice of many lenders of making administration charges, paid by the borrower at the same time as the valuation fee. The existence and size of these charges is not always made clear to the borrower. We see no grounds for objecting in principle to such charges and consider that in a competitive situation it is for lenders to decide how to recoup their costs. We think, however, that the borrower needs to have information on the nature and size of the charge as an element which may affect his final choice of mortgage package. He is more likely to examine critically the administration charge than a valuation fee passed on by the lender. Not disclosing this information distorts competition and increases the danger that borrowers will not select the best mortgage offer for their needs.

1.14. We conclude therefore that the practice of not disclosing the existence and amount of administration charges operates and may be expected to operate against the public interest. We recommend that where lenders refer to valuation fees in their promotional material, including that made available in response to initial enquiries, and in mortgage application forms, they should be required to specify separately and clearly the valuation fee and any administration charges levied in connection with this valuation fee.

1.15. We also point to difficulties for borrowers arising from the presentation of some of the other information they need and draw attention in particular to shortcomings in the APR (Annual Percentage Rate). We suggest the rules for calculating it should be reviewed.

# 2 Background to the reference

2.1.  This chapter considers earlier investigations by the MMC of relevance, the geographic scope of this reference, the legal and regulatory requirements specific to mortgage valuations and recent initiatives on the housing market. Other aspects of the legal framework under which mortgage lending is undertaken are covered in Chapters 3, 4 and 5 where reference is made to various sections of the Building Societies Act 1986, the Consumer Credit Act 1974, the Court & Legal Services Act 1990, the Financial Services Act 1986 and the Restrictive Trade Practices Act 1976.

2.2.  The MMC have in the past inquired into a number of services provided in connection with the property market. In 1977 they reported on the supply of surveyors' services[1] which included property valuations, property management, structural surveys of buildings, and in 1991 on the supply of structural warranty services in relation to new homes.[2] The report on surveyors' services was one of a series of reports by the MMC issued on professional services in the mid to late 1970s.

2.3.  The 1977 inquiry report on the supply of surveyors' services was limited to looking at the scale fees system. At the time representative bodies for surveyors recommended scales of fees for services that their members might supply. Some scales were determined and issued by professional associations, some were negotiated with representative bodies of clients or public authorities and issued by professional associations, and some were issued by bodies of clients. At that time the scale of fees for building society valuations was negotiated between the two main valuers' associations, the Royal Institution of Chartered Surveyors (RICS) and the Incorporated Society of Valuers and Auctioneers (ISVA), and the Building Societies Association (BSA). Historically this approach had been in use since 1945. A sample survey of surveyors by the MMC in the course of the 1977 inquiry indicated that in the case of building society valuations the agreed scales were widely observed.

2.4.  The MMC commented generally in their 1977 report that scales of fees restricted competition if they influenced large numbers of suppliers of the services to charge prices which were not those determined by free and open competition, and that the public interest required that surveyors' clients should be able to obtain surveyors' services of the quality and quantity they required at prices no higher than necessary to elicit the required supplies. The general conclusion of the MMC was that restrictions on fee competition should be removed. They recommended that the rules of the professional associations should be amended to allow surveyors to quote freely for work and that scales determined by the professional bodies alone should be abolished or subject to determination by an independent committee. Fee scales negotiated with representative bodies of clients or public authorities were exempt from the recommendation, provided that it was made clear that the scales were not binding.

2.5.  Against this background the MMC dealt separately with the recommended scale of fees for building society valuations. They recognized features which at that time supported its retention: it was negotiated and the BSA had the necessary expertise and bargaining strength, so that it appeared to be doubtful whether the individual borrower could do better if he were required to negotiate a fee on his own; the overall arrangements for valuation services enabled surveyors to provide a well-defined service economically; and there were considerable administrative and other advantages for the

---

[1] *Surveyors' Services: a report on the supply of surveyors' services with reference to scale fees,* HC 5, November 1977.

[2] *Structural warranty services in relation to new homes: a report on the existence or possible existence of a monopoly situation in relation to the supply within the United Kingdom of structural warranty services in relation to new homes,* Cm 1439, March 1991.

building societies and their borrowers from the existence of a recommended scale of fees. But the MMC were concerned that the arrangements for determining the scale by agreement between the professional associations and the BSA did not ensure that the interests of the borrower who paid the charge were represented in setting the scale. They therefore concluded that the existence of the scale did not operate against the public interest but that the arrangements for determining it might be expected to do so. They therefore recommended that changes to the scale be subject to the approval of the independent committee they had recommended for oversight of other professional fee scales. The recommendation for an independent committee was not, however, implemented by the Government.

2.6. With no prospect of the proposed arrangements to protect the borrower's interest being implemented, the Office of Fair Trading (OFT) gave notice of prospective action over the building society valuation scales under the Restrictive Trade Practices Act 1976 (RTPA 1976). The OFT was concerned that the centrally negotiated nature of the arrangements was a restriction contrary to the public interest and action under the RTPA 1976 would enable this to be examined. The professional associations therefore gave notice to the BSA of their withdrawal from the arrangement in 1982. Neither the associations nor the BSA have since played a role in the setting of valuation fees which is now done individually by the lenders. The current arrangements for setting valuation fees are considered in detail in Chapter 5.

2.7. In making this current reference in May 1993, the OFT made clear that it had been made in response to complaints from surveyors and borrowers over restrictions in the selection of surveyors to carry out valuations and the cost of those valuations. The Director General of Fair Trading (DGFT) commented that 'I am concerned that lenders have little incentive to keep down the cost of the service, because the cost is passed on. And I am concerned that borrowers have little opportunity to keep down the charges they have to pay because of restrictions on their ability to shop around'.

## The geographic scope of the reference

2.8. The present reference covers the supply of residential mortgage valuations in the whole of the UK, and in the course of carrying out this investigation the MMC noted that procedures for transferring residential property in Scotland are different from those in England, Wales and Northern Ireland.

2.9. In England, Wales and Northern Ireland an offer to purchase a property is almost always made 'subject to contract' and becomes binding upon the parties only when contracts in the agreed form have been exchanged. (The main exception to this general rule is sale by auction when the contract becomes binding upon acceptance of the highest bid.) The period before exchange of contracts provides the opportunity for the prospective borrower to arrange a mortgage and for a valuation report to be prepared to satisfy the lender as to the adequacy of the security being offered for the loan.

2.10. In Scotland the prospective purchaser may note interest in the property with the vendor's solicitor as a first step. Any offer to the vendor must, however, be made by way of a formal letter (almost always from the purchaser's solicitor). This may contain conditions but has the status of a valid offer, the acceptance of which would constitute a binding contract. Once the offer is accepted (again by way of letter, usually from the vendor's solicitor) a binding contract is created. Sometimes the vendor's solicitor may send a qualified acceptance to the purchaser's solicitor containing additional conditions, which has the status of a counter-offer. When this has been accepted by the purchaser's solicitor a binding contract is likewise concluded. The prospective purchaser must therefore be satisfied before the initial written offer is made with the condition and value of the property and that he is able to finance the purchase, with a mortgage if necessary.

2.11. Lenders in Scotland observe the same statutory and prudential requirements as apply elsewhere in the UK and will therefore require an acceptable mortgage valuation report before an offer is made. Time pressures can, however, be great. Unlike the rest of the UK the valuation report is therefore usually commissioned at an early stage and frequently commissioned by intermediaries. The role of intermediaries is discussed in more detail in Chapter 3. Typically in Scotland the intermediary will be the purchaser's solicitor or the agency selling the property (usually in the east of Scotland a solicitor, more often in the west an estate agent). It is, however, usual for such intermediaries to have agreed with the lender beforehand which valuers will be acceptable for the valuation report. And while the intermediary may initiate the report, it is usually completed as a report by the valuer to the lender, often on the lender's own particular form.

2.12. Whilst there was a different conveyancing system in Scotland the MMC noted that valuers were usually the same professionally qualified persons as carried out valuations in England and Wales, that they operated to the same professional guidelines, and that they were subject to the same liabilities in law.

## The legal framework

2.13. Building societies are required by law to satisfy themselves that the security for loans they make secured by a mortgage is adequate. Under section 13(1) of the Building Societies Act 1986 (the 1986 Act), they are required to make an assessment of the adequacy of the security on the basis of a report by a competent person on the value of the property.[1] The 1986 Act does not specify who should commission that valuation, the currency of the valuation, ie how up to date it is, or the identity of the competent person conducting the valuation. In practice, directors of most societies have interpreted this as meaning that the duty is not adequately discharged unless the decision as to the competence of the valuer selected to carry out the valuation, and the instruction of that valuer, is taken by the society and not left to the borrower or intermediary.

2.14. Section 13(2) of the 1986 Act does, however, disqualify certain persons from making a valuation report in certain circumstances. In particular section 13(2)(c) provides that where an advance is to be made following a disposition of the property, any person having a financial interest in the disposition and any director, other officer or employee of his or of an associated employer are disqualified. Most societies, on legal advice, have interpreted this provision as disqualifying a valuer directly employed by them valuing for mortgage purposes a property when the society is exercising its own power of sale on the property in question, normally as part of a repossession procedure, but that valuers employed by the society may value and report on a property where the property is subject to an existing mortgage in favour of the society. The scope of section 13(2) is subject to some difference of interpretation considered in more detail in Chapter 4.

2.15. Building societies are also required by section 45 of the 1986 Act to be prudent in their conduct. The legislation sets out 'criteria for prudent management', one of the criteria being maintenance of arrangements for assessing the adequacy of securities for advances secured on property. The BSC (see paragraphs 2.20 and 2.21) has issued a series of Prudential Notes which give guidance on how these criteria can be met. A recent draft note put out for consultation (published 30 July 1993) stresses that societies can go some considerable way to combat serious fraud by having in place 'robust systems' for the selection of valuers. It notes a number of features which can be helpful—establishing a panel who have been thoroughly vetted, making thorough checks of non-panel valuers nominated by the borrower, and being especially wary of any valuations provided by a borrower. It also acknowledges that some societies may prefer to make greater use of staff valuers. The final note will depend on the results of the consultation exercise.

2.16. The 1986 Act applies only to building societies, not other lenders. Many other lenders also observe prudential arrangements in connection with valuations prior to providing mortgages and the Council of Mortgage Lenders (CML) also disseminates advice to its members on valuation arrangements in its Mortgage Law and Practice Manual and its Mortgage Fraud Manual.

2.17. In carrying out the valuation of the security it was generally considered until the early 1980s that the valuer's liability for negligence only extended as far as the lender to whom he was contractually bound. However, in the case of *Yianni v Edwin Evans & Sons* in 1981,[2] the court established

---

[1] The 1986 Act uses the term 'advances secured on land' and defines it in section 10(1). For simplicity's sake the term 'property' is adopted here.

[2] [1981] 3 W L R 843.

that the valuer, instructed by a lender, may also owe a duty of care to the borrower. *Yianni* was approved in the cases of *Smith v Bush*, and *Harris v Wyre Forest District Council*, decided by the House of Lords in 1989.[1] The key test in these judgments was the extent to which it was foreseeable that the intending mortgagor could be expected to rely on the valuation report. In *Yianni* the court held that the applicant for a loan secured on the property in question was almost certainly a person of modest means who would not be expected to obtain an independent valuation; it was therefore reasonable for him to rely on the valuation as communicated to him in the building society's offer. In *Smith* and *Harris*, the House of Lords held that a valuer instructed to carry out a valuation of a modest house owed a duty of care to the mortgagor to exercise reasonable skill and care in carrying out the valuation if he was aware that the mortgagor was likely to rely on that valuation and not have an independent survey; and that any disclaimer by a valuer of liability to the mortgagor would not be fair and reasonable, within the meaning of the Unfair Contracts Terms Act 1977.

2.18. In his judgment on *Smith v Bush* Lord Griffiths commented that it must be remembered that the decision was in respect of a dwelling house of modest value, in which situation it was widely recognized by surveyors that purchasers do in fact rely on their care and skill. He expressly reserved his position in respect of valuations of quite different property, such as industrial property, large blocks of flats or very expensive houses. In such cases he considered it may well be that the general expectation of the behaviour of the purchaser was quite different. He observed that with very large sums of money at stake prudence would seem to demand that the purchaser obtain his own structural survey, and, in such circumstances, with very much larger sums of money at stake, it may be reasonable for surveyors valuing on behalf of those who are providing the finance either to exclude or limit their liability.[2]

2.19. Judgments in the Scottish Courts[3] have paralleled the decisions of the courts in England and Wales in extending a similar duty of care by the valuer to the borrower.

## The regulatory framework

2.20. Under the 1986 Act the BSC is charged with the supervision of the activities of building societies and has a duty to 'promote the protection by each building society of the investments of its shareholders and depositors' and 'to promote the financial stability of building societies generally'. It does this by ensuring that the societies conduct their business in accordance with the criteria of prudent management in section 45 of the 1986 Act. If a society does not do so, then the BSC is entitled to assume that its investors may be at risk and this can be grounds for the use of the BSC's statutory powers.

2.21. Prudential criteria of particular relevance to valuation practices are the requirement to maintain requisite arrangements for assessing the adequacy of securities for advances secured on land, and that the business is conducted with adequate professional skills.

2.22. The Building Societies Ombudsman Scheme, established under the auspices of the 1986 Act, provides a complaints service in respect of the activities of building societies. Its jurisdiction in respect of societies' provision of valuation services is, however, extremely limited. The ombudsmen are not able to consider any complaint that arose before the completion of a mortgage from any person who did not already hold a mortgage with that society at the time the valuation was carried out and they are further constrained in that they can consider only those complaints involving a valuer who is an employee of the society.

2.23. All banks and building societies also observe the Code of Banking which is aimed at setting standards of behaviour and transparency for them to follow in their banking dealings with personal customers. It is, however, directed at customer care rather than borrower protection.

---

[1] [1989] 2 W L R 790.

[2] [1989] 2 W L R 790 at 811C.

[3] *Martin v Bell Ingram*, 1986 SLT 575, *Robbie v Graham & Sibbald*, 1989 SLT 870.

## Other developments

2.24. As part of its response to the Government's Citizen's Charter initiative the Lord Chancellor's Department commissioned a study into what might be done to speed up and simplify the process of buying and selling a house in England and Wales. Its report, based on research amongst the professionals involved in the process, including solicitors, estate agents, surveyors and mortgage lenders, was published on 13 July 1993 for public comment.

2.25. The report considered the costs and duration of the house-purchase process for the consumer. For a typical transaction involving a £70,000 property, and involving just a straightforward purchase rather than a concurrent sale of property, the most significant cost for the buyer was found to be stamp duty. The basic mortgage valuation, on which most purchasers were said to rely, accounted for around 11 per cent of the buyer's costs. Its production was not seen as an important source of delay in the process. But an adverse report was often a cause for initial offers to purchase to collapse, and valuation reports provided a basis for attempts to renegotiate the purchase price at a later stage, a frequent cause for delay.

2.26. The study therefore considered whether the seller should take on responsibility for a survey which would enable information on the property to be available earlier in the process. This seemed to hold out promise of reducing delays and uncertainty in a significant proportion of transactions. However, the report noted that there would be little hope of sellers providing these voluntarily, that buyers might have difficulty trusting them, and that most lenders would not be prepared to rely on them for the mortgage valuation. The lenders reiterated their strong resistance to sellers providing the valuation in the course of this inquiry.

# 3 The market for residential mortgage lending and valuation services

## Contents

## Introduction

3.1. In this chapter, we consider the market for residential mortgage lending, and the associated market for valuation services, which is the main focus of this inquiry, as directed by our terms of reference. We begin, in paragraphs 3.3 to 3.6, by reviewing briefly the demand for the purchase of residential property as the primary source of demand for mortgage lending, and the associated valuation services. We then, in paragraphs 3.7 to 3.18, examine the main types of mortgage lenders—building societies, high street banks and centralized lenders—as well as intermediaries operating in this market; and the entry into and exit from the market that has occurred in recent years in paragraphs 3.19 to 3.21. The nature and complexity of mortgage products, and the way in which they are priced, are considered in paragraphs 3.22 to 3.25, and 3.26 to 3.36, respectively. Against this background, we assess the nature and effectiveness of competition between mortgage lenders in paragraphs 3.37 to 3.48, and the scale of lending and market shares in paragraphs 3.49 to 3.52. We then move on to evaluate the derived market for valuation services in terms of the nature of such services in paragraphs 3.53 to 3.55 and the size of the market in paragraphs 3.56 to 3.61.

3.2. Within this chapter we also indicate briefly and where appropriate the views of the CML and of lenders, particularly on competition in mortgage lending. Their views are summarized more fully in Chapters 6 and 7 respectively.

## Background: the demand for housing, mortgage and valuation services

3.3. Demand for mortgage finance derives more or less directly from the demand for housing and the purchase of residential property. Home ownership, at more than 65 per cent of households, is relatively high in the UK compared with many other countries (though it is lower in Scotland at around 54 per cent). In part, this reflects the effects of past Government policies on housing, including the legislation affecting the market for rented housing, the 'right to buy' policy, and the subsidies to home ownership available, principally in the form of income tax relief on mortgage interest payments. Although a proportion (around 10 per cent) of house-purchase transactions do not involve taking out a mortgage, the great majority do. Currently, around 30 to 40 per cent of borrower demand, in terms of both the number and value of transactions, comes from those buying a property for the first time. The rest is from existing home owners seeking a loan in order to move to a different property; or to remortgage an existing property, sometimes with a different lender; or to take out a further advance to an existing mortgage, often in order to carry out improvement work to the property. These proportions vary from year to year, and also from one lender to another. Demand from new borrowers in the early 1990s has been less than usual as a proportion of the total, for example, whilst demand for remortgages has been, we were told, somewhat higher than in the 1980s. Leaving aside the breakdown between first-time buyers and others, about 75 to 80 per cent of total mortgage lending at present is for the purposes of purchasing residential property, about 10 to 15 per cent is for remortgaging a property, and the balance is accounted for by borrowers taking out a further advance. Lenders and the CML told us that home owners move, and need as a consequence to refinance their mortgage debt, about every seven to eight years or so, on average, in normal market conditions, though the average duration has been longer (up to ten years or so) during the recent recession.

3.4. Home purchase is usually the largest single capital investment made by consumers—the average price of residential property is currently around £55,000 to £60,000 (see also Appendix 5.2)—and, accordingly, mortgage payments for home owners are a major component of their household budgets. Demand for housing and mortgage finance largely follows the general economic cycle and can be affected by various economic factors, including trends in real incomes and unemployment levels, the level of and expectations about future trends in house prices, and the cost of mortgage finance, particularly the nominal interest rate; it is also influenced by demographic factors.

3.5. During the 1980s, housing demand expanded steadily in the first half of the decade, with the number of house-purchase transactions growing from around 1.25 million to around 1.75 million a year, but then grew rapidly in the years 1986 to 1988, when, at the peak, over 2 million transactions a year took place, according to published data available (see Figure 3.1). House prices were also increasing rapidly in the period 1986 to 1988 (see Figure 3.2), and rose to around five times the level of average earnings, compared with the historical relationship of 3 to 3.5 times earnings. Subsequently, when interest rates were increased sharply and the UK economy, particularly that of the South-East, went into recession, the housing market slumped. The number of transactions fell in each of the years 1989 through to 1992, when the total was reduced to about 1.1 million. Over this period, house prices also declined not only in real terms, but also, for the first time in many years, in nominal terms (see Figure 3.2). During this slump, around 200,000 homes were repossessed by lenders because borrowers had defaulted on their mortgage loans; and mortgage payment arrears rose sharply (see Appendix 3.1). Because of the reduction in house prices, over 1 million home owners now owe more to lenders than the resale value of their properties, ie the so-called 'negative equity' phenomenon. Both housing demand and house prices appear now to have stabilized, and there are some signs of a revival in residential property values, according to recent reports on the state of the market by Halifax Building Society (Halifax) and Nationwide Building Society (Nationwide), published in January 1994. Both house prices and mortgage interest rates are relatively low compared with previous years, but demand has been held back, partly because of the existence of negative equity, and partly because the economy as a whole is still recovering from recession. In the longer term, demand from first-time buyers may be limited by demographic factors, in particular the declining proportion of 25- to 30-year-olds in the population. The trend in the amount of mortgage lending each year has naturally followed that of the number of transactions and the trend in house prices. As shown later, in paragraph 3.49 and Table 3.1, new mortgage lending peaked at £75 billion in 1988, and has fallen since then to around £54 billion in 1992. The CML estimated that it fell slightly further in 1993 to £53.4 billion.

3.6. As explained in more detail later, in paragraphs 3.22 to 3.25, mortgage offers are relatively complex because they usually include a number of different components, one of which is the fee for the mortgage valuation of the property. As explained in paragraph 3.29 and Chapter 5, borrowers are required to pay for such a valuation when first applying for a mortgage and the fee paid often also includes or is coupled with a charge for administration costs. As explained in paragraphs 2.13 and 4.1, building societies are required under the 1986 Act to have such a valuation available when making their assessment of an application for a mortgage advance. Other lenders, such as banks and

FIGURE 3.1

**Numbers of residential property transactions, 1980 to 1992**

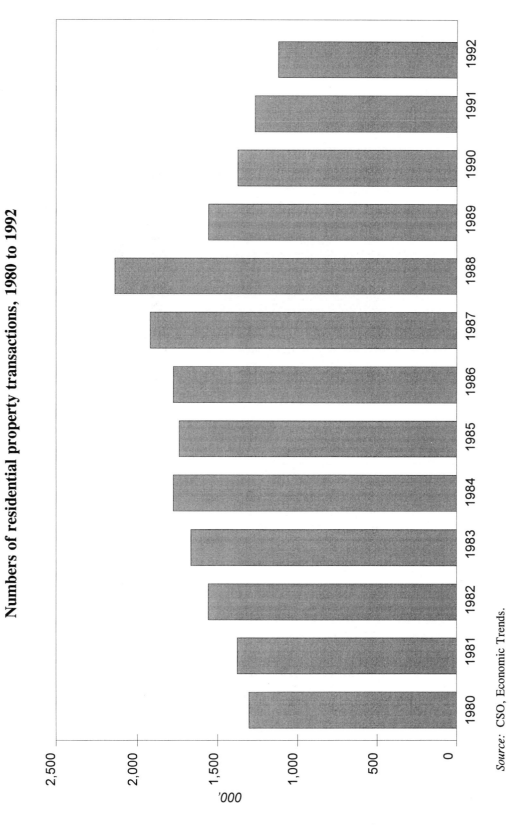

*Source:* CSO, Economic Trends.

FIGURE 3.2

## Annual percentage changes in residential house prices, 1981 to 1992

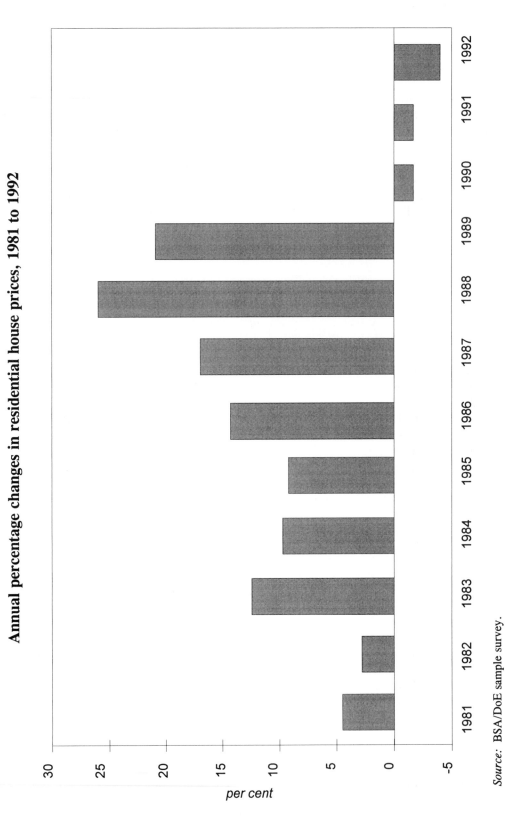

*Source:* BSA/DoE sample survey.

12

centralized lenders, also generally require a valuation for this purpose, though they are not bound by statute or other regulatory controls to do so. Regardless of the source of the mortgage loan, therefore, borrowers do not have a choice over whether a valuation is undertaken. As explained in paragraphs 3.56 to 3.61, the total costs of such valuations and administration charges to borrowers in 1992 were around £160 million and £40 million, respectively.

## Mortgage lenders

3.7. For many years until about 1980, almost all residential mortgage lending was provided by building societies. Since then, most of the high street or commercial banks have entered the market as lenders, as have a number of what are known as centralized lenders (which are mostly owned by banking institutions) and also some insurance companies. Altogether, there are currently more than 150 such individual lenders operating in the UK, most of which are members of the CML. The 15 largest lenders account for over 70 per cent of total mortgage lending (see paragraph 3.50). In the following paragraphs, we provide a brief review of each of these main categories of lender, focusing particularly on building societies, which continue to be the main source of such lending.

### *Building societies*

3.8. A Government Green Paper[1] published in 1984 outlined a number of proposals for changes to the legislation governing building societies, and also provided a summary of both their historical background and their more recent development. Building societies have a long history, beginning in the 18th century. The early 19th century saw the emergence of so-called 'permanent' societies which borrowed money from savers—to whom they paid a rate of interest—and used the funds to provide loans to prospective home owners. The first major piece of legislation affecting building societies was the Building Societies Act 1874. Although it was amended periodically, the basic structure of this legislation remained largely intact for many years. The law was consolidated under the Building Societies Act 1962 (the 1962 Act). At the turn of the century, there were over 2,000 societies, almost all locally based. Since then, the number actively trading has steadily fallen to about 220 in 1981 and to 84 by the end of 1993 (see paragraph 3.19). Although some societies, typically the smaller ones, remain locally based, a number of them now operate either regionally or on a national basis, and the larger societies have become major financial institutions.

3.9. As regards their constitution and main functions, building societies are member-based or 'mutual' institutions. Under the 1962 Act, societies were restricted in the range of financial services that they could offer, their main function being the provision of mortgage lending for house purchase; and the raising of money from members through interest-bearing savings accounts, ie through what is generally known as the retail savings market. The 1986 Act introduced some major changes to the range of financial services that societies could provide and also to their permitted means of financing those services. In particular, societies were legally empowered under the 1986 Act to provide banking, life insurance and pensions services, and to acquire and operate estate agencies. Although conveyancing services were included in the 1986 Act as a permitted service, further (secondary) legislation would have been required to grant societies full legal powers to provide such services: the necessary legislation has not been enacted. The 1986 Act also allowed societies to obtain up to 20 per cent of their total funding from wholesale money markets. This limit on wholesale funds was subsequently raised (in 1987) to 40 per cent, though societies are also generally limited by the BSC (see paragraph 2.20) to having no more than 20 per cent of the value of their loans outstanding in the form of fixed-rate mortgages (see paragraphs 3.22 to 3.25). Societies were also permitted under the 1986 Act to convert to PLC status, with the agreement of their members and confirmation by the BSC. The Deregulation and Contracting Out Bill, presented to Parliament in January 1994, also contains two clauses (13 and 14) amending the 1986 Act which, if enacted, would extend the borrowing and lending powers of societies.

---

[1]*Building Societies: A New Framework*, Cmnd 9316.

3.10. Following the 1986 Act, and particularly in the period 1987 to 1990, many societies greatly expanded their range of activities and the services they provided. Several of the larger societies, including Halifax, Nationwide and Woolwich Building Society (Woolwich), acquired a number of estate agencies which in some instances also had surveying/mortgage valuation departments (see paragraphs 4.29 to 4.31). In recent years, these departments have been consolidated into subsidiary companies. The valuation arm of Halifax, for example, currently trades under the name of Colleys Professional Services (Colleys); Nationwide's valuation subsidiary company trades as Nationwide Surveyors; and Woolwich's trades as Ekins Surveyors. Largely because of the slump in the housing market in the years 1989 to 1992 (see Figure 3.1), the major chains of estate agencies operated by societies have not been profitable over recent years, and some have been sold off. Brief details of the largest estate agencies are included in Appendix 3.2. Some societies have also either acquired or set up life insurance companies; and a number now offer banking services of various types, including the issuing of cheque books and credit cards. The most recent example is Alliance & Leicester Building Society (A&L), which announced in October 1993 that it was planning to offer banking services in the near future.

3.11. Only one society, Abbey National, has converted to PLC status, and it is now authorized under the Banking Act 1987 to provide banking services. Nonetheless, as also explained in paragraph 4.1, like building societies, some 80 per cent of its assets are tied up in mortgages, and, consequently, it told us that it compares itself more with building societies than banks. In accord with this, we treat Abbey National for the purposes of our analysis as a building society, rather than as a high street bank. Abbey National also acquired a chain of estate agencies in the late 1980s, which traded under the name of Cornerstone and which included a surveying/valuing department. However, Cornerstone was sold in August 1993, and Abbey National no longer owns any estate agencies or subsidiary companies providing mortgage valuation services, though it does directly employ a number of in-house valuers (see paragraph 4.30 and Table 4.2).

3.12. As a consequence of these changes, building societies now compete in a range of financial service markets, including insurance, banking, and retail investment products, though these are often related to mortgages on residential property; secured mortgage lending, together with the provision of retail savings accounts, remains their primary business activity. Societies as a whole also continue to be the main source of such lending, accounting (including Abbey National) for over 70 per cent of the gross value of mortgages advanced in 1992 (see paragraph 3.51); and, accordingly, it is still the case that most of the largest lenders are building societies. Many societies are, of course, familiar high street names, the largest six in terms of their shares of the gross value of mortgages advanced in 1992 being Halifax, Abbey National, Nationwide, Woolwich, Leeds Permanent Building Society (Leeds) and Cheltenham & Gloucester Building Society (C&G). These are also six of the seven largest mortgage lenders operating in the UK (see Table 3.1), the other being Barclays Bank plc (Barclays), which is a high street bank.

## High street banks and centralized lenders

3.13. Prior to 1980, high street or commercial banks had virtually no presence in the market for mortgage lending. As explained in the 1984 Green Paper, the abolition of the so-called 'corset controls' (supplementary special deposits schemes) in 1980 led to the entry of banks into this market and for a time (in the early 1980s) they took some 40 per cent of new mortgage business. By 1984 this had fallen back to 25 per cent and their share has fluctuated since then. As new entrants, the banks, particularly the larger ones, had the advantage of existing networks of branches, at which they could promote and sell their mortgage products, though, in practice, much of their business, as with other lenders, also comes from intermediaries. They are also, of course, companies with large financial resources and have considerable expertise in the supply of other financial products. Unlike building societies, however, their access to wholesale money markets for their funds is unrestricted. At times of low interest rates, this may give them a competitive advantage relative to societies, particularly in fixed-rate mortgage products, but this situation may be reversed during periods of high interest rates. Aside from Abbey National (see paragraph 3.11 above), the largest banking lenders in this market include Barclays, National Westminster Bank (NatWest), Midland Bank plc (Midland), Bank of Scotland, TSB Bank plc (TSB) and Lloyds Bank Plc (Lloyds). These and other banks (excluding Abbey National) accounted for around 23 per cent of the gross value of mortgages advanced in 1992 (see paragraph 3.51).

14

3.14. Centralized lenders, as the name implies, are mortgage-lending organizations that do not have branch networks. They attract mortgage business predominantly through intermediaries and borrowers contacting their centralized offices, often in response to media advertising. They are mostly owned by banks or other financial institutions, including insurance companies. Mortgage Services Ltd (Mortgages Services) is owned, for example, by a German bank; The Mortgage Corporation Group Ltd is a subsidiary of Salomon Brothers Inc; and Mortgage Funding Corporation is owned by a consortium of insurance and banking institutions, and managed by Kleinwort Benson Private Bank (Kleinwort Benson), a UK merchant bank. Centralized lenders first entered the market for mortgage lending in the UK in the mid to late 1980s. Notwithstanding the relatively low level of interest rates and the resulting low cost of wholesale funds, some of them have become less active in the market in recent years, particularly during the slump in the housing market. There are currently no central-ized lenders amongst the 15 largest mortgage lenders (see Table 3.1). Centralized lenders along with other miscellaneous financial institutions accounted for around 4 per cent of the gross value of mortgages advanced in 1992 (see paragraph 3.51).

## *Insurance companies and other lenders*

3.15. As mentioned above, some insurance companies participate in this market via ownership interests in centralized lending organizations. Some also offer mortgage-lending products directly to borrowers, but only on a small scale (ie they accounted for only around 1 per cent of the total lending in 1992), albeit that they are large financial organizations in their own right. As with the centralized lenders, insurance companies entered the market during the mid to late 1980s. A number of other miscellaneous financial institutions also provide mortgage loans on a small scale.

## Intermediaries

3.16. Intermediaries have played an increasingly important role in this market during the 1980s and since. They include specialized mortgage brokers, many estate agencies, including those now owned by some of the major building societies, surveying and property management firms, some firms of solicitors (particularly in Scotland), and general insurance brokers. Their function with regard to mortgage lending is to advise on and provide essentially retail services to prospective borrowers, covering a range of different mortgage products available from different lenders. Insurance products have been 'brokered' in much the same way for many years. Individual intermediaries vary in their degree of independence from lenders and the range of mortgage products that they advise on and sell.

3.17. Intermediaries introduce the business of borrowers to lenders, and such 'introduced' business now accounts for around half of all mortgage lending in the UK outside Scotland, where the propor-tion is higher at around three-quarters, reflecting the different procedures for house purchase that apply there (see Chapter 2). In some instances, intermediaries are paid commissions by the lenders for introduced mortgage business, but they mostly cover their costs and earn a commercial profit either from commissions paid (by insurance companies) on insurance products or by making a direct charge to borrowers.

3.18. Intermediaries may also have a role in appointing a surveyor to undertake a valuation for mortgage purposes. This occurs mainly in Scotland, where it is more the rule than the exception, because of the different arrangements for house purchase: intermediaries' selection of valuer is none-theless limited to those valuers on the panel of the lender concerned (see paragraphs 2.8 to 2.12 and 4.19). In the UK apart from Scotland, most lenders will not now permit an intermediary to nominate the valuer.

## Entry into and exit from the mortgage-lending industry

3.19. The legal structure of building societies as mutual institutions is a major constraint on hostile take-overs by other institutions or companies. Nonetheless, they are able to merge with other societies, subject to the approval of their members and authority being given by the BSC. As mentioned earlier, the total number of societies has fallen steadily over many years, mainly as the result of agreed mergers between them. The two largest lenders, Halifax and Abbey National, are both the product of large-scale mergers, Halifax in 1928 and Abbey National in 1944. Since 1980, there have been some 170 such mergers (see Appendix 3.3), mainly between small and medium-sized societies. Amongst the more active in this process of industry consolidation have been Bradford & Bingley Building Society (Bradford & Bingley), C&G, Northern Rock Building Society (Northern Rock), Birmingham Midshires Building Society (Birmingham Midshires), and Britannia Building Society (Britannia). Although many small societies have left the industry as a result, these medium-sized societies into which the small ones have been absorbed now have greater resources and are more secure financially. Neither Halifax nor Abbey National have merged with any others since 1980. Amongst the larger mergers, A&L was formed in 1985; Nationwide and Anglia merged in 1987; and Woolwich and Town & Country merged in 1992. A further 18 or so societies have stopped trading since 1980, whilst only two new societies have been formed in the same period (ie The Ecology Building Society and Kenton & Middlesex Building Society). As a consequence of these many mergers and exits, the number of building societies actively trading has been reduced to 84 by the end of 1993.

3.20. As was also mentioned earlier, most of the main high street banks entered the market in the early 1980s following the easing of regulatory restrictions; and they have continued to offer mortgage products for most of the time since then. However, there have been periods when banks have reduced their mortgage activity. They have been particularly active and successful at times when the general level of interest rates has been relatively low. Similarly, a number of centralized lenders entered the market in the mid to late 1980s at a time when the demand for house purchase and mortgage finance was exceptionally high. Since the slump in the market, some of these lenders have been far less active in seeking new mortgage business and some have withdrawn from the market.

3.21. In summary there have been some major changes in the structure of the industry over the last dozen years. Many smaller societies have left the industry through merger and a number of substantial financial organizations have entered to become significant lenders in their own right. At the same time, those building societies remaining in the market have been able, following the 1986 Act, to expand and diversify the range of financial products they provide. Entry has taken place mainly as a result of the removal of regulatory barriers in 1980, though the boom in demand in the mid to late 1980s was also a major factor in attracting new entrants. There are clearly costs to market entry, particularly the potential sunk costs of establishing the necessary computer systems as well as marketing and advertising costs, but these have not proved to be an effective barrier, at least for the large financial institutions. As regards branch networks, the banks already had such networks in place well before entry into this market, whilst centralized lenders have demonstrated that a physical presence in the high street is not a necessary condition for successful entry. In part, this reflects the greater importance of intermediaries in this market during the 1980s.

## Mortgages and associated products

3.22. Mortgages are long-term loans to cover the cost of buying or developing residential properties, typically over a 25-year period, though they may, exceptionally, be arranged for shorter periods, eg 5, 10 or 20 years. Mortgage products are relatively complex and are of various different types. Traditionally in the UK, the main types of mortgage have been loans at variable rates, arranged either on a repayment basis, where monthly payments cover both interest and capital, or on an endowment basis, whereby interest only is paid monthly and a life insurance policy is used as the means of paying off the capital element of the loan at the end of the mortgage period. Up until the early 1980s, repayment mortgages were the more popular in the UK and accounted for around three-quarters of all mortgage lending, the balance being mainly endowment products. Since then, however, this position has been reversed, with endowment mortgages now accounting for around 60 per cent of the market. Part of this shift has been associated with the introduction, and increased popularity, of fixed-rate mortgages, which generally, though not always, are of an endowment type. The banks and centralized lenders in particular, but increasingly the building societies also, have tended to promote fixed-rate mortgage products, especially at times when the general level of interest rates is relatively low. In addition to these, various hybrid mortgage types have been introduced in recent years, including capped or collared mortgages, mortgages linked to pension plans and other investment products, and mortgages denominated in foreign currencies. We briefly review below the two main types of mortgage, and the three main types of interest repayment arrangements.

*Types of mortgage:*

(a) *Repayment:* Monthly payments cover both interest on the loan and repayment of the capital element. The interest component of the monthly payment declines steadily during the period of the loan as the capital is paid off. Life insurance, in the form of mortgage protection policies, is often linked as part of a package. Lenders (or intermediaries, as appropriate) may receive commission on the sale of such policies. Interest rates may be variable or fixed (see below).

(b) *Endowment:* Monthly payments cover only the interest on the loan, which is payable on the full amount of the capital advanced for the full duration of the loan. A life insurance policy is taken out, with payments by the borrower normally also made monthly, to pay off the capital element at the end of the loan period. Lenders (or intermediaries, as appropriate) may receive commission on the sale of such policies. Early redemption or termination of the life insurance component may result in the loss of benefits to the borrower. Interest rates may be variable or fixed (see below).

*Interest arrangements:*

(a) *Fixed-rate:* Some repayment products are available at a fixed rate of interest, but fixed-rate products are more usually of an endowment type. With these products, the nominal interest rate is fixed at the beginning of the loan for a specified period of typically two, three or five years, after which it often reverts to the variable rate prevailing at that time. Monthly payments are generally more certain than for variable rate products during the fixed-rate period. Redemption or termination of the mortgage during the fixed-rate period usually incurs a penalty payment equivalent to between three and six months' interest.

(b) *Variable rate:* Both repayment and endowment products are available at a variable rate of interest. Under this type of arrangement, the lender may change, or vary, the rate of interest actually charged to the borrower at any time during the full period of the loan. Interest rate changes apply to all existing borrowers with the lender concerned. Monthly payments are adjusted accordingly, though they can often be at a fixed amount for a period of 12 months.

(c) *Capped/collared:* These are variants of fixed-rate mortgages whereby the specified interest rate is variable but, for a fixed period (two, three or five years, for example), it is subject to either a maximum (ie it is 'capped'); or a minimum rate (ie it is 'collared'); or in some instances both.

3.23. In addition to the elements reviewed above, mortgage products often involve other linked services and costs. Where, for example, the loan amounts to 75 per cent or more of the valuation of the property, the lender needs to take out mortgage indemnity insurance, which is paid for by the borrower; and which covers the lender for the excess in the event of loan default or repossession occurring and the full amount of the loan not being repaid from the proceeds of the sale of the property concerned. Similarly, the borrower is sometimes required to take out buildings insurance as a requirement of the mortgage loan. Other costs to borrowers include the legal costs incurred by the lender in relation to the mortgage and also the cost of valuation services. These and other cost elements are considered further in paragraphs 3.26 to 3.36.

3.24. The linking to the mortgage offer of associated financial products offered by a lender, for example insurance products, pensions and the like, is subject to certain regulatory controls. Section 35 of the 1986 Act prohibited the formal linking of these other products to that of a mortgage loan, but this section of the Act has not been brought into operation. Instead, a Code of Conduct was agreed in 1987 between the BSA and the BSC under which building society lenders were permitted to advertise and provide linked packages of products, but subject to the condition that each element of the package was made available and priced separately. Hence, by way of example, a building society lender is currently allowed to offer, say, a fixed-rate mortgage product where the borrower is required to take out a buildings insurance product through that lender, but only if that type of mortgage and that insurance are available separately and priced as separate products. Subject to that condition, the lender is free to set prices as it wishes.

3.25. Additionally, provisions concerning the tying in of other products with mortgages are contained in sections 104 to 107 of the Courts & Legal Services Act 1990 (CLSA 1990)). These provisions have not been brought into operation, however, and are now being further considered under the Department of Trade and Industry's Deregulation Initiative. The DGFT, however, has recently raised the question of whether and how far these provisions should now be implemented, either under the CLSA 1990 or by means of regulations under the Consumer Credit Act 1974 (CCA 1974), designed to achieve the same level of disclosure. This reflects his concerns about possible bias in the information given by lenders to borrowers about ancillary services tied to mortgages.

## Mortgage pricing

3.26. As explained above, most mortgages incorporate a number of different components, the costs or prices of which are typically shown separately in lenders' marketing literature (in illustrative form), in any written quotations to prospective borrowers which are provided on request, and in lenders' formal offer documents. In practice, most borrowers rarely request a written quotation prior to making an application for a loan. They rely in most cases, therefore, on the illustrative figures given in lenders' literature, advice that may be given by lenders or intermediaries in interviews or consultations (including, in some cases, lenders' illustrative quotations) and lenders' formal offer documents. To show the basic pricing structure, we set out below an example for a loan of a typical size (see also Appendix 5.2, which gives details of the distribution of loans made in 1992 for different house price bands) of the main elements that are usually specified by lenders, together with rounded values of typical costs in order to show the orders of magnitude involved and how the different elements compare one with another. The example given is based on a composite of endowment mortgage products, on variable terms, on offer from the largest lenders in August 1993 (when we collected the information on prices and costs).

*A numerical example of mortgage pricing*

**Mortgage product:** A 25-year endowment mortgage (on variable terms) for £40,000 on a property valued at £43,000 (ie a loan:value ratio of 93 per cent), with the nominal interest rate quoted being 7.99 per cent (August 1993).

**Amounts payable:**
1. *Monthly payments* (300 under a 25-year loan):
   *(a)* interest payments (after tax relief) . . . . . . . . . . . . . . . . . . . . . . . . . . . . . £215
   *(b)* life insurance premiums . . . . . . . . . . . . . . . . . . . . . . . . . . . . . . . . . . . . . £50

2. *Once-only charges:* (in order of payment)
       A. Before completion:
           i. Fee for property valuation . . . . . . . . . . . . . . . . . . . . . . . . . . . . . £100
           ii. Administration charge . . . . . . . . . . . . . . . . . . . . . . . . . . . . . . . £35
       B. At completion:
           iii. Lender's legal fees . . . . . . . . . . . . . . . . . . . . . . . . . . . . . . . . . £120
           iv. Mortgage indemnity insurance fee . . . . . . . . . . . . . . . . . . . . . £580
       C. After completion
           v. Accrued interest . . . . . . . . . . . . . . . . . . . . . . . . . . . . . . . . . . . £120
           vi. Cost of mortgage redemption . . . . . . . . . . . . . . . . . . . . . . . . . £50
       D. Total once-only charges (A+B+C) . . . . . . . . . . . . . . . . . . . . . . . . £1,045

**Overall cost:**
    1. Total outlay (interest + all once-only charges, after tax relief) . . . . . . . . . . £80,000
    2. Total amount payable (before tax relief) . . . . . . . . . . . . . . . . . . . . . . . . £120,000
    3. APR: 8.4 per cent

The numerical values shown are rounded and approximate rather than exact; and lenders' literature does not normally use this particular format. The various cost elements included are explained further in paragraphs 3.27 to 3.36.

3.27. For any given set of circumstances, of course, the amounts charged or payable vary to a greater or lesser extent between different lenders. The variation between lenders tends to be larger for the elements of cost relating to insurance (ie mortgage indemnity, life insurance, and also building and contents insurance, if included) than the cost of accrued interest, the lender's legal fees and redemption fees, which generally differ as between different lenders by relatively small amounts. Variations in valuation fees and administration charges, and trends in these charges in recent years, are considered in detail in Chapter 5.

3.28. The costs to borrowers, both in total and for the individual components, also vary between different mortgage products; they vary according to the individual circumstances of the property and the borrower; and there may also be 'special offers' (to first-time buyers, for example) available from different lenders (see paragraphs 3.43 and 5.27 to 5.29). In choosing a particular mortgage, borrowers need, therefore, to consider both which product is most suitable for them and which lender to use. In seeking the lowest price or best offer available, borrowers need to compare:

(a) the initial costs (or 'up-front' payments), including valuation and administration charges;

(b) other 'once-only' charges, whether paid in advance or deducted from, or added to, the amount of the mortgage loan; and

(c) the total monthly charges involved, which are payable over the full period of the mortgage loan.

These cost elements will reflect:

(i) the total outlay, net of tax relief;

(ii) the value of any 'special offers'; and

(iii) the interest charge made for credit, which is by far the largest individual element of the total costs of a mortgage, as spread over the duration of the loan.

3.29. Valuation fees and any associated administration charge (and arrangement fees, in the case of fixed-rate products) are the first charges faced by borrowers and are payable as once-only charges at the time the borrower makes an application for a mortgage loan. Once paid, they are rarely refundable. Valuation and administration charges, which are usually paid together as a single, overall sum, are considered further in Chapter 5. The figures used in the example in paragraph 3.26 are the average charges of the seven largest lenders in 1993. Arrangement fees for fixed-rate products are a form of administration charge which covers the costs to lenders of obtaining the necessary funds from the wholesale funds market, which involves a financial commitment on their part. Such charges are typically around £200 to £250.

3.30. As shown in the example, legal fees incurred by the lender are also a once-only charge which is payable by the borrower, but in this case on completion of the mortgage (ie at the point at which the borrower formally takes up the lender's offer of a loan). They are usually coupled with the borrower's own legal expenses, because the same solicitor is generally used by both parties. Likewise, the mortgage indemnity fee (see paragraph 3.23), if charged, is a once-only charge paid on completion of the mortgage. Usually, it may be paid by the borrower either as an up-front payment or as part of the monthly payments, if the amount of the fee has been included as part of the total amount borrowed. Its purpose is to provide insurance cover to the lender for part of any losses incurred in the event of the borrower defaulting on repayments, and the lender not subsequently being able to recover the full value of the loan through resale of the property, following repossession by the lender. Lenders told us that around 20 to 30 per cent of borrowers are required to pay such a fee and that, when charged, it is a significant element of the costs to borrowers. It may range from £200 to £1,000, the average being about £500, depending on the total size of the loan and the loan:value ratio. Although the fee provides indemnity cover for the first ten years of the loan, if the mortgage is redeemed during that period borrowers are usually not able to reclaim any of the fee paid. Refunds are at the discretion of the insurer rather than of the lender concerned.

3.31. Accrued interest is the cost of interest on the loan arising in the period between receipt of the loan by the borrower and the first interest payment. It is usually payable after completion, as part of the first monthly payment. Although it does not usually vary significantly between lenders, it can vary significantly (ie between near zero and £200, for a typical loan of around £40,000) depending on the actual time period between receipt of the loan by the borrower and the first scheduled monthly payment. Both interest charges and life insurance premiums are each normally paid for on a monthly basis. For repayment mortgages, monthly payments include both interest and capital repayments, and may also include a mortgage protection policy fee, which provides insurance cover to the borrower in the event of his death. Redemption fees, on the other hand, are payable at the end of the mortgage term, or whenever the loan is terminated, to cover the lender's administration costs involved with redeeming the mortgage loan.

3.32. Prior to completion of the mortgage, therefore, valuation and any associated administration fees (and arrangement fees in the case of fixed-rate products) are the main up-front charges arising from the mortgage loan. In the example given above, the valuation and administration charge taken together account for about 16 per cent of all mortgage-related charges paid by the borrower prior to the first monthly payment following completion. If, on the other hand, up-front payment of a mortgage indemnity fee were not required (ie because the loan was less than 75 per cent of the amount of the valuation of the property, or the fee had been included in the amount borrowed), this figure would be just over 50 per cent. As a proportion of the total costs (after tax relief) over the full period of the loan, however, they would amount to less than 0.5 per cent if a mortgage indemnity fee were paid, and less than 0.25 per cent if it were not.

3.33. As regards the calculation of charges for credit, the nominal interest rate (which was 7.99 per cent in August 1993, for each of the seven largest lenders—see also paragraph 3.43) applies only to the interest paid on the loan and, therefore, excludes the cost of any once-only charges, such as valuation and administration charges, as well as the cost of any life and other insurance premia. By contrast, the APR is, in principle, a superior measure of the total cost of credit, because it includes a number of such once-only payments. It does not, however, include all mortgage-related costs and it has a number of other weaknesses which limit its usefulness when applied to mortgage products, as explained in the next two paragraphs. It was because of the general complexity of credit charge arrangements that the Government introduced, in 1980 (in SI 1980/51, under the terms of the CCA 1974), regulations for the calculation of the APR, with the intention that it would enable borrowers to compare more readily, and on a standardized basis, the cost of credit charged by different lenders. All lending and loans, including mortgages, above £15,000 are beyond the ambit of the CCA 1974 and are technically, therefore, unregulated. However, price quotations and advertising which includes prices relating to loans, including mortgages, of any amount fall within the ambit of, and are, therefore, subject to, the Advertising and Quotation Regulations 1989 (contained in SI 1989/1125/6), under which all such advertising is required to include the APR calculated on the basis set out in the 1980 regulations (ie SI 1980/51).

3.34. Under these regulations, the APR quoted on mortgage products includes most of the once-only charges made, including those for valuation and administration, arrangement fees, accrued interest charges, legal charges, and any mortgage indemnity fee, if charged. Nonetheless, as presently calculated, it is subject to a number of defects. It does not, for example, include some of the important costs arising from a mortgage product, such as the monthly premiums for life insurance attached to an endowment mortgage, any mortgage protection policy fees attached to a repayment mortgage, or the potential costs of cancelling a fixed-rate product during the period over which the interest rate is fixed. The way in which interest charges are calculated for the purposes of the APR may also give results which are potentially misleading to borrowers. On mortgage products at variable rates, the APR calculation assumes that the nominal interest rate at the time the mortgage is taken out applies throughout the full term of the mortgage, which is usually 25 years. In practice, of course, the nominal interest rate may change over time, which means that, other things being equal, the cost of credit actually paid may well be different from that quoted. Moreover, following the decisions in June 1993 in two cases in the Divisional Court (involving Abbey National and NatWest), the same assumption is used for fixed-rate products, even though in practice the nominal interest rate reverts to the then current variable rate at the end of the period during which the rate is fixed. As lenders told us, this means that APRs quoted on fixed-rate products give a misleading low indication to borrowers of the real cost of credit. To take an extreme example, a mortgage product which offered a nil rate of interest over the first six months only could legally be advertised as offering an APR of near zero, whatever the actual rate of interest charged over the remaining 24 years and six months. As a further consequence, APRs do not provide borrowers with a meaningful basis for comparing the costs of fixed-rate products with those of mortgage products with a variable interest rate.

3.35. A further weakness of the APR is that it is relatively insensitive to changes in the level of up-front costs, such as valuation charges. This is partly because it is calculated over the full term of the mortgage. In practice, as explained earlier, borrowers replace or refinance their mortgages every seven or eight years, on average. Were the APR to be calculated over this shorter period, up-front charges would have a greater weight in the calculation. As a result, the APR would be higher than normally quoted, and, other things being equal, differences between lenders in the size of up-front and other once-only charges made would tend to be more fully transparent. An additional reason for the insensitivity of the APR, as presently calculated, to up-front charges is that it is calculated and shown in lenders' advertising literature as a 'truncated rate' (or non-rounded rate), rather than a 'rounded rate', which is also normally specified to only one decimal place. As a consequence, two calculated APR rates of, say, 13.09 and 13.00 per cent would both normally be quoted as 13.0 per cent. This reduces the APR's sensitivity to differences between lenders in up-front charges and also, therefore, to any increases in charges made by an individual lender. Lenders provided calculations to us which showed, for example, that for the nominal interest rate then prevailing, an increase in the valuation charge from £100 to £175 would increase the APR by about 0.02 percentage points and would not normally result, therefore, in any change to the APR quoted to only one decimal place.

3.36. As many lenders point out in their mortgage marketing literature, in addition to these up-front charges and the cost of mortgage credit, other costs to, and payments by, borrowers will also, of course, arise from other aspects of the house-purchase process. Such costs may include those incurred when looking for an appropriate property to purchase, estate agency fees (where a property is being sold), the purchaser's conveyancing and other legal costs, stamp duty, removal expenses, and the costs of any redecoration or refurnishing of the property being purchased.

## Competition in mortgage lending

3.37. For many years prior to 1980, there was virtually no price competition between mortgage lenders. Building societies were effectively the only source of mortgage finance for most borrowers, and as explained in the 1984 Green Paper, both mortgage interest and saving accounts rates were 'cartelized', ie they were fixed by agreement between societies at a given rate, such agreements having been specifically exempted (under SI 1976/98) from the requirements of the RTPA 1976. In addition, valuation charges to borrowers and the fees paid to valuers were effectively fixed by agreement between the societies and the RICS. These agreements were not exempt from the requirements of the RTPA 1976. Competition between building societies was, as a consequence, restricted to non-price-competitive factors such as service quality, the availability of funds and local accessibility, which resulted, according to the Green Paper, in a proliferation of building society branches in the high street and there was no effective spur to improve cost efficiency.

3.38. These cartel arrangements were dismantled in the early 1980s and building societies began to compete more effectively both with each other and also with other lenders, principally the high street banks, that had entered the market at that time. The agreements relating to valuation charges and fees to valuers were abandoned in 1982 (see paragraph 2.6). The agreements between building societies concerning interest rates were abandoned around the same time, though their exemption from the RTPA 1976 was not withdrawn until 1986 (under SI 1986/2204). During the mid to late 1980s price competition was further strengthened by the entry of the centralized lenders (see paragraph 3.14). Since then, they have either withdrawn or greatly reduced their new lending, though the banks appear recently to be showing renewed interest in expanding their market share. Lenders in this new environment are able to exercise a degree of individual discretion with regard to the timing and scale of changes in nominal interest rates, but competition in general is greater now than it was a decade ago.

3.39. The largest lenders told us that competition in this market was now intense and that borrowers had a wide choice of lender. There was also a far greater choice of individual mortgage products than ever before, with several hundred available in the form of mortgages at both fixed and variable interest rates, as well as various hybrid products. Entry barriers were low, they told us, as evidenced by the successful entry and subsequent expansion of the high street banks and centralized lenders. Other changes in the market in recent years had also led to greater competition between all lenders and increased the risks that lenders faced. The slump in housing demand, for example, had itself required lenders to compete more vigorously to maintain their share of a smaller market and there was now a surplus of mortgage funds available (in contrast to the mortgage rationing of previous years). Prices and charges by lenders were made fully transparent and the greater importance of inter-mediaries in the market had increased the likelihood that lenders would lose market share unless they offered price-competitive products. Moreover, they stated, borrowers had become generally better informed and discerning than hitherto. As a result, lenders needed to promote their products more actively and to ensure that they were offering good value for money, in order to attract business. A particular feature of the market in the past year was that borrowers had been searching around the market, and switching between lenders if necessary, in order to refinance their mortgage debts at the best rates available. The trend in house prices was also more uncertain now than previously, so that lending and borrowing on the security of property was no longer a one-way bet. Both the largest lenders and the CML told us that, as a consequence of these developments, the commercial risks facing mortgage lenders had greatly increased, as had the risks to lenders of fraud and negligence (see paragraphs 4.58 to 4.74).

3.40. Although there are, according to the information we have collected, more than 150 individual lenders in this market, the seven largest account for around half of all new lending, and the 15 largest account for nearly three-quarters. The average market share of those lenders outside the largest 15 was less than a quarter of 1 per cent, compared with the 15 per cent share in 1992 of Halifax and the 10 per cent share of Abbey National, these being the two largest lenders (see paragraph 3.50). Additionally, whilst most of the 15 largest lenders operate throughout the UK, many of the smaller lenders trade only in particular regions, and some only in local areas. The choice of lender for most borrowers, therefore, is in practice far less than the total number of lenders operating, though in any given locality the choice for borrowers is still considerable. Moreover, those borrowers who use the services of intermediaries may have a still wider range of choice.

3.41. However, because of the complexity and multi-component nature of mortgage packages and the associated credit terms, making clear and unambiguous price comparisons between different products and lenders is far from easy for borrowers. Whilst the APR was intended as a simple and comprehensive means of comparing the overall cost of credit, in practice it suffers from a number of serious weaknesses, as explained in paragraphs 3.34 and 3.35, one of which is that it is insensitive to variations between lenders in the level of once-only charges, such as valuation and administration charges. Because of the requirements of the advertising regulations, lenders give prominence in their advertisements to the APR applying to their products, as evidenced by their media advertising, their marketing literature and the advertisements in the windows of their high street branches. Lenders told us, however, that borrowers do not attach great importance to APRs on their own, and pay more attention to the total monthly outlays involved, the amount of up-front charges and the basic or nominal rate of interest payable.

3.42. On other aspects of price transparency, lenders' mortgage marketing literature usually includes a large amount of information on prices and charges relating to mortgage loans. In many cases, however, particularly in the newspaper and branch-window advertisements we have seen, prominence is given to the nominal interest rate and the APR. Much of the detail on, for example, valuation charges, mortgage indemnity fees, and redemption fees under fixed-rate products are consigned to footnotes which are often written in small print. Similarly, not all of the lenders' brochures contain all the relevant information on charges. Sometimes, for example, separate brochures are available giving details of valuation charges, and sometimes details are provided in explanatory notes included at the end of marketing brochures, again often written in small print. There is also the question of whether the information required by borrowers is always readily available to them when making initial enquiries at lenders' branches. Lenders' commissions on insurance products are currently not disclosed. Moreover, the amount charged to cover administration charges is not always made clear by all lenders (see paragraphs 5.11 and 5.12). More generally, mortgage lending as such is not subject to the Financial Services Act 1986 (FSA 1986), so that lenders are not legally required to give 'best advice' to consumers, with regard to mortgage products. Both the OFT and consumer organizations (eg the Consumers' Association) have publicly expressed concerns about the need for greater price transparency and consumer protection in this market.

3.43. With regard to price competition, the basic or nominal interest rate charged by the main lenders on their variable terms products is often identical. In August 1993, for example, when we collected information on prices and costs, and lenders' advertising literature, it was 7.99 per cent for all the largest lenders. These rates have subsequently been reduced, but different lenders' rates are still either the same or at a similar level. An element of price competition that appears to have become evident over the past year or so is that of 'special offers' by lenders, especially to first-time buyers, in part no doubt reflecting the general reduction in the number of applications for mortgages and the increased difficulty of attracting such borrowers. These special offers often include reduced nominal interest rates for a limited period (eg for 6 or 12 months), and in some cases 'free' mortgage valuations or a contribution towards their cost (see paragraphs 5.27 to 5.29), or the waiving of the arrangement fee for fixed-rate products. To an extent, such offers and special promotions appear to reflect increased price competition in the market, and they may provide genuine savings to those categories of buyers that qualify. These offers rarely amount to 'across-the-board' discounting, however, and therefore not all borrowers are able to benefit. Often, for example, such offers are limited to first-time buyers. Moreover, many special offers of which we have seen details require the borrower to take other associated products supplied by the lender, particularly life insurance as part of an endowment product, or a mortgage protection policy for a repayment mortgage. Where such linked products cost more than comparable products available elsewhere, the net savings to the borrower may, in practice, be less than would appear to be the case at first sight.

3.44. Other forms of competition between lenders continues to be an important feature of this market. As mentioned previously, a number of the major building societies invested heavily in the late 1980s in chains of estate agencies, thereby greatly expanding their presence in the high street. To the extent that these estate agencies acted as intermediaries and brokers for mortgage services, societies effectively expanded their retail network and their potential for attracting mortgage business. In the event, however, and perhaps largely due to the exceptional depth of the slump in demand, these estate agency acquisitions do not generally appear to have been commercially successful, and some have now been sold off.

3.45. Media advertising has also now become a more significant element of competition between lenders in this market, a trend which is likely to have operated to the advantage of the larger lenders. One large lender provided data to us (based on MEAL[1] data) showing that mortgage advertising expenditure by building societies alone (ie excluding the banks and centralized lenders) had increased from £6 million in 1987 to £37 million in 1990, and it had then trebled to £111 million in 1991.

3.46. As mentioned earlier, although mortgages are loans typically made for a period of 25 years, borrowers on average tend to move house about every seven or eight years, at which time, therefore, they have to pay off their existing mortgage and take a fresh advance on their new property. Such borrowers, who account for around half the market, may often find it more convenient to stay with their existing lender unless the service provided by that lender has proved unsatisfactory. Any such 'borrower inertia' may be reinforced by the existence of savings accounts with lenders. Nonetheless, lenders told us that borrowers, whether moving house or simply refinancing their existing mortgage debt, have increasingly tended in recent years to 'shop around' amongst different lenders, in order to seek out the best priced mortgage product. As indicated earlier (see paragraph 3.3), some 10 to 15 per cent of current new lending is to borrowers switching lenders in the process of refinancing their mortgages.

3.47. With regard to the nature and degree of risks involved, the value of mortgage lending is secured against the value of property, ie payment default by borrowers can result in repossession of the property by the lender. The security of mortgage lending is high, therefore, in comparison with other forms of lending, such as unsecured lending, hence the lower interest rate on mortgage loans. The risks associated with mortgage lending have, however, increased. Reduced activity in the housing market and downward pressure on house prices in recent years have resulted in more than 1 million home owners owing more to lenders than the resale value of their properties. Stable or falling prices mean that higher-risk loans (of up to 100 per cent) are less likely to be rescued by the effects of house price inflation than was the case in the early to mid-1980s. Repossessions and arrears increased sharply in the early 1990s, though they fell in 1993 (to under 60,000), and new arrears cases are slowing down, in part reflecting lower interest rates. As a result, problems from arrears are becoming more manageable.

---

[1]Media Expenditure Analysis Limited.

3.48. Moreover, as a matter of lending policy, lenders typically require borrowers to take out mortgage indemnity insurance, where the loan is for 75 per cent or more of the valuation of the property. This effectively reduces further the risk faced by mortgage lenders, with the costs falling primarily on borrowers. The risks of fraud and negligence by valuers occurring are relatively small, but even an individual case can result in significant costs to lenders: these risks and the incidence of fraud and negligence are considered further in paragraphs 4.58 to 4.74. With regard to competitive risks, the potential loss of business for individual lenders due to actions by competitors have probably increased somewhat in recent years, as competition in general between lenders has become more active. Nevertheless, despite the severity of the recent recession, the market currently appears to be poised to resume its long-term growth trend. Building societies are, moreover, subject to prudential controls by the BSC, which limits their exposure to certain types of risk. Lastly, we note that lenders' overall profits on lending on residential property and associated services have remained healthy in recent years, notwithstanding the exceptional severity of the recession.

## Mortgage lending and market shares

3.49. We now turn to our assessment of, first, the size of the market for mortgage lending and the market shares of different lenders (paragraphs 3.49 to 3.52); and secondly, of the market for valuation services provided in connection with mortgage lending (paragraphs 3.53 to 3.61). In Tables 3.1 to 3.3 we set out, for three different measures of mortgage lending, the total value and volume of lending in the years 1988 to 1992, and the market shares of the 15 largest lenders. In Table 3.1 we give data on the total gross value of all new mortgages advanced, which includes the total value of all mortgage loans granted to first-time buyers of residential properties, to borrowers moving house and taking out a new mortgage, to those remortgaging their property with either the same or a different lender, and to existing borrowers taking out a further advance. It may also include mortgage indemnity fees where these have been included in the total amount of the loan. We regard this as the measure, for which data are available, which most closely reflects our terms of reference (see Appendix 1.1). As shown in the table, the total of such lending in 1988—the peak level of demand—was some £75 billion. In the following two years, it was some 6 to 8 per cent lower at about £70 billion, but lending then declined further, in 1991, to around £65 billion, which was 13 per cent below the 1988 peak. The following year saw a further, and even steeper, reduction to £54 billion, nearly 28 per cent below the 1988 level. The CML estimated that gross new mortgage lending was some £53.4 billion in 1993.

TABLE 3.1  **Lenders' market shares based on the gross value of mortgages advanced**

|  |  |  |  |  | per cent |
| --- | --- | --- | --- | --- | --- |
| Lender | 1988 | 1989 | 1990 | 1991 | 1992 |
| Halifax | 14.2 | 14.0 | 13.6 | 13.1 | 15.2 |
| Abbey National | 10.0 | 10.5 | 11.0 | 10.0 | 10.3 |
| Nationwide | 6.7 | 7.3 | 8.0 | 8.4 | 6.6 |
| Barclays | 5.0 | 2.2 | 2.5 | 4.1 | 6.2 |
| Woolwich | 4.7 | 3.8 | 5.1 | 4.7 | 4.7 |
| Leeds | 3.9 | 4.9 | 3.1 | 4.3 | 4.5 |
| C&G | 2.0 | 2.7 | 4.1 | 5.5 | 4.3 |
| National & Provincial | 2.2 | 2.4 | 2.3 | 3.8 | 3.7 |
| NatWest | 2.5 | 2.0 | 1.8 | 2.1 | 3.6 |
| Bank of Scotland | 1.7 | 1.6 | 2.1 | 1.4 | 2.3 |
| A&L | 4.2 | 4.3 | 4.7 | 4.2 | 2.3 |
| TSB | 3.3 | 2.0 | 2.4 | 1.9 | 2.2 |
| Britannia | 2.5 | 2.1 | 2.1 | 2.3 | 2.0 |
| Bristol & West | 1.2 | 2.2 | 1.7 | 2.0 | 1.8 |
| Lloyds | 2.5 | 2.0 | 1.4 | 1.2 | 1.4 |
| Other | 33.3 | 35.9 | 34.3 | 31.0 | 28.7 |
| Total | 100.0 | 100.0 | 100.0 | 100.0 | 100.0 |
| Total (£m) | 75,223 | 69,418 | 70,878 | 65,550 | 53,990 |
| Index | 100 | 92 | 94 | 87 | 72 |

*Source:*  MMC calculations based on data provided by the CML and mortgage lenders.

*Note:*  Lenders selected based on the customary industry ranking.

3.50. The table also shows that the two largest lenders, Halifax and Abbey National, accounted for 25.5 per cent of the total of such new mortgage lending in 1992, whilst the seven largest (Halifax, Abbey National, Nationwide, Barclays, Woolwich, Leeds and C&G) accounted for just over 50 per cent, and the 15 largest lenders for over 70 per cent. The market shares of individual lenders vary to some extent from year to year over the period 1988 to 1992, but the three largest—Halifax, Abbey National and Nationwide—have remained in that position throughout this period. Below the top three, while there is some variation from year to year, the rankings appear to be broadly stable. Treating Abbey National for this purpose as a building society (see paragraph 3.11), ten of these 15 largest lenders are building societies and five are banks. None of the centralized lenders are in the largest 15.

3.51. In 1992 building societies as a whole (including Abbey National) accounted for over 70 per cent of all such lending, high street and other banks accounted for 23 per cent, and insurance companies for 1 per cent. The balance of 4 per cent was made by centralized lenders and other financial institutions. Around 95 per cent of all such lending was for properties valued at not more than £150,000 (see Appendix 5.2).

3.52. Table 3.2 gives figures for the total number of mortgages approved, and in Table 3.3 we give market share figures, as at the end of 1992, based on the total value of mortgage loans outstanding, which is the measure traditionally used by the mortgage lending industry. On both of these measures, ie those in Tables 3.2 and 3.3, Halifax and Abbey National are the largest lenders, and together they account for more than 25 per cent of the market.

TABLE 3.2  **Lenders' market shares based on the number of mortgages approved**

|  |  |  |  |  | per cent |
| --- | --- | --- | --- | --- | --- |
| Lender | 1988 | 1989 | 1990 | 1991 | 1992 |
| Halifax | 16.4 | 16.6 | 13.9 | 15.0 | 16.1 |
| Abbey National | N/A | N/A | 12.9 | 12.8 | 13.1 |
| National & Provincial | N/A | N/A | N/A | 9.1 | 7.6 |
| Nationwide | 9.3 | 6.7 | 9.2 | 8.1 | 7.2 |
| NatWest | 4.0 | 3.0 | 3.6 | 3.6 | 6.6 |
| Leeds | 5.1 | 6.8 | 4.1 | 6.0 | 6.1 |
| Woolwich | 5.5 | 4.8 | 5.9 | 5.3 | 5.7 |
| Barclays | 4.9 | 2.6 | 2.8 | 4.1 | 5.1 |
| C&G | N/A | 1.8 | 3.7 | 3.5 | 3.3 |
| A&L | 5.6 | 4.9 | 6.5 | 5.4 | 3.2 |
| TSB | 2.5 | 2.9 | 3.2 | 2.5 | 2.8 |
| Bank of Scotland | 1.6 | 1.2 | 1.0 | 1.2 | 2.7 |
| Britannia | 2.2 | 1.9 | 1.8 | 1.9 | 2.1 |
| Lloyds | N/A | 1.8 | 1.4 | 1.4 | 2.0 |
| Bristol & West | N/A | N/A | 1.8 | 1.4 | 1.2 |
| Other | 43.0 | 44.9 | 28.2 | 18.7 | 15.3 |
| Total | 100.0 | 100.0 | 100.0 | 100.0 | 100.0 |
| Total ('000) | 1,623 | 1,246 | 1,161 | 1,038 | 879 |
| Index | 100 | 77 | 72 | 64 | 54 |

Source:  MMC calculations based on data provided by the CML and mortgage lenders.

Note:  Lenders selected based on the customary industry ranking.

TABLE 3.3  **Lenders' market shares based on the value of residential mortgage loans outstanding**

| Lender | 1992 (year end) % |
| --- | --- |
| Halifax | 14.8 |
| Abbey National | 11.9 |
| Nationwide | 7.8 |
| Woolwich | 5.4 |
| Leeds | 4.3 |
| A&L | 3.9 |
| C&G | 3.7 |
| Barclays | 3.6 |
| NatWest | 3.5 |
| Bradford & Bingley | 2.9 |
| National & Provincial | 2.9 |
| TSB | 2.2 |
| Britannia | 2.1 |
| Lloyds | 1.9 |
| Bristol & West | 1.7 |
| Midland | 1.6 |
| Other | 25.8 |
| Total | 100.0 |
| Total (£ bn) | 340 |

Source:  MMC calculations based on industry data.

## Valuation services

3.53. In Chapter 4 we examine in detail the nature of mortgage valuations and related services, and the policies of lenders on the use of valuers. The charges made for valuations and related services are considered in Chapter 5, which also includes a financial assessment of the costs, revenues and profits to the seven largest lenders arising from mortgage valuations. Here, we give only a brief account of the main features of valuations and the charges made, and then provide an assessment of the size of the market in terms of both volume and value.

### Services and procedures

3.54. Valuations for mortgage-lending purposes are undertaken principally by professionally qualified valuers, who are usually members of the RICS and/or the ISVA. The valuation in most instances broadly follows the guidelines set out by the RICS/ISVA, with regard to procedures and the scope of the valuation, and its primary purpose is to assess the open market value of the property. Lenders use this as the basis for evaluating whether the property provides adequate security for the loan being sought by the borrower, and the amount of the loan that they are prepared to offer. Homebuyers reports (HBRs) and structural surveys (SSYs) provide a more detailed survey of the condition of the property, and are often also combined with an assessment of open market value. Mortgage valuations are required by the lender whenever the loan being sought is for the purposes of either purchasing residential property or refinancing an existing mortgage which is with a different lender. A reinspection of the property may also sometimes be required by the lender, if the original valuation inspection reveals that work is necessary to remedy defects in the property: the reinspection is to ensure that the work has been carried out satisfactorily. When the loan is by way of a further advance to an existing mortgage, a revaluation of the property is also usually required by the lender.

3.55. As explained in paragraph 5.1 and 5.7, borrowers are generally required by most lenders to pay an up-front charge for the mortgage valuation at the time a loan is applied for. Where an HBR or SSY is undertaken, the borrower is also usually required to pay the valuation fee, either separately or as a composite charge. Many lenders also charge an administration fee at the time of an application for a loan, and this may be specified either as part of the valuation fee or as a separately identified charge. Reinspections also involve a charge which is paid by the borrower. In the case of further advances also, a charge is made by the lender for any revaluation carried out. Charges for both reinspections and revaluations are typically about half that for a mortgage valuation (see paragraphs 5.23 to 5.26).

### Volume and value of mortgage valuation work

3.56. Table 3.4 gives figures, for the years 1988 to 1992, for the total number of valuations, including those where the valuation was combined with an HBR or SSY, carried out on behalf of the seven largest mortgage lenders, together with our estimates of the total number of such valuations for all lenders. As shown in the table, in 1988—the peak of demand for mortgage loans in recent years—some 2.4 million such valuations were undertaken. The total number fell in subsequent years to 1.4 million in 1992, which was 40 per cent or so below the peak in 1988. On most occasions just a mortgage valuation was carried out, ie it was not combined with an HBR or SSY. The data provided by three of the largest lenders indicated that HBRs carried out where a valuation was also provided for the lender account for around 10 to 15 per cent of all valuations. By contrast, SSYs where a valuation was also provided accounted for less than a half of 1 per cent (see also paragraphs 3.60 and 4.11).

TABLE 3.4 **The total number of mortgage valuations\* carried out on behalf of the seven largest lenders, 1988 to 1992**

'000

| Lender | 1988 | 1989 | 1990 | 1991 | 1992 |
|---|---|---|---|---|---|
| Halifax | N/A | N/A | 210 | 228 | 211 |
| Abbey National | N/A | N/A | 159 | 145 | 143 |
| Nationwide | 236 | 294 | 260 | 230 | 102 |
| Barclays | 69 | 27 | 29 | 44 | 39 |
| Woolwich | 107 | 59 | 73 | 62 | 58 |
| Leeds | N/A | 99 | 55 | 72 | 64 |
| C&G\* | 113 | 102 | 90 | 100 | 97 |
| Total | N/A | N/A | 876 | 881 | 714 |
| Industry total† | 2,386 | 2,191 | 1,685 | 1,694 | 1,373 |

*Source:* Mortgage lenders and MMC estimates.

\*Including the number of HBRs and SSYs carried out where a valuation was provided.

†MMC estimates based on the market shares of the largest lenders of the total value of mortgage lending (see Table 3.1).

3.57. The figures in Table 3.4 include all such valuations undertaken on behalf of lenders in connection with applications for mortgage loans. In many cases, however, a loan was not subsequently provided, either because the lender did not make an offer of a loan or because the borrower withdrew the application, for whatever reason. The proportion of the total number of valuations where a loan was not subsequently taken up varies between different lenders, and also, no doubt, from year to year for any individual lender. For some, it has been as high as 30 per cent in some years, whilst others estimated it at around 10 to 15 per cent. For half of the largest lenders, the rate has been around 20 per cent in recent years, and this, we believe is probably a reasonable figure for the industry as a whole.

3.58. With regard to total values of valuations, ie the total costs to borrowers and the total revenues to lenders arising from such valuations, Table 3.5 gives figures for values for the years 1988 to 1992 for the seven largest lenders, together with our estimates for the industry as a whole. These figures include the value of mortgage valuations undertaken, the valuation component of HBRs and SSYs carried out where a valuation was also provided, and also the value of reinspections and revaluations. Data on revenues arising from lenders' charges for administration are not included (see paragraph 3.61). As shown in the table, we estimate the total value of valuations in 1988 to have been around £180 million. This fell to under £150 million in the following year, but it increased to over £170 million in 1991, and then fell again to £156 million in 1992. The figure for 1992 is some 14 per cent below that for 1988, compared with the 40 per cent or so reduction in the number of mortgage valuations carried out over the same period, reflecting the increases in valuation fees by these lenders over this period (see paragraph 5.19). For the seven largest lenders taken together, total revenues from valuation fees are about the same level as in 1990, the main exception being Nationwide, whose revenues in 1992 were significantly lower than in the previous year, reflecting a reduced rate of mortgage lending and the fall in the number of valuations carried out on its behalf.

TABLE 3.5 **Total revenues from lenders' charges for mortgage valuations carried out on behalf of the seven largest lenders, 1988 to 1992**

£'000

| Lender | 1988 | 1989 | 1990 | 1991 | 1992 |
|--------|------|------|------|------|------|
| Halifax | N/A | N/A | 21,857 | 24,299 | 24,358 |
| Abbey National | N/A | N/A | 16,812 | 17,494 | 16,792 |
| Nationwide | 18,923 | 18,072 | 20,422 | 22,202 | 11,364 |
| Barclays | 4,900 | 2,000 | 2,100 | 3,400 | 5,100 |
| Woolwich | 9,770 | 5,568 | 7,777 | 7,141 | 7,067 |
| Leeds | N/A | 9,934 | 5,195 | 8,008 | 7,804 |
| C&G* | 6,179 | 6,354 | 6,962 | 8,034 | 8,703 |
| Total | N/A | N/A | 81,125 | 90,578 | 81,188 |
| Industry total | 180,782 | 145,427 | 156,010 | 174,188 | 156,131 |

*Source:* Mortgage lenders and MMC estimates.

*Fees paid to panel valuers are assumed to have been constant at £6 million for the years 1988 to 1992.
*Notes:*
1. Adjustments to the data have been made so as to include only the mortgage valuation component of HBRs and SSYs.
2. 1988/89 industry aggregates are based on Nationwide, Barclays, Woolwich and C&G; 1990/92 industry aggregates are based on the top seven lenders.
3. N/A = not available.

3.59. With regard to the consumer perspective, we had planned to commission an interview survey of consumers (or borrowers) in order to obtain information on valuations, HBRs and SSYs from the point of view of individual borrowers who had paid for one or more of these in connection with a purchase of residential property and taking out a mortgage loan. We initially undertook a pilot study, during which particular difficulties were found in arranging interviews on this topic, especially with younger property buyers. Moreover, some borrowers had difficulty recollecting accurately the sequences of events, and what had taken place, in their dealings with lenders or intermediaries. These dealings would have involved personal visits and phone calls, as well as written communications over several weeks. Where figures were sought in the study, many borrowers were unable to provide all the information requested, and they were not able to recall details or supply documentation for the purposes of clarification. We concluded from this that a larger exercise would also involve many of these difficulties, so that any findings which emerged might be unreliable and unsatisfactory for our purposes, and we decided, therefore, not to proceed with a full-scale survey.

3.60. As explained in paragraph 4.16, we also obtained information on the market for valuations from a study commissioned from an outside firm of consultants (see Appendix 4.4). This survey collected information on the extent of panel membership, and on the proportion of residential work obtained by surveyors as a result of being on lenders' panels. Some 80 per cent of the firms in the survey were on one or more panels and, on average, these firms said that 49 per cent of their residential work was commissioned via their panel membership. Hence, about half of their work was commissioned independently of their panel membership, as was all of the work of the 20 per cent of the firms in the sample which were not on lenders' panels. Within the total of non-panel work noted in the study, some 61 per cent comprised HBRs (on both houses and flats) and SSYs. Based on this information, we estimate that the total value of such work in 1992 was around £160 million. This would suggest that the proportion of homebuyers seeking further professional advice on the condition of properties may be somewhat greater than indicated by the information from lenders, which was considered in paragraph 3.56 (see also paragraph 4.11).

3.61. With regard to revenues to lenders from charges to borrowers for administration, figures on total revenues for the years 1988 to 1992 for the seven largest lenders, together with our estimates for the industry as a whole, are given in Table 3.5. As there shown, total revenues for the industry were around £33 million in 1988. They rose in the following year, then declined in 1990, but have since risen substantially. In 1992 revenues to lenders from such administration charges were £40 million, which was some 20 per cent higher than in 1988, notwithstanding the 40 per cent or so reduction in the number of valuations. This reflects the increase in such charges made by lenders in recent years, which are considered in paragraphs 5.8 to 5.12, along with other charges made by lenders to borrowers in connection with valuation work.

TABLE 3.6 **Total revenues from administrative charges made by the seven largest lenders in connection with mortgage valuations, 1988 to 1992**

£'000

| Lender | 1988 | 1989 | 1990 | 1991 | 1992 |
|---|---|---|---|---|---|
| Halifax | N/A | N/A | 939 | 3,101 | 4,327 |
| Abbey National | N/A | N/A | 3,060 | 3,450 | 4,692 |
| Nationwide | 1,636 | 3,805 | 5,479 | 5,957 | 3,309 |
| Barclays | 0 | 0 | 0 | 0 | 0 |
| Woolwich | 76 | 38 | 63 | 59 | 1,195 |
| Leeds | N/A | 1168 | 611 | 942 | 918 |
| C&G | 5,625 | 5,083 | 4,879 | 6,517 | 6,361 |
| Total | N/A | N/A | 15,031 | 20,026 | 20,802 |
| Industry total | 33,350 | 40,573 | 28,906 | 38,512 | 40,004 |

*Source:* Mortgage lenders and MMC estimates.

*Notes:*

1. Revenues for 1988/89 are based on MMC calculations for all lenders.

2. Charges for 1990/92 are based on accounting data, apart from Woolwich and Leeds.

3. 1988/89 industry aggregates are based on Nationwide, Barclays, Woolwich and C&G; 1990/92 industry aggregates are based on the top seven lenders.

4. The data exclude revenues from charges by lenders in connection with further advances.

5. N/A = not available.

# 4 Lenders' practices relating to valuation services

## Contents

## Introduction

4.1. We examine in this chapter the various practices of lenders relating to mortgage valuations and associated property surveys on residential property, with emphasis on the two largest mortgage lenders, Halifax and Abbey National (which together account for a quarter of the total market for residential mortgage lending in the UK—see paragraph 3.50), and the next five largest lenders (ie Nationwide, Barclays, Woolwich, Leeds and C&G). These seven largest lenders taken together account for around half of this market. As explained in paragraph 3.11, Abbey National is no longer a building society, having converted to PLC status. It told us that it nevertheless compared itself more with a building society than a bank. Accordingly, we treat Abbey National for the purposes of our analysis as a building society, rather than as a bank. As explained in paragraphs 4.5 to 4.12, virtually all lenders require a mortgage valuation, providing a professional assessment of the open market value of the property, as a condition of granting a mortgage loan, which is, of course, secured against the property concerned. Indeed, all building societies (but not other lenders) are bound by the 1986 Act, sections 13 and 45 (see paragraph 2.13) to have such a valuation available when evaluating a mortgage application. Valuations may be undertaken either on their own or at the same time as surveys of the condition of the property, comprising usually either HBRs or more detailed SSYs (see paragraph 4.10). Valuers are mostly professionally qualified and suitably experienced surveyors who are members of either the RICS (mostly in the General Practice Division) or the ISVA (see paragraphs 4.13 to 4.16).

4.2. Lenders are not bound by statute or other regulation themselves to select the particular surveyor who provides the valuation, but this is their practice in most cases, and ensures the establishment of a contractual relationship with the valuer. Indeed, the major building society lenders stressed to us that the selection of the valuer was a matter for lenders and not for borrowers (see paragraph 4.27). Some lenders, including some of the high street banks, may, however, allow borrowers to choose the valuer, subject to various conditions to ensure that the person nominated to carry out the valuation is acceptable to the lender. Lenders' restrictions on both selection of the valuer and the borrower's permitted contact with the surveyor chosen are considered in paragraphs 4.17 to 4.28. A number of the largest lenders (eg Halifax, Abbey National and Nationwide) employ in-house valuers or valuers in subsidiary companies, or in some cases both, who undertake valuations, as well as using external valuers on their panels (ie lists of lender-approved valuers). Lenders' use of these different categories of surveyor, and the extent to which they allocate valuation work in favour of their own surveyors, is reviewed in paragraphs 4.29 to 4.38.

4.3. We then consider, in paragraphs 4.39 to 4.42, the evidence concerning so-called reciprocity, ie where some lenders may make it a condition of appointment to their panels, or of the subsequent allocation of valuation instructions, that valuers should introduce mortgage business to the lenders concerned. We continue, in paragraphs 4.43 to 4.57, with an evaluation of possible conflicts of interest arising where lenders choose to instruct their own valuers, and the CML guidance on improving market transparency in order to obviate possible detriments to borrowers from potential conflicts of interest. Finally, we consider, in paragraphs 4.58 to 4.75, the evidence on fraud and negligence by mortgage valuers, the increased incidence of which appears to have been associated with the housing market and lending boom of the late 1980s, and its implications for both valuation procedures and the lenders' stated desire to control the selection and appointment of surveyors for mortgage valuation purposes.

4.4. In this chapter we also indicate briefly and where appropriate the views of the CML, of lenders, of valuers and other interested parties on particular practices. Their views are summarized more fully in Chapters 6, 7 and 8 respectively.

## Valuation and surveying services

### Types of services: valuations, HBRs and SSYs

4.5. A mortgage valuation is essentially an assessment of the open market value of a property (see paragraph 4.8), though the report always includes a brief description of any major defects in its condition which may be apparent. HBRs and SSYs are more detailed assessments of the condition of the property (see paragraph 4.10), and are frequently accompanied by a valuation for mortgage purposes. A valuation is required whenever the loan is for the purchase of a property or a remortgage with a different lender but on a property already owned. A reinspection may be required where remedial work to defects in the property are needed: the further inspection is necessary to ensure that the work has been carried out satisfactorily. Where the loan is for a further advance to a borrower with an existing mortgage loan, a revaluation is often required. This involves an additional inspection, which may often be undertaken by the same surveyor who carried out the initial valuation. The emphasis of the inspection is on whether there has been any significant change in either the value or condition of the property since the initial valuation.

4.6. Almost all lenders in this market require a mortgage valuation to be undertaken, both as a prior condition to an offer of a loan being made and to assist in establishing the amount of the loan. Not only are building societies required to have a written valuation available before granting a loan, but they are also for the most part precluded under the 1986 Act from lending more than the total value of the property being offered as security, and in practice 95 per cent is at the present time usually the effective loan:value limit. For loans in excess of 75 per cent (or in some cases 80 per cent) of the property value, lenders also typically require additional security in the form of mortgage indemnity insurance being taken out, which may add considerably to the cost to the borrower of the loan (see paragraphs 3.23 and 3.30). A mortgage valuation involves an inspection of the property, by an appropriately qualified property valuer (see paragraphs 4.13 to 4.16), to assess its open market value, and this requires an examination of its condition to identify any major defects, or other factors, which may affect its value. The principal actions and procedures that the surveyor is required to undertake as part of a valuation, and the definition of open market value, are set out in detail in the RICS/ISVA Guidance Notes for Valuers (see Appendix 4.1). In essence, the on-site inspection is limited to easily visible and accessible parts of the property, and can normally be completed within 30 to 45 minutes. Additional time is necessary, of course, to prepare the report. The valuer is required to assess the property and its condition, having regard to the prices realized recently for other similar properties in the local area. Hence, wherever possible, value is estimated on the basis of appropriate comparable properties.

4.7. Many lenders, particularly the high street banks, centralized lenders and the smaller building societies, require valuers to adhere strictly to the RICS/ISVA Guidance Notes in preparing valuations. A number of the larger lenders (eg Halifax, Abbey National, Nationwide) use the RICS/ISVA Guidance Notes as the main basis for valuation procedures, but also issue their own, often highly detailed, guidance notes, which generally require valuers to use standardized phrases (which may differ from one lender to another) in describing the characteristics of the property and to pay special attention to particular aspects of the assessment (eg signs of subsidence, possible damage from tree roots etc). The seven largest lenders, as well as the CML, have emphasized to us that the quality and consistency of valuation reports has been improved in recent years, partly as a consequence of requiring the use of such guidance notes and partly because of their own monitoring and auditing of valuations provided. The valuation reports themselves are usually relatively brief, typically two pages, and give a summary description of the main features of the property, any major defects (eg rising damp, dry rot, structural movement etc), a valuation figure and an estimate of rebuilding costs for insurance purposes. The report will also indicate whether any retention should be made to allow for the cost of any remedial work to defects in the property that may be necessary. Details of the comparators used as the basis for estimating market value are not given, though they are recorded on file. An example of a valuation for mortgage purposes provided by Halifax is shown in Appendix 4.2.

4.8. As indicated in Appendix 4.1, open market value is taken to be the best price that could be realized within a reasonable period of time (having regard to the nature of the property and the state of the market), but excluding the value of carpets, curtains etc that may be included in the purchase price. Lenders and the RICS/ISVA have both emphasized to us that this is intended as an objective, independent and professional assessment of realizable market value. For lenders, the open market value would be the amount that they could expect to recoup, in similar market conditions, should the borrower default on the loan, making repossession and subsequent resale necessary. The valuation may sometimes differ from, and in particular might well be lower than, the proposed purchase price, either because the buyer had a particular reason for wishing to buy the property, and was therefore willing to pay a premium, or because the inclusion of carpets, curtains and other items in the sale agreement had added to the price (or, indeed, because the purchaser is being asked to pay more than the market value of comparable properties).

4.9. Most lenders require valuation reports to be completed on their own forms, which may include the terms and conditions of engagement. This ensures that the information provided is of the type and in the format desired by the lender, which makes easier the subsequent processing and assessment of the loan application. The largest lenders told us that by commissioning the valuation work, they establish a direct contractual link with the valuer which enables lenders either to take legal action against the valuer (often, in practice, to make a claim against his professional indemnity insurer), should there be evidence of negligence in the valuation. Since the early 1980s, and in particular as a result of the *Yianni v Evans* case (see paragraph 2.17), it has been established that the valuer may in many circumstances have a legal duty of care (in tort) to the borrower. This means that the valuer has, or may have, a legal responsibility in such cases to the borrower (as well as to the lender) to undertake a professionally competent inspection and valuation of the property. The basis for this judgment was that in many cases the valuer could reasonably expect the borrower to rely on the valuation being sound if the lender accepted it in making the loan, whether or not the borrower had sight of the valuation, and independent of the fact that the borrower had paid a fee for it. As a result of this duty of care, should the valuer fail to notice or report on any serious and obvious defects that may have a material effect on the value of the property (eg evidence of subsidence, dry rot etc), he could be sued for negligence by the borrower, in addition to his contractual liability to the lender. Nonetheless, some lenders (eg Woolwich and Leeds) still disclaim, in their valuation reports, any responsibility to the borrower for the contents of the report on the part of the lender or the valuer. Woolwich told us that it does so to emphasize that the prospective borrower should obtain his own survey and because it does not consider itself liable to the borrower for a valuation carried out by a panel valuer. Many lenders, including Woolwich, indicate in their marketing literature that the borrower should not rely solely on the mortgage valuation report, and strongly advise that it is in his own interests to commission a further survey, ie an HBR or SSY (see Appendix 4.5, which gives an example from Abbey National).

4.10. A mortgage valuation contains all the information on the property required by the lender in order to decide on the size of the loan it will make and any conditions it will impose. By contrast, HBRs and SSYs are more detailed assessments of the condition of the property, commissioned in most cases by, and carried out for the benefit of, the borrower. A site inspection for an SSY may take four to five hours and a highly detailed report is usually provided on all aspects of the building, including its structural soundness, the condition of the roof, drainage systems, main services (power and water), etc. The precise coverage of the survey is a matter for negotiation between the house purchaser and the surveyor. Until the 1986 Act, building societies were not allowed to undertake SSYs (or HBRs). An HBR is an intermediate level of report which was first brought into being in the early 1980s. In terms of detail it falls somewhere between a valuation report and a full SSY. Typically, it may require an on-site inspection taking about two hours for an average-sized property, and the written report may consist of between six and ten pages (see Appendix 4.3, which gives an example of an HBR provided by Nationwide). An HBR is more standardized than an SSY, and the RICS/ISVA issue Guidance Notes outlining what is required of surveyors when it is prepared. Nonetheless, HBR products offered by different lenders may differ in content to a greater or lesser extent, and they are often given different names (eg Halifax's 'Scheme 2 Report' and Abbey National's 'Report on Condition and Value' (RCV)). For both HBRs and SSYs, the inspection required and, therefore, the survey work undertaken is more extensive than for a valuation only. As a consequence, the additional work required to produce an assessment of market value is generally quite limited. Indeed, a number of surveyors told us that, if commissioned to prepare an HBR or SSY, they would usually be willing to provide a mortgage valuation at little or no extra charge. A number of the larger lenders, eg Halifax, Abbey National and Nationwide, which employ their own valuers either in-house or in subsidiary companies, often use those valuers to undertake both mortgage valuations and HBRs at the same time, if requested to do so by borrowers. In some cases, those valuers may also provide combined SSYs and valuations, though more often a panel surveyor will be used where an SSY is required. The selection and use of valuers employed by lenders, panel and non-panel valuers is considered further in paragraphs 4.29 to 4.38.

4.11. As explained above, valuations are undertaken for virtually all mortgage and remortgage applications. Although lenders' marketing literature often explicitly recommends or encourages borrowers to have either an HBR or SSY carried out, only a minority of borrowers appear do so. The CML estimated that only about 10 per cent of all borrowers commission their own survey, the majority of which are HBRs. It told us that this figure is influenced by HBRs commissioned by companies when they are relocating their employees. Typically, only 1 per cent or less of borrowers commission a full SSY, and usually these are for older properties or where borrowers have reason to suspect that there may be structural or other serious defects. Such a report is also more likely to be obtained, lenders told us, where the borrower is contributing a high proportion of the purchase price. Whilst such percentages may seem surprisingly small, these figures understate the actual proportion commissioning additional surveys. Some groups of borrowers will have little need for such a survey, including those who are purchasing a new or nearly new property which may be covered by warranty arrangements, such as the National House Building Council or equivalent; those borrowers who are refinancing an existing mortgage, which at present accounts for 10 to 15 per cent of all new borrowing (see paragraph 3.3); and those simply taking a further advance on an existing property. Other information we obtained from the study we commissioned (paragraph 3.60) also suggests that many HBRs and SSYs are carried out independently of lenders. The majority of purchasers, however, do appear to rely primarily on the mortgage valuation report (which is now normally disclosed to them) and their own assessment (or that of friends and relations) of the property's condition, without incurring the additional expense of an HBR or SSY.

4.12. As explained in paragraph 3.57, around one in five (ie 20 per cent) of all mortgage valuations commissioned through lenders do not subsequently lead to a mortgage loan being taken up. In some cases, this may be because the lender is not willing to grant the loan applied for, either because the property offers inadequate security or the status or other enquiries in respect of the borrower do not justify making the loan. More often, however, these aborted applications and valuations reflect a breakdown in the purchase arrangements, with either the purchaser or the vendor pulling out of the proposed sale. As explained in paragraph 4.26, it is rare that any subsequent purchasers are able to use these existing valuations when later seeking a mortgage loan for themselves.

## Surveyors and valuers

4.13. Building societies are required by the 1986 Act (sections 13 and 45—see paragraph 2.13) to have a valuation available that has been undertaken by a competent person, though the term 'competent' is not itself defined explicitly in the Act. In practice, most societies, as well as most other lenders, make it a condition of acceptability that valuers should:

(a) be suitably qualified, which generally means membership of either the RICS (mostly General Practice Division) or the ISVA;

*(b)* have at least two years' post-qualification, professional experience;

*(c)* have adequate local knowledge of the area in which they operate; and

*(d)* have adequate professional indemnity insurance cover.

Though not defined in the 1986 Act, a definition corresponding to the above conditions is included in the recent Leasehold Reform, Housing and Urban Development Act 1993 (section 13, subsection 7).

4.14. The RICS is the main qualifying and self-regulating, professional body for surveyors and valuers (see Chapter 8). Its total membership increased significantly during the 1980s, partly as a result of amalgamations between professional bodies, and also because more surveyors became qualified in this period; it currently comprises nearly 70,000 chartered surveyors practising in a range of specialisms. Of these, some 30,000 are in the General Practice Division, which has primary responsibility for those RICS valuers either undergoing training, including that on valuation procedures, or operating in both the residential and commercial property sectors. Most of these are employed in the non-residential sector on commercial property valuation work and management, by the Government, by industrial or commercial companies, or by building or property companies. Although no reliable statistics are available, the RICS estimated that there are possibly around 5,000 or so qualified surveyors, including ISVA members, who currently undertake residential mortgage valuation or associated work, either as employees of mortgage lenders or in independent firms and companies. Details of surveyors employed, either directly or indirectly, by the largest building society lenders are given in paragraphs 4.29 to 4.31 and Table 4.2.

4.15. The supply of valuers (predominantly surveyors) who are qualified to carry out such mortgage valuations is highly fragmented, within several thousand independent firms. Some of these are sole practitioners, many more are partnerships or larger firms providing valuation and surveying services, and there are also many qualified valuers employed by estate agency firms and by lenders themselves. Some of the larger surveying firms and companies, including those owned by lenders, provide such services on a national or near-national basis, whilst others operate either regionally or local to a particular area. In general, valuers of residential properties are widely dispersed throughout the UK.

4.16. Because information from other sources was limited, and in order to understand the provision of valuation services better, we commissioned a study of firms of surveyors by a firm of outside consultants (see paragraph 3.60). The sample included nearly 900 offices of surveyors who carry out mortgage valuation work, HBRs and SSYs. A summary of the main findings of the study is at Appendix 4.4. Amongst other things (see paragraphs 4.37, 4.38 and 4.41), the study confirmed that the market for valuation services relating to residential properties is highly fragmented, with many small firms and partnerships operating throughout the UK. On average, firms of surveyors in the sample had an annual fee income on all types of residential work of around £100,000 or so, though the turnover for sole practitioners was typically less, at around £60,000 a year. Panel commissions (ie work arising from the valuers being on lenders' panels) was found to be a major source of business and income for many of them. Around two-thirds of firms of valuers are on the panels of up to ten different lenders, though some (7 per cent) were on 50 or more panels.

## Selection of valuer

4.17. In this section, we consider the extent to which it is lenders rather than borrowers who exercise control over the selection of valuer to undertake a mortgage valuation, whether on its own or in combination with an HBR or SSY. Lenders indicate their general policy and approach to the selection of valuers in their marketing literature, some of which deals specifically with valuation services (eg Abbey National's pamphlet on valuation services, shown in Appendix 4.5). The marketing literature of many lenders often state either in general terms that a valuer appointed by that lender will undertake a valuation (eg as in the case of C&G); or that the valuer may be an in-house surveyor, one employed in a subsidiary company of the lender or one from its approved panel (eg as in the case of Halifax). On the mortgage application forms of most lenders, borrowers are neither requested nor required to indicate any choice with regard to the selection of valuer, other than to accept one appointed by the lender concerned. In practice, however, some lenders may, as they told us, be more flexible in certain circumstances than is indicated in their literature.

4.18. A summary of the degree of control exercised by the seven largest lenders is given in Table 4.1. As shown, with the exception of Barclays and, to a limited extent, C&G, each of these lenders selects or nominates the valuer to undertake a valuation when this is done on its own. Lenders also require the valuers to provide the valuation report on the lenders' own forms. These lenders also told us that this ensured that they received the information necessary to suit their own lending policies and internal systems of control. In the case of Barclays, the local branch manager in practice usually selects the valuer, on the basis of his knowledge of suitable valuers operating in the local area. No formal panel, either centralized or local, of valuers is used. Barclays told us, however, that it would normally be willing to agree to the use of a valuer nominated by a borrower, at the discretion of the branch manager, if the valuer so nominated was suitably qualified and otherwise acceptable. This would normally arise in circumstances where the borrower was obtaining his own HBR or SSY. C&G told us that it too would agree, in certain circumstances, to the use of a valuer selected by a borrower.

TABLE 4.1  **Restrictions by the seven largest lenders on the choice of valuer**

| Lender | 1* | 2 | 3 |
|---|---|---|---|
| Halifax | Select | Panel | Panel |
| Abbey National | Select | Select | Panel |
| Nationwide | Select | Panel | Agree |
| Barclays† | Select/Agree | Select/Agree | Select/Agree |
| Woolwich | Select | Select | Panel |
| Leeds | Select | Select | Agree |
| C&G | Select/Agree | Panel/Agree | Panel/Agree |

*Source:* Mortgage lenders.

*Responses apply to the UK other than Scotland, where lenders generally accept valuers selected by intermediaries, if the valuers so nominated are on the lender's panel.
†In practice, Barclays usually selects the valuer from one of those it uses regularly (it does not operate a panel), but will accept a valuer nominated by a borrower, if suitable.

*Key: (a)* Questions put to mortgage lenders:
   1. Do you select the valuer where just a mortgage valuation is involved?
   2. What constraints do you place on the selection of a surveyor by a borrower to conduct an HBR (to include a valuation acceptable to you)?
   3. What constraints do you place on the selection of a surveyor by a borrower to conduct an SSY (to include a valuation acceptable to you)?

   *(b)* Responses:
   Select:  Selected by the lender (either in-house, subsidiary company or panel valuer).
   Panel:  Surveyor from lenders' panel.
   Agree:  Lender has to agree to choice of surveyor made by the borrower or intermediary.

4.19. In the UK, apart from Scotland, it is also the case that most lenders will not now permit an intermediary to nominate the valuer. In Scotland, however, because of the different arrangements and procedures for house purchase (see paragraphs 2.8 to 2.12), valuers are often chosen by such intermediaries, though their range of choice is nonetheless limited to those valuers on the panel of the lender concerned.

4.20. Where a borrower is refinancing an existing mortgage but arranging this with the same lender, eg changing from a mortgage at a variable rate to a fixed-rate product, a revaluation may be required by the lender. In these circumstances, it may be possible in some cases to use the valuer who carried out the original valuation. If so, the borrower would be charged a revaluation fee, which is lower than that for a new valuation. This is unlikely to be possible, however, where the borrower is switching to a different lender, since most lenders in these circumstances require a new valuation to be undertaken by a valuer of their choice, and charged for on the basis of their standard fee scales. Because of the limited overlap between the panels of the seven largest lenders (see paragraph 4.34), the valuer who carried out the original valuation may well not be on the panel of, or otherwise acceptable to, the new lender.

4.21. The majority of other lenders, including many building societies, control the selection of the valuer in much the same way. A summary of this and other practices by a sample of mortgage lenders, including the seven largest, is given in Appendix 4.6. As shown in the table, the Cumberland Building Society and Buckinghamshire Building Society are amongst those societies that do not insist on selecting the valuer, when a mortgage valuation only is commissioned. Likewise, some of the high street banks, including Lloyds and NatWest as well as Clydesdale Bank PLC (whose business is mainly in Scotland) and Citibank Trust Ltd, operate in a similar way to that of Barclays. This means in practice that if the borrower expresses a wish to nominate a valuer when applying for a mortgage, the lender will accept the nominee provided he is suitably qualified and otherwise acceptable to that particular lender. A list of other lenders who we subsequently contacted, indicating which practices they adhere to, is given in Appendix 4.7.

4.22. Where a valuation is to be undertaken at the same time as either an HBR or SSY, the seven largest lenders, again with the exception of Barclays, normally either select the valuer themselves or limit the borrower's choice to that of a panel valuer, as shown in Table 4.1. Where explicitly requested by a borrower, however, some lenders permit a degree of choice. Leeds, for example, will accept a combined valuation and SSY from a non-panel valuer who is suitably qualified and otherwise acceptable. C&G does likewise where a valuation and an HBR (or SSY) are combined. Following discussion with the OFT, the BSA issued guidance in 1979 (in its circular BS2274, which is shown in Appendix 4.8) to the effect that valuations combined with SSYs (HBRs were not in being at that time) from non-panel surveyors nominated by borrowers should be considered for acceptance by building society lenders. During the 1980s, however, many societies ceased to follow these guidelines, which have, however, not been updated or revised since first issued.

4.23. Lenders have emphasized to us that these restrictions on the selection of valuer apply only to the valuation component, though, in examining lenders' marketing literature, one building society made the commissioning of an HBR on any property which had been built pre-1914 a condition of acceptance for one of its mortgage products. Borrowers are normally free to choose their surveyor for an HBR or SSY on its own, but where they do so, and the surveyor chosen is not acceptable to the lender as a provider of the valuation, they are still liable in most cases for a separate valuation fee levied by the lender, as well as the cost of any survey they may have commissioned. Because this involves two surveyors, each making a separate site visit, the overall cost will generally be higher than if the same surveyor is used.

4.24. A further aspect of lenders' control over the use of surveyors is that most of the largest building society lenders, though not some of the banks, restrict borrowers' access to the lender's nominated valuer, both before and during the valuation itself, and also, in most instances, after completion of the report. As a result, borrowers are usually not able to discuss either the property or the details of the valuation report directly with the valuer, though lenders told us that prospective borrowers are permitted to contact the local branch at any stage, either to offer views or to seek clarification of the report. The major society lenders told us that these restrictions were necessary to obviate the possibility of an informal contractual relationship developing between borrowers and valuers; and also to limit any pressure that borrowers might bring to bear on valuers. Some lenders, eg Abbey National, also restrict contact between borrowers and valuers when a combined valuation and HBR is to be undertaken, basically for the same reasons. Lenders do not seek, however, and are not able, to restrict contact between the two when a combined valuation and an SSY is to be carried out, because the detail and scope of the survey has of necessity to be discussed and agreed between the borrower and the surveyor.

4.25. In some cases, house purchasers may have commissioned an HBR or SSY, perhaps with a mortgage valuation included, in the course of negotiating the purchase of a property and prior to an application being made for a mortgage loan. However, the major building societies and most other lenders will generally not accept for mortgage purposes any valuation included in such reports. Nonetheless, some lenders, particularly the banks, may in some circumstances accept such prior valuations, at their discretion. In such cases, they may require the valuation to be transcribed on to their own documentation, and may also still charge the borrower a fee to cover administration costs.

4.26. Similarly, most building societies will not normally accept an existing valuation that was commissioned by another lender. Halifax, Abbey National and Woolwich said that they only accept valuations that they themselves have commissioned from their own in-house subsidiary company and panel valuers, and that each new application requires a separate valuation. As indicated above, some of the banks may in some circumstances be willing to accept prior valuations. Both Nationwide and Leeds told us that they may accept prior valuations commissioned by other lenders, but only if the surveyor had been one of their own subsidiary company valuers or one on their panel, and if the valuation had been submitted on their own forms. As with the other major society lenders, they do not accept previously commissioned valuations carried out by the staff or panel valuers of other lenders.

4.27. In their evidence to us, neither the CML nor the great majority of the lenders contested that these controls or restrictions on the selection of the valuer have been and are widely applied within the mortgage-lending industry. Indeed, they stressed to us that they regarded mortgage valuations as being solely or primarily for the purposes of the lender, to ensure that the property concerned offered adequate security for the loan requested, even though the borrower, since the early 1980s, had generally been given a copy of the report and a fee for the mortgage valuation was paid by the borrower. Moreover, the largest lenders (and the CML) told us that by retaining control over the selection of the valuer they were able to maintain and improve valuation standards and limit their exposure to fraud and negligence by valuers (see paragraphs 4.58 to 4.75, 6.16 to 6.18 and Chapter 7).

4.28. In contrast, bodies representing the interests of valuers, the RICS/ISVA and the Independent Surveyors Association (ISA), as well as individual firms of surveyors, have expressed concern about the restrictions currently imposed by lenders (see Chapter 8). They emphasized to us the need to promote borrower choice, in order to ensure that borrowers receive the best possible professional advice and to foster fair competition in the market for services amongst all suitably qualified and competent surveyors, including those not currently on some lenders' panels. The RICS told us that it recognized that the problem of borrower choice only arises where HBRs and SSYs are commissioned when it is the borrower who is the client.

## Use of in-house, subsidiary company and panel valuers

4.29. Some of the seven largest lenders have had their own, directly-employed, in-house valuers for many years. Prior to 1986 these were relatively few in number, with the great majority of valuations being undertaken by independent panel surveyors, and building societies were not allowed to carry out HBRs or SSYs at that time (see paragraph 4.10). Since 1986, however, and most particularly since the largest societies acquired a number of estate agencies, lenders' employment and use of different categories of valuer has changed significantly in a number of ways. Five of the seven largest lenders (ie Halifax, Nationwide, Abbey National (until August 1993), Woolwich and Leeds) have recently owned or now own subsidiary companies which provide valuation and associated survey services on a national basis, both to their lender parent organizations and also to other lenders. The numbers of in-house valuers directly employed by lenders has also increased in recent years, whilst the number of firms on some lenders' panels has been reduced. As a consequence of these changes, and also the decline in the total number of valuations undertaken each year (see paragraph 3.56), both the amount and the proportion of valuation work done by panel valuers has fallen, and the corresponding share of the work done by in-house valuers and the subsidiary companies of the largest lenders has risen.

4.30. Table 4.2 shows, for the period 1988 to 1993, the numbers of in-house valuers employed by the seven largest lenders, those in subsidiary companies owned by them and the number of firms and practices on their panels. As regards the first category, Barclays is the exception amongst the seven largest lenders in not having any in-house surveyors (nor does it have any subsidiary companies providing valuation services, or a formal panel). The other main lenders increased their employment of in-house valuers in the period 1988 to 1991 from a total of around 400 to about 530. Since then, the overall number has been reduced to around 360 in 1993; the main reason is that two of them, Nationwide and Woolwich, reorganized their valuers and moved all in-house valuers into their subsidiary companies. For those of the largest lenders that have retained their in-house valuers the numbers employed are much the same now as in 1991.

TABLE 4.2 **In-house, subsidiary company and panel valuers used by the seven largest lenders, 1988 to 1993**

| Lender | 1988 | 1989 | 1990 | 1991 | 1992 | 1993 |
|---|---|---|---|---|---|---|
| *Halifax* | | | | | | |
| In-house (staff) | 24 | 72 | 89 | 86 | 119 | 119 |
| Subsidiary (staff)* | 140 | 194 | 231 | 228 | 252 | 262 |
| Panel (firms) | 639 | 738 | 794 | 777 | 770 | 741 |
| (offices) | 1,238 | 1,481 | 1,672 | 1,567 | 1,525 | 1,533 |
| *Abbey National†* | | | | | | |
| In-house (staff) | 122 | 123 | 132 | 132 | 134 | 133 |
| Subsidiary (staff) | N/A | N/A | 88 | 95 | 87 | 82 |
| Panel (firms) | N/A | N/A | N/A | N/A | N/A | N/A |
| (offices)‡ | 1,400 | 1,400 | 1,400 | 900 | 900 | 885 |
| *Nationwide* | | | | | | |
| In-house (staff) | 120 | 116 | 118 | 133 | 0 | 0 |
| Subsidiary (staff) | N/A | N/A | 178 | 235 | 290 | 281 |
| Panel (firms) | 716 | 716 | 716 | 716 | 716 | 716 |
| (offices) | 1,242 | 1,242 | 1,242 | 1,242 | 1,242 | 1,242 |
| *Barclays* | No in-house valuers, or subsidiary companies providing valuation services, and does not maintain a panel. | | | | | |
| *Woolwich§* | | | | | | |
| In-house (staff) | 72 | 75 | 75 | 73 | 73 | 0 |
| Subsidiary (staff) | 0 | 4 | 7 | 61 | 54 | 127 |
| Panel (firms) | 650 | 650 | 650 | 650 | 650 | 650 |
| (offices) | 1,300 | 1,300 | 1,300 | 1,300 | 1,300 | 1,300 |
| *Leeds* | | | | | | |
| In-house (staff) | 46 | 60 | 69 | 70 | 70 | 70 |
| Subsidiary (staff) | 60 | 53 | 48 | 43 | 41 | 39 |
| Panel (firms) | 547 | 568 | 537 | 559 | 581 | 591 |
| (offices) | N/A | N/A | N/A | N/A | N/A | N/A |
| *C&G* | | | | | | |
| In-house (staff) | 19 | 17 | 23 | 37 | 37 | 39 |
| Subsidiary (staff) | 1 | 2 | 4 | 5 | 0 | 0 |
| Panel (firms)¶ | 600 | 600 | 600 | 416 | 430 | 384 |
| (offices) | N/A | N/A | N/A | N/A | N/A | N/A |

*Source:* Mortgage lenders.

---

*Data for 1990 to 1992 are Halifax's best estimates.

†Cornerstone was sold on 31 August 1993. Abbey National no longer has any subsidiary (staff) valuers.

‡The figures given are the MMC's best estimates.

§Woolwich told us that it does not keep historical records of panel movements. It said that the size of the panel had remained fairly constant between 1988 and 1993, and that its panel included around 3,500 individual valuers.

¶Records of years prior to 1991 are not available, but C&G estimated that there were about 600 firms on its panel at that time.

*Note:* N/A= not available.

4.31. The main expansion in numbers of valuers employed by these largest lenders has been in their subsidiary companies, ie Colleys (Halifax), Cornerstone (Abbey National), Nationwide Surveyors (Nationwide), Woolwich Surveying Services Ltd (Woolwich: trades under the name of Ekins Surveyors) and PLUK (Leeds). In 1988 there were about 200 individual surveyors employed in such subsidiary companies, mainly in Colleys (Halifax) and PLUK (Leeds)—see Table 4.2. Since then, other lenders have acquired chains of estate agencies and associated valuers, and then established their own subsidiary companies providing valuation services. By 1993 the total numbers of qualified valuers employed had increased to nearly 800, but Abbey National sold off its Cornerstone subsidiary in August 1993, with the effect that the total number of valuers employed in the subsidiary companies of the largest lenders has been reduced to about 720.

4.32. With regard to panel valuers, the largest lenders were not able to provide accurate figures for the numbers (or the identity) of panel firms in earlier years. The data were also limited to the number of firms and in some cases to the number of individual offices appointed, because this is the basis on which lenders typically establish and maintain their panels. A number of firms of valuers told us however (see paragraphs 8.53 to 8.58), that there had been a number of changes in recent years in the operation of the panel system. Lenders have reduced the size of their panels; it was now almost impossible for other valuers to gain admission to such panels; panel valuers were now getting a reduced share of the more limited valuation work available, because lenders were discriminating in the allocation of work in favour of their in-house and subsidiary companies' valuers; and they were finding that the system was now increasingly dominated by these subsidiary companies.

4.33. As regards the first of these claims, Nationwide and Woolwich told us that the size of their panels had not changed significantly in recent years. Abbey National told us that it had carried out a rationalization of its panel in the second half of 1991 and early 1992, removing firms to which it was not able to provide a meaningful supply of instructions given the decline in housing market activity (and also a few others were removed for failure to provide a high-quality service). Halifax's panel increased in the late 1980s, but has been reduced since 1990 by around 7 per cent. That of Leeds appears to have increased slightly in recent years, whilst that of C&G has been reduced more significantly, from around 600 to nearly 400. Other lenders (eg the centralized lenders and a number of building societies) also told us that they had reduced their panels in recent years, but because of the limited information made available we were not able to estimate the overall effect. A number of the larger lenders told us that there were ongoing costs, including those of training and monitoring, involved with keeping valuers on their panels, and that with the downturn in overall demand they had limited the size of their panels in the interests of cost efficiency as well as of prudential control.

4.34. The seven largest lenders gave us details of the individual firms on their panels in 1993, though in most cases they were not able to provide comparable information for earlier years. We undertook an analysis of these panel lists to determine the extent of overlap or commonality between them. From the data available, it was apparent that each of the main lenders includes on its panel many of the offices of the subsidiary companies of the other main lenders. Thus Colleys, Nationwide Surveyors, Woolwich Surveying Services (Ekins Surveyors), PLUK and also Cornerstone, which was formerly owned by Abbey National, are all on the panels of the main lenders. With regard to other firms of valuers, however, the extent of overlap of the panels of the largest lenders appeared to be modest. We identified some 177 individual offices of these other valuation firms that were common to the three largest lenders, ie Halifax, Abbey National and Nationwide, but these represented, in our estimates, only around 5 per cent of the total of all firms (excluding the subsidiary companies of the largest lenders).

4.35. On the question of whether it had become more difficult for valuers to gain appointment to lenders' panels, each of the largest lenders, excluding Barclays which does not operate a panel, told us that it had made few new appointments to its panel since around 1990. This reflected, they said, the downturn in market demand, the increased availability of in-house and subsidiary company valuers, and the need to contain the costs of panel management. Reflecting this, around four out of five (80 to 90 per cent) of applications by valuers to join their panels were rejected by the largest lenders in 1992. A substantial proportion of the complaints put to us by valuers during our inquiry concerned the difficulty they had experienced in getting appointed to lenders' panels.

4.36. As explained above, a difficulty encountered by those valuers who were on the panels of various lenders was that both the number of instructions and the share of valuation work had declined during the recession, with a larger proportion going to the lenders' in-house and subsidiary company valuers. The largest lenders told us that on average around three-quarters of their panel were used regularly and that they saw benefits from panel valuers undertaking valuations on a regular basis, since this helped to maintain both professional standards and the valuers' familiarity with the changing requirements of lenders. They also provided us with information for 1992 on the proportion of valuation and combined valuation/HBR work undertaken by in-house valuers, those in subsidiary companies and panel valuers, which is summarized in Table 4.3. This shows that, excluding Barclays, around 26 per cent of valuation work, on a weighted average basis, was typically awarded to panel valuers, and around 40 per cent of combined valuation/HBR work, the rest being done by in-house valuers and those in the subsidiary companies of lenders. C&G puts all HBR and SSY work out to external surveyors. In the case of Nationwide, however, some 95 per cent of all valuation and HBR work is carried out by its subsidiary company, with only 5 per cent going to panel valuers. This reflects the order of priority adopted by lenders in the allocation of work. Lenders, again with the exception of Barclays, told us that, unless there were conflicts of interest (see paragraphs 4.43 to 4.56) or other difficulties (for example, of availability), or special circumstances (eg the valuation of country estates), they would normally instruct in-house valuers where possible. If that were not possible, or if it was more appropriate to do so, they would then instruct a valuer in their subsidiary companies. If that were not possible, or it was more appropriate to do so, they would instruct a panel valuer. They explained also that the order of priority might vary between different areas, since in some locations they might not have either in-house or subsidiary company cover; and for SSYs, panel surveyors were more commonly used than their own staff. Overall, however, lenders would seek to use their in-house and subsidiary company valuation capacity as fully as possible, and to use panel valuers only where necessary and appropriate. The lenders also explained that the large reduction in valuation work required because of the downturn in housing demand since the peak of 1988/89 meant that it was inevitable that panel valuers were now getting less work than previously.

TABLE 4.3   **The proportion of the seven largest lenders' valuation and combined HBR/valuation work carried out by in-house valuers, those in subsidiary companies and panel valuers, 1992**

*per cent*

| | Mortgage valuations | | | HBRs/valuations | | |
|---|---|---|---|---|---|---|
| Lender | In-house | Subsidiary | Panel | In-house | Subsidiary | Panel |
| Halifax | 36 | 35 | 29 | 13 | 47 | 40 |
| Abbey National* | 69 | 8 | 23 | 45 | 18 | 37 |
| Nationwide | 0 | 95 | 5 | 0 | 95 | 5 |
| Barclays† | 0 | 0 | 100 | 0 | 0 | 100 |
| Woolwich‡ | 0 | 86 | 14 | 0 | 52 | 48 |
| Leeds§ | 64 | 4 | 32 | 64 | 4 | 32 |
| C&G¶ | 37 | 0 | 63 | 0 | 0 | 100 |

*Source:*   Mortgage lenders.

*Abbey National sold its Cornerstone subsidiary in August 1993.

†Barclays has no in-house valuers or subsidiary companies providing valuation services and does not maintain a panel.

‡Woolwich now has no in-house surveyors; all valuation and HBR work is done through its Ekins Surveyors subsidiary.

§Includes valuations and HBRs under 'in-house' and all three types of reports under 'subsidiary' and 'panel' headings.

¶Includes valuations under 'in-house' and all three types of reports under 'panel' headings.

4.37. The study we commissioned (see paragraph 4.16 and Appendix 4.4), also provided evidence on the operation of the panel system. Over 80 per cent of the sample said that they were on the panel of at least one lender. Two-thirds of the total were on the panels of up to ten different lenders. The average was as high as 18, because it was influenced by the fact that 7 per cent of respondents were on 50 or more separate panels. Those on most panels tended to be the larger firms of surveyors, including those owned by the largest lenders, which were often limited companies. As regards the type of work commissioned, the study shows some clear differences between work commissioned as a result of being on lenders' panels (panel work) and that commissioned independently, which in most cases would have been commissioned directly by individuals considering house purchase, usually with the aid of a mortgage (see Appendix 4.4, Table 17). More than two-thirds of panel work was accounted for by mortgage valuations on their own, most of the remaining work being HBRs and SSYs combined with a valuation. In contrast, and as noted in paragraph 3.60, non-panel work is mostly HBRs and SSYs, with or without a valuation, and only 17 per cent is accounted for by mortgage valuations provided on their own. This is consistent with information provided by the largest lenders (see paragraph 4.36 and Table 4.3). Moreover, panel work on valuations, HBRs and SSYs accounted for around 40 per cent of all work involving residential properties, and over half of the total for those surveyors on lenders' panels. For 20 per cent of the sample, panel work accounted for more than 75 per cent of all residential work. This suggests that there is a rather limited amount of work involving mortgage valuations alone which is available for those surveyors who are not on lenders' panels.

4.38. In part reflecting this distribution, the study revealed (see Appendix 4.4, Table 12) a substantial number of claims of work lost when prospective borrowers wanted a particular surveyor to be used, but could not do so because the valuer was not on the appropriate panel, so that the lender was unwilling to accept a valuation from him. Only 16 per cent of valuers in the sample said that they had lost no work in this way over the past 12 months. Over half of all firms of valuers, and 60 per cent of sole practitioners, claimed that they had lost up to 25 instructions in this period for this reason. The average number per firm of valuers of commissions lost in this way was 39. With regard to lenders' discrimination in favour of their own in-house and subsidiary company valuers, almost two-thirds of valuers on lenders' panels said that the proportion of their work that had come from panel commissions had decreased over the past year (see Appendix 4.4, Table 11).

## *Reciprocity*

4.39. Reciprocity is a practice whereby some lenders may require valuers to introduce mortgage business to them as a condition either of appointment to their panel or of receiving instructions to undertake valuations. We were told that the latter may also involve the lender rationing the number of instructions given in relation to the volume and value of business introduced, for example awarding three instructions for each borrower introduced. This has been a matter of concern for many years both to the RICS and the ISVA and also to those valuers not able to introduce business, because, as they see it, reciprocity results in a distortion of competition between valuers and unfair discrimination against some groups of fully competent valuers, eg those not associated with intermediaries or estate agencies.

4.40. The RICS, and others, told us that introduced business in general—though not necessarily involving formalized reciprocity, and not necessarily by valuers—had long been a feature of this market, and that overall it accounted for probably 40 to 50 per cent of all residential mortgage lending. For some lenders the proportion of introduced business can be as high as 80 per cent, whilst some other lenders (eg Barclays) do not accept any introduced business. We have also been told that it is not unknown, often as a limited-period promotional campaign, for lenders (eg Nationwide) to pay a commission to introducers, though Halifax and Abbey National, for example, both told us that they do not pay such commissions. The RICS expressed concern to us that lenders in recent years, particularly as their panels had been reduced or restricted, had begun to make reciprocity a condition of entry to the panel and for securing valuation work. All the seven largest lenders told us, however, that whilst some of their panel do introduce business to them, it accounted for only a small proportion of the total, and they do not make reciprocity a condition either of appointment to their panels or of receiving valuation instructions. C&G also stated that of its panel of around 400 valuers, three-quarters of them did not introduce any business to it. By contrast, the RICS provided us with a number of examples of letters to valuers from lenders which appear to indicate that at least some lenders do make reciprocity a condition; and a number of individual valuers have also submitted similar evidence to us (see Chapter 8). Some lenders (eg Britannia) have told us that reciprocity has been a feature of the market in the past, but this was no longer the case.

4.41. The study that we commissioned (see Appendix 4.4) also provided evidence on this issue. Three-quarters of the sample who were on lenders' panels said that they do not introduce new business to the lenders concerned (as C&G said is the case with its panel). Of the quarter that do, some 80 per cent introduced up to ten borrowers a year. Most valuers (ie over half of the sample respondents) said, however, that they were aware of lenders who expected to receive introductions in exchange for providing valuation work. The average number of lenders quoted was 14. Of those valuers who did introduce new business, about half of them considered that making these introductions was a necessary condition for inclusion on the panel. Of this last group (ie those who said that introductions were necessary), some three-quarters stated that they had lost business over the past year because they were not able to introduce new business. This group, however, accounted for only some 8 per cent of the total number of valuers in the sample.

4.42. In recent years the OFT has also received complaints about and evidence of reciprocity, and expressed concern to the CML, as has the RICS. Following discussions over several months during 1992 between the CML and the RICS, they issued an agreed 'position statement' in November of that year, which states as follows:

> In respect of the appointment of valuers to lending institutions' valuation panels, it is agreed that the lending institutions' approach should be to make such appointments on the basis of the ability of the valuer to provide the required inspection and valuation service competently,

41

promptly and with the required professional indemnity insurance. In the event of there being more valuers meeting the above criteria than the lending institution requires to cover the subject area, that lending institution may take into account in making its selection the ability of the valuer to introduce other business.

The CML and some of the largest lenders told us that, in practice, this permits lenders to use the potential for introduced business as a 'tie-breaker' in deciding which valuers to appoint to their panels, when there is an excess supply of suitable valuers wishing to join their panels, as has been the case in recent years.

## Conflicts of interest

4.43. As explained above, a mortgage valuation is intended to be an impartial and competent assessment of the open market value of the property concerned. The RICS and others have suggested to us that the independence or accuracy of a valuation may be threatened or undermined where a valuer faces conflicts of interest. The RICS views a conflict of interest as arising in various circumstances: where a valuer is unable to give full, proper and unbiased advice to a client because he acts for another person or has other obligations or pressures that detract from, or affect, his relationship with the client; or because conflicting duties are owed to different clients; or there is an appearance that the valuer is profiting from his own position. Such potential conflicts are most likely to arise where the lender has some form of commercial or financial interest in the sale, which may occur, for example, where the lender either owns the property (eg a repossessed home) or is the selling agent and receiving some form of commission fee (ie when it owns the estate agency).

4.44. The 1986 Act, section 13, specifically disqualifies certain categories of person from making a report on the value of the property in question. It disqualifies:

— building society staff who are engaged in assessing and approving the mortgage application;

— any person who has received a commission from the society for introducing the would-be borrower;

— any person, and associated person, who has a financial interest in the disposition of the property; and

— any person who receives a commission for introducing the parties to the property transaction.

4.45. It is generally accepted that section 13 precludes a valuer employed by a society or by its subsidiary valuing a property for a new mortgage where the property concerned has been repossessed by that society, and is being sold by it. But in the late 1980s the RICS became concerned that other conflicts of interest for valuers may exist as a consequence of societies' involvement in estate agencies. In January 1986 the RICS took legal advice on various situations that could arise and received the following advice:

(a) an in-house surveyor would not be precluded from valuing where a society's estate agency subsidiary was conducting the sale;

(b) a valuer employed by one subsidiary would not be precluded from valuing where the sale was being conducted by another subsidiary; and

(c) a valuer employed by a subsidiary of a society was precluded from acting where that subsidiary was also selling the property on behalf of the building society, for example under its powers of sale under a mortgage deed.

4.46. Lenders have always had to carry out a certain percentage of repossessions but the level increased markedly in the early 1990s. For most of the 1980s, for example, total repossessions were under 20,000 properties a year, but in 1991 this rose to some 75,000. The level in 1992 was not much less, but repossessions in 1993 were down to under 60,000.

4.47. The provision of estate agency services by building societies is a recent phenomenon, arising only after societies were permitted by the 1986 Act to widen their activities in this way. A number of lenders, eg Halifax, Abbey National, Nationwide (see paragraphs 3.10 and 3.11), have acquired large chains of estate agents (and in some cases have later disposed of them).

4.48. There has been a difference of opinion over the interpretation of section 13(2) of the 1986 Act where a valuation report is to be made on a property in connection with a prospective loan where the society in question is already the mortgagee to the vendor. The debate was initiated by legal advice obtained by the RICS in Scotland in January 1987, which concluded that staff and subsidiary company valuers would be precluded from valuing in those circumstances. The RICS in England took further advice. This concluded that a society's own employees were not precluded from carrying out the valuation and preparing the report. The society only had the necessary financial interest when it either owned the property outright, or some other security holder was exercising powers of sale under a mortgage. This view has been contested, but the issue has yet to be dealt with in a court of law.

4.49. In 1987 an RICS working party was established to consider the question of conflicts of interest in residential estate agency. The working party in its deliberations noted that a perceived conflict of interest arose when a staff or subsidiary company valuer was valuing a property that was being sold either through the estate agency arm of the building society which employs the staff valuer or through a subsidiary of the parent organization. It considered the suggestion that there should be a prohibition on staff and subsidiary company valuers taking instructions to value properties which were being sold through the estate agency arm of the parent organization which employs the valuer, but recommended against it.

4.50. Following presentation of its initial report in 1990, the working party was asked to widen its study and look into conflicts of interest generally. It was also asked to reconsider its views on a prohibition on in-house and subsidiary company valuers.

4.51. The working party concluded that the RICS should opt for disclosure rather than prohibition. It considered the legal grounds for disqualification; it recognized that choice of valuer must rest with the lender; it considered the pressure that might be exerted on a valuer and concluded that a panel valuer could feel under similar pressure to enable transactions to go ahead, in order to sustain continuing business, as in-house and subsidiary company valuers; it noted that a valuer who succumbs to pressure and values to order would be dealt with severely under the RICS's disciplinary rules; and it noted that there was little evidence that members of the public complain about valuers' lack of independence.

4.52. The RICS's rules are subject to scrutiny under the restrictive trade practices legislation and it therefore sought an informal view from the OFT. Whilst not wishing to prejudge his position the DGFT commented that disclosure was better than prohibition. He advised that he started from a presumption that prohibition tends to have anti-competitive effects, and went on to say that he would need to be persuaded that there was a problem of such magnitude that prohibition was appropriate despite its anti-competitive effects.

4.53. In the absence of such evidence the RICS concluded that it would be difficult to persuade the OFT that prohibition was in the public interest.

4.54. The RICS simultaneously raised with the CML the question of disclosure and the possibility that if a borrower felt unhappy with the relationship of the valuer with the lender he could ask for another valuer with a different relationship. The CML refused to agree to this but instead agreed to a disclosure of relationship along the lines: 'A valuation may be carried out by a valuer employed by the lender, a valuer from a subsidiary company, or an independent panel valuer from the private sector.' The CML's members were subsequently advised (see Appendix 4.9) to inform borrowers, either in their marketing literature or on the mortgage application form, as they wished, that the valuation might be carried out by an in-house valuer, a valuer in a subsidiary company of the lender, or an independent panel valuer. The CML further advised that prominence should be given to the notice to borrowers, and that it should not be a 'small print' exercise. We have examined the marketing literature and mortgage application forms of a number of lenders and found that many comply with the CML guidance. Halifax, Abbey National and Woolwich, for example, indicate clearly in their marketing literature that the valuation may be either from their in-house staff, from a subsidiary company, or a panel surveyor. Nationwide, on the other hand, includes such information in the notes to its mortgage application form. By contrast, it is on the valuation report that Leeds shows whether it was carried out by one of its own valuers or a panel valuer. We note, however, that borrowers are not positively requested or required to indicate that they have no objection to these arrangements. Lenders told us that borrowers appear to be unconcerned about these arrangements and that borrower complaints on this issue are rare.

4.55. In the course of this inquiry concern has been expressed to the MMC by members of the public and individual surveyors (see Chapter 8) that lenders' valuers might be subject to pressure from lenders to be less than fully objective in their evaluation, leading to either undervaluations or, in some circumstances, to overvaluations of properties. Undervaluations, for example, could in principle, at least, work to a lender's advantage if it wished to minimize risk by reducing its loan:value (equity) ratio. It might also gain financially from an increased take-up of mortgage indemnity insurance. Particularly in recent years there have been a limited number of instances where borrowers have claimed that valuers have undervalued the property, but this might reflect caution following the experiences of the property boom. Alternatively, if the lender were acting also as the selling agent, it might see advantage in a valuation that was not lower than the agreed purchase price, in order to minimize the risk of the sale not going ahead and thereby increasing the chances of it receiving its commission on the sale, as well as any commission that might arise from the sale of any associated insurance products. All the largest lenders, however, told us that there would be no advantage to them from either under or overvaluations: lenders' primary interest is to have available a reliable valuation which is free from any bias. They also told us that such under- or overvaluations by lenders would be in contravention of the terms of the 1986 Act, and that, for valuers, such activity would be contrary to their professional bodies' code of conduct.

4.56. The RICS told us that potential conflicts of interest was a difficult area to deal with but it continues to have concerns. It stated that notwithstanding the lenders' general compliance with the CML's disclosure guidance, the matter was of such concern that it was being kept under review.

4.57. As explained previously, those lenders employing valuers in-house and within subsidiary companies assign much of the work available to those valuers. Major society lenders (eg Halifax, Woolwich and Leeds) told us that in doing so, they believe they comply fully with the requirements of the 1986 Act.

## Fraud and negligence

4.58. The nature and incidence of fraud and negligence in connection with the provision of mortgage valuations are difficult matters to address, at least partly because the evidence available is inherently incomplete. Nevertheless, the subject is of particular importance to some of the central issues in this inquiry. The largest lenders, for example, have emphasized to us that the main restrictions they apply to the selection of valuers are required largely as a matter of prudential control, in order to limit their exposure to fraud and negligence, to accord with guidance under the BSC's Prudential Notes (see paragraph 2.15) and that of some police fraud squads. One lender also told us that those lenders who did not operate such controls tended to charge a higher rate of interest on mortgage loans than those who do.

4.59. In this section, we deal first with the general nature of fraud and negligence in this area; secondly, we look at the economic and other conditions which have led to an increase in such malpractice in recent years; and we then examine such quantitative and other evidence as is available, mainly from the seven largest lenders.

4.60. In its widest sense, mortgage fraud encompasses a broad range of activities and practices involving criminal deception for financial gain. Broadly, there are two main types, ie status fraud and property-related fraud, as explained in a recent research report by Michael Clarke and also in a section of the CML Mortgage Fraud Manual, shown in Appendix 4.10. According to Clarke, status fraud is the most prevalent form. In many cases, this involves individual borrowers exaggerating their true incomes when applying for a mortgage, possibly using forged documentation, in order to secure

a larger loan than would otherwise be granted by lenders. Such borrowers may often have every intention of meeting their mortgage obligations and repaying the loan outstanding, and such cases usually only come to light when something goes wrong (eg they become unemployed) and the borrowers concerned find themselves unable to meet their monthly payments. Another important type of status fraud arises where the borrower has no intention of using the property for his own residential purposes, but instead lets out the property to rent-paying tenants. Again, the borrowers may have every intention of meeting the repayment obligations, and the fraud involved in such cases may only rarely become fully apparent, often as a result of unforeseen circumstances (for example, an Inland Revenue investigation of the borrower, or complaints from tenants to a local authority). Professional fraud of this type in some cases involves multiple purchases of properties, with the borrower perhaps using different identities, and applying for loans from a number of different lenders, or multiple applications in respect of the same property.

4.61. Valuers are most likely to be involved in the second main type of fraud, ie that of property-related fraud. Although such fraud might in principle involve an undervaluation of the property, by far the more likely situation is where the property is wilfully overvalued, in order to secure a mortgage loan in excess of the property's true value. Some of the more extreme examples of which lenders have given us details, for example, have been where the valuation given was substantially in excess of the property's realistic market value, eg the initial valuation was around £500,000, but the subsequent revaluation or realized value following repossession only £100,000. Given this difference between the initial valuation and the subsequent estimate of market price, it is not hard to see that a fraudulent borrower could make a substantial gain once the transaction had been completed simply by defaulting on the mortgage obligations and absconding with the surplus, part of which would presumably be paid to the valuer. In practice, to be fully successful, such frauds may often require either the solicitor or others associated with the transaction to act as an accomplice, in order to prevent evidence of malpractice being exposed prior to completion of the deal.

4.62. Lenders told us, however, that in less extreme cases of valuation fraud, the detection and substantiation of wrongdoing is far more complex. They suggested that some mortgage brokers, for example, might wish to exert pressure on a valuer not to give a valuation that was lower than the purchase price, in order to avoid endangering the sale and the brokers' commission. The difference between a fully objective valuation and that given in these circumstances might be rather modest, and fraudulent behaviour would be difficult to establish. Indeed, both lenders and valuers acknowledge that property valuation is at best a matter of professional judgment, and that different valuers may often differ in their unbiased valuations. Moreover, they also acknowledge that in particular cases, to distinguish adequately between a professional difference of judgment between unbiased valuers, and professional negligence or deliberate fraud by the valuer, may be at best difficult and at worst impossible.

4.63. Many of the instances of professional negligence on which lenders have provided details appear to involve surveyors failing to notice and report on serious defects in the property, such as evidence of dry rot or subsidence. The more serious the defects, the greater, of course, is the potential effect on value. However, the distinction between gross negligence and fraud may be especially difficult to determine. In practice, lenders have found it extremely difficult to meet the high legal standards of proof in fraud cases and, as explained further below, few cases of valuation fraud have been successfully prosecuted in recent years. Moreover, lenders are better able to recoup any losses sustained by claiming for negligence against the valuer's professional indemnity insurer than by pursuing an action for fraud. As a consequence, there are many more instances of alleged negligence than of fraud.

4.64. Turning to the economic and other conditions which have led to an increase in allegations and suspicions of such malpractice in recent years, it would appear from lenders' evidence that prior to 1988 the incidence of detected fraud directly associated with valuations was small, and that negligent valuations were also a rather modest problem. In part, such evidence is misleading, as lenders have told us, because rising house prices would be likely in any event to conceal potential cases of fraud and negligence relating to overvaluations. But the housing boom of the late 1980s gave rise to some exceptional conditions in the housing and associated mortgage lending markets. House prices, for example, were rising very fast at that time, eg on occasions at an annual rate of up to 25 per cent, and the number of transactions also rose in 1988 to a peak level of 2.4 million. Deregulation of the building societies and other lenders in 1986 led to increased competition between lenders, which itself fostered less strict borrowing conditions, such as less exacting checks on borrowers' status and incomes. Given these exceptional conditions, and particularly the high level of transactions, it is perhaps not surprising that the total number of suspected and actual incidents of such malpractice may have increased.

4.65. The subsequent deep slump in the housing market, in terms of both house prices and the number of transactions, as well as the depth of the general economic recession and the increase in unemployment, have exposed these problems. In these circumstances, evaluating whether or not the valuation undertaken at the time was reasonable and competent would, in many cases, have been extremely difficult, and establishing fraud or negligence even more so.

4.66. Lenders both large and small have stressed their concern to us that fraudulent and negligent valuations are a significant problem for them, and that in the past the uncontrolled use of intermediaries and non-panel valuers led, mainly during the recent housing boom, to an increase in the incidence of such malpractice. In normal market conditions, the seven largest lenders taken together deal with over half a million valuations a year, and at the peak it would have been over a million. For these lenders, the number of alleged or suspected cases of malpractice is of the order of 1,000 to 1,500, but these still account for only a small proportion, ie less than 0.25 per cent, of the number of valuations carried out in most years. As explained below, the number of cases where fraud or negligence has actually been proved is far smaller. The largest lenders told us that this reflected the difficulty of establishing such malpractice, that their controls had been effective in limiting its incidence, and that the data they had provided to us excluded any direct actions taken by borrowers against panel valuers, since lenders would not normally have information on such actions.

4.67. As regards the individual largest lenders, one told us that prior to the collapse of the housing market, fraud and negligence had been negligible, but since then a number of cases had been revealed because of the high level of repossessions. In 1992 no cases of fraud involving valuers had been proved, but three cases of suspected fraud involving panel surveyors were currently under investigation. A further 300 cases of suspected negligence were also being examined by this lender, following repossession, of which 50 involved in-house and its subsidiary company valuers and 250 involved panel surveyors. As regards negligence cases against valuers, in 1992, where compensation was paid, 15 cases were against in-house valuers, 8 against its subsidiary company, 12 concerned panel valuers and 1 was against a non-panel valuer. These figures exclude numerous claims settled directly between panel valuers and borrowers where the lender was not directly involved in the settlement and, therefore, does not hold statistical information.

4.68. Another of the largest lenders told us that it had strengthened its internal safeguards against valuer fraud and negligence in recent years and that this had successfully limited its exposure to malpractice. It also said that the number of suspected fraud cases had risen sharply in recent years. In 1992 there were over 2,000 such cases, though it was not able to say how many of these involved valuers and suspected malpractice in the valuation carried out. However, no cases of alleged fraud have been brought to court by this lender in the period 1988 to 1993. In 1992 it pursued claims against its panel valuers in some 24 cases of suspected negligence, almost all of which concerned repossessed properties. In some cases its claims have been dropped, and in others no settlement has yet been reached, so it was not able to quantify the number of successful actions or the amounts recovered. It also said that it had taken disciplinary action, in 1992, against four of its in-house valuers because of suspected negligence; and that six cases were being pursued against valuers in its valuation subsidiary. One of the cases against its in-house valuers involved a property that was initially valued at £1.25 million: the subsequent revaluation was £0.75 million. All the other cases against its in-house valuers and those in its subsidiary company involved properties initially valued at between £200,000 and £300,000. To date, settlements in its favour amount to £170,000.

4.69. Another lender told us that prior to 1988 fraud and negligence case were rare. Since then, there had been, for panel valuers, three cases of proven negligence, no cases of proven fraud, eight cases of suspected fraud, and 62 cases of suspected negligence. Over the same period, non-panel valuers had been involved in 1 case of proven fraud, 11 of proven negligence, 23 of suspected fraud and about 100 cases of suspected negligence. In-house valuers had been involved in only three cases of suspected negligence. It added that a further 400 cases of possible fraud or negligence were yet to be investigated; and that, although fraud cases were few in overall number, the average loss it suffered was in excess of £100,000 for each property involved.

4.70. Another lender told us that since 1988 it had revised its internal procedures in order to minimize its exposure to fraud and negligence. No cases of fraud had been proved, though it provided details to us of two cases arising in 1992 which involved firms of valuers on its panel and which were almost certainly fraudulent. One, for example, involved a forged signature; in the other, the individual concerned was not a qualified valuer. In both cases, the initial valuation had been in the order of nearly £0.5 million, whereas the subsequent revaluations—carried out some two years later—produced a figure of about £100,000. There were also about 450 cases of suspected fraud in 1992, though it was not able to say how many involved valuations. As regards suspected negligence, there were 64 cases involving its in-house valuers, 255 cases involving valuers in its subsidiary company, 49 cases where a panel valuer was involved and 1 case of a dubious valuation by a non-panel valuer.

4.71. Another lender told us that it had stopped accepting valuations from non-panel surveyors in April 1990 because they appeared to be giving rise to a disproportionately large number of overvaluations. Fraud has not been proved in any instance, but it is at present taking legal action in 27 cases, involving 13 non-panel and 14 panel valuers. To date, out-of-court settlements totalling £0.8 million have been agreed, of which £0.55 million was in relation to cases involving non-panel valuers.

4.72. Another lender told us that it had no statistics available on instances of fraud and negligence concerning residential mortgage valuations, though it did not consider such malpractice to be a serious problem. Nonetheless, it said that there were probably several dozen such cases currently under investigation.

4.73. Another lender told us that it had experienced few cases of fraud in relation to valuation reports, though a handful of cases were currently being investigated. It has had more experience of solicitor/conveyancer fraud and negligence, and in 1993 recovered some £2.1 million from the Solicitors' Indemnity and Compensation Fund in relation to fraud, dishonesty and negligence by panel solicitors. In 1992 no cases of fraud or negligence were proved against valuers, though five cases of suspected fraud (all of which involved suspected overvaluations) and two cases of suspected negligence were being investigated. It also provided us with details of 13 claims of negligence against its in-house valuers where it had settled the claims, most of which involved allegations that the valuers had failed to identify serious defects in the property (eg dry rot). It was not able to provide comparable information with regard to either the valuers in its subsidiary company or its panel valuers. It commented, however, that in its experience, claims of negligence were far more likely to involve panel valuers than its in-house or subsidiary company valuers.

4.74. A number of lenders expressed concern that the valuers' professional bodies (RICS/ISVA) did not impose sufficiently high standards of training and quality control on its members, which tended to increase the risk of negligence; and also that there was no indemnity fund to which they could turn in cases of fraud, as there was with solicitors. The RICS told us, however, that technical standards were continuously being improved and that introducing such an indemnity fund was not a practical possibility. The RICS also said that, in practice, very few of its surveyors—less than half a dozen in recent years—had been struck off because of proven fraud; and that many of the lenders' problems with poor loans and the use of intermediaries reflected lax internal controls by lenders concerning borrowers' status, particularly during the housing boom of the late 1980s.

4.75. Lenders did not provide separate statistics on valuer malpractice in Scotland, though they indicated that the numbers were proportionally rather less, mainly because the slump in house prices had been less severe and, as a result, there were fewer repossessions.

# 5 Lenders' valuation and administration charges

## Contents

## Introduction

5.1. Virtually all lenders require prepayment for a mortgage valuation at the time the prospective borrower applies for a loan, whether this is for buying a residential property, for the purposes of refinancing an existing loan, or for a further advance. In paragraphs 5.3 to 5.7 we review the principal costs associated with valuations and broadly how charges are determined. The payment made by the borrower at the time of the application often includes both a valuation fee and an administration charge, the composition, level and transparency of which we consider in paragraphs 5.8 to 5.12. By far the main element of cost involved in the valuation itself is that of employing the valuer who undertakes the on-site inspection and valuation work, whether in the form of a fee paid to an external valuer or the cost of employing an in-house or subsidiary company valuer. Lenders' scales of charges for the valuation component, which are usually set nationally and related to a range of house prices, are evaluated in paragraphs 5.13 to 5.20. In paragraphs 5.21 to 5.29 we provide details of lenders' total charges to borrowers for valuations and administration. These scale charges are also usually set nationally and related to a range of house prices. We also look at lenders' charges for revaluations, and their use of promotional discounts off the standard valuation fee. Charges for HBRs and SSYs are considered in paragraphs 5.30 and 5.31. Lastly, we provide, in paragraphs 5.32 to 5.42, a financial assessment of the revenues of the seven largest mortgage lenders from charges made for valuations and administration, the costs incurred and the profits arising from the provision of valuation services.

5.2. As in Chapters 3 and 4, we also indicate in this chapter, briefly and where appropriate, the views of the CML, lenders and other interested parties on various aspects of charges made. Their views are summarized more fully in Chapters 6, 7 and 8 respectively.

## Valuation charges

### *General: costs and determination of charges*

5.3. When prospective borrowers apply for a mortgage loan, there are three main processes or stages involved, prior to completion of the mortgage. Each of these requires the use of resources and, therefore, results in costs being incurred, falling mainly to the lender in the first instance. The three stages are as follows:

48

(a) the prospective borrower is interviewed, either by the lender or an intermediary, to determine the broad details of the type of advance which is sought and its particular terms;

(b) the lender subsequently evaluates the application made, and most particularly the applicant's income and creditworthiness, to ensure that the loan is within the borrower's ability to repay; and

(c) a suitable valuation is generally carried out to ensure that the property concerned provides adequate security for the advance.

At the interview stage, the main costs to lenders (or intermediaries) are those arising from the use of branch staff and any associated office overheads. Where the interview does not subsequently lead to a loan application being made—which may be the case for a significant proportion of the interviews carried out—the costs are absorbed by the lender (or intermediary) concerned, since no charge is normally levied in these circumstances. Where the borrower does go on to make an application for a loan, the lender incurs office administration costs in stage (b), in the process of checking on the borrower's income and status.

5.4. The valuation itself—stage (c)—is usually carried out at the same time as the lender is processing the borrower's application. The main cost of the valuation is that of employing a valuer to carry out the on-site inspection and prepare a valuation report (see paragraphs 4.5 to 4.12). If an in-house valuer is used or one employed in the lender's subsidiary company, the cost arises from the valuer's salary and any associated employment and overhead costs, including the costs of professional indemnity insurance. The average salary in 1993 of valuers employed by the largest lenders was around £25,000 a year. If an external valuer is used, then the main cost involved is the fee paid to that valuer. Lenders told us, however, that they also incur various other administrative costs which are linked with valuations, eg costs arising in the course of instructing the valuer; in maintaining their panels; in the provision of training to valuers; and in monitoring and auditing valuation reports carried out by their in-house valuers, those in subsidiary companies and panel valuers. The costs incurred by the seven largest lenders, which had risen in recent years, they told us, are considered further in paragraphs 5.32 to 5.42.

5.5. With regard to the scale of fees paid to panel valuers and those charged to borrowers by building society lenders for valuations, these were until the early 1980s fixed by agreement between building societies and valuers under the auspices of the BSA (see paragraphs 2.6 and 3.38). At that time, few lenders made a charge for administration and the fee that borrowers paid was almost invariably the amount that was passed on to the valuer concerned; most of these were external panel valuers. The fee scales agreed within the BSA were, as now, set nationally and related to a range of property price levels (eg £15,000, £20,000 etc). These fee scales applied to all building society lenders and all valuers, and they were widely observed. There was no price competition in valuations, therefore, either between lenders or between valuers.

5.6. As explained in paragraph 2.6, these arrangements were abandoned in the early 1980s, and since then, individual lenders have set their own scales of fees independently of other lenders and without formal consultation with valuers or their representative bodies, the RICS and the ISVA. Virtually all lenders continue, individually, to set scales of fees which, where appropriate, apply nationally and which are related to specified bands of property prices (see paragraphs 5.13 to 5.20). Since around the mid-1980s, many lenders have also introduced an additional charge to cover, wholly or partly, their administration and other costs associated with the valuation and the processing of mortgage applications. This administration charge is usually combined with the fee for the valuation itself, though it is not in all cases separately identified in lenders' marketing literature, and the amount of the charge is not always made clear to borrowers (see paragraphs 5.11 and 5.12).

5.7. Most of the largest lenders told us that valuation services as a whole, and particularly in-house valuers and their panels, are treated as a cost, rather than a profit, centre, though subsidiary companies are natural profit centres in their own right. Charges for the valuation element, they said, are therefore determined largely by the underlying costs involved, particularly those of employing in-house and external valuers, rather than by a requirement to earn a profit margin. Indeed, they told us that when setting fees, their main concern was to maintain the quality of the valuation report rather than to drive costs as low as possible. Some of the largest lenders told us that they were not aware of any instances where panel valuers had declined to accept valuations instructions because lenders' fees were too low. As a result, although individually they have regard to the overall level of fees levied by other lenders, this was not in itself a major factor. An administration charge was also necessary, they said, because around 20 per cent of all applications and valuations do not subsequently lead to a loan being made. A charge was levied, therefore, to recoup some or all of the administrative costs they incurred on failed or aborted applications. This recovery would not be possible if the charge were to be rolled up in the loan itself. The largest lenders also stated that prepayment in the form of an up-front charge was necessary in order to discourage frivolous applications, and to ensure that the valuation element of the cost was paid for in advance by the applicant concerned, rather than by existing borrowers.

## Administration charges

5.8. Many, though not all, lenders currently levy some form of charge to cover some or all of their administration costs in respect of mortgage applications and valuations. Usually, it forms part of the overall charge made for the mortgage valuation, which itself may be variously termed a valuation fee or an application fee. We consider first the nature of the fees levied and the amounts charged in recent years; and secondly, the extent to which such charges are made transparent to prospective borrowers in lenders' marketing literature. The seven largest lenders' revenues from such administration charges are considered in paragraph 3.61.

5.9. Until the mid-1980s, few lenders levied a charge for administration which was in addition to that for the valuation, and where they did, the amount was relatively small. Since then, many lenders have begun to impose such a charge, and the amount of the fee has increased significantly in recent years. A summary of practices relating to administration charges, along with other practices, by all the mortgage lenders from whom we collected information is given in Appendices 4.6 and 4.7. Table 5.1 gives details of the charges made by the seven largest lenders, which together account for about half of the market for residential mortgage lending (see paragraph 3.50). As shown in the table, each of these seven largest lenders, with the exception of Barclays, imposes some form of administration charge. Halifax, Abbey National, Nationwide and C&G each make a charge to the borrower which is additional to that for the valuation itself. Some of these lenders told us that this charge was a contribution towards the costs of processing mortgage applications, as well as other internal administration costs associated with the provision of valuation services. For Leeds and Woolwich, the charge made is in the form of a deduction from the fee received from the borrower before it is paid to panel valuers. C&G also imposes an additional annual lump sum charge on its panel valuers (see the third footnote to Table 5.1).

TABLE 5.1  **Administration fees or charges of the 15 largest mortgage lenders, 1988 to 1993**

|  | 1988 | 1989 | 1990 | 1991 | 1992 | 1993 |
|---|---|---|---|---|---|---|
| (a) The seven largest lenders |  |  |  |  |  |  |
| Halifax | 2 | 2 | 5 | 15 | 25 | 25 |
| Abbey National | 3 | 3 | 20 | 25 | 40 | 50 |
| Nationwide* | 13 | 33 | 31 | 31 | 45 | 45 |
| Barclays |  |  | No administration fee |  |  |  |
| Woolwich† | 0 | 0 | 0 | 0 | 25 | 25 |
| Leeds* | 0 | 10 | 10 | 12 | 13 | 16 |
| C&G‡ | 50 | 50 | 50 | 50 | 50 | 50 |
|  |  |  |  |  |  |  |
| Average (£) | 11 | 16 | 19 | 22 | 33 | 35 |
| Index (base of 1988 = 100) | 100 | 145 | 173 | 200 | 300 | 318 |
|  |  |  |  |  |  |  |
| (b) Other lenders (charges for 1993 only) |  |  |  |  |  |  |
| National & Provincial | £40 |  |  |  |  |  |
| NatWest | No administration fee |  |  |  |  |  |
| Bank of Scotland | No administration fee |  |  |  |  |  |
| A&L | £40 |  |  |  |  |  |
| TSB | No administration fee |  |  |  |  |  |
| Britannia | £60 |  |  |  |  |  |
| Bristol & West | £10–£20 |  |  |  |  |  |
| Lloyds | No administration fee |  |  |  |  |  |

Source: Mortgage lenders.

---

*Administration charges for Nationwide and Leeds vary according to property values. The charges given are unweighted averages for property value bands up to £150,000.

†Woolwich charged a fee of £10 for HBRs during 1988 to 1991. This was increased to £50 in April 1992.

‡Since 1991 C&G has also levied an additional annual charge of £100 + VAT on its panel valuers to cover its costs of maintaining the panel.

50

5.10. As regards the form and amount of such charges, many lenders apply a flat rate charge of, say, £25 or £50 per valuation, though in some cases, for example Nationwide and Leeds, the amount varies, along with the fee for the valuation itself, with the value or purchase price of the property. Table 5.1 gives details of charges for administration by the seven largest lenders in the years 1988 to 1993, together with the comparable charges levied in 1993 by the eight next largest lenders. Most of the seven largest lenders have increased the level of their charges substantially over the period 1988 to 1993. For example, the charges made by Halifax and Abbey National have risen from under £5 in 1988, to £25 and £50 respectively in 1993. Over the same period, Nationwide's average charge has increased from £13 to £45; Woolwich introduced a charge £25 in 1992; and Leeds introduced such a charge in 1989 at an average of £10, which has since risen to £16. That of C&G, on the other hand, has remained constant at £50. Barclays, as well as some other banking lenders, including NatWest, Bank of Scotland, TSB and Lloyds, do not levy a charge to cover their administration costs. On average, the administration component of charges by the seven largest lenders has risen from £11 in 1988 to £35 in 1993.

5.11. Turning to the question of the transparency of such charges to prospective borrowers, we examined the marketing literature of the 15 largest lenders, as well as of a number of others, in order to determine whether the existence of the charge was made clear to applicants for a mortgage loan; whether the amount was specified; and whether the nature of the administration or other costs being charged for was made clear. A summary of our findings is given in Table 5.2, which shows that 10 of the 15 largest lenders levy an administration charge of some sort. Of those ten lenders, four of them (Woolwich, Leeds, National & Provincial Building Society (N&P), and Bristol & West Building Society (Bristol & West)) do not make clear that such a charge is being made, and six of them (including the latter four named societies) do not separately specify the amount of the charge. The two largest lenders, Halifax and Abbey National, do, however, specify the amount (see Appendix 5.1 and Appendix 4.5, respectively). Halifax's current literature also states, albeit in small print, that its £25 fee is an administration charge. The existence and amount of such a charge has been included in Halifax's literature since its introduction in 1981, when valuation reports were first made available to borrowers. Abbey National's current literature, on the other hand, refers to a 'mortgage set up fee' of £50. This was first made clear in its literature in October 1993.

TABLE 5.2  **Lenders' policies on administration charges**

| 15 largest lenders | 1 | 2 | 3 | 4 | 5 |
|---|---|---|---|---|---|
| Halifax | Y | Y | Y | Y | N |
| Abbey National | Y | Y | Y | Y | N |
| Nationwide | Y | Y | N | Y | N |
| Barclays | N | N/A | N/A | N/A | N/A |
| Woolwich | Y | N | N | N | N |
| Leeds | Y | N | N | N | N |
| C&G | Y | Y | Y | N | N |
| N&P | Y | N | N | N | N |
| NatWest | N | N/A | N/A | N/A | N/A |
| Bank of Scotland | N | N/A | N/A | N/A | N/A |
| A&L | Y | Y | N | Y | N |
| TSB | N | N/A | N/A | N/A | N/A |
| Britannia | Y | Y | Y | Y | N |
| | | | | | |
| Bristol & West | Y | N | N | N | N |
| Lloyds | N | N/A | N/A | N/A | N/A |
| | | | | | |
| *Some other lenders** | | | | | |
| Bradford & Bingley | Y | N | N | N | N |
| Yorkshire | Y | N | N | N | N |
| Kent Reliance | Y | Y | N | Y | N |
| West Bromwich | Y | N | N | N | N |
| Dunfermline | Y | N | N | N | N |

*Source:* Mortgage lenders.

*Lenders identified as charging an administration fee but not specifying the amount in their marketing literature.
*Key:* Y = Yes; N = No; N/A = Not applicable.
1. Does the lender impose a charge additional to a fee for the valuation *per se* (ie an application fee or administration charge of some sort)?
2. Is the existence of that charge made clear to the borrower in the lender's marketing literature?
3. Is the amount of the charge specified in the lender's literature?
4. Does the literature specify that the charge is to cover administration costs?
5. Does the literature specify what types of administrative or other costs are covered by the charge?

5.12. More generally, six of the largest lenders and a number of other lenders (see Table 5.2), which together account for more than 25 per cent of all residential mortgage lending, do not separately identify in their marketing literature the amount of the charge being made for administration. Moreover, six of the largest lenders (Abbey National, Woolwich, Leeds, C&G, N&P, and Bristol & West) do not indicate clearly that the charge is to cover administration costs; and none of the ten largest lenders that make such a charge specify or explain what types of administration costs are being charged for.

## Scale fees: the valuation component

5.13. As explained above, the overall charge levied by many lenders on prospective borrowers at the time of a mortgage application includes and usually combines both (a) a fee for administration; and (b) a fee for the valuation, which is the component of the charge that we consider in this section. As it is net of any administrative costs or charges, this component constitutes the amount within the total charge that the borrower pays for the valuation; and also the amount that is paid either to an external panel valuer, or to a lender's subsidiary company. It is also the amount which is retained by the lender, where the valuation is carried out by one of the lender's in-house valuers. As will be explained later (see paragraph 5.42), VAT is generally payable where an external valuer is used, but not where an in-house or subsidiary company valuer carries out the valuation. We start with the general structure of such charges and their relationship to costs. We then look at the amounts charged by the seven largest lenders and the trends in valuation charges in recent years. The selective use by some lenders of promotional discounts from the standard fee is examined in paragraphs 5.27 to 5.29. We then compare the fee scales of these largest lenders with the fees charged by independent valuers for non-panel work, based on information contained in the study which we commissioned (see Appendix 4.4).

5.14. With regard to the structure of such charges, they are in most instances related to specified levels or ranges of purchase price, hence the use of the term 'scale fee'. (Details of the distribution of mortgage loans in the UK in 1992 by different house price bands are given in Appendix 5.2.) Typically, one level of fee is set for properties where the purchase price is, say, up to £25,000; a higher fee applies where the price is, say, between £25,000 to £50,000; and so on. For higher-valued properties where the purchase price is in excess of a given level (this varies between different lenders, but is often around £250,000) the valuation fee is usually negotiable. The pricing intervals that define the scale are not always precisely the same for all lenders, though the two largest lenders, Halifax and Abbey National, use a similar scale based on price bands of £50,000, ie up to £50,000; then up to £100,000; then up to £150,000 and so on (see Appendices 5.1 and 4.5). Each lender sets its own scale of fees, which are typically reviewed each year, and these generally apply throughout the UK. For national lenders such as Halifax and Abbey National, therefore, the valuation charge made for properties of a given value (say £40,000) would be the same, wherever the property was located within the UK. Many of the smaller lenders, however, operate in more limited regional or even local areas, and their scale fees only apply within their own operational areas. A summary of practices relating to the use of scale fees, and other practices, by all the mortgage lenders from whom we collected information is given in Appendices 4.6 and 4.7.

5.15. The scale fee structure incorporates a number of features which tend to weaken or undermine the relationship between the prices actually charged and the underlying costs of carrying out mortgage valuations, and which may as a result involve an element of cross-subsidy between different borrowers. With the use of national scales as currently applied by lenders, for example, the fees charged will vary with regional differences in house prices rather than the underlying costs of the valuation services, which are always provided on a local basis. Specifically, the valuation fee for a property of a given type and size will often be greater in those regions such as, say, the South-East where house prices are higher than the average, even though the time taken by the valuer will not, in principle, be different (though the costs of professional indemnity insurance and other operating costs may be). Similarly, because lenders' scales are based on current property prices, the fees actually levied will tend to rise whenever, as during most of the 1980s, there is general house price inflation. Correspondingly, the rate of price deflation since 1989 has been much greater in the South-East compared with most other parts of the UK. This, in practice, and other things being equal, will have led to greater changes over recent years in the level of fees actually levied in the South-East, on a given property, than in other areas of the UK. These changes in the fees levied will have had little or no systemic relationship to the underlying costs of mortgage valuations.

5.16. Additionally, these scales are related strictly to property values alone and are independent, therefore, of other characteristics of properties which may affect the time taken, or the degree of difficulty involved in assessing their condition and market value. For example, the market value of a small, two-bedroomed flat in central London might well be the same or similar to that of a substantial house in, say, a remote rural area. The scale fee for valuation might also be the same, therefore, even though the time necessary to assess the condition of the house in such a rural area may, in principle, be greater than that required to value the flat in London. Moreover, lenders typically use wide value bands or intervals in their fee scales, eg £50,000 for both Halifax and Abbey National. As a result, properties at the upper and lower edges of a given value band, where the difference in value may be up to £50,000, will attract the same valuation fee, even though the work involved may be greater for the higher-valued property. A consequence of using a scale based on discrete steps, where the fee is higher one side of the step or interval level than the other, is that virtually identical properties either side of a given step will attract a different level of valuation fee. House price inflation will also, of course, have the effect of shifting some properties from just below a pricing interval to just above it, thereby increasing the valuation fee, even though the costs of carrying out a valuation may not have changed at that time.

5.17. The largest lenders told us, however, that setting valuation charges on the basis of a fixed national scale related to property values had several advantages both to lenders and also to prospective borrowers, and that no alternative scheme offered a better or fairer method. For lenders, this approach to pricing avoided the potential complexities of setting charges by area, by type of property (eg having separate fee scales for new and old properties), or by the amount of valuers' time taken. Regional variations in the costs of undertaking mortgage valuations were not considered to be significant in themselves and these were in any event taken into account to some extent, albeit not precisely, through the regional variations in house prices that exist for any given type of property. Thus a three-bedroomed semi-detached house in the South-East, for example, would command a higher market price than an identical property in, say, the North-West. As a result, the actual fee charged for a valuation, and therefore the amount that was paid to a panel valuer, for example, would tend in these circumstances to be higher in the South-East, where labour costs were generally higher than elsewhere. A further advantage of the system was seen by lenders to be greater ease of presentation in their marketing literature. For borrowers, these pricing scales were simple and easy to understand, lenders told us, with the effect that borrowers were able to determine the precise amount of the fee before applying for a loan.

5.18. Turning now to the amounts actually charged by lenders for the valuation component of the overall fee, Table 5.3 gives details of charges made by the seven largest lenders for each of the years 1988 to 1993, covering the main property value bands up to £150,000 corresponding to those used by the lenders concerned. The table also shows the unweighted average fee charged by these lenders in each year, the highest and lowest fees, and the range of fees for each value band. In 1993, for example, the valuation component of Halifax's fee for a property where the purchase price was between £25,000 and £50,000 was £100. The corresponding average charge by these largest lenders was £98: the fees varied between £113 (the highest) and £82 (the lowest), giving a fee range of £31. With regard to the fees for properties of different values, the average fee for properties with a value at the lower end of the range of up to £25,000 was £88; at the other extreme, that for properties valued between £125,000 and £150,000 was £165. We note that this valuation component of the fee has varied between lenders by a significant amount in most years and for most value bands. The variation appears to be least, in most years, for the £25,000 to £50,000 band. For other bands, however, the fees for different lenders has often varied by some 20 to 40 per cent around the average fee for these lenders.

TABLE 5.3 **The valuation component of fees levied by the seven main mortgage lenders, 1988 to 1993**

*Property value bands, £'000*

| | *25* | *50* | *75* | *100* | *125* | *150* |
|---|---|---|---|---|---|---|
| *1988* | | | | | | |
| Halifax | 55 | 75 | 90 | 100 | 115 | 125 |
| Abbey National | 59 | 74 | 89 | 99 | 117 | 129 |
| Nationwide | 55 | 70 | 80 | 90 | 110 | 120 |
| Barclays | 58 | 78 | 95 | 108 | - | - |
| Woolwich | 63 | 81 | 92 | 104 | 144 | 167 |
| Leeds | 61 | 76 | 92 | 104 | 121 | 132 |
| C&G | 50 | 75 | 75 | 100 | 100 | 125 |
| | | | | | | |
| Average (£) | 57 | 76 | 88 | 101 | 118 | 133 |
| Maximum (£) | 63 | 81 | 95 | 108 | 144 | 167 |
| Minimum (£) | 50 | 70 | 75 | 90 | 100 | 120 |
| Difference (max-min) (£) | 13 | 11 | 20 | 18 | 44 | 47 |
| | | | | | | |
| *1989* | | | | | | |
| Halifax | 55 | 75 | 90 | 100 | 115 | 125 |
| Abbey National | 59 | 74 | 89 | 99 | 117 | 129 |
| Nationwide | 60 | 70 | 80 | 90 | 110 | 120 |
| Barclays | 58 | 78 | 95 | 108 | - | - |
| Woolwich | 63 | 81 | 92 | 104 | 144 | 167 |
| Leeds | 67 | 82 | 97 | 112 | 137 | 152 |
| C&G | 50 | 75 | 75 | 100 | 100 | 125 |
| | | | | | | |
| Average (£) | 59 | 76 | 88 | 102 | 121 | 136 |
| Maximum (£) | 67 | 82 | 97 | 112 | 144 | 167 |
| Minimum (£) | 50 | 70 | 75 | 90 | 100 | 120 |
| Difference (max-min) (£) | 17 | 12 | 22 | 22 | 44 | 47 |
| | | | | | | |
| *1990* | | | | | | |
| Halifax | 65 | 85 | 105 | 125 | 155 | 155 |
| Abbey National | 65 | 75 | 92 | 104 | 128 | 140 |
| Nationwide | 65 | 70 | 80 | 90 | 110 | 120 |
| Barclays | 58 | 78 | 95 | 108 | - | - |
| Woolwich | 65 | 84 | 95 | 108 | 146 | 167 |
| Leeds | 67 | 82 | 97 | 112 | 137 | 152 |
| C&G | 75 | 75 | 75 | 100 | 100 | 125 |
| | | | | | | |
| Average (£) | 66 | 78 | 91 | 107 | 129 | 143 |
| Maximum (£) | 75 | 85 | 105 | 125 | 155 | 167 |
| Minimum (£) | 58 | 70 | 75 | 90 | 100 | 120 |
| Difference (max-min) (£) | 17 | 15 | 30 | 35 | 55 | 47 |
| | | | | | | |
| *1991* | | | | | | |
| Halifax | 70 | 90 | 110 | 130 | 160 | 160 |
| Abbey National | 65 | 72 | 90 | 105 | 140 | 140 |
| Nationwide | 77 | 82 | 92 | 102 | 133 | 133 |
| Barclays | 59 | 80 | 98 | 110 | - | - |
| Woolwich | 77 | 97 | 112 | 127 | 157 | 167 |
| Leeds | 72 | 86 | 99 | 117 | 135 | 144 |
| C&G | 80 | 80 | 80 | 105 | 105 | 130 |
| | | | | | | |
| Average (£) | 71 | 84 | 97 | 114 | 138 | 146 |
| Maximum (£) | 80 | 97 | 112 | 130 | 160 | 167 |
| Minimum (£) | 59 | 72 | 80 | 102 | 105 | 130 |
| Difference (max-min) (£) | 21 | 25 | 32 | 28 | 55 | 37 |
| | | | | | | |
| *1992* | | | | | | |
| Halifax | 75 | 95 | 115 | 135 | 165 | 165 |
| Abbey National | 85 | 85 | 105 | 120 | 155 | 155 |
| Nationwide | 77 | 82 | 92 | 102 | 133 | 133 |
| Barclays | 70 | 90 | 110 | 130 | - | - |
| Woolwich | 78 | 98 | 116 | 134 | 164 | 168 |
| Leeds | 90 | 90 | 108 | 126 | 153 | 153 |
| C&G | 85 | 110 | 110 | 135 | 135 | 180 |
| | | | | | | |
| Average (£) | 80 | 93 | 108 | 126 | 151 | 159 |
| Maximum (£) | 90 | 110 | 116 | 135 | 165 | 180 |
| Minimum (£) | 70 | 82 | 92 | 102 | 133 | 133 |
| Difference (max-min) (£) | 20 | 28 | 24 | 33 | 32 | 47 |

|  | 25 | 50 | 75 | 100 | 125 | 150 |
|---|---|---|---|---|---|---|
| *1993* | | | | | | |
| Halifax | 100 | 100 | 140 | 140 | 170 | 170 |
| Abbey National | 90 | 90 | 125 | 125 | 165 | 165 |
| Nationwide | 77 | 82 | 92 | 102 | 133 | 133 |
| Barclays | 70 | 90 | 110 | 130 | 160 | 160 |
| Woolwich | 78 | 98 | 118 | 138 | 168 | 168 |
| Leeds | 113 | 113 | 131 | 149 | 176 | 176 |
| C&G | 85 | 110 | 110 | 135 | 135 | 180 |
| Average (£) | 88 | 98 | 118 | 131 | 158 | 165 |
| Maximum (£) | 113 | 113 | 140 | 149 | 176 | 180 |
| Minimum (£) | 70 | 82 | 92 | 102 | 133 | 133 |
| Difference (max-min): (£) | 43 | 31 | 48 | 47 | 43 | 47 |

*Source:* Mortgage lenders and MMC calculations.

5.19. Table 5.4 shows the data on the seven largest lenders' fees in index form, in order to show the trend over time for different value bands. It also gives, for purposes of comparison, indices over the same period, 1988 to 1993, for both the retail price index (RPI) and an Average Earnings Index (AEI) for service industries, which measures the rate of wage inflation in those industries. As shown in the table, the average charges levied by the seven largest lenders in all these main value bands have risen at or above the general rate of inflation, but less than that of average earnings (in service industries), except for the value band up to £25,000. We consider that the latter is a more appropriate comparator than the RPI, because it more accurately measures wage inflation in employment comparable to that of valuers, and as stated earlier, valuers' salaries or fee incomes are a major cost component of valuations. In the £50,000 to £75,000 band, for example, lenders' fees increased on average by 35 per cent over this period, whilst the RPI and AEI rose by 31 per cent and 39 per cent respectively. We note that whereas fees have risen for most lenders, Nationwide has not increased its fees for the valuation component since 1991. Woolwich's fees actually decreased in 1993, but this was because it imposed a levy in that year on external panel valuers' fees, which it retains as a contribution toward administration costs.

5.20. As mentioned earlier, we commissioned a study of surveyors (see paragraphs 3.60 and 4.16), the main findings of which are summarized in Appendix 4.4. The study provided information on the fees, inclusive of VAT, charged in 1993 by independent valuers for mortgage valuations commissioned other than through their membership of lenders' panels, ie non-panel work. Results from the study are reproduced in Table 5.5. This gives figures for the distribution across various fee levels of charges made for such non-panel valuations, for four value levels, ie for properties where the purchase price was £25,000, £50,000, £75,000 and £100,000 respectively. It also gives the average charge in 1993 for the valuation component of the fees levied by the seven largest lenders (see also Table 5.3) and the average and median charges for non-panel valuations. Although the average charges by the largest lenders were similar at all price bands to the corresponding averages for non-panel valuations, the median level of charges for non-panel valuations was about £10 lower. The table also shows that, for each of the value levels included, an unweighted average of around 60 per cent of the fees charged for non-panel valuations in 1993 were lower than the corresponding average fee levied by the largest lenders. Thus, for a property where the purchase price was £50,000, the average fee of the largest lenders was £98. By comparison, for over one-fifth (ie more than 20 per cent) of the set fee quotations for non-panel valuations in the study, the charge made was £80 or less, which was 17 per cent or more below the average for the seven largest lenders. Correspondingly, around a third of such non-panel valuations were less than £85, which was 7 per cent or more below that of the largest lenders; and, in total, over three-fifths were below the average of £98 charged by the largest lenders. Where valuers are prepared to offer a discount on set fees, actual fees charged would tend to be lower than those shown in Table 5.5.

## *Total fees charged to borrowers for mortgage valuations and administration*

5.21. We have considered separately the administration and the valuation components of lenders' fee scales for mortgage valuations. We now focus on the combined level of fees, which is what

TABLE 5.4  Indices of the valuation component of fees levied by the seven main mortgage lenders, 1988 to 1993

**Property value of up to £25,000**

| Lender | 1988 | 1989 | 1990 | 1991 | 1992 | 1993 |
|---|---|---|---|---|---|---|
| Halifax | 100 | 100 | 118 | 127 | 136 | 182 |
| Abbey National | 100 | 100 | 110 | 110 | 144 | 153 |
| Nationwide | 100 | 109 | 118 | 140 | 140 | 140 |
| Barclays | 100 | 100 | 100 | 102 | 121 | 121 |
| Woolwich | 100 | 100 | 103 | 122 | 124 | 124 |
| Leeds | 100 | 110 | 110 | 118 | 148 | 185 |
| C&G | 100 | 100 | 150 | 160 | 170 | 170 |
| Average (£) | 100 | 103 | 116 | 126 | 140 | 153 |
| RPI | 100 | 108 | 118 | 125 | 130 | 131 |
| AEI | 100 | 109 | 119 | 129 | 136 | 139 |

**Property value of up to £50,000**

| Lender | 1988 | 1989 | 1990 | 1991 | 1992 | 1993 |
|---|---|---|---|---|---|---|
| Halifax | 100 | 100 | 113 | 120 | 127 | 133 |
| Abbey National | 100 | 100 | 101 | 97 | 115 | 122 |
| Nationwide | 100 | 100 | 100 | 117 | 117 | 117 |
| Barclays | 100 | 100 | 100 | 103 | 115 | 115 |
| Woolwich | 100 | 100 | 104 | 120 | 121 | 121 |
| Leeds | 100 | 108 | 108 | 113 | 119 | 149 |
| C&G | 100 | 100 | 100 | 107 | 147 | 147 |
| Average (£) | 100 | 101 | 104 | 111 | 123 | 129 |
| RPI | 100 | 108 | 118 | 125 | 130 | 131 |
| AEI | 100 | 109 | 119 | 129 | 136 | 139 |

**Property value of up to £75,000**

| Lender | 1988 | 1989 | 1990 | 1991 | 1992 | 1993 |
|---|---|---|---|---|---|---|
| Halifax | 100 | 100 | 117 | 122 | 128 | 156 |
| Abbey National | 100 | 100 | 103 | 101 | 118 | 140 |
| Nationwide | 100 | 100 | 100 | 115 | 115 | 115 |
| Barclays | 100 | 100 | 100 | 103 | 116 | 116 |
| Woolwich | 100 | 100 | 103 | 122 | 126 | 128 |
| Leeds | 100 | 105 | 105 | 108 | 117 | 142 |
| C&G | 100 | 100 | 100 | 107 | 147 | 147 |
| Average (£) | 100 | 101 | 104 | 111 | 124 | 135 |
| RPI | 100 | 108 | 118 | 125 | 130 | 131 |
| AEI | 100 | 109 | 119 | 129 | 136 | 139 |

**Property value of up to £100,000**

| Lender | 1988 | 1989 | 1990 | 1991 | 1992 | 1993 |
|---|---|---|---|---|---|---|
| Halifax | 100 | 100 | 125 | 130 | 135 | 140 |
| Abbey National | 100 | 100 | 105 | 106 | 121 | 126 |
| Nationwide | 100 | 100 | 100 | 113 | 113 | 113 |
| Barclays | 100 | 100 | 100 | 102 | 120 | 120 |
| Woolwich | 100 | 100 | 104 | 122 | 129 | 133 |
| Leeds | 100 | 108 | 108 | 113 | 122 | 144 |
| C&G | 100 | 100 | 100 | 105 | 135 | 135 |
| Average (£) | 100 | 101 | 106 | 113 | 125 | 130 |
| RPI | 100 | 108 | 118 | 125 | 130 | 131 |
| AEI | 100 | 109 | 119 | 129 | 136 | 139 |

**Property value of up to £125,000**

| Lender | 1988 | 1989 | 1990 | 1991 | 1992 | 1993 |
|---|---|---|---|---|---|---|
| Halifax | 100 | 100 | 135 | 139 | 143 | 148 |
| Abbey National | 100 | 100 | 109 | 120 | 132 | 141 |
| Nationwide | 100 | 100 | 100 | 121 | 121 | 121 |
| Barclays | - | - | - | - | 120 | 120 |
| Woolwich | 100 | 100 | 101 | 109 | 114 | 117 |
| Leeds | 100 | 113 | 113 | 112 | 127 | 146 |
| C&G | 100 | 100 | 100 | 105 | 135 | 135 |
| Average (£) | 100 | 102 | 110 | 118 | 129 | 135 |
| RPI | 100 | 108 | 118 | 125 | 130 | 131 |
| AEI | 100 | 109 | 119 | 129 | 136 | 139 |

**Property value of up to £150,000**

| Lender | 1988 | 1989 | 1990 | 1991 | 1992 | 1993 |
|---|---|---|---|---|---|---|
| Halifax | 100 | 100 | 124 | 128 | 132 | 136 |
| Abbey National | 100 | 100 | 109 | 109 | 120 | 128 |
| Nationwide | 100 | 100 | 100 | 111 | 111 | 111 |
| Barclays | - | - | - | - | - | - |
| Woolwich | 100 | 100 | 100 | 100 | - | 101 |
| Leeds | 100 | 115 | 115 | 109 | 116 | 133 |
| C&G | 100 | 100 | 100 | 104 | 144 | 144 |
| Average (£) | 100 | 102 | 108 | 110 | 121 | 125 |
| RPI | 100 | 108 | 118 | 125 | 130 | 131 |
| AEI | 100 | 109 | 119 | 129 | 136 | 139 |

Source: Mortgage lenders and MMC calculations.

Note:  Base year of 100 is 1988. Monthly Digest of Statistics, October 1993, No 574, Table 18.11.

TABLE 5.5  Distribution of fees charged in 1993 for non-panel mortgage valuations

| Fee £ | At property value of £25,000 | | | At property value of £50,000 | | | At property value of £75,000 | | | At property value of £100,000 | | |
|---|---|---|---|---|---|---|---|---|---|---|---|---|
| | No of surveyors with fees in range | % | Cumulative % | No of surveyors with fees in range | % | Cumulative % | No of surveyors with fees in range | % | Cumulative % | No of surveyors with fees in range | % | Cumulative % |
| Up to 50 | 14 | 2.7 | 2.7 | 1 | 0.2 | 0.2 | - | 0.0 | 0.0 | - | 0.0 | 0.0 |
| 51–75 | 199 | 38.3 | 41.0 | 66 | 12.7 | 12.9 | 17 | 3.3 | 3.3 | 3 | 0.6 | 0.6 |
| 76–80 | 49 | 9.4 | 50.4 | 48 | 9.2 | 22.1 | 11 | 2.1 | 5.4 | - | 0.0 | 0.6 |
| 81–85 | 40 | 7.7 | 58.1 | 61 | 11.7 | 33.8 | 14 | 2.7 | 8.1 | 3 | 0.6 | 1.2 |
| 86–90 | 61 | 11.7 | 69.8 | 110 | 21.2 | 55.0 | 45 | 8.7 | 16.7 | 11 | 2.1 | 3.3 |
| 91–95 | 13 | 2.5 | 72.3 | 39 | 7.5 | 62.5 | 32 | 6.2 | 22.9 | 10 | 1.9 | 5.2 |
| 96–100 | 26 | 5.0 | 77.3 | 59 | 11.3 | 73.8 | 71 | 13.7 | 36.5 | 31 | 6.0 | 11.2 |
| 101–105 | 3 | 0.6 | 77.9 | 12 | 2.3 | 76.2 | 36 | 6.9 | 43.5 | 8 | 1.5 | 12.7 |
| 106–110 | 4 | 0.8 | 78.7 | 13 | 2.5 | 78.7 | 72 | 13.8 | 57.3 | 24 | 4.6 | 17.3 |
| 111–115 | 4 | 0.8 | 79.4 | 6 | 1.2 | 79.8 | 18 | 3.5 | 60.8 | 28 | 5.4 | 22.7 |
| 116–120 | 15 | 2.9 | 82.3 | 27 | 5.2 | 85.0 | 64 | 12.3 | 73.1 | 96 | 18.5 | 41.2 |
| 121–125 | 6 | 1.2 | 83.5 | 11 | 2.1 | 87.1 | 27 | 5.2 | 78.3 | 40 | 7.7 | 48.8 |
| 126–130 | 2 | 0.4 | 83.8 | 4 | 0.8 | 87.9 | 15 | 2.9 | 81.2 | 76 | 14.6 | 63.5 |
| 131–135 | 1 | 0.2 | 84.0 | 2 | 0.4 | 88.3 | 6 | 1.2 | 82.3 | 22 | 4.2 | 67.7 |
| 136–140 | - | 0.0 | 84.0 | 2 | 0.4 | 88.7 | 8 | 1.5 | 83.8 | 20 | 3.8 | 71.5 |
| 141–145 | 2 | 0.4 | 84.4 | 7 | 1.3 | 90.0 | 7 | 1.3 | 85.2 | 24 | 4.6 | 76.2 |
| 146–150 | 2 | 0.4 | 84.8 | 8 | 1.5 | 91.5 | 13 | 2.5 | 87.7 | 25 | 4.8 | 81.0 |
| 151–200 | 8 | 1.5 | 86.3 | 8 | 1.5 | 93.1 | 25 | 4.8 | 92.5 | 53 | 10.2 | 91.2 |
| Over 200 | 8 | 1.5 | 87.9 | 13 | 2.5 | 95.6 | 19 | 3.7 | 96.2 | 29 | 5.6 | 96.7 |
| Not stated | 63 | 12.1 | 100.0 | 23 | 4.4 | 100.0 | 20 | 3.8 | 100.0 | 17 | 3.3 | 100.0 |
| Total | 520 | 100.0 | 100.0 | 520 | 100.0 | 100.0 | 520 | 100.0 | 100.0 | 520 | 100.0 | 100.0 |
| *Sample* | | | | | | | | | | | | |
| Average charge (£) | 86 | | | 99 | | | 119 | | | 136 | | |
| Median charge (£) | 76 | | | 90 | | | 110 | | | 125 | | |
| Average charge of the seven largest lenders (£) | 88 | | | 98 | | | 118 | | | 131 | | |

*Source:* An outside firm of consultants (see Appendix 4.4).

prospective borrowers are in most cases required by lenders to pay up-front when applying for a loan to purchase a property or to refinance an existing mortgage, before a valuation is carried out and before the lender evaluates the borrower's application. We also consider lenders' fees for revaluations, which might be charged when borrowers seek a further advance to an existing mortgage loan (see paragraphs 5.23 to 5.25); and examine the selective use by some lenders of promotional discounts off the standard valuation fee (see paragraphs 5.27 to 5.29).

5.22. Table 5.6 gives details of the total amount of lenders' standard fee scale charges for mortgage valuations, including administration charges, in 1993, for both 14 of the largest mortgage lenders and also a sample of 19 other lenders. These were included in the earlier analysis of lenders' practices with regard to the use of valuers, in paragraph 4.21 and Appendix 4.6. As indicated in Table 5.6, a wide range of fees was charged by these 33 lenders for each of the value bands included. For properties up to a value of £50,000, for example, the highest charge (by C&G) was some £160; whilst the lowest (by First National Bank plc (First National)) was only £58, and several other lenders charged under £100. The fees charged by the largest lender, Halifax, were mostly at or above the average in the sample. We note that the fees of virtually all lenders increase, though less than proportionately, with the value or purchase price of the property; and that the average fees of the seven largest lenders are 10 per cent or more higher than for the sample as a whole.

TABLE 5.6  **Total fees charged by mortgage lenders in 1993\* for mortgage valuation including administration charges**

*Value of the property, £'000*

| Lender | 25 | 50 | 75 | 100 | 125 | 150 | 175 | 200 | 250 | 300 | 400 | 500 |
|---|---|---|---|---|---|---|---|---|---|---|---|---|
| Halifax | 125 | 125 | 165 | 165 | 195 | 195 | 225 | 225 | 255 | 285 | 345 | 405 |
| Abbey National | 140 | 140 | 175 | 175 | 215 | 215 | 250 | 250 | 285 | 320 | - | - |
| Nationwide | 100 | 120 | 140 | 160 | 190 | 190 | 220 | 220 | 250 | 290 | 355 | 415 |
| Woolwich | 100 | 120 | 140 | 160 | 190 | 190 | 220 | 220 | 250 | 275 | 330 | 390 |
| Leeds | 125 | 125 | 145 | 165 | 195 | 195 | 225 | 225 | 255 | 285 | 340 | 420 |
| C&G | 135 | 160 | 160 | 185 | 185 | 230 | 230 | 230 | 275 | 275 | 330 | 375 |
| Barclays | 70 | 90 | 110 | 130 | 160 | 160 | 160 | 190 | 220 | 250 | - | - |
| A&L | 130 | 130 | 140 | 155 | 175 | 190 | 215 | 220 | 250 | 280 | 340 | 440 |
| Bank of Scotland | 100 | 100 | 110 | 130 | 170 | 170 | 210 | 210 | 250 | 300 | 400 | - |
| N&P | 125 | 125 | 165 | 165 | 195 | 195 | 225 | 225 | 255 | 285 | 345 | 405 |
| NatWest | 71 | 85 | 109 | 129 | 165 | 188 | 223 | 247 | 306 | 365 | 483 | 601 |
| Britannia | 115 | 140 | 140 | 165 | 190 | 190 | 215 | 215 | 215 | 265 | 315 | 315 |
| Bristol & West | 110 | 140 | 140 | 160 | 190 | 190 | 230 | 230 | 270 | 310 | 380 | 450 |
| Lloyds | 110 | 130 | 130 | 160 | 190 | 190 | 220 | 220 | 278 | 335 | - | - |
| Yorkshire Bank | 150 | 150 | 150 | 150 | 150 | 150 | 150 | 150 | 150 | 150 | 150 | 150 |
| Yorkshire | 100 | 120 | 140 | 160 | 190 | 190 | 220 | 220 | 250 | 280 | 340 | 400 |
| Mercantile | 85 | 105 | 125 | 150 | 190 | 210 | 240 | 260 | - | - | - | - |
| Bank of Ireland Home Mortgages | 110 | 110 | 110 | 110 | 170 | 170 | 240 | 240 | 240 | 240 | 300 | 375 |
| First National | 58 | 58 | 86 | 115 | 144 | 173 | 201 | 230 | 288 | 335 | 460 | 575 |
| BNP Mortgages | 82 | 82 | 88 | 118 | 147 | 176 | 206 | 235 | 294 | - | - | - |
| Cumberland | 70 | 85 | 105 | 125 | 135 | 135 | 150 | 150 | - | - | - | - |
| Kent Reliance | 125 | 125 | 125 | 150 | 175 | 175 | 200 | 200 | - | - | - | - |
| Buckinghamshire | 80 | 80 | 110 | 125 | 140 | 155 | 170 | 185 | 200 | 250 | 300 | - |
| The Ecology | 125 | 140 | 160 | 170 | 185 | 200 | 210 | 230 | - | - | - | - |
| The Mortgage Corporation | 90 | 90 | 100 | 125 | 125 | 160 | 160 | 210 | 250 | - | - | - |
| Citibank | 100 | 100 | 125 | 125 | 180 | 180 | 207 | 236 | 295 | 354 | 472 | 590 |
| Household Mortgage Corporation | 125 | 125 | 160 | 160 | 195 | 195 | 230 | 230 | 265 | 300 | - | - |
| West Bromwich | 120 | 140 | 160 | 190 | 190 | 220 | 220 | 250 | 300 | 300 | - | - |
| Northern Rock | 115 | 130 | 150 | 150 | 180 | 180 | - | - | - | - | - | - |
| Ulster Bank | 80 | 100 | 100 | 125 | 150 | 150 | 150 | 150 | 150 | 150 | 150 | 150 |
| Royal Bank of Scotland | 100 | 100 | 120 | 120 | 155 | 170 | 170 | 200 | 240 | 240 | 280 | 375 |
| Tipton & Coseley | 65 | 80 | 100 | 115 | 125 | 135 | 145 | 155 | 195 | - | - | - |
| Dunfermline | 80 | 95 | 115 | 125 | 150 | 150 | - | - | - | - | - | - |
| Average of seven largest lenders | 114 | 126 | 148 | 163 | 190 | 196 | 219 | 223 | 256 | 283 | 340 | 401 |
| Maximum | 140 | 160 | 175 | 185 | 215 | 230 | 250 | 250 | 285 | 320 | 355 | 420 |
| Minimum | 70 | 90 | 110 | 130 | 160 | 160 | 160 | 190 | 220 | 250 | 330 | 375 |
| Average of full sample | 103 | 113 | 130 | 145 | 171 | 179 | 204 | 215 | 249 | 280 | 338 | 402 |
| Maximum | 150 | 160 | 175 | 190 | 215 | 230 | 250 | 260 | 306 | 365 | 483 | 601 |
| Minimum | 58 | 58 | 86 | 110 | 123 | 135 | 145 | 150 | 150 | 150 | 150 | 150 |

*Source:* Mortgage lenders.

\*Charges as at August 1993.

5.23. As explained above, when borrowers seek a further advance to an existing mortgage loan, often for improvement work to the property, a revaluation charge is usually, though not always, made by most lenders. If, for example, a valuation had been carried out recently, the lender might not require a further valuation, and, accordingly, no charge would be made. Where the lender, at its discretion, decides that a revaluation is required, it will normally arrange, where possible, for the inspection to be carried out by the same valuer that undertook the previous valuation. Where that is the case, the inspection required would usually focus on any significant changes since the previous valuation as to the value and condition of the property. Most lenders charge a fee in such circumstances which is lower than their standard fee for a first valuation.

5.24. Some of the largest lenders charge a flat rate fee of about £60 to £75 (mostly excluding any administration charge) per revaluation, which is around a half to two-thirds of the average full valuation fee for a property where the purchase price is £50,000. Those lenders which charged such a flat rate fee in 1993 included Nationwide (£75, including a charge for administration: this was increased to £85 in November 1993), Leeds (£65), and C&G (£60). For three others of the largest lenders, the revaluation fees are *ad valorem* rather than flat rate, ie related to the size of the additional loan being sought. Woolwich changed its fees during 1993. Prior to 1 September it charged £25 if the loan was less than £2,500, and £75 for larger loans. Since then, its charges, including both administration and the revaluation, have been 1 per cent of the amount of the further advance, subject to a minimum of £50, for loans under £15,000. For larger loans, the fee is at a flat rate of £150. Halifax's charges in 1993 were £65 against a loan of £10,000 or less. An extra £5 was charged for each additional £5,000 of the loan up to £20,000, and thereafter an extra £5 for each additional £10,000. Where the further advance was £30,000, for example, Halifax's revaluation fee would have been £80. Likewise, Abbey National charged £55 for a further advance of up to £10,000, and £70 for larger loans up to £25,000. For loans greater than this, its charge was its standard valuation fee, less the £50 administration charge. Barclays takes a slightly different approach to revaluation fees. No revaluation would be needed and no charge would normally be made if the further advance did not increase the total loan:value ratio to 80 per cent or above, thereby requiring mortgage indemnity insurance cover (see paragraph 3.23). If, on the other hand, the loan was expected to exceed this 80 per cent level, a further valuation would be required and it would be charged for on the basis of Barclays' standard fee scale.

5.25. Some lenders include details of their revaluation charges in their marketing literature, in other cases, borrowers are informed on request. Most lenders do not make available the revaluation report to borrowers, though they may be informed of the amount of the valuation itself. In addition to these revaluation charges, borrowers may face added costs if the further advance increases the loan:value ratio to the point where the lender requires mortgage indemnity insurance cover to be taken out or the amount of existing cover to be increased (see paragraph 3.23). We note also that borrowers face a limited choice of lenders when taking out a further advance, since in most cases he will not be able to switch to another lender without refinancing the entire mortgage loan.

5.26. As mentioned in paragraph 4.5, where a mortgage valuation has been carried out in respect of an application for a loan a reinspection of the property may be required, by the lender, if remedial work to defects in the property are needed. The reinspection is necessary to ensure that the work has been carried out satisfactorily. Revenues from lenders' charges for reinspections are included in the data on the total value of valuation work given in paragraph 3.58. In this inquiry we did not collect detailed information on the charges for reinspections made by individual lenders, though they generally appear to be of the same order of magnitude as those made for revaluations.

5.27. With regard to promotional discounts, a number of lenders periodically offer reduced, and in some cases nil, charges for valuations as a means of attracting mortgage business. Usually with such offers, the fee or some proportion of it is refunded to the borrower on completion of the mortgage. Refunds are not made, therefore, if the mortgage is not taken up. Other conditions are also often attached: borrowers may be required, for example, to complete the mortgage before a given date to qualify for the refund. Halifax told us that it occasionally offers, for a fixed period of time, free or reduced price mortgage valuations as part of its marketing strategy. In 1993 Halifax offered a £200 cash refund to first-time buyers, and £250 cash plus a refund of the valuation fee of up to £405 to other borrowers. Abbey National has used similar marketing promotions directed at particular categories of borrower in each of the last three years. Its 'market mover' discount schemes were available from May to August 1991, April to June 1992, November 1992 to May 1993, and June to August 1993.

Its most recent scheme offered a £200 cash refund (on completion of the mortgage) plus a free mortgage valuation to new borrowers, and to those wishing to refinance with Abbey National an existing mortgage with another lender. A condition of the offer was that the loan could not exceed 75 per cent of the valuation of the property.

5.28. Nationwide told us that it occasionally offers discounted valuations in promotional schemes, which are usually available for fixed and limited periods of time. It offered, during 1993, a refund on completion of the mortgage of £275 to borrowers wishing to refinance with Nationwide their existing mortgage with another lender. Existing Nationwide borrowers were offered a full refund of the valuation fee, including the administration component, if they were moving house and took out a new mortgage with Nationwide. C&G also offers special discount schemes from time to time as part of its marketing programmes. In November 1993 it introduced its 'action repay' scheme, under which the entire valuation and administration fee is refunded to borrowers on completion of the mortgage, and which is available to all borrowers taking a variable rate mortgage product.

5.29. By contrast, Barclays and Woolwich have not used free or reduced valuation fees in any promotional schemes in recent years. Woolwich told us, however, that it might do so in the future, if it considered that such a scheme might attract a worthwhile volume of new mortgage business.

## Charges for HBRs and SSYs

5.30. The nature of HBRs and SSYs, and lenders' policies with regard to acceptance of any associated valuations, are considered in Chapter 4. Where an HBR is carried out by a surveyor nominated by the lender, the surveyor will usually also provide a mortgage valuation. Most firms of surveyors are able to provide HBRs, but any associated mortgage valuation may not be accepted by lenders if the surveyor is not on their approved panel. As with mortgage valuations, most lenders have their own national fee scale which is related to different levels of purchase price, and which often includes a charge for administration. The full scales of fees used by Halifax and Abbey National are at Appendices 5.1 and 4.5 respectively: Halifax's HBRs are known as 'Scheme 2 Reports' and Abbey National's as 'Reports on Condition and Value'. Table 5.7 gives details of fees for HBRs by the seven largest lenders in 1993, for a range of property values up to £150,000. Hence, for a property where the purchase price was less than £25,000, for example, the average charge made by these lenders, excluding Barclays, was £230; where the purchase price was between £50,000 and £75,000, the average charge for an HBR was £292. For each of the value bands, the average charge by these lenders for an HBR was about twice the cost of a mortgage valuation alone. Lenders' charges for HBRs have risen in recent years at a similar rate to that of mortgage valuations. The ISA gave us examples of fee scales used by some of its members which showed fees for HBRs for a £50,000 property ranging from £150 to £230 (inclusive of VAT), compared with the largest lenders' comparable charges which range from £194 to £260 (again, inclusive of VAT), the average charge being £238 (see Table 5.7).

TABLE 5.7 **The seven largest lenders' charges for HBRs (including administration), 1993**

| | Property value bands, £'000 | | | | | |
| Lender | 25 | 50 | 75 | 100 | 125 | 150 |
|---|---|---|---|---|---|---|
| Halifax | 250 | 250 | 330 | 330 | 380 | 380 |
| Abbey National | 260 | 260 | 335 | 335 | 395 | 395 |
| Nationwide | 194 | 194 | 235 | 266 | 317 | 317 |
| Barclays | | | Negotiable with surveyor | | | |
| Woolwich | 225 | 225 | 275 | 325 | 375 | 375 |
| Leeds | 250 | 250 | 325 | 325 | 440 | 440 |
| C&G | 200 | 250 | 250 | 300 | 300 | 350 |
| Average charge for HBR (excluding Barclays) | 230 | 238 | 292 | 314 | 368 | 376 |
| Average charge for mortgage valuation (including administration) | 114 | 126 | 148 | 163 | 190 | 196 |
| Ratio of average HBR to mortgage valuation | 2.02 | 1.89 | 1.97 | 1.93 | 1.94 | 1.92 |

*Source:* Mortgage lenders.

5.31. Few if any lenders have a scale of charges for SSYs, because the coverage and depth of the survey work is a matter for negotiation between the borrower who commissions the survey and the surveyor who carries it out. The cost is also dependent on the size, age and condition of the property. From the examples we have seen, charges for SSYs are often twice or more those for HBRs, ie typically in the range of £450 to £800, including the cost of the mortgage valuation. Some individual surveyors told us that their charges for SSYs were substantially less than those of surveyors on lenders' panels.

5.32. Lenders' restrictions on the use of non-panel surveyors undertaking SSYs combined with mortgage valuations are considered in paragraphs 4.22 to 4.25. Where a valuer nominated by the lender is used, many lenders (including Halifax and Abbey National) require the borrower to pay the lender in advance their standard, overall fee for the valuation (including any charge for administration), and to negotiate separately with the surveyor over the cost of the survey work. The lender subsequently pays the surveyor the mortgage valuation element of the overall fee.

## Financial assessment

### *Introduction*

5.33. Financial questionnaires were sent to the seven largest mortgage lenders and we set out below a summary of the data received from these and their subsidiary companies providing valuation services, ie Colleys (Halifax), Cornerstone (Abbey National), Nationwide Surveyors (Nationwide), Ekins Surveyors (Woolwich) and PLUK (Leeds). The questionnaires to the lenders sought information on the income, costs and profits arising from valuations undertaken by them in-house, by their subsidiary companies and by external (mainly panel) valuers. The questionnaires to the subsidiary companies sought similar information. Initially we asked all the lenders to provide us with information on all their valuation activities including valuations for house purchase, refinancing and further advances. In the event, all the lenders (excluding Barclays) included data on repossessions in the results reported to us. Subsequently we asked all the lenders to provide us with information on valuations for house purchase separately from other valuation activities. Abbey National, Nationwide and Woolwich were able to provide us with this information. Halifax provided us with substantially the same information but did not exclude the costs of reinspections, revaluations, and repossessions valuations. In this section, where aggregate results are shown, these exclude valuations for repossessions and revaluations for Abbey National, Nationwide and Woolwich. For Halifax, they include the costs of reinspections, revaluations and repossessions valuations. The individual results of these four lenders are reported on these bases.

5.34. Each of the seven largest lenders organizes its mortgage valuation activities differently and, although in this section we have dealt in aggregate with some of the information supplied to us, the bulk of it is summarized in Appendix 5.3 where we set out individual factors affecting each company and its subsidiary's results. For control purposes all the lenders (except Barclays which has no in-house valuers and passes all valuation fees collected directly to its external valuers) treat their mortgage valuation activities as cost centres (or parts of cost centres). The responsibility for the efficient running of these activities is usually that of the chief surveyor who, typically, seeks, they told us, to minimize the costs of the operations rather than to make a profit on them. The information we obtained on costs relates to the valuation work arising in these cost centres and also overheads and other costs arising in other departments allocated by the lenders to mortgage valuation work. So far as the lenders are concerned, overheads and other costs (eg expenses of accommodation at branches and at head office and sometimes computer and related expenses) tend not, as a matter of practice, to be allocated to valuation activities and are the responsibility of different departments. Further, because the valuation activities and the income and costs of these activities of the lending organizations are small in comparison with the rest of their business, the lenders do not produce information on these activities on a 'stand-alone' basis. One lender, for example, stated that 'when considering the financial information provided by the society it is important to be aware that no accounts are prepared for valuation services as a matter of course, due to the relative size of the valuation function as a proportion of the society's total operation'. Consequently, the allocation of non-direct costs to valuation work proved a source of difficulty for the lenders as did the division of income and, particularly, costs between residential mortgage valuation work and other activities of the departments concerned. Also, one lender could not identify the division between the number of valuations made by in-house employees, by the lender's subsidiary and by its external (panel) valuers. Accordingly, the analyses in this section are subject to the qualifications set out above and the figures taken as an indication, rather than an exact record, of the income, costs and profits arising from these activities.

5.35. We decided not to undertake a survey of the income and cost profiles of external valuers. We foresaw even greater difficulties, than the difficulties encountered in identifying lenders' costs, in seeking to segregate external valuers' costs and returns on valuations of residential property from those on their other activities. We did not consider that the exercise was likely to provide us with data of sufficient quality to support conclusions or to justify the expense entailed.

## Income from valuation activities

5.36. Set out in Table 5.8 is a summary of the income figures in respect of all valuations undertaken by, or on behalf of, the seven largest lenders from 1990 to 1993. We have allocated company data to the calendar year in which the major part of that company's financial year falls. The financial year ends for Halifax, Nationwide and Leeds on 31 January, 31 March and 30 September respectively. The other four companies end their financial year on 31 December. Over the period, between 74 and 78 per cent of income arose from mortgage valuations alone (ie 'stand-alone' valuations which were not undertaken at the same time as HBRs or SSYs).

TABLE 5.8 **Income from valuation fees, HBRs, other valuation work including SSYs and administrative charges collected by the seven largest lenders, 1990 to 1993**

|  |  |  |  | £'000 |
| --- | --- | --- | --- | --- |
|  | 1990 | 1991 | 1992 | 1993 estimated |
| Mortgage valuations | 65,928 | 70,532 | 68,004 | 78,641 |
| HBRs (incorporating a mortgage valuation) | 15,844 | 19,472 | 17,974 | 19,221 |
| Sub-total | 81,772 | 90,004 | 85,978 | 97,862 |
| Other mortgage valuation work* | 337 | 308 | 302 | 340 |
| Total | 82,109 | 90,312 | 86,280 | 98,202 |
| Administrative charges | 14,357 | 19,025 | 18,689 | 23,056 |
|  |  |  |  | per cent |
| Mortgage valuations | 80.3 | 78.1 | 78.8 | 80.1 |
| HBRs (incorporating mortgage valuations) | 19.3 | 21.6 | 20.8 | 19.6 |
| Sub-total | 99.6 | 99.7 | 99.6 | 99.7 |
| Other mortgage valuation work* | 0.4 | 0.3 | 0.4 | 0.3 |
| Total | 100.0 | 100.0 | 100.0 | 100.0 |

*Source:* MMC from company data.

*'Other mortgage valuation work' includes SSYs which the respondents that undertake this type of work state is a very small part of their total valuation work.

5.37. Set out in Table 5.9 is the income of the seven largest lenders from valuation fees broken down between valuations carried out in-house, by subsidiary companies and by external valuers. The table shows that external valuers have taken a progressively smaller percentage of the valuation income of these lenders over the period under review. Their share has dropped from 39 per cent in 1990 to an estimated 30 per cent in 1993. We have not obtained similar figures for other lenders.

TABLE 5.9  **Income from all types of valuation services commissioned through the seven largest lenders broken down by in-house, subsidiary company and external valuers, 1990 to 1993**

|  | | | | £'000 |
|---|---|---|---|---|
|  | 1990 | 1991 | 1992 | 1993 estimated |
| Total income | 82,109 | 90,312 | 86,280 | 98,202 |
| Percentages of which were undertaken by: | | | | per cent |
| in-house employees | 47.5 | 49.5 | 42.5 | 34.2 |
| subsidiary firms | 13.3 | 14.5 | 22.8 | 31.8 |
| Sub-total for in-house and subsidiary firms | 60.8 | 64.0 | 65.3 | 70.3 |
| External valuers | 39.2 | 36.0 | 34.7 | 29.7 |
| Total | 100.0 | 100.0 | 100.0 | 100.0 |

*Source:*  MMC from company data.

5.38. In Table 5.10 we summarize the surpluses and deficits of the lenders as a percentage of all income received from valuations and, in Table 5.11, the surpluses and deficits for in-house activity only.

TABLE 5.10  **Surpluses and deficits accruing to the seven largest lenders as a percentage of the income received by them from fees for all types of residential valuation undertaken by them or on their behalf, 1990 to 1993**

|  | | | | per cent |
|---|---|---|---|---|
|  | 1990 | 1991 | 1992 | 1993 estimated |
| Halifax | [ | | | |
| Abbey National | | | | |
| Nationwide | | *Figures omitted.* | | |
| Barclays | | *See note on page iv.* | | |
| Woolwich | | | | |
| Leeds | | | | |
| C&G | | | | ] |
| Total | 3.1 | 8.3 | 5.5 | 6.8 |

*Source:*  MMC from company data.

TABLE 5.11  **Surpluses and deficits accruing to the seven largest lenders as a percentage of the income received by them from fees for in-house residential valuations undertaken by them, 1990 to 1993**

|  | | | | per cent |
|---|---|---|---|---|
|  | 1990 | 1991 | 1992 | 1993 estimated |
| Halifax | [ | | | |
| Abbey National | | | | |
| Nationwide | | *Figures omitted.* | | |
| Barclays | | *See note on page iv.* | | |
| Woolwich | | | | |
| Leeds | | | | |
| C&G | | | | ] |
| Total | 7.3 | 17.7 | 18.2 | 21.4 |

*Source:*  MMC from company data.

5.39. Taking the seven lenders together, they cover their costs of mortgage valuation work. Returns are earned mainly on work undertaken in-house. For 1992 the overall surplus for the seven largest lenders for all valuations, and for in-house valuations alone, was 5.5 per cent and 18.2 per cent respectively, but not much weight should be placed on these overall averages partly because the comparison of these figures is affected by [      *      ]. These figures are on the basis of total revenues received and exclude surpluses and deficits arising in their subsidiary companies (which ultimately accrue to their lender parents). The range of results around these averages is wide and they include Barclays which transfers all fees direct to outside valuers and report no earnings. Looking at the spread of results for the individual lenders, for 1992 on all valuations these range from a surplus of [ * ] per cent ([    *    ]) to a deficit of [ * ] per cent ([   *   ]).

5.40. However, the overall results bring together two very different types of transaction. For external valuers the lender acts primarily as a handling agent for the fee and itself determines both the levels of valuation fees it collects from applicants and the amount it pays over to subsidiary companies and external valuers. It is important therefore to distinguish between the information we have obtained from lenders on the surpluses arising from each type of valuer and information on the lenders' results from all types of valuers taken together. On in-house valuations, the results for the five lenders who undertook them ranged from [ * ] per cent ([ * ]) to [ * ] per cent ([   *   ]). The variations in the results reported to us can in part be attributed to at least two factors: first, as explained in paragraph 5.34, the lenders told us that they do not look on their mortgage valuation departments as profit centres, and secondly, different bases of allocations of costs to these activities have affected the levels of surplus and deficit reported. For instance, [   *   ] applied four times as many man-hours and related direct costs to preparing HBRs than to mortgage valuations only, resulting in reported losses on HBR work. In contrast, [   *   ] assumed that the man-hours required to carry out HBRs, in comparison with those required for valuations alone, were proportional to the fees charged, ie that about twice as much time was required for an HBR as for a mortgage valuation. As a consequence the surpluses or deficits arising for each type of valuation, as a percentage of income, tended to be the same.

5.41. Table 5.12 sets out the surpluses and deficits of the subsidiary companies for all valuations undertaken by them for their lending parent companies as a percentage of income received from their parents. Despite this activity generally being part of a profit centre, this work remains a small part of the total work of the firms concerned. Similar problems of cost allocation arose in the subsidiaries as in their parent companies and the cost allocation basis chosen in any particular case could have a disproportionate effect on comparative rates of surplus or deficit. Again, as an example, there is a significant difference between the results of the subsidiaries of [   *   ] and [   *   ], because each adopted the allocation basis of their respective parents. [

*Details omitted. See note on page iv.*

]

TABLE 5.12   **Surpluses and deficits accruing to the subsidiaries of five\* of the seven largest lenders as a percentage of the income received by them for all residential valuations undertaken by them on behalf of their parent companies, 1990 to 1993**

|  | | | | *per cent* |
| --- | --- | --- | --- | --- |
|  | *1990* | *1991* | *1992* | *1993 estimated* |
| Colleys (Halifax) | [ | | | |
| Cornerstone (Abbey National) | | | | |
| Nationwide Surveyors (Nationwide) | | *Figures omitted.* | | |
| Ekins Surveyors (Woolwich) | | *See note on page iv.* | | |
| PLUK (Leeds) | | | | ] |
| Total | 2.8 | 13.6 | 1.4 | 8.7 |

*Source:* MMC from company data.

---

\*Barclays does not have a subsidiary undertaking valuation work. C&G disposed of its subsidiary in 1991 and could not provide us with information for the subsidiary's results.

---

\*Details omitted. See note on page iv.

5.42. Another general aspect of financial returns from mortgage valuation work is the way that VAT applies. Lending on the security of residential property is an exempt transaction for VAT purposes. Since valuing the property is part of the lending process this too is exempt. As a result the lender does not charge VAT to the borrower and cannot recover VAT on any services or goods that it purchases. This principle extends to any intra-group transaction so that valuations by subsidiary companies are also exempt from VAT. However, where a valuation is carried out by an external valuer, he has to meet the VAT charge out of the amount received from the lender. Borrowers pay the same valuation fee whether or not the valuation is to be carried out by an external valuer. Some lenders told us that in calculating the level of fees to borrowers they take into account an estimate of the amount of VAT that they expect to have to bear where external valuers are to be used. For them the process is one of spreading total valuation costs over all valuations. For six of the seven lenders (but not including Barclays, which pays over all valuation fees it collects to its external valuers) the fees reflect the VAT element that will be incurred if the valuation is undertaken by an external valuer. Thus, where valuations are carried out in-house or by a subsidiary either the lender or the subsidiary firm retains that part of the fee (the VAT element), which would be paid by an external valuer if the valuation had been carried out by him. The result is that a component of the profit on valuations carried out in-house or by subsidiary companies can be attributed to this. As a percentage of the income received, this component is less than the full VAT imposition since, unlike VAT-registered independent valuers, lenders and their subsidiaries are unable to recover VAT on those of their inputs subject to VAT. We made only limited enquiries to identify more exactly the advantage accruing to lenders and their subsidiaries in respect of in-house valuations because of the way the VAT system applies to mortgage valuations. From these enquiries it appeared that external valuers which are registered for VAT can claim back about 20 per cent of the VAT they are liable to pay HM Customs and Excise because of the extent of their inputs which bear VAT and which they can recover. This reduces the apparent advantage enjoyed by lenders from a maximum of 14.9 per cent (ie 17.5 as a percentage of 117.5—the full 'VAT element' as a percentage of the total fee charged to borrowers) to about 12 per cent (ie 17.5 *less* 3.5 as a percentage of 117.5—the net VAT payable to HM Customs and Excise as a percentage of the total fee charged).

# 6 Views of the Council of Mortgage Lenders

## Contents

## Introduction

6.1. The CML is a national representative association for the mortgage-lending industry, and membership is available to any institution which undertakes mortgage lending in the UK as part of its business. As at 30 May 1993 there were 152 members and altogether the CML membership accounts for about 95 per cent of all outstanding mortgage balances.

6.2. Building societies account for 87 of the members of the CML. Banking institutions make up another significant tranche of the membership including all four large clearing banks. Other members are drawn from insurance companies and their subsidiaries, finance houses and the centralized mortgage lenders which developed in the mid-1980s. Organizations interested in the operation of the mortgage market such as legal and accountancy firms or residential asset management companies may also be admitted as associates.

6.3. The CML has its origins in the BSA which, in turn, has its origins in the Building Societies Protection Association established in 1869. In the deregularized financial markets of the mid to late 1980s building societies faced competition from new lenders entering the market for the first time and from the banks which had entered the mortgage market in the early 1980s. As a consequence the BSA and others saw the need for a new, broader-based, representative body. This body was to operate alongside the BSA which would continue to serve the specific interests of the building societies in connection with other aspects of their activity not directly concerned with mortgage lending. The CML was established on 1 August 1989 as an unincorporated body. In its mission statement it pledged to provide 'a service to mortgage lending institutions by helping to establish a favourable operating environment, by providing a forum for discussion on non-competitive issues, and by providing information to assist them in their business'.

6.4. The CML is directed by an Executive Committee whose composition is based on a representative cross-section of the institutional sectors of the membership. There are currently 25 members who elect a Chairman and two Deputy Chairmen both for the CML and the Executive Committee, each person to come from a different institutional sector of the membership. The CML also has three standing subcommittees dealing with fraud prevention, secondary markets and statistics and business information. In addition, there are a number of specialist panels and working groups. Amongst these is the valuation panel, the eight members of which are all Chief Valuation Surveyors of their respective organization. The panel advises the CML on all issues relating to valuations. The secretariat of the BSA provides all secretariat services to the CML.

6.5. The CML has no regulatory or disciplinary powers as such apart from the power to expel members. Its Executive Committee provides guidance for the membership but it falls to the members individually to decide whether they follow that guidance or not.

6.6. The CML has the following five objectives:

(a) to be a central representative body, to put the views of mortgage-lending institutions to government departments and other relevant bodies;

(b) to be a research and statistical centre, to aggregate and publish statistics, and to provide analysis on mortgage lending and other relevant market information;

(c) to be a technical centre providing commentary, guidance and advice on all legal, fiscal, financial and other regulatory developments of relevance to mortgage lending;

(d) to provide a forum for the exchange of non-competitive information, including the subject of mortgage fraud; and

(e) to provide a focus for media relations stemming from (a) to (d).

6.7. At the start of the inquiry the members of the CML's Executive Committee instructed the CML to co-ordinate an industry response to the MMC on behalf of the membership and an advisory group was set up to oversee this work. At the same time the CML recognized that the MMC could call for any information and evidence from individual lenders that it thought necessary, as in fact it did, and that individual members might wish to make their own individual representations, as many did. The MMC held two hearings with the Advisory Group and on both occasions detailed written submissions were provided in advance.

6.8. Membership of the CML Advisory Group comprised the Chairman of the CML, representatives drawn mainly from the largest building societies and staff of the CML.


## The UK mortgage market

6.9. In its initial submission to the MMC the CML drew attention in particular to the changes that had taken place in the UK mortgage market, and to a number of other factors. These included the effect of the recession on lenders, the valuation report as a lender's means to satisfy itself as to the adequacy of the security offered by a property and the availability of other reports for the borrower, the need for a lender to control the provision of its valuation services, the influence of fraud on lenders' behaviour, and the competitive and cost influences on the charges for mortgage valuations and associated administrative charges.

6.10. The CML explained that the UK mortgage market had changed significantly over the last 15 years. Formerly building societies had been forced to employ rationing devices to ensure that scarce funds were allocated as fairly as possible between competing borrowers; there was little innovation in the mortgage product and price competition was limited by the BSA's recommended rates system. The removal by the Government of remaining non-market controls on the banks in the early 1980s led them to enter the market in a significant way, competing with their own pricing strategies. Under this competitive pressure the BSA's recommended rates system came to an end in 1983. The mid-1980s saw the arrival of a number of centralized lenders operating without branch networks and drawing funds, not from depositors, but from the wholesale money market. A wide range of institutions, therefore, now competed to provide mortgage finance; mortgages were advertised extensively in the media and the introduction of new products had become relatively common.

6.11. The CML explained that the late 1980s and early 1990s had been difficult years for all UK mortgage lenders; building societies' provisions for losses were low until the late 1980s, but in 1991 they had amounted to £1.2 billion and in 1992 to £1.8 billion. Much of this was due to the slump in the residential property market rather than to problems with mortgage valuations. Insurance companies which provided mortgage indemnity guarantee insurance to lenders the CML said had also suffered. Following large losses in recent years they had tightened up or substantially increased their premiums and sought even tighter lending criteria. Some now placed restrictions on the acceptance of mortgage valuations from valuers who were not on a lender's approved panel.

## Mortgage valuations

6.12. The CML emphasized that the fundamental characteristic of a mortgage was that the loan was secured on the property which was pledged by the borrower, to the lender. Although only building societies had a statutory duty before lending to satisfy themselves of the adequacy of the security offered and to acquire a written valuation of that security, other lenders generally did so as a prudential matter. The mortgage valuation report was therefore provided for the lender in the course of the lender's assessment of the adequacy of the security offered. In addition, the courts had decided that valuers owed a duty of care to the borrower in tort. The CML said that, in applying for a mortgage, the borrower would normally be advised, initially by way of the lender's literature but possibly also during an interview, that the mortgage valuation report was for the lender's purposes in assessing security and that, if the borrower required a report on the structure and condition of the property, he should commission an HBR, or a full SSY.

6.13. In the CML's view the need to ensure the adequacy of their lenders' security meant that it was necessary for them to maintain control over the arrangements for obtaining accurate and honest valuation reports. It pointed to the need, in a competitive situation, for the lender to know that valuation reports would be produced quickly and in a convenient format suitable for its own requirements, that the lender needed to be satisfied as to the competence of the valuer and that the valuer was properly insured against subsequent claims. The industry's concerns over fraud and negligence had also led a greater degree of control.

6.14. The CML said that lenders had employed staff valuers since before the Second World War but that these teams of valuers had expanded substantially over the last six or seven years. Since the 1986 Act, societies had been able to sell surveying and valuation services and some had increased their staff valuers for that reason, or incorporated subsidiaries offering these services to their parent or other clients including other lenders. A further reason for the expansion of staff valuers was the need to improve the quality and consistency of valuations and reports. The CML said that staff valuers also had the advantage of providing immediate advice on property matters to the lender in accordance with the lender's specific requirements; they had access to a database of all the valuations carried out for that lender. The proportion of work carried out by staff valuers would vary according to the state of the property market. Lenders would aim to keep their staff valuers fully employed, using external panel valuers to handle valuation instructions that could not be absorbed by the in-house valuers which could more appropriately be done by panel members. Also panel members were instructed if a conflict of interest might otherwise exist. The proportion of valuations done in-house would tend to fall in a buoyant market and rise in a depressed market.

6.15. The CML pointed out that most lenders operated panels of approved valuers, as opposed to accepting valuation reports from any qualified valuers. By giving instructions only to firms and individuals whose competence had already been established, the lender was said greatly to increase its ability to control mortgage valuations. It would, however, be inefficient for lenders to operate panels which were larger than necessary to meet operational requirements. The CML explained that, whilst there had been a shrinkage in the number of transactions, this had not necessarily resulted in all lenders reducing the number of valuers on their panels; some of their members had reported increases, whilst others reported that the number of firms on their panels were static. Lenders periodically reviewed their panels as part of a continuing process of managing their businesses. Where panels had been reduced, this might have been because of fraud or negligence, reduction in operational requirements or mergers of firms of valuers.

## Fraud and negligence

6.16. In guarding against fraud and negligence, the CML was clear that the lender must be able to rely on the valuer's competence and integrity. In the vast majority of cases the valuer would be the only professional who actually saw the property to be mortgaged. During the peak of the property boom towards the end of the 1980s, the volume of business being undertaken by lenders had enabled unscrupulous valuers to take advantage of weakness in lending and conveyancing procedures. Many examples of fraud did not come to light until some time later; property values fell and lenders suffered losses on some of the properties concerned when they took possession and placed the mortgaged properties on the open market.

6.17. The CML observed that the dividing line between fraud and negligence was thin. A valuer would not be able to claim on his insurance if he had been fraudulent; consequently there had been a tendency for lenders, when faced with a case which could be argued on the basis of fraud or negligence, to argue that overvaluations had been due to negligence which was easier to prove than fraud. Insurers took a contrary view in resisting claims.

6.18. The CML said that there was statistical evidence that the incidence of both fraud and negligence was higher where a panel valuer was instructed as opposed to a staff valuer, and higher still if a non-panel valuer was involved. The fact that using non-panel valuers left lenders more vulnerable had been acknowledged by the police, who had issued a 'recommended code' of lending practice, reproduced at Appendix 6.1. Any lender which failed to follow that advice ran the risk of the police being unwilling to investigate the reported fraud. The police had established, in a number of major cities and regions, special units devoted to the investigation of mortgage fraud which, the CML considered, was an indication of its importance.

## Standards of valuation

6.19. The CML pointed to the industry's long-running concern that the main professional bodies representing valuers and surveyors, the RICS and the ISVA, were not able to guarantee that their members complied with their respective rules on insurance cover and had insufficient sanctions against those of their members who were either fraudulent or negligent. This contrasted with the Law Society, which operated a compulsory indemnity and compensation fund. The CML said that there were many examples of insurance arrangements for valuers proving to be worthless. One of the reasons for this was that insurers avoided claims on which there had been material non-disclosure of facts. Another reason was failure by some valuers to maintain their professional indemnity insurance cover. It was therefore important for lenders to be sure that they were dealing with reputable valuers who maintained adequate insurance cover which was unlikely to be called into question. Lenders therefore needed to exercise caution both when making appointments to their panels and also when accepting individual valuations from valuers and surveyors with whose work they were not familiar.

## Fees for valuation services and mortgage administration charges

6.20. On fees for mortgage valuations and associated administration charges the CML pointed out that up until 1982 valuation fees were the subject of periodic negotiation between the BSA and the two professional associations (the RICS and the ISVA) resulting in one national scale. In the present situation, individual lenders set their own scales of fees for the valuers they used. CML evidence demonstrated a wide range of fees being charged currently by lenders for mortgage valuation. This reflected the variety of practice which could be expected in a competitive market. Some lenders used discounts from their valuation fees as a marketing tool, others competed by reducing other costs or by offering incentives. Administration charges were levied partly as a result of the increased competition between lenders based upon the mortgage rate, partly as a result of the obvious increases in the degree of formality and regulation associated with processing a mortgage application, and partly in order to avoid cross-subsidy between successful applicants and those applicants (amounting to between 20 and 30 per cent of all applicants) whose application had been processed but, for one reason or another, had decided not to proceed. The growth of the adoption of an administration charge was part of a general development toward identifying costs and charging them to those on whose behalf they were incurred as opposed to spreading them across the ranks of those who took out mortgages with any one lender.

6.21. The practice of requiring payment in anticipation of processing the application and the valuation obviated any credit risks which would otherwise be associated with an application. There was a growing trend toward multi-applications to many lenders (reflecting the competition in rates and types of mortgage products) and it was quite common for applicants, in good faith and in pursuit of the best mortgage arrangements for themselves, to accept the most favourable offer and abandon the others. Advance payment ensured that there was no difficulty in recovering the costs incurred in such applications. Not all lenders made an administration charge although the practice had become more widespread in recent years. It reflected the growing costs to the lender of processing mortgage applications, with more emphasis on verifying the application. In addition a significant proportion of transactions (on average, about 20 per cent) fell through, for one reason or another, before completion but after valuation and after some administration costs had been incurred; requiring an initial payment enabled the lender to make certain of recovering some of these costs. The level of charge would, however, rarely cover the full cost to the lender of processing the application. Lenders' practice in making these charges fully transparent to the borrower varied.

6.22. The CML acknowledged that the average valuation fee had risen from around £45 in 1983 to £117 in 1992. It said that much of this was because of inflation. If the figures were deflated by an appropriate measure, for which it used the AEI, the real growth was shown to be from around £45 in 1983 to around £59 in 1992. The trend in real terms had been for the average fee to change little between 1983 and 1985, then to rise in 1986 and 1987 before stabilizing again until 1990, and to increase sharply in 1991 and 1992. The main reasons for the sharp increase were the increased standards and greater detail being asked of valuers, the identification and inclusion of administration charges and the sharp increase in the costs of professional indemnity cover faced by valuers. On the first point, CML told us that over the period in question the nature of a valuation had changed significantly. As a result of the greater risks in the business of mortgage lending facing the lenders from the onset of the housing recession in 1988, a more structured inspection was now required by most lenders covering more matters, in more detail. This might involve more equipment required for inspection, for example for dampness, and also, for some lenders, the provision of a photograph of the property and evidence of 'comparables', that is, the transaction prices for similar homes. The CML argued that higher standards of valuation were responsible for the bulk of the increases in the costs of valuation. One yardstick of the extra cost of valuation was that the daily average number of valuations which each valuer could undertake reasonably had fallen. For example, in the case of one of the larger lenders the number had fallen from five to four.

## The complex monopoly situation

6.23. In its response to the provisional finding by the MMC of a complex monopoly and the issues that arose from that, the CML disputed that the conditions in section 7(2) of the Fair Trading Act for the identification of a complex monopoly had been fulfilled. It argued that the MMC had not shown that the practices they had identified prevented, restricted or distorted competition in connection with the supply of residential mortgage lending. The CML argued further that the state of competition in the market-place was very high and the market was very transparent. Moreover, the MMC, in its view, had not recognized the difficulties which the hypothetical remedies put forward by the MMC would have on the operation of the prudential policies of the lender.

*(a) Limiting a prospective borrower's choice of valuer by refusing to accept valuations by any competent valuer*

6.24. In relation to practice *(a)* the CML argued that a valuation was essential, either under the provisions of section 13 of the 1986 Act, or in accordance with ordinary prudential mortgage lending for the purposes of the lender assessing the adequacy of the security. Under section 13 of the 1986 Act, a statutory duty was placed on building societies to obtain valuations in a prudent manner. It had never been contemplated that this duty could be discharged by allowing borrowers or intermediaries to determine the choice or competence of valuers. As the borrower had never enjoyed the right to a choice of valuer, the lender's behaviour could not be held to affect competition. Borrowers were free to choose and pay for a surveyor for their own purposes if they so wished.

### (b) Discriminating in the allocation of valuation business in favour of valuers that are employed by the lender, or associated firms or companies

6.25. On practice *(b)* the CML argued that individual lenders were entitled to make their own judgment on how to obtain the services they required most economically and, where appropriate, to use their own resources. Provided the undertaking was not in a dominant position, and effective competition existed between lenders, the practice did not prevent, restrict or distort competition. No rational lender, it said, would seek to pay more than was necessary by using its own internal services as opposed to better value valuation services supplied externally. Nor had the MMC revealed evidence of a systematic policy of 'discrimination' in the procurement of valuation services by lenders. Some lenders obtained all their valuation services externally, others obtained varying proportions of their needs from valuers employed directly or indirectly by them. The CML therefore did not believe that effects arose which were adverse to competition.

### (c) Requiring the prospective borrower to pay a set fee based on a national scale established by the lender

6.26. With practice *(c)* the CML explained that lenders typically offered mortgages throughout the UK on rates and conditions which did not differentiate between borrowers: there was no good reason why administrative and valuation charges should be treated any differently. These conditions were advertised nationally and could not be varied locally without administrative difficulty and exposing the advertisers to sanctions for breaches of the financial and trading standards regulations. They brought certainty at the stage of the application and convenience to borrowers and, provided lenders set individual scales which could easily be compared by borrowers, competition would not be affected.

### (d) Paying external valuers a set fee based on a national scale established by the lender

6.27. On practice *(d)* the CML saw nothing restrictive in individual lenders operating their own set national scales for paying valuers. The establishment of a 'price list' on a national basis by buyers was widespread and unexceptional, and there was no evidence that lenders colluded in the setting of national prices for valuation services. For some lenders the establishment of local charging scales would be an administrative nightmare.

### (e) Requiring prospective borrowers to pay fees in connection with valuation services which also contain administrative charges for the valuation or for other services, and which are not separately identified

6.28. The CML suggested that the wording of the practice was unclear: was it the charging of a fee, the 'bundling' of administration and valuation fees, or the failure to disclose the size of the components which created an alleged anti-competitive effect? On the administration charge the CML said that lenders were entitled to charge for the service they offered prospective borrowers since they would be incurring costs in providing that service. As many as 20 per cent of all mortgage applications did not proceed to completion and, in the CML's view, it would be wrong if the costs of those non-completions were simply loaded on to existing borrowers. They saw no good reason why such a cross-subsidy should be seen as acceptable.

6.29. In connection with the allegation of 'bundling' of charges the CML considered that the lender was offering one service, the mortgage loan, and costs were incurred in the provision of that mortgage loan. It was not clear why those costs had to be separated out; they would all be recoverable from the borrower and how this was done was best left to the discretion of the lender. Moreover, there was considerable variety of practice in the way lenders dealt with such charges. While the level of up-front charges was clearly a factor in the borrower's choice of lender, it was irrelevant to him whether the components making up the up-front charges were separately specified. Many lenders did, in fact, separate valuation fees and administration charges but this was a matter properly left to the discretion of lenders.

6.30. Following the MMC's amendment to their original provisional list of practices the CML commented that it was pleased to see the deletions to the list of practices but repeated its earlier concern that Parliament had deliberately left the definition of 'competent valuer' to the lender, and that it had yet to be demonstrated that the suggested lack of transparency in charging affected competition.

6.31. The CML commented generally on the issues identified by the MMC that it saw no adverse effect arising from the current arrangements and consequently saw no necessity for remedies to be applied to lenders' practices.

## Issues

### *Selection of valuer*

6.32. A number of the issues sprang from the question of the selection of the valuer. In commenting on those issues the CML reiterated that the valuation report was required for the lender's purposes and it was imperative that lenders retained control of the valuation process, and selected and instructed the valuer. If lenders were obliged to surrender control, the CML believed lenders would have much less confidence in the valuation reports commissioned by others, especially financial intermediaries, as establishing the adequacy of the lender's security for the borrower's loan. It followed that other means would have to be adopted to restore the lenders' confidence. This would take many forms, for example higher provision for mortgage indemnity insurance, reduced percentage loans and greater efforts made to monitor the valuations commissioned by others (as in Scotland). Any of those expedients would impose additional costs on the lenders and, therefore, on borrowers.

6.33. The present arrangements allowed the lender to make an informed choice of valuer and to bargain over fees and the coverage of the valuation from a stronger commercial position than a borrower. In the CML's view the borrower had a primary interest in securing an advance and could have little or no interest in the adequacy of the lender's security. The costs of selection, and the valuation charge itself, were lower than would otherwise be the case. If those arrangements were changed, borrowers would be unable to make informed choices of valuer and incapable of bargaining on charges to the same degree and effectiveness as lenders. Such choices as would be made by borrowers would be based upon an imperfect understanding of valuer quality. Valuers' costs would also increase, as they deployed more resources into marketing and advertising, and it was likely that valuer concentration would increase, and therefore local borrower choice would diminish.

6.34. The CML suggested that it would be folly for the MMC to base recommendations on assertions by a few aggrieved valuers that valuation work could be conducted more cheaply by them, especially given the concerns that lenders had over the quality of valuations and risks from fraud and negligence.

6.35. The CML noted that no evidence had been presented by the MMC to show that excessive profits were being made in the provision of valuation services and argued that lenders had no interest in inflated valuation fees, whether the valuations were provided by panel members or by in-house valuers. Borrowers were sensitive to differences between lenders in threshold charges, thus ensuring that competitive pressures would keep down the price of valuations.

6.36. The CML maintained that limiting the number of approved valuers on a particular lender's list brought clear benefits. It allowed the lender to maintain a regular and close relationship with the valuers, permitted the rapid accumulation of comparative data on house prices and greater accuracy in valuations, and ensured an appropriate understanding of the lender's specific requirements and working practices. It also provided the lender with greater reassurance that the valuer had, and main-tained, the requisite insurance to meet any legal claims and that he was unlikely to expose the lender to fraud. Even without a panel the lender would still have only a limited number of instructions to distribute amongst valuers; in a depressed market the expectations of some valuers would inevitably be disappointed. The CML believed that the size of the panel and its composition was best left to the lender to judge.

6.37. In response to the suggestion that borrowers were put to unnecessary expense by lenders refusing to accept existing valuations by competent valuers, the CML acknowledged that lenders would not normally accept a report prepared by someone not on their panels. This would be for all the prudential reasons already given. The lender would also incur expenses in satisfying itself that a non-panel valuer was competent, of integrity and had adequate insurance arrangements. It believed there would almost certainly be extra delays involved. However, where the report was by a valuer on the lender's own staff or by panel valuer, and was reasonably current, then, with few exceptions, lenders would generally be prepared to accept it.

6.38. In the CML's view, the lenders' selection of valuer had not discouraged borrowers from seeking their own more detailed reports. It said that many lenders positively advised borrowers to do so and actively promoted HBRs and SSYs. The CML suggested that if lenders had not been promoting these more detailed survey reports, hardly any of them would have been sold.

6.39. If persons other than lenders, for example intermediaries such as estate agents or brokers, were able to select and instruct a valuer, the CML considered that the incidence of fraud and negligence would undoubtedly increase. These bodies, with no interest in the adequacy of the lender's security, would be in a position to abuse their position. The CML said that all informed commentators placed the actual fraud figure, notwithstanding the present arrangements, as very high; in the absence of the present guarantees and system for ensuring lenders' control of valuations it would be higher still. The policy of lenders in England and Wales not generally to accept valuations commissioned by third parties was supported, and influenced, both by the police and the mortgage indemnity guarantee insurers. Metropolitan Police advice to lenders was to use a panel valuer, while one of the major mortgage indemnity guarantee insurers specified that an applicant's or introducer's suggested valuer was not to be used.

6.40. The CML believed it would be wrong to assume that the Scottish system of accepting mortgage valuations commissioned initially by third parties worked well and should be adopted generally throughout the UK. The system worked reasonably well in Scotland because lenders made it work but at some considerable additional cost to themselves. Experienced Scottish practitioners and lenders had suggested to the CML that perceptions as to the desirability of the Scottish system might well be very different had the Scottish market experienced the same degree of upheaval as that shown in England over the last five years.

6.41. On the issue that lenders' control of the valuation process deprived borrowers of direct contact between the borrower and the valuer, the CML pointed out that there was no evidence that any legitimate interest borrowers might have in details arising from a valuation report was not provided for by current practice. Lenders would be concerned about the possibility of borrowers seeking to influence valuers on the level of valuation. Lenders were looking for a long-standing relationship with their borrowers and were naturally anxious to maintain good relations and therefore took responsibility for dealing with borrowers' queries. Lenders believed they could provide a better service if queries were routed through them. A further advantage of this procedure was that it avoided the legal problem of valuers exposing themselves to additional risks of liability in tort to the borrower; generally professional indemnity insurers advised valuers not to enter into any communications with borrowers. Ultimately, if borrowers were unsatisfied and continued to have concerns arising from a lender's valuation report, they could always commission another valuation or an HBR or SSY.

## Valuation fees

6.42. The CML submitted that no scheme of charging was perfect. The overriding priority in establishing methods of charging valuation fees for borrowers was that they be ascertainable in advance and thus easily calculable by all concerned at the initial stage. Alternative bases existed such as 'quantum meruit', time costing or regional scales; but all these would lead to uncertainty, complexity and the creation of difficulties in marketing mortgage products nationally, especially as mortgage valuation costs were incorporated in the APR.

6.43. The CML drew attention to the fact that in the MMC's 1977 report on *Surveyors' Services*, on the question of scale fees, the Commission had not discussed the possibility that any regional differences should be taken into account. Moreover, it was not obvious to the CML that the costs borne by valuers did, in fact, differ markedly between regions. There was no simple association between low house prices, low overheads and lower costs of valuation.

6.44. The CML did not agree that the use of a national scale by lenders for valuations deprived borrowers of the ability to negotiate a lower price. The report was for the lender and lenders were efficient purchasers of valuation services for their own purpose, which was to assess the adequacy of the security offered by the borrower. Lenders were often able to offer borrowers cheaper packages for combined mortgage valuations and HBRs if borrowers chose to take advantage of that option. If the borrower required a structural survey the lender would generally be willing to assist by suggesting surveyors who were also competent to carry out the valuation, giving the borrower the opportunity to negotiate a lower price for the combination of valuation and SSY. The CML pointed out that not all valuers were competent to survey a property and not all surveyors were competent to value a property at all, or in a particular area. The CML said that lenders had no interest in inflating the costs of valuations. Equally, lenders had a notion of the costs incurred in obtaining proper valuations and were not necessarily attracted toward the promise of the lowest cost valuations which were, in their view, often associated with substandard or inaccurate valuations of the security offered.

6.45. As regards convergence of valuation fees, the CML noted that its own evidence showed there were still significant differences between the valuation fees charged by different lenders. If there were to be a degree of convergence over time this was not surprising. It arose naturally as part of the competitive process in the same way the lending interest rates themselves converged.

## Reciprocity

6.46. The CML believed this issue had been elevated out of all proportion as a result of the lobbying by disaffected valuers. Reciprocity was used as a criterion for making appointments or giving instructions only as a tie-breaker, when all other factors were equal. As such, it was unexceptional and indeed normal in a variety of commercial settings. The CML reiterated that the overwhelming desire of lenders was to have an accurate valuation. Reciprocity was therefore the last, rather than the first, consideration lenders employed.

## Conflicts of interest

6.47. On the issues on conflicts of interest the CML emphasized that the valuer's primary duty was in contract to the lender. The lender's overriding interest was in obtaining an accurate valuation. The CML could not understand why any lender would wish to frustrate the giving of an advance by encouraging an undervaluation if its lending criteria were otherwise satisfied. If the lender did not wish to make an advance, all it had to do was to say so, and the borrower could go elsewhere. Nor could the CML understand why lenders would be willing to be satisfied with the overvaluation of a security. This would simply mean that the lenders' security was inadequate with all the imprudence, irregularity and illegality that implied. It pointed out that the lender's valuation function, even (or perhaps especially) when supplied in-house, was discharged independently of the loan function. The CML said that lenders had a high reputation for straightforward behaviour.

6.48. The CML dismissed the suggestion that conflicts of interest were increased by the use of in-house valuers, associated company valuers or panel members. In lenders' experience, in-house valuers were more independent than panel members as they were under no economic pressure to consider future instructions or to facilitate a transaction which would not otherwise take place. Lenders ensured that the various subsidiaries in their group structure were kept and operated separately. Building societies were careful to preserve the valuers' ability to stand apart from the lending process itself, given that criminal penalties could apply if they failed to give a proper valuation. With panel members there was no evidence to show that the actual allocation of work to panel members was influenced by a consideration of the level of mortgage introductions. Adequate security was at the heart of lending culture and the advent of wholly-owned estate agency chains had not changed this.

## Use of in-house valuers

6.49. With the concern that valuations conducted by in-house and subsidiaries' valuers were exempt from VAT but panel valuers attracted VAT, the CML argued that lenders simply employed a standard scale charge irrespective of who conducted a valuation. Notwithstanding the apparent difference in margin in the use of the two sources of valuation, the CML said that there was no evidence that the selection of valuers was based upon the incidence of VAT, as opposed to operational requirements.

## *Transparency*

6.50. On the suggestion that information on valuation and administration charges was withheld from borrowers, the CML stated that the provisions of the CCA 1974 applied to such charges. This ensured that the overall cost of valuation and administrative charges were made known to the borrower. The component elements might not always be broken down and identified specifically, and lenders' practices varied. Faced with a total level of charges, the CML took the view that it was a matter of indifference to borrowers how the charge was constituted as between valuation and administration and the MMC had provided no evidence of any borrowers' decisions being affected by lack of information. It was the total charge which influenced borrowers and if one lender's charge was too high, irrespective of its composition, there were other lenders to which that borrower could turn.

## CML response to RICS statement of views

6.51. At a late stage in the inquiry a meeting took place between the CML's valuation panel and the RICS. The statement of views from the RICS which emerged from that meeting was subsequently seen by the CML and it strongly endorsed its contents (see paragraph 8.39).

## Summary

6.52. In conclusion, the CML took the view that the current arrangements were beneficial. It was essential for lenders to satisfy themselves of the adequacy of the security offered, and a valuation conducted on their behalf, and independently of the borrower, was a key element in this. Lenders were able to procure cheaper and better valuations than any borrower. If they lost this control, lenders would require extra assurance that the security offered was adequate: this would inevitably mean higher costs to borrowers. The existing arrangements met lenders' needs, provided a high-quality valuation for the lender (and, incidentally, the borrower) and, in confirming the value of the security, reassured investors, regulators and the capital markets of the financial soundness of the lenders.

# 7 Views of individual mortgage lenders

## Contents

## Introduction

7.1. During the course of the inquiry the MMC held hearings with eight lenders, representative of the largest building societies, banks and other lenders. In addition some lenders not seen by the MMC submitted comments to the inquiry directly.

## Halifax Building Society

7.2. Halifax is the world's largest building society. In 1992 it had a 15 per cent market share of the UK residential mortgage market. It operates out of over 700 branches throughout the UK and has now expanded into Europe. Its subsidiary company, Halifax Estate Agencies Ltd, has 600 offices. In 1990 it adopted the name of Colleys as the trading name of its survey and valuation division. Valuers employed by Colleys also undertake work for other building societies, banks and other financial organizations. The volume of instructions undertaken for external clients in 1992 was some 56 per cent of their annual workload. During 1992/93 Halifax commissioned in excess of 200,000 mortgage valuation reports.

7.3. Halifax said that changes in business practices relating to the commissioning of valuation advice had to be seen against the background of the purchase by building societies of estate agencies, the effects of litigation against valuers that had occurred during the 1980s and the more definitive information and advice on valuation now given by the professional institutions and required by Halifax. These circumstances had led to building societies issuing detailed guidance to valuers and demanding higher standards of them. There had been increased pressures by the professional indemnity insurers as a result of the decline in the property market which had resulted in some valuers having difficulty in obtaining cover.

7.4. The decline in house values since 1988 illustrated the importance of stringent procedures to ensure that property offered adequate security. The key issue for the lender was risk management. Assessment of each advance was a legal and prudential requirement on the lender, and a valuation was an essential part of this assessment. If the lender relinquished control of the valuation process, Halifax's recent experience showed that the risks associated with lending increased.

7.5. Halifax said that its policies and practices conformed with the law and were in the best interests of its depositors and borrowers. Its policies were consistent with best business practice and did not operate against the public interest. It reserved the right to decide for itself what precautions it needed to take to assess the adequacy of the security offered for loans and whether it should select and instruct the valuers upon whose reports it relied in making loan assessment decisions.

## The complex monopoly situation

7.6. Halifax endorsed the views expressed by the CML on issues of jurisdiction. It did not consider that its practices prevented, restricted or distorted competition and therefore no complex monopoly situation existed. Nor did it believe that its practices were against the public interest. It acknowledged that whilst its own requirements were fully met by the mortgage valuation report it commissioned on its own behalf, its endeavours to encourage prospective borrowers to commission HBRs or SSYs may have led it to become identified with the need for, and provision of, such reports. Halifax had introduced its triple-option scheme 'Scheme 1, 2 and 3', to illustrate to borrowers the relative levels of inspection and report and thus the limitations of the mortgage valuation and, as a service to introduce customers to a surveyor given that few, if any, would have retained a surveyor. It was essential for lenders to assess a borrowers' security independently, free from the influence of borrowers and intermediaries.

## Competition

7.7. Halifax said that the home loan market was highly competitive and likely to remain so. Borrower choice was probably wider than it had ever been. Lenders had to be able to respond to changes in market conditions. Interest rates and product range were likely to remain of paramount interest. Market share, however, depended on remaining competitive in all areas. Failure to compete effectively in any one area would lead to a fall in market share so there was a continuing need to balance all factors, including valuation fees and practices and administration charges, in the light of market conditions.

7.8. The entry of the banks and centralized lenders into the mortgage market had increased competition. At different times since the mid-1980s they had accounted for significant percentages of total annual mortgage lending. This had led to a loss of market share for the building societies, particularly during the early period when the banks concentrated on large value mortgages. When mortgage rates returned towards the level of wholesale money rates, building societies had regained market share.

7.9. A borrower's main consideration was the amount of loan that could be obtained and the cost of the monthly repayment. In recent years, product range and interest rates had taken on increasing importance and incentives related to up-front costs could be seen as orientated towards the marketing of particular financial products, for example fixed-rate mortgages. On their own, such incentives might be of little importance to the average borrower. Halifax did occasionally offer incentives such as waiving or reducing the valuation fee. It was not likely that, in isolation, a borrower would base his choice on such incentives but if a lender did not offer an incentive and a competitor did, it was necessary to react to the competitive threat or else lose business. The incentives were part of the marketing mix and they assumed greater or less importance from time to time.

## Selection of valuers

7.10. Halifax said that it reserved the right to select the valuer for mortgage valuation purposes. It was bound by statute to obtain such a report prior to making its decision on whether or not to make an advance. This need was reinforced by the importance placed on adequacy of security by credit-rating organizations and mortgage indemnity insurers. Its success in reducing risk was reflected in its high credit rating and thus lower cost of capital. Experience showed that few customers were concerned about the process of the lender satisfying itself that the security offered was adequate. Equally borrowers were bound to be far less well informed than Halifax as to what it required from a valuation report. Halifax said that if a borrower (or intermediary) were free to select a valuer of his choice there would be a tendency for him to select the valuer on the basis of facilitating the transaction (and for the intermediary to receive a commission). Neither would have the paramount interest of the lender in the adequacy of the security offered. If this were forced on the lenders, Halifax would need to introduce further checks on valuations and extra audit procedures to reduce the increased risk. This would increase administrative costs, put pressure on its credit rating and lengthen the time before mortgage offers were made. Costs would increase throughout residential lending and there would be no benefit accruing to anyone, least of all the borrower.

7.11. Halifax employed about 120 staff valuers and Colleys about 262. The benefits of employing its own staff included direct control and management of properties held in its possession. The introduction of staff valuers' expertise into this area of work over the past two years had been a significant factor in minimizing loss. Staff valuers were also reinforcing the training of panel valuers. 35 per cent of valuations were undertaken by its own staff.

7.12. Halifax also used valuers chosen from a panel of external firms whose staff were chosen for their competence and experience. The panels in England, Wales and Northern Ireland were reviewed in 1989. Halifax said that the review was occasioned by its recent experiences of inaccurate, negligent or fraudulent valuations and greater risks in the property market. The review gave Halifax the opportunity to remove valuers who were no longer practising and those who were unable or unwilling to effect the necessary professional indemnity insurance cover. One hundred and sixty-seven firms had their appointments terminated and of these 21 had complained to Halifax. The panel continued to include a significant number of sole practitioners and smaller locally-based firms. The 1990 panel review in Scotland resulted in the removal of 13 firms of which five had complained. Few members had been admitted to the panel since 1992 because of the large reduction in mortgage applications.

7.13. When allocating work where a choice of valuer was available, priority was given first to staff valuers, secondly to Colleys and lastly to panel valuers. In all cases it was imperative that valuers had sound proven local knowledge. Halifax prescribed the post-code areas within which all its valuers were able to operate.

7.14. At one time Halifax had agreed to accept reports prepared by non-panel valuers. This facility had been withdrawn in 1990 following an analysis of arrears and possession cases. The proportion of problem cases that arose from such valuers had been disproportionate to the numbers involved. Halifax was also aware that non-panel valuers were increasingly routed through intermediaries.

7.15. It would not be acceptable to Halifax for the borrower to choose the mortgage valuer. A borrower could not be expected to be aware of the requirements of the lender, nor could he be relied on not to try to influence his chosen valuer if he thought there was a risk that the valuer would report in such a way that a purchase might be in jeopardy.

7.16. If a customer had instructed a surveyor to undertake a private structural survey prior to an approach to Halifax and the surveyor was not acceptable to Halifax, it would consider charging a discounted fee for its own valuation report (subject to a copy of the original report being made available). The report for mortgage purposes would be arranged through one of its staff valuers.

7.17. Halifax advised borrowers of the limitations of mortgage valuation reports and advised them to commission HBRs or full SSYs if they required additional assurance. There were many occasions, however, when it might not be imprudent for a borrower to forego this safeguard. If the house were new, for example built by an NHBC-registered builder and covered by an NHBC warranty, that and a mortgage valuation report would normally be adequate assurance of the value and condition of the property.

7.18. Halifax recognized that not all banks insisted on selecting the mortgage valuer. It said that if a bank were content that the security offered was adequate as a result of factors such as the local manager's knowledge of the borrower, house prices in the area and the local reputation of the valuer, so be it. It, however, did not enjoy these benefits and chose to reduce risk in other ways. The credit risk of a known bank customer was probably lower than the average building society applicant and a bank manager was likely to have full knowledge of a borrower's financial situation. Building societies handled a limited range of personal transactions and had far less knowledge of the financial and personal affairs of their borrowers.

## Standards of valuation

7.19. Halifax had taken measures to improve the professionalism of the valuers it used. This had been achieved by:

(a) Establishing its own valuing group. Its staff not only carried out valuations but also monitored and regulated the work undertaken by members of its panel. Staff valuers were better able to function in this role as direct employees because they were not seen by panel members as direct competitors in the external market-place.

(b) Using professional valuers employed by Colleys and endorsing their quality.

(c) Training valuers. Panel members were offered training courses to reach Halifax's standards.

There was tight quality control by staff surveyors. This included sampling of reports, checking of key controls, and senior staff periodically accompanying surveyors on site visits.

7.20. Halifax was concerned about the professional training of valuers. The RICS and other professional organizations had been reluctant to become involved in some of its more progressive ideas. It was not content to rely on the RICS as a body to train or judge the competence of any valuer. In its opinion, the level of competence of the average valuer was low. Despite the depressed market conditions for homes and therefore valuation services, there was a shortage of experienced valuers. The retention of competent and experienced staff was seen as a priority.

7.21. Halifax considered that the level of professional indemnity insurance limits required by the RICS was wholly inadequate. It required for its own panel valuers a minimum level of cover in the sum of £500,000 for each and every claim, with the exception of the more distant parts of Scotland and Northern Ireland where, upon application, a lower level was sometimes agreed. Halifax wanted the RICS to make its guidelines on indemnity insurance mandatory and to ensure that they were observed.

## Valuation fees

### Fees charged to borrowers

7.22. Halifax said that the fees it charged borrowers were fair. It would be most unlikely that a borrower could negotiate a better fee and at the same time satisfy the lender's requirements. It operated a national scale of fees. This had clear benefits in terms of operational efficiency and enabled fees to be collected at the application stage. The fees reflected the expertise of the valuer, the time the task would take, and competition in the market. The fees were based on the purchase price of the property but the range of property values across the UK for broadly similar accommodation resulted in a range of fee payments which broadly reflected regional differences in valuation costs. Valuers' salaries were much the same everywhere in the UK. The work involved was often disproportionate to the actual property value. Averaging out, through the use of a national scale, was a fairer system. Halifax had no interest in maintaining an inefficient scale structure and kept the position under review. It was satisfied that the present scheme was the least unsatisfactory and cumbersome to operate.

7.23. Halifax did not favour a *quantum meruit* as a basis for payment, that is, calculated according to individual circumstances, as this would bring uncertainty and possible confusion to both borrower and valuer. If national scales were abandoned, the risk of non-payment would increase. This problem had been observed in the private market for surveys and valuations.

## *Fees paid to valuers*

7.24. There were dangers in making direct comparisons between lenders on fees alone in view of the differences in the reports they required. The expertise required for residential valuations had increased over the past few years.

7.25. The need for more detailed inspection meant that fewer valuations could be undertaken in a given period. Halifax did not want to see a situation arise in which, in order to maintain their income, its valuers were forced to increase their workload and possibly prejudice the standard of their work.

7.26. An indicator of the appropriateness of fee levels would be the profitability of the panel members and staff valuers. Halifax believed that profitability levels were modest and acceptable.

7.27. Some valuers might offer discounted rates from time to time to win short-term business, but this could put the long-term viability of the firm in question. This could leave the lender at risk. And it might expose the borrower to a situation in which a legal remedy, should problems arise later, would be of no value, especially in the absence of adequate, or any, mortgage indemnity protection.

7.28. The separate administration charges paid by borrowers to Halifax were not attributable to the valuation process alone. Their universal application partially offset the burden of administrative charges relating to abortive applications and resulted in keener mortgage rates. The costs of aborted applications would otherwise fall on existing borrowers and members. It also reflected extra burdens in the application process brought about by financial regulation, including the need to enhance the procedure for obtaining references.

7.29. Halifax was opposed, on grounds of inefficiency, in equity and on cost, to the MMC's hypothetical remedy of a two-tier pricing system which would permit the total cost of administration and valuation charges to be included in the amount of the loans made to new borrowers only. Also its policy was not to refund fees in those cases where mortgage applications were cancelled.

## Transparency

7.30. Halifax regularly reviewed its documentation so that it should be accessible to, and understood by, its customers. At the initial interview with Halifax, the lender's need for a valuation and the type of valuation and survey reports available were explained to the customer, as was the need to pay any administration charges appropriate to the type of mortgage required.

## Reciprocity

7.31. Halifax said that the potential for reciprocity was an accepted part of normal business life. Reciprocity had not, and did not, influence the enforcement of the controls Halifax used in respect of panel management, including the geographical allocation of work. In the event of there being a surplus of suitable valuers in an area, it might take into account the ability of a valuer to introduce other business as a tie-breaker. But, in practice, it was Halifax which was subject to pressures from estate agents and intermediaries regarding their offers of introductions in return for valuation instructions.

## Conflicts of interest

7.32. Halifax accepted and incorporated within its codes of practice the recommendations on conflict of interest made by the RICS and the CML. Its internal guidance went beyond the RICS requirements and had been in place prior to CML guidance. It included, *inter alia*, that lenders should make clear to borrowers that in-house valuers, or those employed in subsidiaries, might be instructed. It also issued guidance to panel valuers on which instructions they might properly accept to avoid actual or perceived conflicts.

7.33. Halifax's policies, marketing documentation, and the alignment of its estate agency companies did not raise any cause for concern. The management and control of its staff valuers was wholly separated from the departments which were involved in the loan assessment process. Its staff, and those employed by Colleys, were statutorily prohibited from acting in valuations for mortgage purposes of properties which Halifax had repossessed. However, they did play a leading role in recommending the appropriate course of action in respect of the selection of the estate agent, the pricing policy and marketing strategy.

7.34. Parliament had addressed the question of subsidiaries through the 1986 Act. This allowed building societies to have subsidiaries and did not prohibit those subsidiaries from valuing property to be mortgaged to the societies. In Halifax's view there was no doubt that valuers acting on its behalf worked only to provide accurate valuations for the building society for prudential/statutory and business reasons and not to achieve the subsidiaries' sales targets.

7.35. Halifax gave the borrower full details of the content of the valuation report including the appropriate fee and other charges to be made. It believed it was the only lender to give the borrower the name of the valuer and the firm for which he worked.

## Use of in-house valuers

7.36. Halifax agreed that it could not recover the VAT paid to panel valuers and that it paid no VAT in respect of in-house and subsidiary valuers. However, VAT incentives did not affect its choice of valuers. It was neither necessary nor practicable to have a two-tier fee structure reflecting which instructions were given to panel valuer and which were not. It was not possible to determine in advance whether a valuation would be undertaken by a staff member or a panel valuer.

## Fraud and negligence

7.37. Halifax said that it was sometimes difficult to distinguish between fraudulent and negligent valuations. The worst excesses of overvaluation had occurred during the period when the property market was enjoying a period of high inflation and were revealed when house prices fell. Steps it had taken, in conjunction with other lenders and by itself in more recent years, had been instrumental in reducing the risk of exposure to fraud.

## Intermediaries

7.38. During the late 1980s, Halifax had been under pressure from intermediaries to accept the valuer's report as part of a package, and in these cases the valuer had been nominated by the intermediary. The use of intermediaries brought increased risks of subverting the valuation process. The majority of intermediaries operated within the statutory and regulatory framework but cases did arise when short-term financial reward displaced customer interest.

7.39. The growing influence of intermediaries had put additional pressure on Halifax to train and develop its own staff. Halifax now took the initiative in dealing with prospective borrowers and there was evidence of a reverse of the trend to use intermediaries or brokers. However, 63 per cent of its mortgage applications in England, Wales and Northern Ireland arose from its own estate agency or members of its introducers' panel which had been established in December 1992. The BSC, as part of its advice on prudential lending, had made a recommendation that the degree of the lender's business originating from intermediaries should be monitored.

7.40. The legal position in Scotland had enabled solicitors and other intermediaries to play a dominant role in the property market, including the valuation process. Halifax accepted that in many instances a valuation would have been prepared for the prospective purchaser before the identity of the lender was known. Halifax's response had been to heighten its controls and enhance its monitoring. The Scottish conveyancing system operated in a smaller, less volatile, market than in other parts of the UK and it would not be appropriate to consider its wider application.

## Remedies

7.41. Halifax commented that it was wholly unacceptable that borrowers should be free to commission mortgage valuations required by the society. Its underlying concerns about such freedom were equally applicable to the suggestion that borrowers should be offered a choice of valuers from the lender's list. Borrowers' choice was a fundamental threat to the objectivity of the valuations and reports on which loan assessment decisions were based.

7.42. It would be perverse to require that all valuations should be obtained from valuers not employed by the lender. Halifax would be denied access to the expertise of those surveyors best placed to value and report on its behalf. Controls were in place to prevent conflicts of interest and there was a total absence of any examples which suggested that borrowers or its own position had been prejudiced.

7.43. In response to the suggestion that the panels should be opened to any suitably competent valuer and that there should be a ban on the use of reciprocity, Halifax told us that no external organization existed which had the capacity to maintain a satisfactory list of competent valuers for use by lenders. Halifax made a major commitment to the administration and support of its panel (which, in the difficult market conditions in recent years, had operated below capacity). Valuers were placed on the panel through merit, and their ability to offer reciprocity was taken into account only as a secondary factor. Reciprocity was less significant than might appear.

7.44. Halifax was prepared in certain limited circumstances and at a valuer's discretion to accept a previous valuation undertaken on behalf of a lender only if it had been undertaken by a member of Halifax's panel. If so, the normal fee would be charged and a Halifax report would be completed based on the previous report but ensuring that all the matters required or specific to Halifax were covered. The valuer would have total discretion whether or not to carry out another full inspection. A previous report commissioned by a borrower direct from a valuer would not be acceptable to Halifax.

7.45. Halifax said that it might accept a valuation not yet carried out (but proposed or agreed between a borrower and a valuer) if the borrower had commissioned a surveyor who was a Halifax panel member to undertake a structural survey and subsequently requested that the same firm should be instructed by the society for its mortgage valuation instruction.

7.46. Halifax fully supported the concept of transparency in respect of valuation fees and charges. The fact that its administration charges were collected at the same time as the valuation fee should not be taken to imply that they were wholly or directly related to the administration of the valuation and survey service. The administration charges made a contribution towards all overheads involved in the processing of applications which Halifax believed to be equitable especially given that, for Halifax, some 30 per cent of applications did not proceed to completion. There was consumer resistance to high administration charges, whereas the valuation fee was known to be in respect of a valuation and therefore acceptable.

7.47. Halifax saw problems with the suggestion that the valuation charge made at the outset should be refunded in respect of all applications which become loans and included as part of the overall loan. The disadvantages included the non-MIRAS (Mortgage Interest Relief at Source) eligibility of the fee, the additional overall cost of the loan, the administrative complexity, and the likelihood that indemnity insurers would not agree to cover that portion of the debt which represented the valuation fee. It was also contrary to the desirable trend that costs should be identified and charged to those incurring them and not bundled into the mortgage rate. Further, it seemed odd that monies should be paid to Halifax and then paid back to the borrower, only to be recouped over the term of the loan.

7.48. Halifax was opposed to the suggestion that the cost of valuation should be absorbed in general overheads for the following reasons:

(a) It would require an increase in the interest rate charged, the incidence of which would increase the shorter the effective term of the loan.

(b) The report would be treated as a report prepared solely for the lender with the result that it need not be disclosed to the borrower. He would have to commission his own HBR or SSY if he required an assurance as to value, thus adding further to the time needed to complete a house purchase.

# Nationwide Building Society

7.49. Nationwide is one of the top seven lenders with around 7 per cent of the residential mortgage market. In 1992 it instructed 102,000 valuations (mortgage and revaluation). Nationwide operates out of 721 core retail and 303 estate agency branches throughout the UK.

7.50. As well as providing mortgage lending Nationwide also provides valuation services and estate agency services. It expanded into estate agency in 1987 and operates a subsidiary company, Nationwide Estate Agents. With the acquisition of estate agents Nationwide also inherited surveyors who were formed into a professional services division of the estate agency subsidiary. Nationwide has also had its own staff surveyors since 1930. On 1 April 1992 the staff surveying team were merged with the professional services division of Nationwide Estate Agents and a new subsidiary company was formed called Nationwide Surveyors. This company employs some 217 surveyors on mortgage valuations.

## The complex monopoly situation

7.51. Nationwide noted the MMC's provisional findings regarding the existence of a complex monopoly situation and said that it fully supported the CML's submission on jurisdiction and the various practices. It also supported the points made by the CML on the issues and remedies identified.

7.52. On the practices, Nationwide pointed out that competition in the mortgage market was unrestricted and the choice for the consumer was vast; that the lender was the client for the valuation; that it was no more discriminatory to employ its own staff for valuations than for secretarial services and employing its own staff ensured a superior service; that setting national scales was the fairest approach to charging; and that a requirement for separate identification of administration charges would be acceptable to them.

## Competition

7.53. Nationwide considered that competition in the mortgage market was much greater now than it had ever been, reflecting not only the large number of lenders active in the market but also the broader product range. Borrowers looked at the overall picture, the interest rate, monthly repayments, up-front costs and the service received, and lenders had to be competitive in all these. Nationwide acknowledged that there was now a much greater degree of complexity in the choice facing borrowers. But at the same time it was aware of considerable movement of borrowers between lenders and that consumer loyalty to a particular lender was not as strong as it used to be.

7.54. Nationwide saw the factors influencing its competitive position as price, product, promotion and distribution (its branch network and the service it provided). Borrowers did shop around and it had conducted consumer research which suggested that up-front costs, particularly valuation fees, did not rank highly among factors which influenced a borrower's choice. The main criterion was the interest rate. In response to the shopping around, Nationwide had developed its quick quote system so that a more accurate outline of the key elements of a proposed loan than a general leaflet could be made available to the borrower at an earlier stage.

## Selection of valuer

7.55. Nationwide referred to the statutory obligations on it, pointing out that section 45 of the 1986 Act stipulated criteria for prudent management, including the maintenance of arrangements for assessing the adequacy of securities for advances. In its view the lender could not relinquish control of the lending process, since the relationship was fundamental to prudential management. It believed that the only way it could fulfil its statutory obligations was by means of a direct contract between itself and the valuer.

7.56. Nationwide had severe reservations about borrowers instructing valuers direct. It had concerns over the valuer being put under pressure to value to order, and had received evidence to support this contention. It pointed out that there were in fact two separate transactions in the valuation process and two parties with different interests. The lender wished to secure its loan prudentially against a property valued by a professional valuer to its specific requirements. The borrower by contrast often wished to buy at the agreed price without any delay or problems. He was often emotionally involved in the transaction and influenced by how well the property had been marketed to him. His own financial interest in the property might be very small, if he were seeking to buy with the aid of a loan whose amount was very close to the market value of the property. These two different interests were only reconciled by a valuer acting on behalf of the lender, with a limited duty of care to the borrower. It accepted, however, that some advertising, which referred to giving the borrower a free valuation on his home, might leave some confusion in the borrower's mind over who owned the valuation.

7.57. Nationwide could rely on the integrity of its approved panel and subsidiary staff. There would be considerable extra costs involved in any move away from current arrangements. Nationwide would need to be satisfied that the reports prepared were properly audited to ensure that these were satisfactory. All additional costs would need to be passed on or reflected in interest rates; it considered that this would be against the public's best interest.

7.58. Nationwide did not consider that its control of the valuation process discouraged borrowers from having more detailed reports. It encouraged borrowers to have much more detailed reports and not to rely on the valuation, and made sure that all its valuers could offer the full range of survey services.

7.59. Nationwide believed quality could only be achieved by having a panel of a manageable size. It pointed out that it had not reduced the size of its panel (which stood in excess of 1,000 firms) over the last few years. There was, however, an operational limit on the size of the panel and once it grew beyond that it became a very costly burden on the society to administer, to monitor and to guard against fraud. Any increased costs from this cause would need to be passed on to its borrowers, or reflected in the interest rates charged. It did not consider that this would be in the public's interest.

7.60. Nationwide did not believe that accepting another lender's panel valuer would help since it had its own specific requirements for valuations; for instance it required all its surveyors to carry out an energy audit in properties on which HBRs were carried out.

7.61. Nationwide questioned whether in practice banks were more flexible than building societies as had been suggested. Its own surveyors worked for all the major banks and were not aware of any using an open panel approach. In its view branch bank managers effectively ran their own local panels. Furthermore Nationwide valuers were advising banks in connection with claims against valuers; some banks had lost substantial sums of money, perhaps because they had been too relaxed in the past.

7.62. In Nationwide's experience, requests from borrowers to accept existing valuation reports were very rare. It needed to instruct a valuer directly to create the contractual relationship and to satisfy its prudential concerns. It would be prepared to accept a previously prepared valuation by a valuer on its panel if it was not more than one month old, but in all other circumstances such reports would be unacceptable.

7.63. Nationwide did not consider that the borrower's interests were adversely affected by the lender instructing the valuer. If the borrower wanted a more detailed report he could instruct a surveyor to produce one. If he wanted clarification of a point in the courtesy copy of the valuation report which he received, his query was routed through the lending branch. If there was a need for the surveyor to speak to the borrower that could be arranged.

## Valuation fees

7.64. Nationwide believed that because of the vast number of mortgage valuations the administrative burden of local fee scales would be too cumbersome, especially as fees were collected up-front of the transaction. For a financial organization as large as Nationwide, it saw it as more cost-effective to its customers to set average application fees in relation to house price-bands. It did not see that setting regional variations, with the problems and the additional cost involved, would be in the best interest of its customers. Nationwide also pointed out that there was quite a close correlation between operational costs and property prices and this was reflected in the method of setting fees.

7.65. It did not see that operating its national scale of charges for valuations harmed those borrowers who wished to commission their own SSY or HBR since it required Nationwide Surveyors and all its panel firms to be able to offer the full range of survey services. Borrowers thus had the opportunity to negotiate with the surveyors concerned and cost savings could be obtained by the borrower on the overall cost by allowing the valuer to carry out both inspections at the same time. It believed the combined cost was cheaper than going into the open market-place.

7.66. For a given level of quality, Nationwide did not see that valuation costs would be any lower. There were valuers in the market-place who would carry out valuations at uneconomic prices because of the state of the housing market, but at such heavily discounted prices it did not see that an adequate quality of valuation could be maintained. Nationwide pointed out that it earned nothing on valuations where panelled, while for valuations carried out by Nationwide surveyors the overall return was less than 10 per cent.

7.67. Nationwide considered that the true increase in valuation fees had been quite small in recent years. There had been a substantial amount of additional work required of its valuers, reflecting both its own prudential interest, increasing professional guidance and to some extent liabilities to the borrower imposed on the valuer by the courts. As an illustration of the growth in workload Nationwide pointed out that its in-house valuers, who used to be able to complete five full mortgage valuations (plus two further advances) in a day, now only undertook four mortgage valuations (and one further advance) a day. As to any convergence of valuation charges amongst lenders, Nationwide pointed out that they varied considerably at the present time. It considered that some convergence was inevitable since lenders' charges were based on costs and their valuers followed standard professional guidance.

## Transparency

7.68. Nationwide believed in transparency of costs to customers and considered that its documentation was clear in this respect in that it disclosed the existence and size of such charges. However, it pointed out that in its experience borrowers chose lenders on the basis of interest rates and not application fees.

## Reciprocity

7.69. Nationwide made clear that reciprocity played no part in the placing of its own mortgage valuation business. Its lending branches and outlets were separate from Nationwide Surveyors, which handled all instructions for valuations. Appointment of panel surveyors by Nationwide Surveyors was strictly on the basis of professional criteria and reciprocity of business would not have any effects on membership of the panel or the continued supply of instructions to them. If a panel firm with which it had established a relationship came to it with mortgage introductions, it would be prepared to consider that business but it was not a requirement it had ever stipulated.

## Conflicts of interest

7.70. On concerns over overvaluation or undervaluation, Nationwide pointed out that mortgage valuations were governed by the RICS/ISVA guidance notes which were followed by all its subsidiary company valuers and panel valuers. All that it asked for was a true reflection of open market value (which was defined in the guidance notes) on which to base its lending decisions.

7.71. In its experience panel surveyors could on occasion be subjected to pressure to value to order by brokers or intermediaries for fear of losing business; by comparison valuers in the lender's subsidiary company had simply to meet the lender's requirements to satisfy section 13 of the 1986 Act. It said that influencing a valuer to be generous or hard with valuations would be a criminal offence under the 1986 Act, to which Nationwide would not be a party. It was not in its best interests to influence a value up or down, as its overriding responsibility was to protect its depositors.

7.72. Nationwide complied with the disclosure guidelines on who might do the valuation agreed with the RICS, and this was made clear in the mortgage application form. If a borrower then had concerns it would try to accommodate him by using a panel valuer. Nationwide had had no complaints in this area.

## Use of in-house valuers

7.73. Commenting on the concern that the rules on VAT created an incentive to use in-house rather than external valuers, Nationwide said that it did not consider that VAT was a material consideration. The scale fees were assessed without taking VAT into account, and the charge remained the same to the borrower whether an in-house or external valuer was used. Nationwide regarded the additional costs of VAT associated with using an external valuer as a cost that Nationwide had to find from within its own resources. If lenders used external valuers exclusively the overall cost would have to rise and it did not see that this was in the borrower's best interest.

7.74. Nationwide did not consider that the use of its own valuation staff gave rise to additional conflicts of interest. Nationwide's policy was to require valuations complying with professional association guidance. If anything it believed that panel surveyors were more of a risk. Its own in-house surveyors were kept totally independent from the rest of the organization.

## Fraud and negligence

7.75. Nationwide registered that its processes were geared to minimize any impact of fraud and negligence. It separated the valuation process from the assessment process and exercised strict quality control over panel and Nationwide surveyors.

## Intermediaries

7.76. Nationwide considered that quality and reliability would be suspect if intermediaries commissioned valuations from non-panel surveyors. It needed to exercise prudential control over valuers on panels to protect not only investors and borrowers, but ultimately the public at large. Nationwide believed there was much evidence of intermediaries and estate agents influencing valuers to value at price and to limit repair retentions to a minimum.

7.77. In Scotland Nationwide still operated a panel system to ensure that valuers were aware of its requirements and it ensured that there was a direct contractual link between itself and the valuer by having the report written on its own form. Its administrative costs in operating a wider panel in Scotland were high and Nationwide Surveyors audited every report submitted by intermediaries.

## Remedies

7.78. Nationwide said that approximately 20 per cent of mortgage applications were abortive and unless application fees in connection with processing a mortgage application, which included the valuation element, were collected up-front, the costs of borrowers who did not proceed to take an advance would have to be recouped from its membership or other borrowers. Whilst there might be marketing promotions which would give discounts or refunds of charges to new borrowers at particular times, and whose cost was borne as a management expense, such promotions could not be sustained for lengthy periods without impacting on the rate paid to the Society's investors or the rate of interest charged to its borrowers.

7.79. In conclusion Nationwide considered that the current arrangements had beneficial effects in reducing overall costs through control of fraud, through customer care via its customer complaints process, through a reduction in claims on valuers, and through ability to keep interest rates as low as possible by using employees who were fully aware of lending policy and guidelines.

# Woolwich Building Society

7.80. Woolwich is the third largest building society and has a 5.5 per cent share of the UK residential mortgage market. In 1992 it gave instructions for 52,000 mortgage valuations.

7.81. In 1987 it established an estate agency subsidiary, Woolwich Property Services Ltd. In January 1993, following further acquisitions, including 190 estate agency branch offices from Prudential Property Services, it separated its estate agency and surveying businesses. All its former staff surveyors, and those employed by Woolwich Property Services, are now employed by Woolwich Surveying Services Ltd, which trades as Ekins Surveyors.

## The complex monopoly situation

7.82. Woolwich supported the views expressed by the CML. It did not believe that the lenders or organizations (of which it was one) that were referred to in the issues letter, or which were within the terms of reference, so conducted their activities in a way which prevented, restricted or distorted competition. It was also concerned that some of the remedies suggested by the MMC would be against the public interest and could increase costs to its members.

7.83. Woolwich said that there was a clear distinction between a valuation commissioned by it as a prospective lender (and required under the 1986 Act) and any survey which might be commissioned by a borrower. The purpose of a mortgage valuation was to ensure that there was sufficient security for the funds which could be lent against the property. It was a valuation for the lender and not the borrower.

7.84. It considered that self-interest lay behind some of the views expressed to the MMC by the members of the valuation profession; they failed to acknowledge that it had been the severity of the downturn in the housing market which had been the primary reason for the decline of valuation opportunities.

## Competition

7.85. Woolwich said that the impact of deregulation and the ensuing interest in rate-led competition had been the main factors affecting the mortgage market over recent years. The market would remain highly competitive in the short term, especially in terms of rates and discounts. Fixed-rate lending would continue to play a dominant role. Quality of service and the lender's reputation and integrity would assume greater importance in a borrower's choice of lender.

7.86. The popularity of fixed-rate mortgages could disadvantage building societies which were having to compete with banks which were not subject to the same financial limits on wholesale funding. Centralized lenders were currently less of a competitive threat but their presence should not be overlooked particularly if the housing market made a marked recovery. Woolwich's approach had been to offer potential borrowers a choice of competitively price fixed-rate and variable-rate mortgage products. The quality and speed offered by its surveying subsidiary helped it to maintain its competitive advantage.

7.87. Woolwich said that borrowers considered three cost-related matters when deciding on a particular lender. These were:

*(a)* the cost of the monthly repayment net of tax relief;

*(b)* the up-front costs of obtaining the mortgage including the valuation charge; and

*(c)* the basis on which the lender was able to vary the interest rates and monthly repayments during the mortgage term.

The APR formed a basis of comparison between lenders' products but was not generally understood by borrowers. The valuation fee was not of sufficient size to affect the APR.

7.88. The 1986 Act had widened the powers of building societies and Woolwich had taken advantage of this by offering additional surveying services to potential borrowers. In 1986 it had introduced a scheme, known as the Woolwich Home Purchase Report, which provided for a report to be undertaken specifically for the homebuyer. It also provided a limited in-house service of full SSYs.

7.89. It did not consider that the availability of these additional surveying services restricted competition. Nor did they increase costs to borrowers. Woolwich would not normally accept a mortgage valuation report from a valuer who was not a member of its panel. But it was prepared to accede to requests by borrowers to combine mortgage valuations with structural surveys undertaken by surveyors not on its panel in certain circumstances. It would take into consideration the loan:value ratio and whether the valuer was a member of a practice known to Woolwich Surveying Services.

7.90. Woolwich did not offer incentives to borrowers on valuation fees. It had always taken the view that the benefits would not justify the substantial financial commitment involved. Its view could change if the experience of other lenders were to show that there were competitive advantages from such offers.

## Selection of valuer

7.91. Woolwich Surveying Services (Ekins Surveyors) employed about 130 staff valuers who also acted as panel surveyors to other lenders. Mortgage valuations were their first priority. Additionally, Woolwich used the services of a panel of external valuers.

7.92. Responsibility for allocating Woolwich's valuation inspections rested with Ekins Surveyors. If one of its staff valuers was not available, the instruction would be given to a local panel surveyor. In 1992 Ekins Surveyors carried out 84 per cent of the mortgage valuations commissioned by the society. The size of the panel had not been reduced in recent years. Seventy new applications to join the panel were received in 1992, of which 60 were rejected because of lack of demand in the locality.

7.93. Both Ekins Surveyors and panel valuers operated within individually defined geographical areas. Its controls were also mirrored by professional indemnity insurers who were imposing their own requirements in the light of claims experience in recent years.

7.94. Woolwich said that it required a new valuation report to be prepared in the case of each main mortgage advance. It would not accept a report previously prepared for another prospective borrower. It acknowledged that there could be a situation, albeit unusual, when a valuer might not need to reinspect the property to prepare a report.

## Standards of valuation

7.95. Ekins Surveyors and panel valuers were required to be Associates or Fellows of the RICS or the ISVA with a minimum of two years' post-qualification experience. In addition to meeting Woolwich's standards of competence, panel valuation firms were required to have professional indemnity insurance cover in the sum of £500,000. Ekins Surveyors staff all received training and their performance was monitored on a regular basis. They also had responsibility for monitoring the work of panel valuers.

7.96. Woolwich said that the work and responsibility undertaken by a valuer had grown as a result of the following factors:

*(a)* the release to borrowers of a courtesy copy of the valuer's report;

*(b)* the Courts' decisions as to duty of care owed to the borrower;

*(c)* the Courts' decisions as to the validity of disclaimer clauses;

*(d)* mortgage valuation guidelines published by the RICS and the ISVA;

*(e)* the detailed specific requirements of all lenders;

*(f)* the fall in property values resulting in losses to lenders and negligence claims against valuers; and

*(g)* the attitude of professional indemnity insurers following the increase in claims in recent years.

7.97. The number of valuations carried out by most surveyors had decreased in recent years as a direct consequence of the decline in demand for the work to be done and the increased standards and responsibilities involved. This meant that fewer inspections were able to be undertaken in a given period.

## Valuation fees

7.98. Woolwich said that it did not seek a specific level of profitability from mortgage valuations but expected to fully cover the costs associated with them.

### *Fees charged to borrowers*

7.99. Woolwich charged according to a national scale of fees. It said that this was necessary because of the size and scale of its operation. It also gave borrowers a figure against which to budget. It did not levy administration charges *per se* although there was an element for administration built into the overall charge.

7.100. It did not consider that there were any adverse effects on the borrower in being required to pay for the valuation at the outset of the proposed transaction. It enabled a borrower to gauge the competitiveness of the price and make an informed choice.

## Fees paid to valuers

7.101. Until 1992 its panel valuers were paid the whole of the fee which had been collected from the borrower. But Ekins Surveyors now retained £25 as a contribution towards the time and cost involved in dealing with panel matters.

7.102. Where an SSY had been commissioned by a borrower from an external valuer, the borrower paid the valuation fee to Woolwich, which in turn paid the surveyor. The borrower negotiated, and agreed direct with the surveyor, the separate additional payment to be made in respect of the SSY.

## Transparency

7.103. Woolwich said that it had endorsed the practice which had developed within the industry of disclosing the valuation report to the borrower, leaving him free to rely upon its contents or seek a survey of his own. It acknowledged that this had led to some confusion over the purpose of the report.

7.104. A full breakdown of fee scales was shown in the information given to the borrower. Woolwich also produced a guide to moving home which gave a breakdown of the different forms of survey available. An individual leaflet was produced on valuation and survey. Its mortgage application form advised borrowers that it was important that they should not rely on the valuation report in deciding whether to proceed with the purchase. It recommended that they obtain their own more detailed survey report on the condition and value of the property.

7.105. Its valuation report included a disclaimer concerning the limited nature of the report. Woolwich recognized the existence of a duty of care to the borrower but said that this did not create a contractual relationship between the valuer and the borrower in relation to the preparation of the report.

## Reciprocity

7.106. Woolwich said that it did not impose any requirement in respect of reciprocity. The overriding criterion used was the competence of the surveyor to carry out the valuation and the highest percentage of valuations which had been carried out for it by any one firm in 1992 was approximately 3 per cent. 12 per cent of Woolwich's mortgage business had been introduced by Woolwich Property Services and 48 per cent by other intermediaries.

## Conflicts of interest

7.107. Woolwich said that it had adopted the recommendations of the RICS and the CML on possible conflicts of interest. There were no direct links between Woolwich Property Services Ltd and Ekins Surveyors. Parliament had addressed the subject of conflict of interest in the 1986 Act and Woolwich adhered to that statutory provision.

## Fraud and negligence

7.108. Woolwich said that maintaining control of the valuation process was one of the most effective methods of preventing mortgage fraud. It had not had much experience of fraud or suspected fraud but was investigating some cases involving panel valuers where it believed the valuations had been negligently prepared. Its experience of professional negligence and fraud had tended to centre on solicitor and licensed conveyance fraud and negligence. It attributed the low numbers of cases involving valuers to the strict requirements which applied under its present arrangements.

7.109. As a safeguard against fraud, Woolwich did not allow the borrower to discuss the valuation directly with the valuer before it was undertaken.

## Intermediaries

7.110. Woolwich considered that there was a role for intermediaries. However, borrowers were able to make their own decisions and often contacted several lenders before deciding which to choose.

7.111. In England and Wales, Woolwich did not normally accept valuations that were incorporated within a mortgage application prepared by intermediaries as part of a package arrangement. It was concerned about some of the practices and procedures which had become established in Scotland because of the different legal system. Here, the valuer's fee was normally paid by the introducer, sometimes on a discounted basis, although often the valuer charged the lender a transcription fee. Woolwich believed that this practice could raise the possibility of collusion between the valuer and the introducer. It would accept a mortgage application through an introducer where the valuation had already been commissioned from a panel valuer. The valuer would be required to complete a Woolwich *pro forma*. Woolwich would not accept a valuation commissioned by an intermediary from a valuer who was not on the Woolwich panel.

7.112. Woolwich paid a fee to Woolwich Property Services for each completed mortgage introduced. No commissions or other payments were made to any other intermediary.

## Remedies

7.113. The suggestion that borrowers should be free to commission valuations from any suitable qualified valuer was not acceptable. Woolwich was unable to delegate to the borrower its responsibility of ensuring that the assessment of the value of the security was accurate. To do so would be in breach of the statutory provisions and against the criteria of good lending practice.

7.114. It would understand a recommendation by the MMC that adjustments should be made to the fee scales to reflect a more localized assessment of the cost. In its view, however, this could lead to an increase in some areas and a decrease in others which would cause confusion to the borrower and lead to an increase in the cost of administration. Its preference was for fees to be standardized on a flat-rate basis.

7.115. It did not believe that the use of national fee scales had led to charges to borrowers being higher than would otherwise be the case. An element of its scale fee did comprise certain administrative costs. It had concluded that it would be in the interests of transparency for the size and nature of that element to be disclosed.

7.116. Woolwich did not believe it to be necessarily in the interest of a borrower to add the valuation cost to the loan; it would result in interest accruing over that element of the advance.

7.117. Woolwich could see certain arguments for absorbing valuation costs into overheads but was against the suggestion. It would lead to the costs being met by its members and depositors and give encouragement to multiple or spurious applications. A scheme offering a refund only to borrowers whose applications had proceeded would still incur costs to the lender. This would result in a reduced level of profitability and at some point in time the consumer would have to pay.

7.118. Woolwich said that qualifications alone could not be the sole criterion for appointment to the panel. Integrity, local knowledge, specialist expertise, adequate professional indemnity insurance and competence all had to be considered. Its selection methods had ensured that its members, depositors and borrowers were as fully protected against fraud and negligence as possible.

7.119. Woolwich noted and shared the concerns of the RICS in Scotland and agreed with that body its preference for the lender to issue instructions to the valuer.

7.120. Woolwich could not accept the suggestion that a valuation carried out in connection with an earlier abortive mortgage application should be acceptable.

# Cheltenham & Gloucester Building Society

7.121. C&G is one of the 15 largest lenders and has a 4.5 per cent share of the mortgage market. In 1992 it commissioned about 80,000 mortgage valuations. In 1991 C&G disposed of its subsidiary estate agency business, C&G Estate Agents, which had been established in 1988.

7.122. C&G said that it placed great emphasis on cost control. It concentrated on core investments and mortgage markets. It had fewer branches than the majority of its competitors. Its assets had increased threefold since 1988. This had been achieved chiefly through organic growth. Its cost:income ratio was typically half that of its main competitors. Only 15 per cent of its borrowers were first-time buyers. Most customers were primarily interested in purchasing good-quality properties. At present about 40 per cent of its business involved remortgages but this varied significantly depending on how competitive its product was at a given time.

## The complex monopoly situation

7.123. C&G did not accept that a complex monopoly existed, nor that it was one of the parties to it. It noted that more valuers than members of the public had voiced concern to the MMC about the present arrangements. It believed this was an attempt by some members of the profession to bring about changes for their own financial advantage. It saw no need to change existing practices relating to mortgage valuations. C&G supported the views expressed by the CML.

## Competition

7.124. C&G said that banks and centralized lenders had rapidly gained market share in the 1980s through their ability to raise funds more cheaply through the wholesale money markets. The decline of centralized lenders had been almost as quick but it expected both to regain share.

7.125. C&G thought the main growth in competition in the next five years would be from non-building-society lenders. New distribution channels would be opened and there would be an increase in money-market-derived products such as fixed-rate mortgages. A successful lender needed a good reputation, financial strength, a large distribution network and the ability to cope with complex legislation.

7.126. The contraction in the mortgage market had increased competition resulting in greater product ranges and lower rates. Some borrowers had moved between lenders to achieve more favourable interest rates while others were committed to one lender having accepted fixed-rate mortgages. The market was still volatile.

7.127. C&G did not make general or life assurance product sales conditional upon obtaining a mortgage. But other lenders insisted upon this requirement. Its policy was to maintain a competitive product range of discounted and fixed-rate mortgages.

7.128. Lenders must be able to respond to market trends and not be constrained by overly prescriptive regulation. C&G's ability to respond to market changes and developments was a clear sign of a healthy and openly competitive market. It anticipated that, as the mortgage market continued to diminish, lenders would seek to offer more incentives and valuation services would become more competitively priced.

7.129. However, borrowers paid little attention to valuation fees which were viewed simply as a pre-requisite for a mortgage. A borrower's prime concern was the nominal interest rate and the cost of his monthly repayments. Once these were satisfied, up-front costs then became a factor in his choice. Since a High Court decision in 1993, comparing APRs across products or lenders had become a lottery and not a genuine comparison of mortgage costs. Most applicants were more aware of headline rates.

7.130. Since 1992 C&G had been offering a cash-back incentive to all applicants who attended interviews at a C&G branch. It was offering currently a refund of the application and valuation fees for variable rate mortgages.

## Selection of valuer

7.131. C&G said that it adopted an aggressive pricing policy and worked on narrow profit margins. It could not afford to take risks in the assessment of the quality of its security. It was essential that it retain control over the valuation process.

7.132. It employed about 40 in-house surveyors and used a panel of external valuers, many of whom were employed by subsidiaries of other financial institutions and building societies. The panel was reviewed annually. No one firm was given more than 5 per cent of its valuations. The appointment of valuers to its panel was handled at Chief Office by its Chief Valuer but the choice of either panel valuer or in-house valuer for a particular valuation was made at its local branch level.

7.133. In-house valuers were responsible for 40 per cent of C&G's valuations and were given priority over external valuers. This was seen as sound business practice. If market conditions were to improve, its policy would be to increase the number of staff surveyors rather than extend its panel. It would consider reports from non-panel valuers but such requests were rare. During 1993, 34 were accepted and six rejected. A sole practitioner would be acceptable if it could be demonstrated that he was well known in a locality and had a good reputation.

7.134. C&G accepted valuations undertaken on behalf of other lenders if the request were made within a reasonable time-span and the valuer met its criteria. It would enter into its own contract with the valuer concerned and would still require the borrower to pay the fee. The borrower was then free to negotiate a discount directly with the valuer if he so wished.

7.135. Only about 6 per cent of its borrowers requested an HBR or an SSY.

## Standards of valuation

7.136. C&G had reduced the content of its valuation report which was now more closely focused on its requirements. Despite the brevity of the report, standards of inspection had been raised. However, greater efficiencies in the processing of the reports had enabled valuers to maintain their previous level of inspections. Borrowers were advised to seek HBRs or SSYs if they required further information.

7.137. C&G said that its criteria for the appointment of valuers were stricter than some other lenders. Where non-panel valuers were used, each one was investigated separately. No charge was made for this service but this policy would need to be reviewed should the number of requests increase substantially.

## Valuation fees

### Fees charged to borrowers

7.138. C&G used a national scale of valuation fees. It believed that this had resulted in significant cost savings to the borrower. It was in a better position than the borrower to obtain an appropriate rate, having discussed with the valuer the quality of service and standards that it required. Quality was considered before price.

7.139. C&G's valuation fee did not include an administration charge. A separate administration charge was made as a contribution towards the costs of a mortgage application. It was not convinced that borrowers would find it more acceptable to pay higher fees for valuation reports rather than pay a general administration charge. The trend was for all prices to be forced down to remain competitive.

## Fees paid to valuers

7.140. There was no consultation with the valuation profession on the level of fees but C&G might send information on proposed changes to some valuers for their comments. Because of the differences in property values across the country, C&G used a system of fee-banding, weighting regional price differences against the complexity of the job.

7.141. The valuation fee was identified as a separate item and paid to the valuer without any deduction. The savings in VAT which accrued when in-house valuers were used were put into its general funds for the benefit of its members.

## Transparency

7.142. C&G thought it likely that lenders had contributed to some borrowers' confusion over the status of the valuation through their failure to explain the purpose for which the valuation was intended. A lender required a valuation to assess the risk on the security offered, but the borrower's main interest was the condition of the property. This conflict was the reason for most complaints.

7.143. C&G said that there was ample information available describing the various products in the mortgage market. Borrowers were sophisticated and able to identify those products which were uncompetitive. It was not difficult for them to compare the total up-front costs of all lenders. It provided a detailed quotation to all its customers giving information on costs at all stages of the application.

## Reciprocity

7.144. C&G told us that it received less than 5 per cent of business from firms on its valuation panel. Reciprocity was not a major consideration in the choice of valuer. In 1992, 75 per cent of valuers on its panel did not introduce any business at all to the society. The only significance of reciprocity was to act as a determinant of the choice between equally competent valuers in an area.

## Conflicts of interest

7.145. During the time that C&G operated its own estate agency business it did not consider that there had been any conflicts of interest. The estate agency subsidiary had placed more business with other lenders than itself, possibly because the subsidiary dealt in the first-time buyers' market for which C&G did not have a product. It had received no complaints.

## Intermediaries

7.146. C&G received a significant proportion of its business through intermediaries. This did not pose undue problems but stricter controls were necessary on appraising business from this source.

7.147. In Scotland, the wider use of intermediaries had led C&G to impose a more stringent control procedure on valuation than applied in England and Wales. It operated a panel in Scotland and would only accept reports from valuers on that panel. The valuation report was sent to the C&G branch and not to the intermediary.

## Remedies

7.148. C&G noted the suggestion that valuation fees should be absorbed into general overheads. It had recently introduced a scheme called 'Action Repay' which provided a refund of valuation fees for successful applicants who chose variable mortgages. The borrower was still required to pay the

94

fee at the application stage but was given a refund if the application resulted in a completed mortgage. C&G bore the costs of the scheme; they were not incorporated within the interest rate.

7.149. The suggestion that up-front costs should be absorbed into overheads was not welcomed. It would result in successful applicants, existing borrowers and depositors subsidizing those whose applications did not proceed. C&G preferred to operate its 'Action Repay' scheme.

# Leeds Permanent Building Society

7.150. Leeds is one of the top seven lenders. It maintained that it did not conduct its affairs so as to prevent, restrict or distort competition in the supply of residential mortgage lending. On the selection of valuer, Leeds submitted that prudential concerns and the needs of the 1986 Act dictated that the lender should control all the procedures leading to an offer. The lender was the client for the report and he required an impartial report. As a matter of courtesy, a copy of the report was disclosed to borrowers but it had never been the intention that borrowers should base their decisions to purchase on the strength of that report. Borrowers were always advised to consider obtaining a more detailed report since the lender required far less information on which to base his particular decision to lend. Leeds saw dangers in allowing borrowers to choose the valuer or for it to accept reports in packaged business from intermediaries, illustrating the latter with a fraudulent case it had reported to the police.

7.151. Leeds employed staff surveyors and did not consider that their use was discriminatory in the provision of valuation services. The valuation was for the society and staff surveyors provided the best possible quality and consistency of reporting, and an increase in the efficiency of processing loans. Fee scales needed to reflect a requirement for high-quality reporting and maintenance of professional standards. Its fee scales were competitive with those of other major lenders. The reduction of fees in 'a free for all' would increase pressures on surveying firms and put standards at risk. Increases in insurance claims would increase premiums and many firms would go out of business, restricting the choice available to lenders and to borrowers wanting more detailed surveys. Leeds said that it did not make any charge within its fee scale which was not related to the valuation.

7.152. On the other issues, Leeds also said that no pressure was ever imposed by it on staff or panel surveyors to influence valuations. The experience over recent years indicated that the competence of many independent valuers was open to question, and that statistically the number of surveyors and members of the public who had voiced concerns to the MMC were negligible.

# Alliance & Leicester Building Society

7.153. A&L, one of the 15 largest lenders, did not consider that its arrangements operated or might be expected to operate against the public interest. It pointed out that the valuation was for the purpose of the society, and that to comply both with the 1986 Act and to provide a prudent approach to lending it needed to instruct a valuer of its choice. It had established criteria for competence, and controlled the quality of the valuation service by using its own staff or staff in an associated company. Where this was impossible it used the services of a panel whose members had been evaluated by its staff and who were subject to specific controls. Borrowers were free to obtain a more detailed report for their own purposes, and were recommended to do so. If it had to accept valuations obtained by borrowers A&L would need to establish substantially enhanced control procedures which would add to costs passed on to the customer.

7.154. A&L believed it was good business practice to establish an appropriate and uniform fee scale for valuations. It was also the most efficient approach, and any attempt to regionalize fees would increase administration costs which would feed into fees. It believed it needed to offer a competitive rate of fees to obtain the services of appropriate valuers and it took into account the comments made by valuers providing those services. It collected an administrative charge of £40 with its valuation fee, which partly covered the administrative costs of applications which aborted before a valuation was carried out, and partly contributed to the costs of the valuation arrangements. The charge was made clear in its notes for applicants which the borrowers specifically acknowledged.

7.155. Commenting on other issues that had been raised, A&L said that the borrower's freedom of choice could not be inhibited by its arrangements since those arrangements were made for a report solely for its own purposes. The borrower could make his own arrangements. Where a borrower obtained an HBR or SSY A&L would consider a valuation report from that valuer, but this was on the basis that it only occurred exceptionally. A&L made clear that in the selection and use of a valuer, taking into account a business connection between the firm of valuers and the society was very much a secondary consideration after operational needs and quality criteria had been met. On conflicts of interest, it stressed that its interest was in obtaining a proper valuation, bearing in mind the professional guidance given to valuers. It did not seek to influence valuers in their valuation. A&L said that in obtaining valuation reports it had to protect the interests of its membership. This was a primary duty for its directors.

# Britannia Building Society

7.156. Britannia, one of the 15 largest lenders, said that it had a duty to protect the interests of its investors and members and indeed to act prudentially in all matters. In taking a property as security for a mortgage it must therefore be absolutely certain that the valuation it received had been carried out by a valuer who was more than 'competent' or 'qualified'; hence the need to carry out strict vetting and auditing of procedures. The experiences of the 1980s and the early 1990s had led it to tighten its control of its valuation function. Britannia had introduced a staff valuer network in 1992/93, transferred responsibility for instructing the valuer out of the branch network to its staff valuers, and reduced its panel membership in England and Wales from 1,000 surveying offices to just under 300.

7.157. Britannia pointed out that the valuation was commissioned for its needs under the 1986 Act and that the selection by it assisted in combating fraudulent valuations and limiting losses that might occur where valuers bowed to pressure to value-to-order. It saw the use of staff valuers as improving the quality of reports produced and found that complaints were far more likely to occur with reports from panel firms than staff valuers. Britannia also found that limiting the size of the approved panel had increased the quality of valuation services since those valuers knew the specific requirements of the lender, received guidance, and were monitored. If an open panel were to be adopted this would lead to additional costs: from higher instances of fraud; enhanced checking procedures and staffing; increased distribution of guidance; and the need for greater involvement by the professional bodies in regulating their members for which there would be a cost. This additional cost would have to be recovered through higher interest rates to borrowers and lower rates for depositors. It pointed out that in the present limited number of cases where it accepted a non-panel valuer report additional guidance was involved which could result in lengthy exchanges of correspondence to clarify aspects of the reports, possibly leading to delays in the house-purchasing process.

7.158. Britannia disclosed the limited nature and scope of the valuation report to its borrowers at three separate stages in the lending process. It promoted to the borrower the option of a more detailed survey and explained that commissioning it simultaneously with a valuation resulted in savings to the borrower. Its fee scales for valuations had regard to the competitiveness of the market, as well as reflecting the quality of report it required. Borrowers would compare mortgage packages so there was an incentive to keep application fees (including the valuation fee element) competitive. The introduction of administration charges as part of the application fee was a relatively new occurrence. In its literature it made clear the breakdown between valuation and other charges. As to whether a fee needed to be collected up-front, Britannia pointed to the need to meet the costs of abortive applications and possible complications over MIRAS claims if the fee were incorporated within the loan.

7.159. Britannia made clear that reciprocal business was not a criterion for panel membership. It did not see that its selection of the valuer created conflicts of interest since both the interests of the depositor and the borrower were best served by employing a valuer who had been vetted for adequacy, competency, professionalism and service. On acceptance of prior valuations, Britannia would be prepared to accept a report provided it was from a valuer on its panel and was within a reasonable period of time.

7.189. Abbey National stressed that none of its activities acted to prevent, restrict or distort competition in the reference market and that its activities operated in the public interest. Abbey National considered that its activities in relation to the practices outlined by the MMC did not justify inclusion in the list of parties to the provisional complex monopoly.

7.190. Abbey National said that borrowers were free to commission a property valuation, or, more likely, a survey for their own purposes from any surveyor of their choice. The valuation for mortgage purposes, however, was a service required by the lender and not the borrower. Abbey National pointed out that, as recently as November 1991, the OFT had written to the CML recognizing 'the lender's right to choose from whom to obtain that service or, of course, whether to provide it himself'. The client/professional relationship for a mortgage valuation was therefore between Abbey National and the valuer. There was no market distortion in this, since Abbey National pointed out to the borrower, on at least four occasions in the lending process, the advisability of obtaining more detailed survey services concerning the property he was acquiring.

7.191. Dealing with the argument that because the borrower paid for the valuation he should have a say in the arrangements made for it, Abbey National pointed out that in making such a charge it was recovering a cost from the borrower of a service required to facilitate prudential lending to its borrowers, in the same way that the costs of taking up credit references on the borrower were recovered as part of the mortgage set-up fees charged to its customers.

7.192. It was also Abbey National's view that it was, on the basis of its considerable experience in procuring valuation services, best placed to select the valuer to be used for its mortgage valuation. Abbey National supplied the MMC with a paper on the market failure that could result from borrowers exercising choice. Its view was that consumers would have highly imperfect information, that the costs of 'search' for comparative price and quality information were high and that valuers could take advantage of this through price discrimination, that consumers would have little bargaining power, and that barriers to entry would appear, meaning that existing suppliers of valuation services would make it difficult for new entrants to appear.

7.193. On the suggestion that their practice in the allocation of mortgage valuation instructions between surveyors was a cause of concern, Abbey National pointed out that the service was provided for the lender, and that the lender had to operate objective standards, checks and safeguards in the allocation of work. Furthermore, there were cost advantages for the company of having in-house valuers and utilizing them as fully as possible. These cost advantages help keep fees charged to borrowers as low as possible.

7.194. Abbey National told us that panel systems did not restrict or distort the way in which mortgage lenders competed in connection with the supply of reference services (ie mortgage loans) to borrowers. Its freedom to determine who was on its panel, and from whom it would obtain valuation services, was not restricted or distorted in any way by the manner in which other lenders conducted their respective affairs. Accordingly, the ways in which it allocated mortgage valuation instructions should not be regarded as conduct which could form the basis of a 'complex monopoly situation'.

7.195. Turning to the practice of fee scales, Abbey National pointed out that adopting an individualized cost-based approach to fees would be very complicated and would raise administrative costs. It exercised the freedom to decide its own scales without any anti-competitive restrictions or constraints such that it believed it was not a party to any 'complex monopoly situation'. It considered that the MMC's findings in their 1977 report on surveyors scale fees still held, that is, that a scale system was a reasonable, efficient and administratively simple way to operate. Overall Abbey National believed the use of a scale system ensured that charges to borrowers were lower than they would be under an alternative system, given the relative negotiating and bargaining power of Abbey National compared with that of an individual borrower.

7.196. On the practice of failing to identify for the borrower the amount of any administrative charge made to him, Abbey National pointed to the wide variations in behaviour in the market-place, the difficulty of easily drawing comparisons between lending institutions, and its own change of practice as a result of which the borrower is not told the amount of the charge which is now described as a 'mortgage set-up fee'. Furthermore, there were wide variations in behaviour in the market-place, making it difficult to draw comparisons between lending institutions. Abbey National said that it informed prospective borrowers of the level of the 'mortgage set-up fee' and that the change in terminology from 'administration fee' to 'mortgage set-up fee' was so as to improve the transparency of the charge, given that it related solely to the costs of processing the mortgage application. Abbey National pointed out that it had no objection to any recommendation made by the MMC that lenders should be required to show administration charges separately from the valuation charge. However, in so far as lenders may make an administration charge separately from any valuation charges, to ensure a level playing field and assist comparisons for borrowers, such charges should be detailed consistently across all lenders.

## Competition

7.197. Abbey National emphasized the importance of understanding that the mortgage market was highly competitive, so that any significant anti-competitive practices in respect of any part of the mortgage package could not be sustained.

7.198. It pointed out that different customers would have different considerations in selecting a mortgage product. Abbey National based its competitiveness on a range of factors: pricing, product range and development, advertising, promotion and corporate image, and quality of service. Borrowers tended to shop around by selecting three or four lenders from the wide range available and comparing the packages they offered.

7.199. It tried to develop a strong corporate image in an attempt to ensure that it was one of the lenders considered at this stage. To improve customer service it had invested heavily in its branch network and computer technology and established a new unit offering advice and sales by telephone, Abbey National Direct. Abbey National had also developed its contacts with intermediaries, who were responsible for an increasing proportion of business, and had established Business Development Units to meet their information and support needs.

7.200. Demand was, however, extremely sensitive to the costs of the mortgage package and price competition remained a key factor. Abbey National estimated that a [ * ] per cent reduction in the mortgage rate would lead to a [ * ] per cent increase in mortgage market share. Borrowers attached equal importance to the up-front costs of a mortgage, the monthly payments and how much they could borrow.

7.201. Abbey National believed that the costs of search for mortgage finance were relatively small due to a number of factors, such as lenders' high street presence, lenders' literature, frequent advertisement of mortgage products and the presence of intermediaries who can undertake the search for the prospective borrower.

7.202. As competition intensified the lender had to compete across the whole range of the mortgage package. It was no longer enough for lenders to compete just on price, they also had to compete on quality and on other elements of the mortgage package such as mortgage valuations.

7.203. In this context Abbey National drew attention to the large number of suppliers, the strong price competition, the high degree of substitution in that prospective borrowers can obtain a mortgage from a variety of different lenders, the strong competition on levels of service provided by lenders, the low barriers and costs to entry and the frequent and varied promotional activity in the market. This, it said, resulted in fluctuating inter- and intra-sector market shares for mortgage lenders. Lenders therefore needed to constantly pay attention to competitiveness in all aspects of the transaction.

7.204. It also drew attention to the results of customer research which suggested that up to 60 per cent of borrowers were highly satisfied with the service provided by lenders. In its view this high level of satisfaction provided a further measure of competition being effective in the mortgage market.

---

*Figures omitted. See note on page iv.

## Selection of valuer

7.205. A number of the issues related to the selection of valuer. Abbey National reiterated that the mortgage valuation was for the lender's purpose, not the borrower's, and that for prudential reasons it must have the right to commission the mortgage valuation of the property which was to be the security for the loan.

7.206. It pointed out that the borrower could commission his own independent survey for his own purposes from any surveyor of his choice, but it would not be prudent for several reasons for Abbey National to rely upon a valuation commissioned by him for its mortgage purposes. One of those reasons was the uncertainty as to what recourse (if any) in tort Abbey National would, in such circumstances, have against a valuer if negligent. This would also assume that it would be worth suing the valuer and that he had adequate professional indemnity insurance. Moreover, if the valuer had acted fraudulently then no such professional indemnity insurance would exist to meet such a claim. It was, therefore, advisable for the lender (or borrower) to ensure that it was able to rely upon a clear contractual (rather than a questionable tortious) relationship with the valuer.

7.207. Further concerns would arise as to the influence that the borrower or any intermediary would have over any valuer instructed by him rather than by the lender: the lender's likely unfamiliarity with the valuer and his approach to valuation, uncertainty over the adequacy of his professional indemnity insurance and the lack of any safeguards in the event of fraud by the valuer in the absence of any professional indemnity against fraud by the RICS and the ISVA. These concerns would remain even where the borrower's valuer was prepared to agree (whether for valid consideration or at no extra cost) to a direct contractual relationship with Abbey National.

7.208. Abbey National cited the experience of some centralized lenders and others to support the need for tight prudential controls, pointing to the higher interest rates that such lenders were now charging. It took the view that, if its controls were relaxed by allowing borrowers to commission its mortgage valuations, the costs of mortgage indemnity insurance could rise. This could increase costs to the borrower, while the mortgage-lending process would be delayed and become more costly due to the need for lenders to check on the soundness of the valuers and their reports.

7.209. Abbey National questioned the suggestion that if the borrower could actually select the valuer this would automatically lead to lower valuation charges. Borrowers did not have the same bargaining power to deal with valuers as had Abbey National. Moreover, Abbey National was concerned that a lower price might be at the expense of quality. Borrowers generally had highly imperfect knowledge of the market for valuation services, coming into the market only once every five years on average. All valuers were not of equal competence and the professional bodies did not monitor insurance requirements nor competence, which was why Abbey National itself needed to restrict its valuation service to certain approved valuers. It was not in Abbey National's interest to charge borrowers high valuation fees, since it faced competitive pressure from other lenders and in order to compete effectively must offer good value across all elements of the mortgage package.

7.210. Furthermore, it feared that the outcome of lenders giving up the responsibility for instructing valuers would not be the borrowers taking on the role but that third parties such as estate agents, who had an interest in the sale of the property, would move into the void left by the lender. This would raise serious conflict of interest problems and would be contrary to the interests of borrowers. There were, therefore, risks to the quality and integrity of the service offered.

7.211. Abbey National believed that limiting the number of approved valuers on its panels was beneficial both in terms of the quality and the price of mortgage valuation services, thus enabling it to keep down the costs to the borrower. There was a limit to the number of mortgage valuers which a lender was able to supervise effectively and administer economically. There was a close correlation between the volume of work and the size of the panel, and to preserve the quality of its mortgage valuation service it believed it was essential that valuers worked with a regular flow of instructions in order that they may be familiar with the details of and any changes to Abbey National's specific requirements as regards its mortgage valuations. If business increased so that the standard, quality and speed of service were affected it would consider increasing the size of the panel.

7.212. In reply to the suggestion that some of the other banks might, in operating lending to residential purchasers, have a more flexible approach to the selection of valuer, Abbey National suggested that these banks tended to have an ongoing business relationship with their clientele, so based their assessment of risk more on the customer's creditworthiness. Moreover, local bank branch managers sometimes enjoyed a significant degree of autonomy such that the decision to accept a valuer by a local branch manager might well be from some kind of informal panel. The risk management perspective also might well be different, as banks had a much smaller proportion of their assets tied up in mortgages than building societies and Abbey National.

7.213. As to the suggestion that lenders should accept existing valuation reports from any competent valuer, Abbey National pointed to the prudential risks, the question of how 'competent' would be defined and how would an appropriate period of time between the original valuation and acceptance by a lender be defined.

7.214. On the question of contract between the valuer and the borrower, it stated that it did not allow direct contact between the valuer and the borrower to discuss the valuation report commissioned for Abbey National's own mortgage purposes. This avoided problems of advice given outside contract. This, it said, was in the borrower's and lender's best interests but if points of clarification arose they encouraged the borrower to speak to his local Abbey National branch staff.

## Valuation fees

7.215. Abbey National was concerned by any suggestion that lenders' scales gave rise to higher charges to borrowers. It did not accept that there were massive regional variations in surveyors' costs, pointing out that it employed valuers throughout the UK. In setting its own scales it had regard to its own costs and, with considerable cost reductions in recent years, was only now covering its costs with the valuation and mortgage set-up fees charged. Any move away from national scales towards setting price according to the circumstances of an individual property would complicate matters and raise administrative costs leading to higher average charges to borrowers.

7.216. Abbey National told us that its national scale of charges to borrowers for valuations did not operate to deprive borrowers of a better price or to raise the total cost to borrowers when mortgage valuations were combined with a more detailed survey. Should a borrower wish to have a structural survey Abbey National advised the borrower of a suitable panel firm which could also carry out the mortgage valuation, enabling the borrower to negotiate direct with the valuer for a lower fee for the survey. Abbey National did not make an overall profit on its valuation services; the aim in setting the level of its valuation fees was to broadly recover the costs it incurred.

7.217. Abbey National had carried out its own analysis of trends in valuation fees using as an index the costs associated with the survey and mortgage-lending process. It drew the conclusion that fees had increased very much in line with these costs. After making allowances for discounts paid to borrowers under Mortgage Movers promotions, its average valuation fees had increased by only [*] per cent between 1990 and 1992, less than the rate of general inflation. As to any convergence of lenders' charges, Abbey National pointed out that this could well be evidence of the high degree of competition in the market-place.

7.218. Abbey National suggested that the MMC's analysis of valuation fees was suspect in that the MMC had considered only scale fees and not the actual fees charged by lenders. It did not, therefore, consider the impact of changes in house prices or refunds made to borrowers under promotions such as Abbey National's Mortgage Mover promotions.

## Transparency

7.219. Abbey National pointed out that in its literature it presented administrative charges clearly and did not withhold information on charges from borrowers. The fact that there was an administration fee, its amount and that it covered general administration costs associated with the mortgage application were now all made clear to borrowers.

---

*Figure omitted. See note on page iv.

## Reciprocity

7.220. Abbey National made clear that reciprocity was not a condition for its use of particular surveyors. Such a policy would be seen by it as potentially jeopardizing the quality of the valuation and the prudential control provided to it by the valuation service.

## Conflicts of interest

7.221. Dealing with concerns that there could be conflicts of interest for the valuer carrying out the valuation, leading to either overvaluation or undervaluation of property, Abbey National took the view that lenders required a realistic, well-substantiated valuation which did not obstruct sound mortgage business and which did not jeopardize prudential control. Abbey National said that it had written to all staff and panel valuers in 1991, informing them of this fact. It pointed to the structural separation of its valuation services from the local branch network, and to the responsibility branch managers had for ensuring the quality of Abbey National's mortgage book. It therefore did not accept any allegation that it would apply pressure on its valuers to undervalue or overvalue. Furthermore, Abbey National had specific guidelines of its own regarding actual conflicts of interest and how they should be handled.

## Use of in-house valuers

7.222. Abbey National had employed in-house valuers since 1935 and did not consider that the use of staff surveyors led to higher valuation charges or gave rise to any 'complex monopoly situation'. It indicated a number of measures it had introduced to control and reduce the costs of its survey operations, for example a major project to introduce new information technology systems which would lead to a reduction in administrative costs and time savings. As a result it believed the cost of valuations carried out by staff surveyors was lower than the cost of obtaining valuations from external firms. Nor did it see that any conflicts of interest for valuers referred to above were increased by the use of staff surveyors.

7.223. With regard to the concern that the rules on VAT created an incentive to use in-house rather than external valuers, Abbey National pointed out that the implications of the VAT rules were taken into account from a global perspective in setting its scale charges, to the overall benefit of all its borrowers. The alternative would be two-tier charging with external valuers becoming a less attractive proposition.

## Fraud and negligence

7.224. Abbey National said that when deciding whether to grant a mortgage advance it was necessary to assess the degree of both credit risk and asset risk associated with the loan. Credit risk it assessed by looking at the borrower's income and outgoings, savings, previous tenure, length of time in employment etc. Asset risk it assessed by commissioning a valuation for mortgage purposes on the property.

7.225. On its experience of fraud and negligence, Abbey National considered that it had been relatively fortunate because of the controls it had in place. Without the control on valuations it exerted it believed it would have faced considerably greater losses in recent years.

7.226. It pointed to the BSC draft note on Prudential Lending of June 1993 (see paragraph 2.15) and the views of the police in support of its policies with respect to prudential control.

## Intermediaries

7.227. Abbey National made clear that it would not want the system prevailing in Scotland, whereby intermediaries commissioned many of the valuations, replicated in England and Wales. Abbey

National pointed out that the market in Scotland was fundamentally different from that south of the border.

7.228. Abbey National was concerned by the power or influence held by intermediaries in the Scottish market. Often they were solicitors who dealt with the housing transaction and also with the mortgage funding. Also in many instances they instructed the surveyor on behalf of the borrower, so the borrower did not in fact exercise any choice in Scotland.

7.229. The higher costs of quality controls and incidence of fraud in Scotland as a result of valuations being commissioned by third parties were in its view distinct disadvantages. The levels of prudential control, measured by the amount of time spent by its surveyor checking valuations, were about four times higher in Scotland than in England and Wales.

## Remedies

7.230. Abbey National did not see that removing the up-front nature of the valuation fee or requiring the lender to absorb the cost were preferable to the current situation. It did not consider that it would lead to more borrowers commissioning any more detailed surveys, it might diminish the duty of care owed to the borrower, it would not add to transparency and it meant that frivolous and abortive applications would be paid for by Abbey National's existing customers.

7.231. In conclusion Abbey National maintained that it did not conduct its affairs in a manner which restricted or distorted competition between mortgage lenders or in a way that justified the label 'complex monopolist'. If, contrary to its views, the MMC were to conclude that Abbey National was a complex monopolist, it contended that its behaviour did not operate contrary to the public interest, but rather in its favour.

# Barclays Bank

7.232. Barclays has loaned money for mortgages since 1980, in part through its branch network and in part through its centralized lending division, Barclays Direct. In 1992 its gross lending for residential properties in 1992 was £2.36 billion and its share of the UK residential mortgage market was about 6 per cent. Mortgage valuations totalled 39,000.

7.233. Barclays pointed out that it did not itself operate a panel of valuers in connection with its granting of loans for residential purposes. It agreed with the views put forward by the CML in general but added some comments of its own about the market.

## Competition

7.234. Barclays said that it had firmly established its position in the highly competitive mortgage market and intended to retain it. Its reputation and wide network of branches enabled it to compete effectively. Its policy was to concentrate on retaining existing customers and attracting first-time buyers. The majority of its borrowers were existing current account customers.

7.235. One of the chief concerns of a borrower was the cost of the monthly mortgage repayment. The high interest rates of the early 1990s had led to the popularity of fixed-rate mortgages. There had been some evidence of customers choosing high street lenders in preference to the smaller building societies. Further increases in fixed-rate mortgages could lead some lenders into difficulties and prevent new lenders from entering the market.

7.236. A customer considering a mortgage offer had two main concerns: the competitiveness of the mortgage interest rate, and the size of the monthly repayment. The APR was intended to be a recognizable and fair way of making comparisons and could not be faulted in technical terms. However, most borrowers, and some within the industry, had little or no understanding of the concept.

## Selection of valuer

7.237. Barclays said that it obtained valuations for its own purposes to ensure that a property was acceptable as security for the mortgage advance. Customers were provided with a copy of the valuation.

7.238. It did not employ in-house valuers. Its branch managers were responsible for selecting a suitable valuer. Their broad experience and regular contact with the local business community gave them an advantage over local managers of other types of lender in assessing suitability. Basic conditions had to be fulfilled. A valuer had to be a member of the RICS or the ISVA and be in private practice with appropriate professional indemnity insurance. However, provided that these criteria were met, it would allow the borrower to decide on the choice of valuer. If a valuer was unknown to the bank, it would enquire about his suitability.

7.239. Barclays was not interested in competing with external firms by employing in-house valuers. It was likely that a chosen valuer might be a customer, or potential customer, of the bank. It had no objection to sole practitioners. It could understand the reasons that had led other lenders to establish panels of valuers and might have done so itself had it not had such an extensive branch network with the associated benefits of sound, local knowledge. Barclays Direct had, however, used a panel.

7.240. Customers were advised to have HBRs or SSYs undertaken if they had any doubts about the properties they intended to purchase. In practice, however, few did so. Where a customer did commission an HBR from an acceptable valuer, a mortgage valuation was appended. The borrower and the surveyor negotiated the fee for the combined report. Barclays considered that the surveyor was not likely to be influenced by the borrower's views on the valuation, because the surveyor would have entered into a contract with Barclays. The valuation report which was sent directly to the bank established Barclays' contractual rights.

7.241. It would consider a valuation report prepared for a previous mortgage application to Barclays provided that the valuation was not more than three months old. In this case, there would be no additional cost to the borrower. It would not, however, rely on a valuation carried out for another lender. But, provided that the valuer met its criteria, it would request him to carry out a further mortgage valuation for Barclays and, if possible, negotiate a lower fee.

## Standards of valuation

7.242. Barclays was generally content with the monitoring and quality enforcement standards of the RICS and the ISVA but not with their speed of response when problems arose. However, it attached importance to valuers maintaining 'run-off' cover after they had ceased to practise. It was concerned that the RICS did not make this a requirement for practice. It would also have liked the surveyors' professional bodies to operate a compensation scheme.

7.243. There could be many reasons for a branch manager deciding not to continue to use a particular firm of valuers. Probably the commonest reasons were failure to comply with acceptable service standards, such as unacceptable delay in producing reports, and doubts about professional competence. Controls exercised by local managers should ensure that firms had sufficient professional indemnity insurance cover.

## Valuation fees

7.244. Barclays applied a national scale of valuation fees charged to borrowers. The charge collected was passed in full to the valuer. Fees had been increased last in 1991. The present level was about right, enabling the bank to obtain a service from valuers which fully met its needs. Some lenders had increased their fees above the rate of inflation, probably to recover overheads.

7.245. Barclays' branch managers did not have the discretion to agree fees locally. This would be administratively inconvenient and run counter to the bank's philosophy of retaining central control over pricing policies. Administration charges were made on some types of loan but none were added to the cost of valuation.

7.246. Barclays' customer research indicated that in customers' minds the size of valuation fees was secondary to the offer of a competitive mortgage rate. It had considered providing incentives on valuation fees but had not found it necessary.

7.247. It was not in favour of adding the valuation fee to the mortgage repayment. The effect of this suggestion would be that only those customers who proceeded with loans would bear the charges. Additionally tax problems could arise. There was a limit on the amount of fees the Inland Revenue would allow to be added on to a loan to qualify for MIRAS. If this limit were exceeded, the lender would need to establish a second loan account covering valuation fees.

## Reciprocity

7.248. Barclays said that it did not instruct valuers on the basis that they provided reciprocal business.

## Fraud

7.249. Barclays said that there was probably more fraud perpetrated in connection with the valuation than in relation to other aspects of the mortgage application. But it had found that the incidence of fraud on the valuation of domestic properties was low probably because of its system of local control and monitoring and the fact that many of its borrowers were customers of the bank. Fraud might have been more prevalent when house prices were increasing rapidly but Barclays considered that it was still essential to maintain rigorous controls.

7.250. Barclays maintained a database for fraud prevention purposes and arranged to obtain audit valuations on a random basis at the bank's cost.

## Intermediaries

7.251. Barclays said that intermediaries were a powerful force in the market-place. It preferred to deal with its customers directly as it was a better use of capital resources at the present time. In May 1993 it decided not to accept any further business through Barclays Direct, partly because of its experience of bad debt, but chiefly because it preferred to lend money to its customers through its branch network rather than give insurance companies the benefit of developing relationships with its customers.

# Lloyds Bank

7.252. Lloyds is one of the 15 largest lenders in the UK. It entered the mortgage market in 1979, the first of the major clearing banks to do so. In 1982 it established an associated estate agency company, Black Horse Agencies (BHA) (a subsidiary of its life assurance company, Lloyds Abbey Life). In 1992 its gross lending for residential mortgages was £760 million, representing a market share of about 2 per cent. In the same year 19,500 valuations were carried out on its behalf. Lloyds joined the CML in December 1993.

7.253. Lloyds said that mortgage valuation was important to both the lender and the borrower. The lender needed confirmation that its security was protected and the borrower wanted reassurance that the property was suitable for mortgage purposes.

## Competition

7.254. Most of Lloyds' borrowers were existing customers. The increased use of fixed-term mortgages had widened its customer base, including borrowers who had moved their mortgages from other lenders. Lloyds said that mortgages were a standard product; it was pricing and packaging that created competition. Incentives offered by lenders could disguise the true costs of a mortgage and it was difficult for borrowers to make an informed choice.

7.255. Lloyds said that the APR was not widely understood; the average borrower was more concerned with the monthly mortgage repayment. Use of the APR should assist in indicating different rates to customers during highly-discounted short periods but problems arose because there were two acceptable methods of quoting the rate.

7.256. It did not believe that the level of up-front payments influenced prospective borrowers in their choice of lender. However, it was necessary for Lloyds to offer incentives from time to time, to remain competitive and to ensure that its customers were not disadvantaged.

## Selection of valuer

7.257. Lloyds did not employ its own valuers directly, nor did it operate a panel of external valuers. 40 per cent of its valuations were undertaken by valuers employed by BHA. In most cases the borrower was content to leave the choice of valuer to Lloyds. But, if a borrower preferred to use his own valuer, Lloyds had no objection provided the person chosen was competent. It was important that the valuer should respond quickly. Lloyds believed its present arrangements worked satisfactorily.

## Standards of valuation

7.258. Lloyds said that its branch managers normally would know the local valuers and be able to judge their competence. But Lloyds could always obtain views on a valuer's reliability and acceptability from other sources (for example, BHA).

7.259. Lloyds had experienced few problems with the professional standard of valuers. It believed valuers now tended to be more cautious. One of the most common complaints from customers was that valuations were understated. It did not ask valuers about their professional indemnity cover. It believed the disclaimers and qualifiers on most valuation reports would deter a borrower contemplating legal action against a valuer for negligence. Lloyds' experience of inaccurate valuations linked to fraud was minimal. It believed dishonest introducers or legal advisers were often involved in such cases.

## Valuation fees

7.260. Lloyds applied a national scale of valuation fees. An external valuer recovered the whole fee charged to the borrower. For valuations undertaken by BHA valuers, borrowers were charged the appropriate scale fee but Lloyds itself was charged an internal discounted rate. The difference between what the borrower paid Lloyds and what Lloyds paid to BHA was retained by its branches. Its fee levels reflected information about other lenders' charges and from BHA. Lloyds charged a commitment fee to borrowers who opted for fixed-term mortgages, but no administration charge was made in connection with mortgage valuations.

## Transparency

7.261. Lloyds believed lenders should not absorb valuation fees into overheads and the constituent costs of a mortgage, including the valuation fee, should be quoted separately. It noted that the Courts and Legal Services Bill would require banks to be more transparent in their dealings with customers.

The Code of Banking Practice required banks to disclose the fees for services they provided. Borrowers were told about Lloyds' national fee scales but not about the discounted rate that BHA valuers' charged it.

## Reciprocity

7.262. Lloyds believed it was inevitable that relationships between its branch management and valuers known to them would be of mutual benefit. But it had no arrangements which required reciprocity.

## Conflicts of interest

7.263. Lloyds had robust safeguards against conflicts of interest. In cases of repossession it strove to meet its duty of care to the former owner. BHA Asset Management Unit handled most repossessed properties but independent valuers inspected them. The selling agent would be asked to recommend a price. The valuation report and all other information was then considered by Lloyds' Corporate Client Unit, which told the selling agent the price to ask. The Estate Agents Act required all offers to be submitted to Lloyds, and if they were lower than the independent valuation it might seek further valuation. At all times Lloyds represented the former owner. The objective of the selling agent and itself was to obtain the maximum price available. There had been no substantiated allegations that Lloyds or BHA had jointly failed in their duty of care to the borrower to obtain the best price for the property.

## Fraud

7.264. Lloyds thought it was less at risk from fraud than some other lenders because it knew its customers better. It maintained an internal audit team which exchanged information with other lenders and was in regular contact with the police.

## Intermediaries

7.265. In 1992 Lloyds received about 4 per cent of its mortgage business through BHA. It did not accept introductions from any other intermediaries.

## Remedies

7.266. Lloyds said that it would respond positively if the MMC recommended that the internal commission element of its valuation fee should be transparent when associated valuers were used.

7.267. Lloyds thought the suggestion that the valuation costs could be added to the loan was reasonable provided the borrower did not lose tax relief obtained through MIRAS. It already allowed its branch managers the discretion to add certain fees to the loan when MIRAS limits were not affected. This was particularly helpful for customers who were in a 'negative equity' situation.

# National Westminster Bank Group

7.268. NatWest, one of the 15 largest lenders, provides mortgage lending through its branch network, but mainly through its subsidiary National Westminster Home Loans Ltd. It expressed surprise at any suggestion that the way it conducted its valuation arrangement prevented, restricted or distorted competition in the supply of residential mortgage lending. NatWest commented that the valuation report was central to its assessment process, its need to assess the adequacy of the property as security for the loan being sought. Its experience had shown that this area of the lending process was particularly vulnerable to fraudulent activity. In line with recommendations from both the police and the Law Society it had therefore introduced a valuation panel. However, it would consider accepting reports undertaken by 'non-panel valuers' and in practice only a small minority of such requests were turned down.

7.269. In the selection of valuer, NatWest pointed out that it had no staff or associated company valuers, the size of its comprehensive panel (in excess of 1,500) ensuring that effectively it did not limit borrowers' choice although it would limit the numbers of valuers in any one particular area to facilitate monitoring and good service. It was usually willing to accept the use of a non-panel valuer. It operated a scale of fees for valuations of properties up to £200,000. But its perception was that the majority of its borrowers took comfort from having a known fee, and avoiding the necessity of stressful negotiation with the valuer (given that the borrower actually paid the valuer the payment, albeit that the payment was routed through NatWest). It therefore protected the borrower from unscrupulous firms. At the same time the scale of fees had not been revised since 1986 and the scale fee paid by the borrower was what the valuer received. There were no 'hidden' fees and NatWest did not make any administration charge for the valuation.

7.270. NatWest said that it always encouraged the borrower to obtain an HBR or SSY. If a borrower was having a more detailed survey then the cost of providing the valuation report for NatWest's purposes could be wrapped up in the overall negotiation between the valuer and the borrower direct. It did not see conflicts of interest as a problem since the valuers were independent. If it foresaw that conflict of interest might arise it would not instruct that valuer. Nor did it see reciprocity as an issue since it did not make the ability to provide reciprocal business a condition for joining its panel.

7.271. NatWest believed the benefits of having a national scale were that it helped to keep fees down and that the use of a panel of valuers ensured quality and consistency of reports which was of benefit to the borrower who received a copy of the report. NatWest commented on hypothetical remedies that it must have some control over the nomination and instruction of the valuer both to protect itself and the borrower, by for instance ensuring that the valuer had suitable indemnity cover. Much of its practice was in line with the hypothetical remedies, that is, it allowed scope for a borrower to exercise choice and it was transparent over charges. It did, however, consider that accepting every potentially suitable valuer on to its panel would in practice be unmanageable in terms of monitoring and ensuring quality of service to itself and its borrowers. NatWest doubted whether it was practicable to require all administration charges levied in the valuation fee to relate solely to the cost of the valuation service, since it doubted that all organizations could distinguish the costs involved. Nor did it see merit in the suggestions that borrowers could have the valuation fee rolled into the loan or that valuation fees be absorbed into general overheads.

# Bank of Scotland

7.272. Bank of Scotland, one of the 15 largest lenders, operates in the mortgage market via its branches in Scotland and a centralized service, Centrebank, in England and Wales. It interpreted the concerns raised as principally applying to the activities of Centrebank, and its response therefore focused on Centrebank. It considered that in looking to protect its shareholders' interests it had to adopt appropriate policies for valuation arrangements, but saw no material disadvantage to its customers. Centrebank operated with a restricted panel of valuers of three main firms with eight other firms to handle any extra work and had no in-house valuers. Its decision to operate in this way was driven by a need to establish consistency in valuation reports, a need for control given that it was 'lending at a distance', and concern over the increasing incidence of fraud and negligence in recent times. It was also concerned over problems with ensuring that professional indemnity insurance cover was there to meet any claims and considered that the most prudent strategy was to use a small number of large national firms which it could check economically.

7.273. Centrebank saw no disadvantage to borrowers in its arrangements. Its valuation fee scales had been and remained competitive with industry norms and it doubted that a borrower could obtain a significant advantage by instructing the valuer himself. It would accept a prior valuation report at a nominal fee provided the valuer was on its panel and the valuer was agreeable to transcribing the report on to its stationery. It made clear to borrowers the limitations of a valuation report and, if an applicant wanted an HBR or SSY, it encouraged direct contact with its valuer so that the overall cost could be negotiated. Centrebank was transparent over the valuation fee, publishing its fee scale. There was a 12.5 per cent deduction made to the sums passed on to the main panel of valuers representing the cost of collecting the fees on behalf of the valuers and administering the collection account service, but it did not consider this disadvantaged the prospective borrower. It was satisfied that a restricted panel system did not prejudice the price of a valuation and that it enhanced the quality of reporting. It considered that the requirement for the valuation fee to be paid at the outset was necessary in case the borrower decided not to proceed with the transaction.

7.274. On other aspects of the selection of valuer Centrebank said that it did not practise reciprocity (acknowledging that such a practice would possibly be interpreted as restricting choice of lender), and that at no time would a valuer be encouraged by it to arrive at a valuation in a manner which conflicted with his duty of care to the borrower. It did not see why commissioning of valuations by intermediaries should necessarily affect quality or reliability, providing appropriate safeguards were taken on the risks of fraud and negligence.

7.275. Centrebank saw the beneficial effects for the public in the efforts of lenders to reduce the levels of fraud and negligence. It commented on the hypothetical remedies that it would be difficult to draft and enforce legislation which forced lenders to use valuers in whom they had no confidence and/or to prevent the use of in-house valuers. Either move it saw as restricting competition. It also commented that valuers might help themselves by creating a stronger, more representative body that would stand behind its weaker members, particularly in terms of training and indemnity.

# TSB Bank

7.276. TSB, one of the 15 largest lenders, noted the provisional finding of a complex monopoly and indicated that it supported the CML's submission on this. TSB arranges its valuation service through its subsidiary company, TSB Property Services (which handles around 15 per cent of its valuations in England and Wales), and valuer panels for Scotland and for England and Wales. The latter had only been in existence since 1993. Suspected and proven fraud and negligence had had a material effect on its current procedures and it highlighted the experience of its direct lending subsidiary, Mortgage Express, and its branch network prior to the establishment of a panel in England and Wales.

7.277. TSB considered that its arrangements had beneficial effects in that: a limited panel facilitated quality and control; knowledge of its lending policy prevented abortive costs on properties unlikely to be acceptable to it; it could ensure, through control of the report that the borrower was aware at the earliest opportunity of any factors that might affect the granting of a mortgage; and the risk of fraud and negligence would be reduced through the controls applied to a finite panel membership.

7.278. It did not see that its procedures disadvantaged the borrower. TSB would consider any request from borrowers on the valuer to be used. It encouraged borrowers to consider an HBR or SSY and to minimize costs it recommended they be conducted by the same valuer as for the valuation, it believed that individual contracting was more likely to result in an increase in charges compared with the estimated fee it provided to borrowers, and was actively considering a national scale of charges. It was transparent over likely fees in the quotation it provided to borrowers.

7.279. On other aspects of the selection of valuer, it did not as a policy consider the appointment of firms to its panel on the basis of reciprocal business, and it endorsed the statement of reciprocal business agreed with the RICS. On conflicts of interest, it pointed to the professional guidance notes from the RICS and commented that its own internal audit procedures on valuers could be expected to ensure compliance. TSB would consider prior reports from a valuer on its panel list and transcribed to its own form.

7.280. With the hypothetical remedies identified, TSB commented on proposals to allow the borrower more say, that it would be reluctant to see choice left to the borrower to select any suitable valuer considering that a suitable valuer would need to be defined and that it would involve TSB in introducing checks which would extend time-scales and increase costs. It had no objections in principle to a borrower selecting from an approved list but noted that borrowers would have little meaningful information on which to base their choice, and that administration costs would increase. It saw excluding in-house and associated valuers as denying borrowers a comprehensive choice of service and undermining competitive benefits accruing to those lenders with in-house staff. While in principle it had no objection to accepting any suitably competent valuer on its panel, it pointed out that there were practical limitations from the point of view of control and cost to the size of the panel. TSB supported proposals for transparency in charging and for confining any administration element in a valuation fee solely to costs of administering the valuation service. It saw any proposals for rolling up the valuation cost in the loan or absorbing it in general overheads as commercial matters for the individual lender.

# Other banks

7.281. The chief points made by other banks which offered loans for residential mortgages were similar to those expressed by the larger lenders. Most commented on the contractual relationship between the valuer and the lender. Some reinforced the point that this did not prevent the borrower from entering into a separate arrangement with a valuer for other types of survey. Others said that a valuer's membership of the RICS or the ISVA did not automatically guarantee his competence.

7.282. *Bank of Ireland Home Mortgages Ltd* (BoI) said that it would be disturbed if the MMC did not interpret the statutory obligations placed upon building societies to obtain valuations on property offered for security as also placing an obligation on them to instruct valuers. Building societies were expected to act prudently and BoI believed this should include their ability to control valuations undertaken on their behalf. BoI, although not bound by the statute, had a duty of care to its shareholders. This included the prevention of a possible compromise of the validity of a valuation by the influence of a borrower.

7.283. BoI said that it was an indictment of the surveyors' professional institutions that they were not able to verify the competence and standards of their members engaged in mortgage valuation. It was left to the lenders to adjudicate on competence and this could only be achieved by developing a proven panel of appointed valuers who were closely monitored by appropriate formal auditing procedures. Not all valuers able to undertake HBRs or SSYs had the competence to report on the value of a property to a lender; not all valuers could be relied upon to cease valuing when their professional indemnity insurance cover ceased.

7.284. *Banque Paribas* was concerned that there would be a lowering of standards due to lack of control if borrowers were responsible for instructing mortgage valuations. This would increase the risk to the lender of fraudulent and negligent valuations. A lender would find it difficult to take legal action against a valuer for negligent work in the absence of a contractual relationship being established between itself and the valuer. Banque Paribas believed it would be necessary for the lender to determine the geographical limits within which the valuer operated. It said that the costs of borrowing were likely to increase if valuation fees had to be absorbed in general overheads. Lenders would need to maintain their profit margins and would need to reflect additional costs, probably increasing the mortgage rate payable as a result.

7.285. *Western Trust & Savings Ltd*, part of the Manulife Group, said that there was ample competition in the mortgage market. It found unacceptable the suggestion that borrowers should be free to commission valuations directly because of the potential for fraud on an individual basis or collusion on a wider scale. It would consider accepting a previous valuation report that had been undertaken for itself but valuations previously undertaken for other lenders or commissioned by borrowers were open to fraud and were unacceptable.

# The Mortgage Corporation Ltd

7.286. The Mortgage Corporation Ltd (TMC) is a centralized lender (see paragraph 3.14). It has been operating in the UK mortgage market since 1986. TMC said that it was concerned about only two issues arising from the issues letter. The first, and most important, was the potential loss of its right to select a valuer. The mortgage valuation was for the sole purpose of the lender so that he might determine whether the property represented adequate security for the proposed loan. Secondly, TMC believed it should not be precluded from operating a national scale of fees.

7.287. TMC said that borrowers were most interested in the interest rate when selecting a lender. The increase in remortgages that had occurred in the late 1980s had encouraged borrowers to consider new lenders. Centralized lenders, who financed their operations through the wholesale money markets, had taken market share from the building societies when interest rates were low because they did not have obligations to depositors. But they had been disadvantaged when interest rates rose.

7.288. TMC had no in-house surveyors or associated companies. It operated only through an external panel of valuers. Since 1991 it had reduced the size of its panel to exercise greater control over the quality of valuation reports. The panel currently consisted of 18 firms, most with multiple branches. TMC now exercised closer control over its valuers. Most of its panel firms operated nationwide but it did not rule out small independent firms. Valuers were permitted only to undertake inspections in geographical locations with which they were familiar. TMC said it was unlikely that it would accept a borrower's choice of valuer even if the valuer were a panel member.

7.289. TMC said that it was understandable that lenders used their own staff in preference to external valuers. Centralized lenders, who did not have this capacity, were more susceptible to fraud and negligence. It was probably true that centralized lenders were more active in pursuing recovery actions against valuers than other lenders.

7.290. Prior to 1991 TMC had accepted packaged business and it was its experience that sometimes business links between an intermediary and a valuer had led to a higher incidence of poorer-quality valuation reports.

7.291. TMC said that the RICS arrangements for monitoring the professional indemnity insurance status of valuers was highly unsatisfactory. In TMC's experience, the RICS was not able to confirm whether or not a particular member firm had insurance cover despite the fact that RICS rules required a valuer to have a minimum level of cover and six years 'run-off'.

7.292. All firms on its panel were required to carry professional indemnity insurance cover. It was concerned about the increasing number of cases where insurance cover was no longer in force at the time a claim for negligence against a valuer was made. The RICS had suggested that some lenders had acted irresponsibly by putting valuation firms on notice. TMC had categorically refuted this. However, in any event it was required by its own indemnity insurers to show that it was exercising adequate control.

7.293. TMC operated a national scale of valuation fees. It was opposed to any suggestion that individual fee arrangements should be introduced because of the administrative implications. It also believed a national scale was to the borrower's advantage; the lender was able to negotiate lower rates. TMC identified its valuation fee separately from administration charges and all fees were disclosed to the borrower. It paid the valuer the whole of the valuation fee that was charged to the borrower.

7.294. It set its fee levels by reference to those of its competitors. But the recent upward revision in its fees had come about as a result of representations from its panel members who had said that an increase was necessary to ensure that quality was maintained.

7.295. TMC said that valuation fraud was more prevalent on remortgages. In some instances intermediaries had introduced borrowers to valuers who were prepared to collude with the borrowers to support the loan . It was likely that the valuers in question were seeking to ensure further business from the intermediary concerned.

7.296. There were two main categories of negligence. One was where a valuer overvalued a property by failing to notice significant faults. More often the negligence stemmed from a wrong assessment of the market and a failure to check upon comparable properties.

## Mortgage Trust Ltd

7.297. Mortgage Trust Ltd, a subsidiary of Skandinaviska Enskila Banken, now limited its own lending to the provision of further advances in the residential mortgage market. It used a limited panel of valuers so that it could control the quality of valuations and ensure that all valuers had current professional indemnity insurance cover. It now charged borrowers an arrangement fee which included the cost of the valuation when arranging loans for third parties.

## Household Mortgage Corporation plc

7.298. Household Mortgage Corporation plc (HMC) was concerned that, by the MMC taking comments only from the larger lenders, the extent of fraud and negligence was likely to have been seriously understated. The larger lenders had either staff surveyors and/or subsidiary organizations providing valuation services and as such there was likely to be an unwillingness for those lenders to recognize negligence by their staff valuers or subsidiaries which did not apply when external, independent firms were used. HMC's experience was that whilst the absolute level of fraud or negligence might be relatively low, the losses sustained could be substantial. HMC believed lenders should not be forced to accept valuations commissioned by borrowers. It was also opposed to absorbing valuation fees into overheads.

7.299. HMC had not found operating in Scotland difficult despite the difference in practices surrounding house purchase. It believed that any requirement to define the separate elements in an application fee would be artificial. It would impinge upon the commercial sensitivity of the lender's negotiations on fees with valuers.

## The National Home Loans Corporation plc

7.300. The National Home Loans Corporation plc (NHL)'s chief point concerned the lack of consistent standards of competence amongst valuers. NHL withdrew from new lending in 1991. Over the last two years, when many repossessions had occurred, it had suffered significant losses following the resale of the most properties. It said that the poor standard of valuations undertaken at the time the original mortgage had been granted was a major factor in the level of the loss incurred. Fraud and negligence had played a part but by far the largest proportion of problems uncovered had been due to the lack of competence of the valuer. NHL had since reviewed its policy on the use of valuers. The fact that the RICS would not accept a role in monitoring the competence of its members had influenced this decision. It now relied on an in-house team of valuers for advice on its existing book of mortgages together with a tightly controlled panel. Experience had shown that a lender would be irresponsible to make a loan decision on the advice received from an unknown surveyor. It would not consider such a suggestion until the RICS and the ISVA improved the monitoring and training of their members, many of whom had had no specific training in mortgage valuations.

## UCB Home Loans Corporation Ltd

7.301. UCB Home Loans Corporation Ltd (UCB) said that it had investigated over 200 cases of suspected mortgage fraud in the past four years. It had never encountered pressure by lenders on valuers to influence the outcome of a valuation. But it had heard of many cases in which borrowers and intermediaries had sought to have valuations increased to enable borrowers to obtain the loans they required. UCB said that the level of fees paid to valuers was barely enough for valuers to make a profit. It did not consider that it would be prudent to accept valuations from a borrower but considered that improvements could be made to the procedures applicable when a borrower required a combined survey and valuation report. UCB emphasized that the valuation was obtained to assist the lender to assess the risk before agreeing to make a loan.

## Co-operative Insurance Society Ltd

7.302. Co-operative Insurance Society Ltd (CIS) said that it conducted its residential mortgage business through its 7,000 agents who operated from 224 district offices throughout the UK. It operated a panel of valuers. It believed the risk of collusion between borrower and valuer would increase if a borrower were able to select the valuer. It said that it must retain control of the valuation to protect the funds of its policy-holders to whom it owed a duty of care. It would consider adding a valuer to its panel at a borrower's request if the valuer satisfied its criteria.

7.303. CIS said that valuation fees were competitive because of the large number of lenders in the market-place. It used a national scale of fees which had been established with the members of its panel. Its fees were lower than those charged by many of its competitors; they were also lower than the level of fees which would be charged to a borrower if he negotiated directly with a valuer. Its agents discussed valuation fees with borrowers at the time the mortgage application form was completed. CIS requested valuers who undertook combined SSYs and mortgage valuation reports to ensure that valuation fees were taken into account when the costs were being negotiated with borrowers. It favoured administration charges being separately identified from valuation fees. It said that this would have the effect of making the lender accountable and would stimulate competition. It did not levy a separate administration charge within its valuation fee or elsewhere.

## Sun Life of Canada Home Loans Ltd

7.304. Sun Life of Canada Home Loans Ltd was concerned about the role of the intermediary. It said that pressures arose from:

(a) intermediaries regularly using a particular valuer so that the valuer became dependent upon this source of introduction;

(b) potential vendors who selected from a group of competing estate agents on the basis of the highest indicated price, and the agent, with his vested interest in the price, instructing a dependent valuer when an offer was accepted; and

(c) borrowers being directed to valuers from estate agents or other intermediaries with a financial interest in the transaction completing.

It was less than satisfied with the way in which it was able to manage the valuation process under the Scottish system and was currently reviewing its position.

# 8 Views of valuers and other parties

## Contents

## Representative bodies

### Incorporated Society of Valuers and Auctioneers

8.1. The ISVA has about 7,500 members of which there are 4,500 corporate members. Most have received the training needed to carry out mortgage valuations. The ISVA estimated that between 1,200 and 1,500 of its members were engaged in mortgage valuation for residential properties as their principal activity.

8.2. The ISVA drew attention to a number of points of concern. The chief concern was over the lack of choice for the consumer. It accepted that any client should have the right to choose his or her professional adviser. Consequently, it was quite reasonable that lending institutions should select valuers for their panels provided the reasons for selection were on the grounds of local knowledge, expertise and the necessary professional indemnity cover. However, it was equally right in the Society's view that the consumer should be able to choose his own professional adviser, most particularly in the case of the commissioning of an HBR or SSY. If the consumer had more choice to enable him to choose his own surveyor or valuer to complete the HBR, this service would be more competitively priced. It would then be simpler for the lending institution's valuation form to be completed along with this HBR for a nominal fee. This would achieve a substantial saving for the consumer by comparison with the likely totals payable if separate valuers had to be instructed for the mortgage valuation on the one hand and the HBR/SSY on the other.

8.3. The ISVA said that fee arrangements laid down by lending institutions were not totally clear to prospective borrowers. Whilst in most cases written literature available to prospective borrowers might be quite clear, it was apparent that staff in the offices of lending institutions frequently asked for a valuation fee although in fact part of this was actually an administration fee to the lending institution and was not paid to the valuer.

8.4. Some lending institutions expected staff valuers to cover wide areas where their personal experience and access to comparable valuation evidence was limited, even though there were in most cases competent, qualified valuers with local experience available, often already on the lending institution's panel.

8.5. The ISVA accepted that in many cases reciprocal arrangements reflected a normal commercial situation but was particularly concerned when reciprocity effectively denied instructions to locally-based valuers with relevant local experience and expertise and necessary professional indemnity. The growing influence of national chains of surveyors and valuers, many linked to or wholly owned by the lending institutions, meant that local panel valuers were seldom, or in some cases never, used. Most panel valuers had provided excellent service over many years and obviously had a greater degree of experience and local knowledge that the conglomerate organizations which were replacing them, mainly for commercial rather than professional reasons.

8.6. The ISVA believed that sole practitioners were being unreasonably excluded from lenders' panels. The suggestion that smaller organizations were more prone to fraud and, furthermore more likely to value the security incorrectly was, in its view, without foundation; the ISVA had, for many years, set standards of examinations and training for its members which should ensure the competence of both the independent members and those who worked for large organizations on mortgage valuations. Opportunities for fraud were greatly reduced by compliance with its mandatory members' accounts rules and professional indemnity requirements, which were monitored annually.

8.7. The ISVA said that conflicts of interest could arise when a single company owned both an estate agency and a survey and valuation department; this was of particular concern if the company was also a lending institution.

8.8. During considerations of the public interest issues the ISVA gave further evidence. It accepted that a lender should choose his valuer for mortgage valuations. It was the arrangements for carrying out the other type of work, ie HBRs and SSYs, with which the ISVA was mainly concerned. However, it saw little prospect of widening the panels and accepted that the lenders should have the right to choose who was on them. But within that framework the public should have a choice of surveyor to provide an HBR or SSY, with an associated valuation that would satisfy the lender. The ISVA said that it had tried to promote a common valuation form acceptable to all lenders for many years but without success. In view of the concerns over adequate insurance being in place for valuers, the ISVA was actively considering the issue of run-off cover. It had not itself experienced many problems in this area but acknowledged that it was of serious concern to lenders. The ISVA saw as unlikely a compensation fund for surveyors along the lines of that operated by The Law Society. It was a subject of constant debate but the resourcing entailed would be a problem for its membership. Given that, the ISVA understood the desire by lenders to operate their own controls. It noted, however, that very few major losses for lenders had not been covered by insurance. It was especially concerned with the consequences of fraud and negligence for smaller clients and the public.

## Independent Surveyors' Association

8.9.  The ISA was formed in October 1992 by a number of surveyors who were concerned at developments in mortgage valuation practices. Current membership consisted of some 300 firms, totalling in the region of 500 individuals. About half of the member firms are sole principals. The ISA considered that the building societies by virtue of their market domination (and particularly the large national societies) were able to dictate the choice of valuer to consumers who they would use as valuers, the level of fees that would be applied and to a lesser extent the package that the purchaser would accept. This substantially restricted the purchaser's freedom of choice even before the effects of inherent conflicts of interest and possible dubious practices within the system were taken into account.

8.10.  Valuers were not accepted by lenders on the basis of competence, expertise or competitiveness but simply on whether they were on the building societies panels' or, more commonly, because they were in fact staff surveyors. The present system operated against the consumer's interest in terms of choice. The cost paid by the borrower was open to abuse; building societies acted only as intermediaries between purchaser and valuer where valuation fees were concerned, as the full cost was recovered from the purchaser and as such could only be partly involved in the choice of surveyor, the consumer also being entitled to choice as the person actually paying the fee.

8.11.  In particular the ISA drew attention to the following concerns:

(a) The present system prevented prospective purchasers obtaining independent advice by restricting the choice of surveyor and often by requiring the mortgage valuation to be carried out by a staff surveyor who had no direct contact whatsoever with the purchaser. It was often the case that the purchaser was not allowed to know the name of the surveyor who actually carried out the inspection.

(b) Prospective purchasers were not advised of suitable available options for the types of survey that were available. This might be partly through ignorance on the part of the building society staff but was also in some cases a result of deliberate policy by the building societies.

(c) Many mortgage lenders did not abide by their own regulation BSA 2274 which recommended them to accept valuation reports by suitably qualified valuers where that valuer had already carried out an independent private report for the purchaser. Out of 22 building societies polled by the ISA, nine had said that they would not accept any report from a surveyor who was not on their panel, two stated that they would be a little more flexible if an SSY (not an HBR) had been independently carried out, but only three said that they would be prepared unconditionally to accept non-panel surveyors' reports. The remaining ten had indicated that there would be some flexibility. The failure of building societies to implement BSA 2274 had led to duplication of fees. Where a prospective buyer had instructed and obtained an independent survey and valuation from the surveyor of his choice, he was often then required by the building society to pay a second mortgage valuation fee so that an additional valuation would be carried out. This was unreasonable and worked against the consumer interest.

(d) There was no incentive for mortgage lenders to keep down costs, as they passed on the surveying fee directly to the prospective purchaser through their scales of charges plus any administration fee which they added on, acting simply as an intermediary.

(e) As most building societies employed staff surveyors, they were effectively setting their own scales of charges so as to pay high fees to their own staff surveyors (or to their own subsidiary companies of surveyors and valuers) at the expense of the house purchaser. A poll of members of the ISA had indicated that in a number of cases, the mortgage valuation scale fee payable by the borrower (either to the panel or staff surveyor) was as high as the charge that many independent surveyors would make for carrying out an HBR and valuation.

(f) Valuers were often instructed on the basis of reciprocal business and not on a basis of competence.

(g) The present system was rife with potential conflicts of interest. The situation could arise where a building society acting as mortgagee in possession could instruct its own estate agency firm to sell the property; the purchaser would then be advised by an in-house financial services adviser, the mortgage valuation could be carried out by a subsidiary firm of surveyors and the building society would also issue instructions to the solicitor; the latter would probably be the only independent in the whole transaction. Where building societies sold properties through their estate agency subsidiaries and those properties were valued by their surveying subsidiaries or staff valuers, the system was open to abuse.

(h) A number of valuation firms did not abide by the RICS Valuation Guidance Notes, in particular the provisions relating to valuation outside geographical areas. Whilst the problem was not restricted to building society staff valuers or subsidiary surveyors, this was an area where there were particular problems within the building society valuation organizations, particularly where applying holiday cover, etc.

(i) The use of limited panels of surveyors and the refusal to accept reports from surveyors who were not on those panels, and in particular the refusal to accept reports from sole practitioners, ruled out a substantial body of surveying expertise. Many small independent firms were run by well-qualified, very experienced surveyors, and if building societies refused to accept reports from these surveyors then that experience was denied to the purchaser.

(j) The restriction of valuers to a small panel could lead to those panels of valuers over-influencing the market, and might bring about a possibility that mortgage lenders could dictate the attitude of their valuers according to fund availability. The large building societies, by virtue of their domination of the residential market, could wield considerable influence over it.

8.12. The ISA said that in the short time since its formation, it had received complaints from the public, its own members and other interested parties, varying in format and detail. Many members had indicated that they had had some difficulties in getting the public to make written complaints. House purchasers often felt very aggrieved at the time they experienced delays and encountered extra costs when trying to expedite a house purchase but, at a later date after the purchase and mortgage had been completed, they were content to let the matter rest. However, ISA members had on frequent occasions indicated that their clients had not wanted to make too much of a fuss for fear of upsetting their mortgage lenders and in some way prejudicing their financial status. Some firms of independent surveyors had expressed a similar view in that they did not wish to be seen to be openly criticizing building societies and other mortgage lenders' practices, this being an indication of the amount of influence many of the larger lending institutions appeared to wield in the current economic climate.

8.13. However, the ISA had gathered a good number of complaints in a very short time-scale. Many of the complaints dealt with recurring themes and certain patterns had emerged, and were often interlinked. Complaints generally dealt with one or more of the following problems:

(a) a restriction of the consumer's choice of a valuer/surveyor, particularly where the consumer (as potential house purchaser) had commissioned, or wished to commission, a more detailed report than the mortgage valuation (eg an RICS HBR or a detailed SSY);

(b) unnecessarily high fees and/or duplication of fees payable in connection with valuation and survey reports, usually as a result of (a) above;

(c) hidden administration fees levied by mortgage lenders, often within published 'valuation fee scales' making the fee payable for a valuation and/or survey report appear higher than the fee which is actually paid to the valuer or surveyor;

(d) misrepresentation (either deliberate or accidental) by mortgage lenders' staff over the adequacy of the different types of report—mortgage valuation, HBR and SSY;

(e) appointments of valuers and surveyors' appointments to mortgage lenders' panels of valuers being terminated or restrictions on such appointments being made, the mortgage lender usually requiring reciprocation of mortgage business as a condition of a panel appointment or, in some cases, even payment for the privilege of being given a panel appointment;

(f) conflicts of interest and suggestions of improper (even fraudulent) behaviour within large corporate groups of estate agency/surveying firms having parent financial institutions; and

(g) valuers undertaking mortgage valuation work in areas where they did not have sufficient local knowledge, contrary to the guidance given in the Mortgage Valuation Guidance Notes issued by the RICS and the ISVA.

## *Royal Institution of Chartered Surveyors*

8.14. The RICS is the main qualifying and self-regulating professional body for valuers. It comprises nearly 70,000 Chartered Surveyors practising in a wide range of specialist areas. Of the total, some 30,000 practise in the division that covers valuation expertise, whether in the residential or commercial market sectors. A large proportion of these are in private practice firms, both large and small, either as partners or directors or as employees with considerable involvement in residential and valuation matters. Valuers are also employed by building societies and other lenders. Entry to the profession is now generally through a degree with an additional two-year mandatory period of relevant, structured and assessed practical training and experience.

8.15. In its initial submission the RICS identified four areas of concern:

(a) reduction in panel appointments;

(b) lenders providing business to surveyors in return for reciprocal introductions;

(c) lack of transparency in charges; and

(d) impartiality of advice and the potential for conflicts of interest.

8.16. Over the last three years the RICS had received numerous complaints from its members which confirmed the trend by lenders to reduce the size of their panels. Complaints were received from members practising in small and large firms where they had had their panel appointments cancelled. In other cases panel appointments had not been cancelled but some of the surveyors on the panel had either received no instructions or at most only a minimal number.

8.17. There were a number of consequences of the reduction in the size of panels. Whilst a reduction in panels might have little consequence if the service was a service for the lenders only and was paid for by them, this was no longer the case. The service of a valuer now fulfilled a dual purpose since the report was now provided to the prospective borrower and as a result of case law the valuer usually now owed a duty of care to the purchaser in the tort of negligence.

8.18. An area of current potential difficulty was where a borrower might wish not to rely only on the valuation commissioned by the lender but decided that he or she would like a more detailed report of their own on the property in the form of an HBR (which would have a valuation as part of the report) or an SSY. In both cases there were likely to be efficiencies and cost savings if the valuation service for the lender were to be provided by the same surveyor. The problems arose where the borrower instructed a surveyor before seeing the lender, or where, after the lender commissioned a report from a surveyor, the borrower was unhappy with the choice from his own viewpoint. In both cases the borrower might face increased costs if the lender refused to accept the mortgage valuation from the valuer commissioned by the borrower.

8.19. If the surveyor selected by the borrower was not on the panel of the particular lender, even if the surveyor could satisfy the lender's criteria, a number of lenders refused to permit the surveyor to provide the valuation. The prospective borrower, if he decided to go ahead and obtain more detailed advice, then had to pay the additional fee for the valuation without being able to benefit from any price economy that there might be for carrying out a joint service, ie a mortgage valuation plus an HBR or SSY.

8.20. The RICS believed that if the trend to reduce panels were to continue, there was a danger that a private sector residential valuation service (ie valuations carried out by those other than staff valuers) might not be viable, thereby depriving the public of independent sources of advice where they wished to have more detailed advice other than rely on the valuation only provided for the lender and no measure against which to judge in-house service.

8.21. The RICS said that the seeking and the provision of reciprocal mortgage business was, and had been for many years, part of the commercial business world. Estate agents and surveyors had introduced mortgage applicants to lenders for a long time and a procurement fee might have been charged as a result. More common, however, had been the normal business and professional relationship of mutual and reciprocal understanding between a local estate agent or surveyor and a local building society manager. Such arrangements had existed for many years and the RICS saw no difficulty with these.

8.22. In recent years, however, the RICS has been provided with clear evidence that at least some lenders appeared to have made the provision of reciprocal mortgage business a condition of firms being placed on their panels and, once on the panel, a condition of issuing continuing instructions for valuation work. Although, when challenged, this had often been denied, the RICS had received comments to the contrary from members and had reason to believe that this practice was now common.

8.23. It was the conditional nature of these arrangements that concerned the RICS. They were likely to exclude competent surveyors who were able to assess both the condition and value of the property. The ultimate effect on members of the public was that they were then obliged to pay an additional fee that might not be charged at all, or might be significantly reduced, if lenders were prepared to accept their valuations (subject to the individuals having adequate professional indemnity insurance, local knowledge and being competent to undertake the valuation based on the lender's own particular requirements and the prior agreement of the lender having been obtained).

8.24. The RICS had sought to agree with the CML a statement to the effect that lenders should, in principle, accept more detailed inspection reports commissioned by a purchaser provided the agreement of the lender was obtained in advance. This would enable the lender to check, in advance, those matters upon which it would wish to be satisfied. The grounds on which the lender might decline to accept a report would be inadequate professional indemnity insurance cover, lack of competence or local knowledge. It considered, initially at least, that lenders could cater for their legitimate concerns by operating, in addition to panel valuers under their strict control, a system of approved valuers, accredited perhaps by the professional bodies concerned, from whom the public might obtain more detailed advice and whose advice on valuation would be acceptable to lenders. The RICS was willing to play an important role in this process from the regulatory point of view whilst recognizing that the special requirements of lenders varied considerably.

8.25. In the event the RICS was not able to achieve agreement with the CML on a statement relating to the acceptability of more detailed reports which prospective purchasers required. It was in this area where the RICS believed the public's right to choose for more detailed survey work its adviser, at a price that properly reflected the degree of competition in the market, was being unduly restricted and was therefore against the public interest.

8.26. A further area of concern related to the lack of transparency in the way in which some lenders charged for services. The RICS said that in some instances lenders were making a hidden administrative charge, or were having valuations carried out at a discount to lenders' published scales, but without, in either case, this being disclosed to the borrower. These charges were hidden within the so-called 'valuation fee' which the purchaser had to pay. This lack of transparency meant that the borrower believed that the fee he or she was paying was the cost of the professional time which was being devoted to the valuation. It followed that the borrower might believe the lender to be commissioning a more detailed report than was actually the case. There was therefore a danger that the borrower would place more reliance on it than was prudent.

8.27. Although many lenders made it clear in their literature that a separate identifiable but inclusive administrative fee was being charged, this might not always be apparent at the point when the borrower paid. Nor was it always made clear at this point how much of the charge related to the valuation with the result that there were abuses of the system which were not in the interests of the public.

8.28. The RICS had received information about instances where full scale fees as laid down by the lenders were being charged for valuations but the lender had imposed a lower fee upon the valuer, and the difference was then retained by the lender or, more often, the broker. The difference appeared to range between £30 and £100 in most cases. This might represent an overhead of 50 per cent or more in many cases.

8.29. The RICS saw a number of reasons why the potential for conflicts of interest, which might jeopardize the purchaser's position, was likely to arise in the house-purchase process. These included:

(a) the desire of owners of residential estate agency practices, whatever the size of firm, to package a number of different services together within the same related transaction. Often these were aimed at different clients or customers. These services now included agency, valuation and survey and financial services;

(b) the acquisition by the financial conglomerates of residential estate agency practices leading to a greater concentration of offices under a single ownership. The build-up of major chains of estate agency offices increased the likelihood that different, and potentially conflicting, services, linked within the same related transaction and offered within the same corporate identity, would be more widespread; and

(c) that, in the main, the client or customer would have little or no specialist knowledge and might be unaware of the possibility of conflicts of interest arising; this differed from the position in the commercial property sector where the client usually had a greater awareness of the issues. It was important, therefore, that not only should such clients and customers be protected but that they should clearly be seen to be protected. The RICS believed the reason for the small number of complaints from the public was a result of lack of appreciation of the relationships involved and the potential for conflicts of interest.

8.30. An RICS Working Party had published a major report on the subject in June 1991. This recognized that it might appear that staff valuers and group valuers[1] felt under the greater pressure because lenders and financial intermediaries might be anxious to lend or arrange for the lending of money on mortgage, or to provide some other financial services connected with the transaction, or because the selling agent might be anxious to make a sale. Panel valuers, however, could feel under similar pressure to overvalue or to produce biased reports or not to reject properties for mortgage if they were to remain on the lender's panel, at a time when some lenders were reducing their use of panel valuers and seeking to retain their share of the lending market.

8.31. The RICS Working Party had proposed to the CML that at the time that a mortgage application was made, the lender should explain carefully the types of valuer that might be used and their relationship, if any, with the lender. If the borrower felt unhappy with that relationship, he or she could then ask to have another type of valuer. In the event the CML would not accept this pointing out that, in strict law, there was no conflict of interest and that section 13(2) of the 1986 Act did not prevent a staff valuer, or a valuer employed by an estate agency subsidiary, from valuing a property being sold by an agent owned by the same lender. The CML therefore refused to implement the RICS suggestion.

8.32. Instead the CML agreed to suggest to its members that they should tell borrowers, where relevant, that they might use staff valuers, group valuers or a panel valuer in order to value property by issuing information on the following lines: 'A valuation may be carried out by a valuer employed by [the member], a valuer from a subsidiary company, or by an independent panel valuer from the private sector.'

---

[1]For example, one who is employed by a subsidiary of the parent organization that owns the estate agency and who may or may not be the lending source for the mortgage.

8.33. The phrase would be included in the lender's mortgage documentation. There was no specific agreement where it should be inserted in the documentation; that would be for each lender to decide. It might, for example, be placed on the mortgage application form. It was agreed, however, that a degree of prominence should be given to the notice—ie it should not be hidden in 'small print'.

8.34. In addition the Working Party had recommended strengthening RICS rules on conflicts of interest to require members not only to disclose the facts to the client in a conflict of interest situation but to advise him to take independent advice; to require a degree of separation between functions which might give rise to conflicts of interest; if the required separation was not achieved, making it a disciplinary offence to offer services giving rise to a conflict of interest without disclosure. This was now enshrined in the Institution's code of conduct implementing the recommendations of the RICS Working Party.

8.35. The RICS was aware of a few cases where both staff and panel valuers had been brought under pressure to provide a valuation of property or a 'gloss' on a report which would prevent the property being valued from being turned down as unsuitable security upon which to lend money by way of a mortgage. The cases involved instances where the lender was in possession of the property and where the property was being sold through the estate agency arm of the lender.

8.36. Subsequently, at the time the MMC were considering public interest issues, the RICS gave further evidence. It said that on further discussion its views had hardened. It now felt that there was only one clear solution to resolve all the issues of concern to the RICS. This solution would be one which left the lender to commission and pay for the valuation that it needed for its purposes. The lenders' statutory obligations and prudential approach to lending meant that it was right that the choice of valuer should be for the lender. This had always been the RICS's view. As the valuation was undertaken to meet lenders' requirements, the RICS saw the cost as a straightforward administrative expense, comparable to offices or staff salaries, which should be borne by the lender as an incidental overhead. This would help remove some of the confusion in borrowers' minds over the purpose of the report and its limitations. The RICS also suggested that the borrower should consequently no longer receive a copy of the report. The borrower would then not be lulled into a false sense of security, through having paid for and received a report which was not intended for his purposes. The RICS hoped this would lead to more borrowers commissioning HBRs or SSYs which would give them the fuller information on a property, tailored to meet the needs they required as appropriate protection. In this connection the RICS drew attention to a survey carried out by the Consumers' Association which had suggested that one in five of HBRs or SSYs carried out for housebuyers revealed significant defects.

8.37. On the selection of the valuer by the lender, the RICS commented that it had never wished as an institution to try to determine the size or composition of panels that lending institutions might have in any area. What it wished to see was proper criteria for determining membership. It did have a concern over the impact of decisions on size of panels for the future in that there was a danger that the base of practising valuers would become too narrow. The RICS had reflected further on the idea of an approved list of valuers for mortgage valuations drawn up by a peer group of RICS members and had moved away from this to a preference for separating and clarifying the two parties' interests set out in the preceding paragraph. It recognized the problems in how an approved list would be selected to meet lenders' individual requirements and that it would be difficult to exclude any appropriately qualified member. The RICS said that the question of whether it ought to judge the continuing competence of its own members other than through education standards and a requirement on members to undertake continuing development was one of continuing debate in the Institution. Recently its General Council had concluded that competence could be handled under existing powers rather than through new powers being added to its constitution. Work to take this forward continued within the RICS.

8.38. On the insurance concerns raised by lenders, the RICS acknowledged that, in the absence of the ability of the Institution to monitor all competence and guarantee insurance cover, it was understandable for the lenders to want to rely on their own controls, particularly since the lenders' requirements might differ in some respects from those of the Institution's. The RICS was looking at ways of improving the current situation such as working with the insurance market on run-off cover, rather than establish a compensation fund along the lines of that established by The Law Society.

8.39. In the final stages of the inquiry the President of the RICS wrote to the MMC setting out the Institution's views on a number of issues which formed the subject matter of the inquiry. The letter was written following a meeting between the President and representatives of the CML's Valuation Panel and its contents have been strongly endorsed by the CML. It reiterated its views that the client for the mortgage valuation was the lender, that the client for the services should pay for its commissioning, that reciprocity was acceptable as a tie-breaker for panel appointments and that there should be absolute transparency where any charge was made on the borrower. The statement also developed further proposals to ensure that the distinction between the interests of lender and borrower was recognized by proposing that where a mortgage valuation and a more detailed report, such as an HBR or SSY, was involved the two services should be the subject of separate instructions and conditions of engagement, even where the same valuer was involved (see paragraph 6.51).

8.40. The RICS made clear that it continued to have concerns on the consequences of reducing the size of panels, the use of reciprocity by lenders as the primary and conditional factor in placing business and on the potential for conflicts of interest inherent in the bringing together in one group the provision of mortgage finance, house sales, valuation and financial services.

## Representatives of Scottish surveyors

8.41. Representatives of the RICS in Scotland expressed concern at the practice in Scotland of intermediaries commissioning valuations. As a consequence of the Scottish system for house purchase, it was a long-standing practice for intermediaries, usually solicitors, acting for the purchasers to commission valuations on their behalf. The Financial Services Act 1986 had led to a substantial growth in financial intermediaries and to the practice of 'mortgage packaging' under which the lender received from intermediaries, usually estate agents or mortgage brokers, completed mortgage applications with supporting valuations and references. Much of this business was introduced to brokers by sources with an interest in the sale of the property, either directly or indirectly, and significant numbers of instructions for residential mortgage valuations were being received from those with an interest in the sale and also involved in the provision of mortgages and other services to the purchaser.

8.42. The RICS in Scotland was concerned that such conflicts of interest might lead to undue pressure on surveyors to provide compliant advice and drew the MMC's attention to a report by a Mortgage Packaging Working Party of the General Practice Division of the RICS in Scotland, prepared in February 1992, which listed a number of examples of such pressure:

(a) requests to provide a compliant valuation and report which would not frustrate the sale of the property involved;

(b) statements to valuers intimating that the level of valuation was of crucial importance, particularly in cases involving new houses, the sale of property on a fixed-price basis and transactions where 100 per cent mortgages were concerned;

(c) the termination of business from an intermediary, either temporarily or permanently, after the submission of a report, the terms of which were unacceptable to the instructing source;

(d) the dismissal of firms of valuers, from the panels of estate agents and mortgage brokers, for failing to provide reports and valuations which met the wishes of estate agents and mortgage brokers; and

(e) insistence by intermediaries on preferred valuers being included on lenders' panels.

8.43. The report pointed out that RICS Insurance Services had reported a rise in the incidence of claims involving overvaluation and that fraud had been alleged in some instances. A study of mortgage fraud by Birmingham University had identified intermediaries as being a problem. Lothian and Borders and Strathclyde Police had also advised lenders not to accept valuations presented to them by intermediaries.

8.44. The Working Party report recommended that a residential mortgage valuation should not be commissioned by agents referred to sell the property, or by mortgage brokers in the direct employment of the selling agents or an associated company. It suggested that the best way forward might be for all mortgage valuations to be instructed directly by lenders.

## Other representative bodies

### Architects and Surveyors Institute

8.45. The Architects and Surveyors Institute (ASI) represents both architects and surveyors and has a total membership of approximately 6,000. The ASI complained that the BSA and the CML were directing their members to accept only those valuations submitted by members of the RICS or the ISVA, and in doing so were setting a standard which effectively permitted them to be the accreditation agencies for professional qualifications. By encouraging their members to accept valuations from only two professional bodies, the BSA and the CML were implying that no other professional was competent to carry out the exercise. The ASI stated that its code of conduct which governed members' professional behaviour insisted that members only operated within the discipline in which they were qualified and, in the case of mortgage valuations, within a specified geographical area where their experience had been established.

8.46. The ASI said that it was significant that the restrictions placed on its members had become much more evident following the entry of building societies into estate agency and property surveying, thereby limiting an applicant's access to independent advice. Prospective borrowers had lost their right of choice; they could not choose their own valuer who might be locally-based and familiar with the area, thus having the best opportunity to assess a property's worth. If lenders would not consider valuations or surveys already prepared by surveyors nominated by borrowers, it was likely that borrowers would incur additional expense by having to pay for a separate report by the lender's chosen surveyor. Borrowers were required to pay the lender's valuation fee and, in some cases, an administration fee in advance. And this had to be paid to a lender which might also be acting for the vendor *and* providing the mortgage for the purchaser. The ASI said that under those circumstances conflicts of interest arose which acted against the public good, and despite the abolition of the old set fee scales, prospective borrowers had no opportunity to 'shop around' for the best deal.

8.47. The ASI said that it had evidence of local building society managers indicating acceptance of survey reports and applications for finance only if the valuer could offer reciprocal business. The fact that sometimes young and relatively inexperienced branch managers used reciprocal business as a condition for admission to a valuation panel had caused the ASI great concern. It stressed that valuers should be accepted for their professional ability, and not for their ability to provide reciprocal business.

### Royal Institute of British Architects

8.48. The Royal Institute of British Architects (RIBA) said that it had received numerous complaints from long-established practising members that valuations made during the course of SSYs were often not accepted by building societies. It was the RIBA's view that many of its members were competent, through a combination of experience and local knowledge, to value residential properties, and this was evidenced by the RIBA's publication of standard valuation forms for architects' use and the availability of professional indemnity insurance to cover the liability involved in making a valuation. Many experienced and competent valuers were effectively excluded from undertaking valuation business because they were not employed by building societies or their subsidiaries, or because they could not offer reciprocal business.

8.49. The RIBA said that the present system was unfair to the housebuying public. In some cases building societies were charging a more than nominal administration fee, to the benefit of the society. Borrowers were obliged to pay scale fees agreed by the building societies, and there was no scope to seek alternative fees from other valuers. This was less important in respect of valuations, but could be significant in the case of HBRs, particularly on larger properties.

8.50. The RIBA believed the present system could be improved if each town (or appropriate geographical area) were to maintain a list of valuers who were competent, having regard to their qualification, experience and insurability, to value residential properties in that area. Such lists would be prepared by independent regional committees comprising representatives of the RIBA, the RICS, the ISVA, lenders and consumer organizations. Lenders would be obliged to accept valuations undertaken by any valuer on the list within the designated area. On applying for a mortgage, borrowers would be given a list of the approved valuers covering the area within which the subject property was located. This would give borrowers the freedom to use a valuer of their own choice with whom they could make their own arrangements.

## Chartered Institute of Building

8.51. The Chartered Institute of Building expressed concern that Chartered Surveyors essentially had a monopoly of residential mortgage valuations and SSYs and that other suitably qualified and experienced professionals were not accepted by building societies to carry out such work. The Institute argued that professionally qualified Chartered Builders with professional indemnity insurance and suitable experience should have equal opportunity to be employed for SSYs and valuations of domestic property in connection with residential mortgages.

## Royal Incorporation of Architects in Scotland

8.52. The Royal Incorporation of Architects in Scotland recorded concern that, while Chartered Architects, particularly in areas outwith the urban central belt of Scotland, had in the past undertaken property valuation work, lenders had in recent years increasingly developed policies which excluded them. The Incorporation would support moves to open this area of the market to Chartered Architects.

## Surveyors and valuers

8.53. Eighty-two firms in the surveying and valuing professions wrote to the MMC voicing concerns with the current arrangements for the provision of valuation services.

8.54. Well over half the complaints related to the restrictions being placed on the consumer's freedom to choose a surveyor. Often this was allied with the complaint that a surveyor had found that he had not been accepted for a lender's panel of surveyors, or that his panel appointment had been terminated, or instructions to value property were no longer forthcoming. This could happen after years of service to a lender. Two firms stated that they had been on one particular lender's panel for decades but then found in the early 1990s that they were no longer sent valuation instructions.

8.55. There was a widespread belief among surveyors that the cause of this was a demand by lenders that, in return for being placed on a panel and given valuation instructions, a surveyor should provide reciprocal business in the form of mortgage introductions; almost half the correspondents mentioned reciprocity as a cause for concern. One correspondent cited various ratios of business required; these ranged from one valuation instruction in return for one mortgage introduction to six instructions for each mortgage introduced. There was also concern that firms with a sole principal were being discriminated against. About a quarter of the letters received were from correspondents who identified themselves as sole principals. Some correspondents were concerned that reciprocity involved more than a mutual exchange of business between surveyors and lenders for their mutual benefit and that independent surveyors were being effectively squeezed out of the market by lenders appointing one another's estate agency/surveying firms to panels and channelling valuation work to them.

8.56. Correspondents generally believed that restrictions on consumers' choice of surveyor led to consumers incurring higher costs than necessary. Correspondents cited examples where they could provide an HBR or SSY together with a valuation more cheaply than the lender's nominee or where their client was faced with an additional fee for having a separate valuation report done. Some indicated that they could carry out a valuation alone more cheaply than the valuer selected by the lender while others commented that there was no incentive on lenders to keep down fees. There was also concern that lenders were discouraging consumers from having more detailed surveys done by quoting excessive estimates of their costs to consumers.

8.57. The majority of correspondents believed that the move away from independent firms had affected the quality of valuations provided. The main complaint was that in-house valuers were inspecting properties in areas in which, it was suggested, they were not familiar, and therefore did not have the adequate local knowledge professionally required. One correspondent cited a lender's nominee from the Home Counties being sent to value a property in central London; another cited valuers travelling from North London, North Kent and Dorset to value property in the extreme south-west of Surrey. Correspondents were also often concerned that quality was being affected by the use of in-house and corporate surveyors who were inexperienced rather than the experienced local surveyors who had been carrying out such work for many years. Some surveyors cited a propensity by such valuers to seek unnecessary specialist reports on matters which they themselves would expect to cover in a report or to make unrealistically critical comments about perceived structural faults. All of these, it was said, could frustrate house-purchase transactions or add to their cost.

8.58. Over one-quarter of correspondents were concerned that the growth of conglomerates carrying out mortgage lending, house sales and surveying created conflicts of interest which were likely to inhibit the duty of care which they believed surveyors owed to the borrower. It was suggested that the borrower needed reliable independent advice and several correspondents criticized subsidiaries of lenders for not making clear to the borrower that they were not independent agencies. One correspondent, commenting on conflict of interest, gave an example of a case in which, as a panel surveyor for a lender, he had advised an applicant against a purchase, the applicant had then turned to the lender's associated surveyors and the mortgage had gone ahead.

## Estate agents

### *National Association of Estate Agents*

8.59. The National Association of Estate Agents (the Association) identified three main areas of concern:

*(a)* the appointment of panels of surveyors by lending institutions and the fact that membership of the panels was sustained through the volume of new business introduced by the surveyors;

*(b)* clients being forced to employ the services of surveyors from appointed panels; and

*(c)* the practice of lending institutions retaining part of the valuation fee as an administration charge.

8.60. The Association accepted that lenders should be free to decide who they appointed to their panels, provided there were no restrictive practices. Panel appointments were often limited to valuers who were able to offer reciprocal business. The refusal by some lenders to accept surveys or valuations carried out by non-panel valuers was clearly restrictive. Where a client had chosen to use an independent surveyor who was suitably qualified and had professional indemnity insurance, the Association believed it was wrong in principle that the client should have to pay an additional fee to the lender for the duplicate work involved. If lenders chose not to accept valuations or reports carried out by independent surveyors, and insisted instead on using panel members, then the lenders should bear any additional costs.

8.61. The Association stated that it had developed a Certificate in Estate Agency in the expectation that it would be recognized and widely accepted by lenders. While professional work should be undertaken by those suitably qualified, the Association argued that valuations could be undertaken by those qualified by experience. It was common practice for panel valuers to seek advice on the value of properties from members of the Association in areas where the surveyors did not have local knowledge.

## Individual estate agents

8.62. Four estate agents wrote to us about the current arrangements. One commented that surveyors were attempting to determine the market price of properties with the effect that many sales were being lost by totally unrealistic undervaluations. Another said that clients should be allowed to select a surveyor of their choice as this would enable them to negotiate fees rather than having to accept the fixed fees demanded by lenders. A third believed lenders should value properties purely for their own purposes, using valuers of their own choice (and at their expense) leaving the client free to choose his own surveyor at his own expense. The vendor of a property should be able to commission a valuation for mortgage purposes, at his own expense, from an independent and suitably qualified surveyor. The valuation would then be utilized and relied upon by potential clients and lenders for a set period of three or six months. To prevent any conflict of interest, the surveyor should not thereafter be allowed to act as an estate agent in the sale. A fourth agent considered that surveys (not valuations) should be carried out by suitably qualified and insured surveyors and the report relied upon by all parties, ie the vendor, borrower and lender. Valuations should be undertaken by similarly qualified surveyors chosen by the lender but able to be relied upon also by the borrower.

# Regulatory bodies

## Building Societies Commission

8.63. The BSC explained that its general functions under the 1986 Act were 'to promote the protection by each building society of the investments of its shareholders and depositors' and 'to promote the financial stability of building societies generally'. It needed to be satisfied that the directors and other officers of building societies conducted their business in accordance with the criteria of prudent management specified in section 45 of the 1986 Act; in particular, the criterion that the requisite arrangements must be maintained for assessing the adequacy of securities for advances secured on land. The Act required the person making the assessment to have furnished to him a written report on the valuation of the land made by a competent person.

8.64. The BSC said that the statutory requirements meant that societies had a duty to be satisfied that the valuations they obtained for their purposes were made by competent persons in whom they could have confidence. It would be imprudent, and in breach of law, for a society to accept a valuation made by a person of whom it had no knowledge. It noted that too many frauds had recently been perpetrated on lenders who had accepted valuations provided by borrowers' nominees. Societies generally, therefore, had close relations with firms on their panels as providers of valuations in accordance with the statutory requirements. Some of the firms also acted as agents for the collection of retail funds and mortgage repayments, and as intermediaries providing mortgage business. The BSC had encouraged societies to keep the performance of intermediaries under review, and not to use the services of those which had consistently referred poor-quality business. These arrangements, therefore, tended to promote the protection of investors' funds by securing reliable valuations and good-quality assets in conformity with the duties of directors and the BSC's prudential guidance.

## Office of the Building Societies Ombudsmen

8.65. The Office of the Building Societies Ombudsmen pointed out that many complaints connected with mortgage valuations were outside its terms of reference. It could not recall having received any complaints that the practices of building societies had limited the freedom of housebuyers who wanted more detailed reports in nominating their own surveyor. Nor had it dealt with any cases where it was alleged that a society was unwilling to accept, for valuation purposes, surveys already carried out for a potential borrower.

# Legal profession

## The Law Society

8.66. The Law Society said that it had no evidence of significant numbers of complaints about valuers' fees, but that if there were dissatisfaction, it would not necessarily expect complaints to be made to its members or to itself. The Law Society was aware that members of the public tended to have difficulty in distinguishing between the role of a valuer providing services to a lender, and that of a surveyor, who may be the same person, providing services to a borrower. It was not uncommon for misapprehensions about this to lead to annoyance or resentment when a borrower, or prospective borrower, discovered the nature of a valuer's report. Some of the complaints about the level of valuers' fees might have derived from borrowers' reactions on discovering that a separate, and additional, fee had to be paid in order to obtain a surveyor's structural report. Anything which could be done to educate prospective borrowers in this respect was desirable.

8.67. The Law Society emphasized that, although lenders should clearly apply objective and justifiable criteria in deciding which valuers they were willing to instruct, it was important to bear in mind the general principle that lenders should be entitled to be selective, within reason, in choosing. Thus, any criteria which they applied should not unduly limit a borrower's choice; nor should they unnecessarily restrict competition, on the grounds of price in particular, between valuers. However, the valuer's function was a responsible one, which, if not carried out conscientiously and scrupulously, could expose a lender to considerable risk. In The Law Society's view, therefore, the criteria which should apply related to standards of skill, care and integrity. Lenders were entitled to refuse to accept services which did not reach the standards which were set. The criteria should not be based on the amount of business which the valuer's firm might introduce to the lender, nor on the size of the valuer's firm.

8.68. Furthermore, it was of considerable concern to The Law Society that lenders should exercise proper care in selecting valuers to act for them. Mortgage-related fraud had given rise to significant losses by lenders in recent years. In a number of frauds, lack of care by the lender in making a choice of valuer had, in its view, made an important contribution to the ability to execute the fraud, a deliberate overvaluation of the property involved being a typical feature.

8.69. The Law Society said that, to its knowledge, in several cases of fraud a solicitor had also been involved, sometimes having negligently failed to exercise adequate vigilance, and sometimes also involved in the dishonesty. As valuers were not covered by indemnity and compensation arrangements to anywhere near the level of solicitors, The Law Society's indemnity and compensation funds had often been called on to meet the major proportion of the lender's claim in respect of its loss. Its indemnity fund covered claims arising out of the negligence of all solicitors, and the dishonesty of those in partnerships (broadly speaking), while its compensation fund, which was a fund of last resort, existed to meet valid claims against solicitors which could not be met by indemnity insurance, for example claims due to dishonesty against sole practitioners. It was The Law Society's aim so far as possible to ensure that those who used the services of solicitors were compensated in the event of loss caused, or contributed to, by a solicitor.

8.70. The claim which the two funds had had to meet had imposed a substantial burden on the profession, to the extent of millions of pounds. So long as the Society continued to have more generous arrangements than others for the compensation of those who had suffered loss, it was inevitable that it might be called upon to pay a major and disproportionate part of the cost of a default in which a valuer or surveyor was involved, if a solicitor had also in any way contributed to the default. It did not seek to change this but would therefore oppose any changes to lenders' arrangements which were likely to increase the risk of fraud by valuers or surveyors. It seemed to The Law Society that to restrict the ability of a lender to select its own valuers and surveyors would be likely to increase that risk.

8.71. The Law Society told us that it had been reviewing ways of reducing claims on its Compensation Fund. To reduce the risk of fraud, it would be sensible for a lender not to instruct a valuer recommended by the borrower or one which the lender had been led to instruct by the borrower; so that any valuation should be carried out by a valuer of the lender's choice.

8.72. The Law Society would therefore be unhappy if the MMC made recommendations which prevented it, in the event of a claim, from considering whether certain common sense prudential measures had been implemented by lenders. The result might well be a further increase in mortgage fraud and consequent claims on its funds, the cost of which would eventually impact on the house-buying public.

## Individual firms of solicitors

8.73. Two firms of solicitors commented on the current arrangements. The first said that lenders had consistently refused to accept valuations carried out for other lenders, and in some cases they had instructed the same valuer who then charged another fee. This was not related to the date of the valuation but purely a matter of policy on the part of the lenders. The second firm commented that there was an undoubted tendency to pursue self-interest in house valuations, whether directly on behalf of the clients through suggesting inflated prices as being obtainable, or by virtue of payment on a scale related to the sale price. In this system of self-interest there were a limited number of estate agents all valuing each other's sale properties, and it was clear that this would encourage valuers to support each other and each other's valuations when carrying out what was intended to be an independent survey/valuation exercise. The effect was to create an artificial spiral of increasing house prices to the benefit of all interested parties whether through insurance commission levels, estate agency fee levels or levels of leading business.

# The police

## Metropolitan Police

8.74. The Metropolitan Police Company Fraud Department (Fraud Department) formed a squad in 1989 to combat the growing problem of mortgage fraud. In view of the number of reported instances of suspected fraud the Fraud Department had found it necessary to prioritize its attention to cases involving solicitors. Other cases were dealt with by local police stations. Resource considerations led it to limit its enquiries to those sufficient to substantiate prosecution of the main offenders, and to target only the main participants. If a prosecution was brought then any others involved would be prosecuted alongside the solicitor.

8.75. The Fraud Department said that, in the year since the CML guidelines on mortgage fraud had been issued, there had been a 34 per cent reduction in reported fraud. This it considered could be due to a number of factors: fewer mortgage advances, lenders being more careful in checking applications, lenders being aware that police would only attach a low priority to investigating cases where the guidelines had been breached, or lenders recognizing that failure to comply with the guidelines might prejudice any civil action against either the borrower or any negligent professional. The defence would be that failure to observe the guidelines was reckless.

8.76. It was the view of the investigators within the Fraud Department, and a view shared by other Fraud Squads, that lenders must be able to secure their loan by having a trusted professional valuation completed at the time of the advance. The Fraud Department considered that this could only be achieved by each lender selecting individuals or companies to protect his interest, ie by establishing a panel, which all might apply to join but which would be selected by that lender. Any other situation would not secure the lender's interest and, in the case of building societies, their statutory duty to safeguard the interests of its depositor. The Fraud Department therefore supported the panel system.

## Strathclyde Police

8.77. Strathclyde Police told us that it had regular meetings with banks and building society liaison groups, The Law Society of Scotland and the Glasgow and District Valuers' Association and the common theme it pursued was to encourage all the links in the mortgage chain to conduct rigorous checks and to tighten their procedures. It pointed out that the Procurator Fiscal at Glasgow had made clear that he would not pursue a criminal case of fraud if the element of deception was one which might reasonably have been expected to have been detected by the lender during the assessment of the mortgage application. If the panel system was thought restrictive, and the lender's right to impose it was removed, then the Strathclyde Police believed some form of guarantee would be required to protect the lender from dishonest or incorrect valuations.

131

8.78. Commenting on statistics on mortgage fraud in recent years the Strathclyde Police made the point that the nature of mortgage fraud enquiries was such that the investigations tended to be spread over several years in many cases and often came to light a considerable time after being perpetrated on the lenders. In 1991 it had reported nine cases involving alleged mortgage fraud to the Procurator Fiscal involving 34 charges of fraud and attempted fraud to the sum of £1.4 million. Five of the charges, all occurring in the same fraud case, involved alleged false valuations being submitted in support of mortgage applications and the funds obtained amounted to £276,000. The same surveyor was involved in four out of the five instances of false valuations. In the other instance of false valuation, a surveyor on a lender's panel was asked to transcribe on to his firm's letterhead a completed valuation from a colleague in another firm, in order that it could be submitted to that lender. In 1992 Strathclyde Police had reported five cases involving alleged mortgage fraud to the Procurator Fiscal involving 28 charges of fraud and attempted fraud, to the sum of £1.8 million. The most significant case in 1992, accounting for £1.2 million, involved a firm of intermediaries preparing allegedly fraudulent mortgage packages and presenting them to building societies.

## Consumer bodies

### Consumers' Association

8.79. The Consumers' Association (CA) considered that there was a lack of transparency in the function of mortgage valuations and in the operation of the market. While mortgage valuations were paid for by borrowers, it was not clear that the valuations were primarily for the benefit of the lenders. It was also not apparent why many lenders would accept valuations only from those valuers whom they had chosen. Also, despite the fact that borrowers paid for the valuations, most large lenders would not allow borrowers to choose *any* suitably qualified surveyor. Instead, the valuer was either chosen from the lender's panel or was employed by the lender. Entry to a panel might depend on the valuer's ability to provide reciprocal business. CA said that consumers also lost out if staff/ panel valuers had limited local knowledge. An unrealistically low valuation could mean that the lender's mortgage offer was too low for the prospective buyer to be able to afford to buy.

### National Association of Citizens Advice Bureaux

8.80. The National Association of Citizens Advice Bureaux welcomed the inquiry but did not make any specific comments. Evidence obtained by the Association relating to the purchase of property indicated that there had been little or no concern expressed by members of the public about house valuations.

### National Consumer Council

8.81. The National Consumer Council did not make any representations in response to our invitation to comment.

## Members of the public

8.82. Thirty-eight members of the public wrote to the MMC voicing concerns about the current arrangements for the provision of valuation services. Lack of freedom to nominate the surveyor to conduct the valuation was a grievance mentioned by half the complainants. This was usually tied to a belief that this had led to increased cost either through having to use the lender's nominee or through incurring the cost of the lender's valuation in addition to any survey and/or valuation work they had themselves commissioned.

8.83. Correspondents were mystified why on occasions a valuation by a surveyor acceptable to one lender was not also acceptable to other lenders. In one case a valuation carried out by a valuer employed by a subsidiary of another building society was not acceptable. One correspondent, commenting on costs, cited a situation in which his solicitor was able to arrange a cheaper valuation by directly instructing the same surveyor who had been nominated by the lender. Another correspondent thought the lender should pay for the valuation. One angry correspondent thanked a lender for proving how expensive and stressful buying property can be.

8.84. Another key theme was criticism of the quality of the service. Over a quarter of complaints alleged that lenders' valuers had undervalued property. Complaints on undervaluation came not only from potential vendors but also from purchasers who had been faced with increased costs by having to pay for mortgage indemnity cover required by the lender, because the loan required amounted to a larger proportion of the value of the property than they had expected. Similar complaints were made by borrowers wanting to remortgage to take advantage of mortgage products. In one remortgage case the correspondent cited the same firm of surveyors as having within seven days given one valuation to him as the potential seller and a lower valuation by 25 per cent to the proposed lender. Others questioned the adequacy of the valuer's analysis of 'comparators' (ie the prices of comparable properties), the cursory nature of the surveyor's visit and the lack of local knowledge of the surveyor chosen. One correspondent raised the converse situation where a surveyor overvalued the property, allegedly at the behest of the lender's estate agency arm which was selling the property, thereby forcing the borrower to pay more. Two other correspondents were concerned that they were unable to approach the surveyor for clarification on the valuation that had been undertaken and for which they had paid.

# 9 Conclusions

## Contents

## The mortgage and valuation markets

### *The residential mortgage lending market*

9.1.  Most residential mortgage lending is for the purchase of residential property, but the market also includes remortgages, ie the refinancing of existing mortgage loans, which may involve the borrower switching from one lender to another, and further advances secured on the borrower's existing property. We estimate that currently almost four-fifths of total advances are made in connection with the purchase of a property, with remortgages accounting for over half of the remainder and further advances for probably less than 10 per cent of the total.

9.2.  There are more than 150 lenders currently providing residential mortgages. We estimate that in 1992 the gross value of new lending on residential property was £54 billion. The seven largest lenders account for about half of new residential mortgage lending and the 15 largest for almost three-quarters; other lenders range from substantial lenders operating throughout the country to some small building societies operating regionally or even locally. There are three main types of lender: building societies, banks, and the centralized lenders. The greater part of lending, over 70 per cent of new lending in 1992, was provided by building societies,[1] the traditional suppliers of residential mortgages. Following the loosening of controls on their lending in 1980, the banks entered the market in the early 1980s and quickly took a substantial share of business, through both their branch networks and intermediaries. Within a short period the banks had 40 per cent of new lending, although this level was not maintained (see paragraph 3.13). Banks draw funds mainly from the wholesale money markets, and have been particularly successful in times of low interest rates. The centralized lenders, who entered the market during the mid to late 1980s, also draw their funds from the wholesale money markets and attract business primarily through intermediaries. Many have withdrawn from the market altogether or cut back operations in the more difficult conditions of the last few years.

9.3. The entry of these new lenders was accompanied by the relaxation of controls on building societies under the Building Societies Act 1986 (the 1986 Act) which allowed them to provide banking, life insurance and pension services, structural surveys (SSYs) and homebuyers reports (HBRs) for borrowers, and to establish and acquire estate agencies. Controls on their sources of funds, which had meant that most funds were raised from depositors and rationed to borrowers, were also relaxed. Currently building societies can obtain up to 40 per cent of funds from wholesale money markets.[2] The changes in the market were accompanied by a large number of mergers of building societies, totalling 170 in the last ten years or so; the Council of Mortgage Lenders (CML) told us that currently 84 remain as active lenders (see paragraph 3.19).

9.4. These changes have had major effects in the market. The range of mortgage products available has increased. The borrower now has a wide choice between different kinds of endowment and repayment mortgages, available at fixed or variable rates. The recent decline in the housing market, accompanied by continuing availability of funds for lending, has intensified competition between lenders. There has been some switching by borrowers between lenders in search of better terms and a number of lenders have been actively seeking this business.

9.5. Most lenders tend to quote the same or a very similar basic interest rate. There is, however, a range of differing packages available featuring the different types of mortgage and a variety of special inducements, for example interest rate discounts or a contribution to the borrower's costs, which will be offered for a limited period or to particular classes of borrower. The costs incurred by the borrower in securing the mortgage include not only the valuation fee but lenders' legal costs and, where the loan:value ratio is high, a substantial mortgage indemnity premium. Many building societies charge an administration fee as a contribution to their costs, and where a fixed-rate mortgage is negotiated, an arrangement fee may also be charged at the point when the funds are booked by the lender. While some of these costs can be included in the mortgage advance and thus in the monthly payment, and others settled on completion, the valuation fee is traditionally paid by the borrower when he submits his application form and before any mortgage offer is made. The more recently introduced administration charge is also usually levied at this point. We describe these fees and charges, which have to be incurred by the borrower before he knows whether the mortgage transaction will proceed, as up-front costs.

9.6. Buying a home and taking out a mortgage to finance it involve some of the most important financial decisions in the borrower's life. He needs not only to make appropriate financial arrangements but to satisfy himself that he has made a sound purchase; we discuss the role of the valuation in reassuring him on this aspect later (see paragraph 9.49). Until the market changes described above there was little choice of product and the chief hurdle for the borrower was to be accepted by a building society. Today, in choosing a mortgage a borrower is faced with a variety of lenders and a far wider range of products than in the past. He is provided with a great deal of information on terms and costs, including the up-front costs described above. These costs are included in the APR (Annual Percentage Rate) which all lenders are required to quote under Consumer Credit legislation (see paragraph 3.33). The APR, however, although it may be well-suited to shorter-term credit transactions, is less informative when applied to long-term mortgage transactions. Given the way in which

---

[1]For the purposes of this chapter we group Abbey National plc (Abbey National) with building societies rather than banks or other lenders (see paragraph 3.11).

[2]There are proposals in the Deregulation and Contracting Out Bill, published on 20 January 1994, for relaxing this limit.

the relevant legislation has been interpreted, for example on truncated rates and fixed-rate mortgages, the APR is now of even less use to borrowers. There was general agreement on these points among those who gave evidence to us on the subject. Moreover, regulation under the Financial Services Act 1986 does not extend to mortgage lending as such; for example, there is no obligation, as there is on insurance or pensions, to offer best advice.

9.7. Given the range of products and the amount of information available about them, many consumers prefer to rely on intermediaries, who are now responsible for over half of the business coming to some major lenders. The evidence from a number of lenders, however, and observation of shop window, newspaper and other forms of advertising, including pamphlets, suggest that most of those borrowers who do go direct to a particular lender will nowadays obtain initial information from a number of others. Borrowers examine the packages offered by the individual lenders and are principally concerned with the monthly outgoings on the mortgage, the interest rate, whether it is fixed or variable, and the size of any up-front payments; the first of these is generally the most important. While lenders are required to state costs to borrowers, the extent to which they break these costs down and the way the information is presented will vary.

9.8. It is clear, therefore, that the recent changes in the residential mortgage market have promoted active competition between lenders offering mortgages. This does not mean, however, that this competition is always fully effective. The range of factors to be taken into account by the borrower is particularly complex and, as indicated above and referred to in more detail in paragraph 3.41, the information he receives is not always presented in the most useful way to help him.

## The valuation market

9.9. We now consider the valuation market. The cost of the valuation—the arrangements for which are the main subject of our inquiry—is likely to be an element in a borrower's calculations but not a major one; it is only part of the costs which the borrower will have to meet before the transaction is completed. Some lenders, however, now see the valuation as an element in the mortgage offer on which it is worth offering rebates as an incentive to attract potential borrowers. The cost of, and the arrangements for, the valuation will also be a factor for those borrowers who have already decided on, or commissioned a survey of, the property and who hope to save money by having their selected surveyor accepted also to provide the valuation.

9.10. A valuation report is essentially a professional assessment of the open market value of the property, to provide reassurance to the lender that the advance is adequately secured. It will take account of information on values of comparable properties and will note any major observable defects in the property which may affect its value. The lender may require these to be put right as a condition of making the loan (and this may lead to a reinspection by the valuer). More detailed assessments of the condition of the property are available to the borrower through an SSY which should give him a full picture of the condition of the property, or an HBR, which is a less detailed and less expensive report in a form drawn up by the Royal Institution of Chartered Surveyors (RICS) to encourage more borrowers to opt for their own advice (see paragraph 4.10). In broad terms an HBR, including a valuation, can be expected to cost about twice as much as a valuation carried out on its own and an SSY (again including the valuation) twice as much again.

9.11. On the basis of information provided by the seven largest lenders we estimate the total cost to borrowers of valuations carried out for all lenders in 1992 at £160 million. Other information we collected through a survey (see paragraph 3.60) suggested that the total value of all valuations carried out for lenders and other clients, together with the value of HBRs and SSYs commissioned, whether carried out with a valuation or separately, may have been twice as much as this figure.

9.12. Virtually all lenders require a valuation when they are lending on residential property. It is one of the two key elements in the decision to grant a mortgage, the other being the applicant's status (ie income and creditworthiness). There is a statutory requirement on building societies that before making an advance they satisfy themselves on the security for the advance and for that purpose have in their possession a written valuation made by a competent valuer. The requirement, currently in section 13 of the 1986 Act, is longstanding. While there is no comparable statutory obligation on other lenders such as banks and centralized lenders, virtually all follow the same practice. The statutory obligation requires only that the person carrying out the assessment of the security of the advance be in possession of a valuation. Building societies, however, and other lenders regard it as essential that they establish a contractual relationship with the valuer by directly commissioning the valuation themselves and all retain the final say over the selection of the valuer. He will virtually always be either an in-house surveyor (or one employed by a subsidiary) or one drawn from a panel of approved surveyors established by the lender. Lenders have been under pressure to maintain strict controls by outside bodies including the Building Societies Commission (BSC), The Law Society and police fraud squads, and by their indemnity insurers. The views of these bodies have been taken into account in the guidelines issued by the CML to its members.

9.13. In Scotland, in part as a result of the different housebuying system, most mortgage applications are packaged by intermediaries who make arrangements for the valuation, but the surveyor is almost always from the lender's panel. A contract is established between lender and surveyor before the final arrangements for the mortgage are made.

9.14. Until the early 1980s the valuation report was not shown to the borrower and he was not considered to have a legally recognizable interest in its contents. However, as a result of a series of cases from 1981 onwards,[1] the courts have established a duty of care by the valuer to the borrower in respect of his report in cases where it is foreseeable that the borrower will rely on it. In the first of these cases (the *Yianni* case) the court took into account that the house concerned was at the lower end of the market, purchased by a person of modest means who would be expected to rely on the building society's valuation, for which he had paid, and not to obtain independent advice. The extent to which purchasers of more expensive properties or in different circumstances might benefit from a duty of care on the part of the valuer remains untested.

9.15. Shortly after the *Yianni* case Abbey National decided to disclose valuation reports to borrowers. Other lenders followed suit. It has now become normal practice for them to pass copies of valuation reports to the borrower. Most lenders' reports now contain more information about the condition of the property than the earlier undisclosed ones.

9.16. While the lender commissions the valuation, it is for the borrower to negotiate the terms and conditions for any SSY or HBR he may require and commission it directly from the surveyor. (However, at least one lender requires a prospective borrower to commission an HBR on pre-1914 property.) As noted above, such a fuller report is usually combined with the valuation. In the majority of cases the borrower will be content to commission his more detailed report from the same surveyor as the lender has selected for the valuation. Where, however, he wishes to use a surveyor who is not included on that lender's panel and the lender will not accept his choice of surveyor, he will either have to abandon his choice or pay separately for the lender's valuation, thus incurring additional cost.

9.17. Lenders normally require that the person carrying out a valuation for them be a member of either the RICS or the Incorporated Society of Valuers and Auctioneers (ISVA), have a minimum of two years' experience, and possess local knowledge of the area where he is carrying out the valuation, which will cover both comparative prices and local planning or physical conditions which may affect the value of the properties. Where independent valuers are employed they must satisfy the lender that they have adequate professional indemnity cover.

9.18. As noted in paragraph 9.12, valuations are provided to lenders by three main groups:

*(a)* in-house employees of the lender who provide valuations solely for it;

*(b)* valuers in a subsidiary company who may work both for the controlling lender and for other lenders; and

*(c)* external surveyors, who are usually on the panel of the lender commissioning the valuation.

---

[1] *Yianni v Edwin Evans & Sons* [1981] 3WLR843; *Smith v Bush* and *Harris v Wyre District Commission* [1989] 2WLR790.

9.19. Until the mid-1980s almost all valuations were undertaken by external surveyors. Since 1986, when lenders were allowed to buy and run estate agencies and to provide SSYs and HBRs, they have made increasing use of valuers in subsidiary companies then acquired, which often provide a national chain of surveying and valuation offices. The use of surveyors directly employed in-house has also increased; these staff, however, do not usually provide SSYs. Apart from Barclays Bank plc (Barclays), which has no in-house or associated surveyors, and Cheltenham & Gloucester Building Society, the other five of the seven largest lenders from whom we sought information now carry out the great majority of their valuations through in-house or subsidiary company surveyors. It appears, however, that other lenders still continue to rely more on external valuers.

9.20. At the same time the number of surveyors grew rapidly through the 1980s and, although reliable statistics are not available, the RICS estimates that currently about 5,000 of the 30,000 members in its General Practice Division undertake mortgage valuations or associated work, of whom about 1,150 are employed directly or indirectly by the seven largest lenders.

9.21. These changes, combined with the fall in total valuations required, have led to a reduction in numbers on panels and a further continuing decline in the volume of business going to non-panel valuers.[1] In addition, lenders have been increasingly reluctant to use sole practitioners or small partnerships, because of the perceived additional risk on any claims arising, and this group of surveyors appear to have been hit particularly hard by the cut-backs (see the views of the ISVA, the ISA and individual surveyors in Chapter 8).

9.22. While lenders have always been aware of the possibility of fraud and negligence in relation to valuations, the boom in the late 1980s followed by the fall in prices and an increase in repossessions brought to light a number of cases, some of which might otherwise have remained undiscovered. Proven cases of fraud are few; however, it is often difficult to draw a clear line between fraud and negligence and it may be more effective to pursue a case as one of negligence. Evidence from the seven largest lenders suggested that in this recent period they had between 1,000 and 1,500 cases of suspected fraud and negligence. While the numbers are small in relation to the number of valuations carried out for these lenders each year they are large enough to explain the increased attention being given by lenders to precautions against both fraud and negligence.

9.23. Until 1982 an industry-wide national scale for payments to valuers, based on property values, was negotiated between the RICS, the ISVA and the Building Societies Association (BSA); the arrangements were abandoned in the face of possible action by the Office of Fair Trading (OFT). Since then the fees collected from borrowers and paid to independent valuers have been set by the individual lenders. While they are still set by reference to scales based on property values, as shown in paragraph 5.18 fee scales may now differ significantly between lenders. In many cases the fee charged to the borrower will include an administration charge which may or may not be separately specified. When allowance is made for these the range of charges made for the valuation itself can vary by 20 per cent or more around the average.

9.24. Information from the seven largest lenders suggests that over the last five years the level of fees to borrowers has risen faster than inflation or earnings (see paragraph 5.19) although the lenders suggested that this was in part the effect of court decisions, leading to higher standards and more detailed reports.

## The monopoly situation

9.25. Under the terms of reference made by the Director General of Fair Trading and dated 6 May 1993 (see Appendix 1.1) we are required to investigate and report on whether a monopoly situation exists in relation to the supply in the UK of services consisting of the lending of money on the security of any residential property (residential mortgage lending). In so doing we are required to limit our consideration to agreements and practices relating to the making or procuring of mortgage valuations and the making of charges, including administration or other charges, to borrowers in connection with such valuations. We have first to consider whether a monopoly situation exists and, if so, by virtue of

---

[1]An external valuer who is not on the panel of the lender commissioning the valuation. Such a valuer may well be a panel valuer for other lenders.

which provisions of sections 6 to 8 of the Fair Trading Act 1973 (the Act), and in favour of what person or persons the situation exists. If we identify such a situation we have to consider whether any steps (by way of uncompetitive practices or otherwise) are being taken by that person or persons to exploit or maintain the situation, whether any actions or omissions by them are attributable to the situation and, finally, whether any facts found in pursuance of our investigations operate, or may be expected to operate, against the public interest.

9.26. Under the provisions of sections 7(1)(c) and 7(2) of the Act a complex monopoly situation is taken to exist when at least one-quarter of all the services of a particular description in the UK are supplied by, or to members of, one and the same group, consisting of two or more persons (not being a group of interconnected bodies corporate) who, whether voluntarily or not, and whether by agreement or not, so conduct their respective affairs as in any way to prevent, restrict or distort competition in connection with the supply of these services.

9.27. In September 1993 we notified 41 residential mortgage lenders, and subsequently notified almost a hundred further lenders, that we had provisionally concluded that a complex monopoly situation existed in relation to the supply of residential mortgage lending, in that these lenders were members of a group who appeared to conduct their affairs so as to prevent, restrict or distort competition in connection with the supply of residential mortgage lending, in that they engaged in one or more of the following practices:

*(a)* limiting a prospective borrower's choice of valuer by refusing to accept valuations by any competent valuer;

*(b)* discriminating in the allocation of valuation business in favour of valuers that are employed by the lender, or associated firms or companies;

*(c)* requiring the prospective borrower to pay a set fee based on a national scale established by the lender;

*(d)* paying external valuers a set fee based on a national scale established by the lender; and

*(e)* requiring prospective borrowers to pay fees in connection with valuation services which also contain administrative charges for the valuation or for other services, and which are not separately identified.

9.28. We also informed these lenders of the provisional finding that this monopoly situation existed in their favour.

9.29. In commenting on the provisional finding, a number of lenders and the CML argued that the practices had no anti-competitive effects and that there was therefore no complex monopoly situation. They drew attention to the strength of competition in the mortgage lending market and to the fact that the valuation report was the property of the lender, secured by him for his own purpose, with, in their view, no recognizable borrower's interest in the selection of valuer.

9.30. In relation to practice *(a)*, they argued that a statutory responsibility was placed on building societies to obtain a valuation and that it had never been contemplated that any choice should rest with the borrower. As the borrower had never enjoyed the right to a choice of valuer the lenders' behaviour could not be held to affect competition. Borrowers were free to choose and pay for a surveyor for their own purposes if they so wished.

9.31. On practice *(b)*, it was argued that individual lenders were entitled to make their own judgment how most economically to obtain the services they required and, where appropriate, to use their own resources and again no adverse competitive effects would arise.

9.32. On practices *(c)* and *(d)*, it was argued that the use by individual lenders of set national scales for charging borrowers and paying valuers brought convenience and certainty to borrowers and, provided lenders set individual scales and these were made known to borrowers, competition would not be affected. Price lists were established by buyers on a national basis for many products and generally accepted without challenge, and a pricing policy which discriminated on the basis of borrower or locality would obviously attract a finding that it prevented, restricted or distorted competition.

9.33. On practice *(e)*, the CML argued that, while the level of up-front charges was a factor in the borrower's choice of lender, it was irrelevant to his choice of lender whether the components of up-front charges were separately specified.

9.34. A number of lenders pointed to the desirable effects of practices *(a)* to *(d)*.

9.35. We reviewed our findings in the light of the various comments and further information submitted. As a result we simplified practice *(a)* to read 'refusing to accept valuations by any competent valuer'. We removed practice *(b)*, although the use of in-house and subsidiary valuers remained, as an aspect of selection of valuers (practice *(a)*), a matter for examination as possibly raising public interest issues for the inquiry. We also slightly reworded practice *(e)* to read 'requiring prospective borrowers to pay fees in connection with valuation services which do not separately identify any administration charges levied in connection with or incorporated in the fee' to make clear that the restriction or distortion of competition provisionally identified was based on lack of transparency, ie the withholding of information.

9.36. In relation to practice *(a)* as revised, lenders' refusal to accept any competent surveyor as a provider of valuations, means that competent surveyors who might otherwise receive business are deprived of the opportunity to compete. A lender's refusal to accept the borrower's nomination, where he wishes to use his own choice of surveyor to carry out an SSY or HBR and to provide at the same time a valuation, can lead the latter to incur extra expense. To avoid this cost the borrower may be influenced to agree to instruct a surveyor whose valuation will be acceptable to the lender. These constraints distort competition in the provision of valuations and thus in connection with the supply of the reference services of residential mortgage lending. Moreover, to the extent that the borrower attaches importance in selecting a lender to being able to nominate the valuer, the failure of lenders to offer such a choice also distorts competition directly in the supply of residential mortgage lending.

9.37. In considering practices *(c)* and *(d)*, we interpret national scales as those applied by lenders to mortgage transactions within their normal area of operation. Smaller societies will only apply their scales within a limited area. The use of set fees to borrowers based on a national scale established by the individual lender (practice *(c)*) results in fees to the individual borrower that do not necessarily reflect the cost of the individual valuation or take account of variations in the cost of valuations, either between regions or between properties of the same value. In combination with practice *(a)* the practice deprives individual borrowers of any opportunity to benefit from lower costs and fees that might otherwise be available and thus distorts the basis on which lenders compete to supply valuations to the borrower in connection with the supply of the reference services.

9.38. The lenders' practice of using their individual national fee scales to pay valuers (practice *(d)*) deprives surveyors of the opportunity of competing on price for valuation business. In combination with practice *(a)* it deprives many qualified surveyors of any opportunity of competing for valuation business from a large number of individual lenders. It therefore distorts competition in the supply of valuation services and thus distorts competition in connection with the supply of the reference services.

9.39. Requiring a borrower to pay a fee for the valuation which contains an unidentified amount for administration fees (practice *(e)*) deprives the borrower of information on the composition of an important component of the mortgage offer. Competition is distorted or restricted if borrowers have access to unequal or misleading information about the different mortgage packages available to them. The borrower knows that a valuation fee is charged for a specific professional service and in many cases this fee will be passed to an independent professional. He is likely to examine more critically the size of, and the reasons for, any administration charge levied and to look at the alternatives offered by other lenders particularly since, if the information is made available, he will find that many lenders make no such charges. Without information on the existence and amount of the administrative charge, he will be unaware, or may gain a misleading impression, of the element of the up-front payment required of him that is a true valuation charge. He is thereby prevented from making an adequately informed assessment of the lender's package and the competitive process is thereby distorted.

9.40. As set out in paragraph 3.50, the seven largest suppliers of residential mortgage lending accounted in 1992 for over 50 per cent of the gross value of all new residential mortgage lending. On the basis of the evidence set out in Appendix 4.6 it appears that all these lenders conduct their affairs in one or more of the ways described above. On the basis of the evidence set out in Appendices 4.6 and 4.7 it appears that most other lenders also conduct their affairs in one or more of the ways described. We therefore conclude that a monopoly situation exists by virtue of sections 7(1)(c) and (2) of the Act (a complex monopoly) in that the 129 lenders listed in Appendix 9.1 (being members of one and the same group for the purpose of these provisions) supply at least one-quarter of the residential mortgage lending supplied in the UK and, as set out in that appendix, each engages in one or more of the following practices:

— refusing to accept valuations by any competent valuer (practice *(a)* as revised);

— requiring the prospective borrower to pay a set fee based on a national scale established by the lender (practice *(c)*);

— paying external valuers a set fee based on a national scale established by the lender (practice *(d)*); and

— requiring prospective borrowers to pay fees in connection with valuation services which do not separately identify any administrative charges levied in connection with or incorporated in the fee (practice *(e)*, as revised).

9.41. We have also concluded that the monopoly situation exists in favour of the lenders listed in Appendix 9.1. The appendix lists all the major lenders, together with a large number of other lenders. We accept that, given the large number of lenders and their different channels of operation, there may be some other small lenders engaging in one or more of the practices whom we have not identified. If so, however, such lenders do not play any significant role in this market and we took account of this commercial reality in coming to our conclusion.

9.42. We stress that the finding that a practice restricts, distorts or prevents competition, in the terms of section 7 of the Act, carries no implication that the practice in itself has any adverse or beneficial effects. Considerations of this kind arise in the discussion of the public interest, which we now address.


## The public interest

9.43. Having found that a complex monopoly situation exists we are now required by our terms of reference to consider whether any steps (by way of uncompetitive practices or otherwise) are being taken by any of the persons in whose favour the complex monopoly situation exists, for the purposes of exploiting or maintaining that situation, and whether any action or omission on the part of those persons is attributable to the existence of that situation. Finally, we are required to consider whether any facts found in pursuance of our investigation operate, or may be expected to operate, against the public interest. We first, in paragraphs 9.44 to 9.69, set out the issues in relation to the various practices identified above, and then in paragraphs 9.70 to 9.111 we address the above questions and assess the public interest.


### *The selection of valuer*

9.44. Practice *(a)* relates to the selection of valuers by lenders. One of the main reasons for this inquiry was complaints to the OFT from valuers that lenders were refusing to give them valuation business, either by excluding them from the lender's panel, or by refusing to accept them on a borrower's nomination. Almost all lenders operate panels of approved valuers for specified geographic areas who they consider have adequate competence and local knowledge. The extent to which lenders restrict choice to the approved panel varies. Some of the larger building societies adhere rigidly to their rule that valuations from external surveyors are only acceptable if made by panel valuers. Others, including most of the banks and centralized lenders, are prepared to consider a valuation by a surveyor nominated by the borrower who is not on their panel, subject to satisfactory checks on competence, particularly in cases where the borrower may already have commissioned an SSY or HBR from that surveyor before making a firm offer or seeking a loan. Over the last few years the number of valuations has fallen sharply through the recession; lenders have made increasing use of in-house valuers and valuers in subsidiary companies and some panels have been cut back. At the same time pressure from surveyors seeking work has increased. Sole practitioners and small firms have found it particularly difficult to gain admission to or be retained by lenders on their panels and have expressed their concerns throughout the inquiry.

### The lender's interest in selection

9.45. Lenders represented strongly to us, both through the CML and individually, that the valuation report belonged to them and not to the borrower. It was required for their purposes, to determine whether the property was adequate security for the proposed loan, and any borrower interest was incidental. The selection of the valuer and the standards of valuation required were therefore for the individual lender to determine.

9.46. Lenders told us that standards of valuation required had become more rigorous for two reasons. First, the establishment by the courts over the last decade of a valuer's duty of care to the borrower had led to more detail being provided in reports. Secondly, the experience of rapidly falling house prices in the late 1980s, after a long period of price inflation which had masked problems, had brought to light a number of unsatisfactory valuations, due either to fraud or more often negligence. Although small as a proportion of total valuations, these had led to significant losses and increased insurance costs and had caused much concern to lenders. This experience had led lenders to improve their valuation procedures and devote more resources to vetting valuers' competence. To accept valuations from a wider range of valuers would increase lenders' costs in training and monitoring valuers, which would have to be passed on to borrowers through increased charges.

9.47. In addition, lenders said that experience of fraud and negligence had shown that valuers' professional indemnity insurance cover was sometimes inadequate. While the RICS required members to carry professional indemnity insurance cover, including 'run-off' insurance (to cover claims arising after the valuer has retired from practice), the RICS relied on self-certification to check that this was in place. Once a valuer had retired, or a firm had been wound up, there was no way of ensuring that 'run-off' cover was maintained for claims which could take some years to come to light. Lenders therefore saw some advantage in relying on established firms which might reasonably be seen as more likely to stay in business than sole practitioners. A further consideration was that fraud by a sole practitioner, unlike negligence, could not be covered by his insurance. Nor had the RICS established a compensation scheme of the kind run by, for example, The Law Society, to meet claims arising from fraud or negligence by its members in cases where individual firms or their insurers were unable to meet their obligations. Lenders therefore felt obliged to protect their interests and to keep down their own mortgage indemnity premiums by adopting a selective approach to valuer approval and thoroughly vetting those whom they accepted.

9.48. We accept that without lender controls there would be increased opportunities for both fraud and negligence. The removal of such opportunities benefits lenders, depositors and borrowers and the public interest generally. Equally, however, we think that such dangers should not be used as a justification for any or all restrictions lenders might choose to introduce, if adequate protection of their interests might reasonably be expected from less stringent restrictions on selection.

### The borrower's interest

9.49. The borrower's interest in the valuation may at first sight appear the same as that of the lender since both have an interest in knowing the market value of the property. There are, however, important differences. The lender is interested only in satisfying himself that the property represents adequate security for the loan he contemplates making. The borrower may also reasonably expect a valuation to provide reassurance that the property is worth what he proposes to pay for it, should he wish to resell. But the borrower also appears in many cases effectively to rely on the valuation to give him a general reassurance on the condition of the property, eg that it is free from major defects. Evidence from lenders, and detailed figures from some of the largest lenders, suggested that only a small proportion, perhaps 10 to 15 per cent or so, of borrowers take out a further HBR or SSY on the property. It is at first sight surprising that this proportion is not larger, given the serious consequences of major defects in a property and an earlier survey suggesting that one in five more detailed inspections reveal significant defects (see paragraph 8.36). There may be a number of explanations. First, our own study (see paragraph 3.61) suggests that the proportion indicated by lenders above may be an underestimate of the numbers taking their own advice. Secondly, some borrowers switching lenders or taking out a further loan will already be familiar with the condition of the property and will not need a further survey, while those buying newly-built properties are usually protected at least against major structural defect for the first ten years by the National House Building Council or an equivalent guarantee. Finally, the proportion may be an indication of the extent to which borrowers still think their interests are fully covered by the lender's valuation report. Even allowing for these factors, however, it is clear that only a minority of those who could benefit from further advice commission it. In spite of the frequent warnings in lenders' literature that valuations are prepared for their own purposes and not for the borrower's, there may well still be some confusion in the borrower's mind, strengthened by the fact that he pays for the valuation, about the extent to which he is entitled to rely on it. Recent court decisions,[1] by recognizing a degree of borrower interest and a duty of care to him, together with lenders' policy of disclosing reports to borrowers, have probably strengthened the borrower's inclination to rely on the lender's report.

9.50. In practice therefore the majority of borrowers appear content to rely on the lender's valuation and on its choice of valuer. Many of the minority who do decide to commission an SSY or HBR will already be in discussion with the prospective lender and will make a choice from the lender's panel for a combined survey or report and valuation. However, a number of instances were drawn to our attention where the borrower had either already commissioned a survey or report before submitting a mortgage application or wished to use a surveyor already known to him by reputation or past experience. In such cases, if the lender refuses to accept a mortgage valuation from that surveyor the borrower finds he has to pay two separate fees and his costs are significantly increased.

## The cost of valuations

9.51. It was also argued by many surveyors that the lenders' refusal to accept a wider range of valuers deprived consumers of the benefit of the lower prices that surveyors not on their panels were prepared to charge for composite reports. In the course of the inquiry we received complaints from surveyors about individual cases where they had quoted for composite reports and then lost the business, and where the charges of the lender's approved valuer were claimed to be substantially higher (see paragraph 5.30). We collected information through our own survey about the charges for independently commissioned valuations, and compared these with the seven largest lenders' charges (see paragraph 5.20). There was a wide dispersion of charges but the average of larger lenders' charges appeared higher at all levels of property prices than the median figure for valuers' quotations for independently commissioned work, by approximately £10 on average. For valuing a house in the £25,000 to £50,000 price bracket, one in five of the fees quoted by valuers were at least £20 less than the fee charged by the lender. Our information on levels of total charges, ie including administration charges, collected from a wider selection of lenders suggests that the charges of the seven largest lenders tend to be higher than those of smaller lenders (see paragraph 5.22). This may to some extent reflect their need as national lenders for more detailed and therefore costly checking procedures. We therefore think it unlikely that, on average, quotations by surveyors for independently commissioned work are significantly lower than lenders' charges.

9.52. We noted that valuation charges had risen over the last five years faster than either the retail price or earnings indices. Lenders, however, linked this to the fuller inspection and more detailed reports now being prepared; some produced evidence of the consequential decline in numbers of valuations carried out per day.

---

[1]See paragraph 2.17.

9.53. We looked at the profitability of valuation business to the seven largest lenders. As explained in paragraph 5.33, there are difficulties in trying to isolate the results of this comparatively small part of lenders' business, which they do not separately account for, and the different accounting treatment of lenders make aggregation difficult. There are also problems in trying to produce an overall measure of profitability for an activity where some fees are transferred directly to third parties and others set against work in-house. Subject to these reservations the information collected suggests that overall modest margins are being made, mainly due to returns on in-house valuations. Part of this, however, was due to the treatment for VAT purposes of lenders' valuation activities, a matter to which we return later, in paragraphs 9.59 and 9.80.

## Acceptance of earlier valuations

9.54. We received complaints, mainly from valuers rather than borrowers themselves, that the latter are put to unnecessary expense because, where an earlier prospective transaction has been frustrated, lenders are unwilling to accept a valuation recently made on the property which may have been prepared either for the same borrower or for a different prospective borrower. We were given estimates (see paragraph 3.57) that about 20 per cent of applications fail to result in a completed mortgage and in most of these cases a valuation will have been carried out. Lenders' practice varies: some will only accept valuations already carried out for them; others will in certain circumstances accept valuations carried out for other lenders. In this respect banks appear more flexible than building societies. Because of past experience, however, all lenders tend to be wary of earlier valuations carried out for the seller or the prospective borrower rather than commissioned by a lender.

9.55. It was suggested by some surveyors that lenders should be prepared to accept any valuation carried out for another lender within a set preceding period, say one month or six weeks previously. Some lenders told us that they were ready to consider such requests from borrowers. Where they had commissioned a valuation for a transaction that did not then take place and another borrower contacted them, or where two prospective borrowers were trying to buy the same house, they would normally offer a reduction to the unsuccessful purchaser. All lenders insisted, however, that they must retain the ultimate responsibility for deciding when an earlier valuation was acceptable. They would not be prepared automatically to accept a valuation acceptable to another lender whose standards or coverage of the valuation form might be different; some of the largest lenders would not necessarily accept valuations prepared for another equally large lender. Nor did lenders think it possible to lay down set time periods within which an earlier valuation should remain acceptable.

## Reciprocal business

9.56. We received complaints from individual surveyors that valuers were appointed to lenders' panels, and valuation instructions were allocated, on the basis of the valuer's ability and willingness to provide reciprocal mortgage introductions. The RICS also expressed strong concern about the practice and submitted a dossier of evidence from members on its extent. Our own survey of surveyors (see paragraph 4.41) suggested that most were aware of the practice, and that a significant minority provided introductions or considered that they had lost business as a result of failure to do so. Some lenders told us that reciprocity played no part in their choice. Most, however, told us that, while this factor did not determine their selection of valuer, nonetheless if all the essential criteria of professional competence, local knowledge etc were satisfied, this was a factor which could be taken into account. While the RICS condemns the practice of choosing valuers purely on grounds of reciprocity, it has agreed a joint statement with the CML which accepts that, in considering appointments to its panel, reciprocity may be used by a lender as a determining factor in choosing between equally suitable valuers.

## Use of in-house valuers

9.57. While some building societies have employed their own valuers for many years, until the 1986 Act most valuations were carried out by external surveyors. Since then the numbers of in-house valuers employed have grown and some major lenders now have subsidiary companies which carry out valuations both for them and for others. Information from the seven largest lenders suggested that (excluding Barclays which has no in-house valuers) about three-quarters of their valuations are now commissioned in-house or from associated valuers. A number of independent surveyors expressed concern that increasing use of in-house valuers was a major factor in the decline of business going to them, thus depriving borrowers of a source of well-qualified advice. It was claimed that in-house surveyors frequently had less local knowledge than the independent valuer and were less able to comment on structural matters. They therefore tended to call for additional technical advice, involving the borrower in further expense. Concern was also expressed by the professional bodies and individual surveyors about the potential for conflicts of interest arising and this is discussed further below.

9.58. Lenders argued that the extent to which in-house valuers were used was a matter of commercial judgment. They denied that their staff were less well-qualified and claimed that because they were trained specifically to meet the needs of the individual lender the quality of their reports was often higher. Given their wish to make full use of in-house valuers economically it was inevitable that the proportion of work carried out in-house rose when total numbers of valuations fell, as in the recent recession.

9.59. As indicated in paragraph 9.53, the financial information we collected from the seven largest lenders suggests, subject to the qualifications there indicated, that their returns on valuations, which vary widely between lenders, are earned on in-house valuations. A contributory factor here is the different treatment for VAT purposes of valuations carried out in-house or by subsidiary valuers as compared with those carried out for the lender by other valuers. External valuers liable for VAT have to charge and account for at the 17.5 per cent rate on the valuations they carry out for lenders, and this has to be allowed for in the level of fees set by lenders. The provision of loan finance and associated costs, however, including the provision of valuations in-house or by subsidiaries, are exempted from VAT. A standard fee is charged to borrowers, irrespective of whether the valuation is carried out by an independent valuer or not, and, even allowing for the fact that lenders, unlike independent valuers, cannot reclaim VAT paid on inputs, a financial benefit arises for the lender from using in-house or subsidiary valuers (see paragraph 5.42).

## Conflicts of interest

9.60. The RICS, as well as individual valuers, drew our attention to the potential for conflicts of interest where lenders have a direct or indirect commercial interest in the sale of the property on which the mortgage is being sought, which might lead to pressure on the valuers to value to order, so that a property transaction might proceed. The potential scope for such pressures had grown with the increasing ownership by lenders of estate agents and the extension of their activities to other financial areas such as banking, life assurance and pensions which provided a wider range of profit opportunities from the transaction.

9.61. There are statutory constraints in the 1986 Act which prevent building societies using as a valuer 'any person having a financial interest in the disposition of the [property]'. These provisions, which were enacted before the great increase in the use of in-house or subsidiary valuers, preclude the use of in-house valuers or of valuers in associated companies to value for a mortgage advance properties repossessed by the lenders. Legal advice has been sought by the RICS on other circumstances in which lenders might be deemed to have an interest which precluded valuation by their employees, and there has been some difference of view. It is generally accepted, however, that in those other circumstances in-house valuers or those in other subsidiaries can legally value where an agent within the same corporate group is selling the property.

9.62. The RICS put to the CML in 1991 the proposal that the lenders should explain the types of valuer that might be used and their relationship with the lender, allowing the borrower, if concerned, to ask for another type of valuer. The CML rejected this proposal; it did, however, advise lenders to make clear to borrowers that in-house or associated valuers may be used without suggesting that borrowers had any choice in the matter.

9.63. Lenders told us that their overriding interest was in a good-quality valuation and that it would not be in their interests to allow pressures on valuers to adjust valuations to arise which would lead to unreliable valuations. They followed the CML guidance in one form or another and told borrowers that in-house or subsidiary valuers might be used but they had found that borrowers did not appear concerned by the problem.

## Lenders' use of scale charges to borrowers

9.64. Virtually all lenders use a set scale of charges payable by the borrower for valuations, linked to the purchase price of the property. The level and spread of these charges is discussed in paragraph 5.22. The valuation fee charged may include an administration charge towards the general administration costs associated with granting the mortgage. While some lenders make clear the existence and size of the administration element, others do not and the effects of this practice are discussed further in paragraphs 9.109 and 9.110.

9.65. These scales, and the scales for payments to valuers discussed in the following section, stem from the original industry-wide scale for payments to valuers negotiated between the RICS and the BSA. All lenders now have their own individual scales but all still use a set scale linked to property prices although the actual amounts charged differ.

9.66. Lenders' scale fees clearly involve cross-subsidy between borrowers since the amount of work involved in a valuation may be largely unrelated to the price of the property. For example, an expensive new property on an estate may involve far less work for the valuer than an older city property or a character cottage in the country. Moreover, the large lenders' scales, which apply throughout the country, take no account of variations in valuation costs between different regions.

9.67. The lenders argued that the borrower above all required clear information on the up-front charge that he had to pay. To attempt to charge on the amount of work involved or by the hour would be administratively complex and the latter might lead to inefficiency. While larger lenders might be able to operate local or regional scales this would introduce complexity and would create difficulties in the marketing of mortgage offers, which was usually done on a national basis. Lenders argued, moreover, that cost differences between regions were not a major factor and since they tended to be reflected in house price levels, the linkage of the fee to the house purchase price provided a rough adjustment which accommodated such regional variations.

9.68. We also received a number of complaints from valuers that if given the opportunity they were prepared to offer borrowers lower fees than lenders' current scales for valuations, either for valuations on their own or provided with an HBR or SSY. The lenders argued that their bargaining strength *vis-à-vis* surveyors enabled them to keep fees below those which the average borrower would be able to negotiate. As indicated in paragraph 9.51, there is some evidence that lenders' charges to borrowers tend on average to be a little above those quoted by independent surveyors. However, the range of individual quotations can be large.

## Lenders' scale fees to valuers

9.69. Most lenders establish set fee scales for payment to valuers which, like their valuation charges to borrowers, are linked to the selling price of the property; indeed many lenders simply pass on to the valuer the valuation fee received from the borrower. The level of fees is set by the lender without negotiation, although representations are received from valuers, and occasionally from the RICS, on the level of fees. Lenders told us that in setting fees they took into account the fees charged by other lenders and the need to set their own at the level necessary to secure the quality of valuations required; where in-house valuers were employed fees were set to cover costs, and in some cases to achieve targeted margins. We received no direct complaints from panel valuers about the level of fees offered and we heard of no work being refused on the grounds that fees were too low. Although independent valuers criticized lenders' fees as being too high, we were told of no offers by non-panel valuers to try to secure work or a place on the panel by offering to accept lower fees. However, they may have been influenced by the attitude of lenders, who told us that they would be wary of offers to work at cut rates in case standards were compromised; lenders considered that their bargaining power, accompanied by the need to compete with other lenders on fees to borrowers, enabled them to set competitive fee levels to the benefit of borrowers.

## Assessment

### *General effects of selection on borrowers*

9.70. The various features of the arrangements for valuations made by lenders discussed in the preceding paragraphs are all aspects of the arrangements made by lenders which involve the selection of valuers from the pool of those competent to carry out the work. We accept that the prudential responsibilities of lenders to their depositors, which for building societies are set out in section 45 of the 1986 Act (see paragraph 2.14), require them to retain the ultimate responsibility for selecting the valuer in any particular instance. In so doing they take into account their own circumstances and the balance of costs and benefits in deciding what principles of selection to follow. We have, however, to consider whether lenders' selection practices and charging arrangements operate in a way which has effects adverse to the public interest in respect of the consumer in his role as borrower.

9.71. There is clearly a borrower's interest to be taken into account, first at the general level and secondly in specific cases. First, the lender's practice of requiring the borrower to pay for the valuation, together with the valuer's duty of care to the borrower in many cases, established by the courts, gives the borrower a recognizable interest in the choice of valuer. Lenders' selection, combined with their practices in setting fee scales, also determines the prices paid by borrowers for valuations. There is thus a general borrower interest in the choice in so far as this affects the price and the quality of the valuation. Secondly, there is the interest of those borrowers who wish to commission their own survey advice by way of an HBR or SSY and hope to lessen the combined costs of valuation and survey by having their own personal choice of surveyor accepted to carry out both. We look first at the general aspects.

9.72. Lenders' prudential responsibility requires them first and foremost to be satisfied on the valuer's competence. It is generally accepted that to be regarded as competent and acceptable a valuer must have professional training, experience, local knowledge and adequate professional indemnity cover. There is at present no outside agency or professional body which checks whether surveyors meet all these tests, nor any power, apart from the ultimate sanction of expulsion from the professional body, to require valuers to carry adequate professional indemnity cover; nor is there any professional compensation scheme to provide run-off cover. The lender's responsibility can therefore only be met by satisfying itself by its own investigation that the individual surveyor whose valuation it accepts meets the necessary standards. In such circumstances we consider that it is not unreasonable for lenders to limit the costs of administering and checking such procedures by operating a panel of approved valuers and for each lender to limit its panel to the number it considers appropriate to give it adequate coverage geographically and by type of property.

9.73. We have considered whether the restrictions on panel appointments operate in a way which leads to higher costs or poorer service to consumers, bearing in mind particularly the interests of those borrowers who wish to have a say in the choice of valuer. We have noted criticisms by independent surveyors that some in-house valuers and even panel valuers lack local knowledge of the areas they work in. The lenders explained to us their systems for controlling the areas in which their valuers work and for monitoring the quality of their reports. Given the large number of valuations commissioned there will inevitably be some individual cases of poor-quality reports and examples of these were given to us. We were satisfied, however, that the valuers used by lenders, whether employed in-house or in subsidiary companies or on panels, are generally competent, and that the arrangements result in reports that are satisfactory for the lenders' purposes.

9.74. While all lenders appear to use broadly the same tests of competence, they differ in their willingness to accept sole practitioners as valuers and to consider requests for use of a surveyor not on their own panel. On both of these aspects building societies tend to take a more restrictive approach than banks and centralized lenders.

9.75. The reluctance to accept sole practitioners arises from the lenders' concern over possibilities of fraud and negligence. There may be concerns that if a sole practitioner has to meet claims for negligence or gets into other difficulties he is less likely to be able to maintain cover than a larger firm. He may have problems in maintaining run-off cover to meet liabilities arising after he retires and his insurance cannot cover fraud by him. We think it reasonable, however, that lenders should take account of both factors in establishing a panel, and that it is for the individual lender to decide how much weight to put on these dangers.

9.76. In practice, there is a broad distinction between building societies[1] and banks, both in the way they draw up their panels and in their willingness to accept valuers who are not on their panels. The banks tend to leave greater discretion to local managers to select panel valuers and to vet requests for use of non-panel valuers, which they are usually prepared to entertain. Building societies usually insist on their own choice of surveyor where a valuation alone is required but will often be prepared to accept a borrower's choice, where he has selected a surveyor for an SSY or HBR, provided the choice is already on the lender's panel; a non-panel valuer is not usually acceptable. The more flexible attitude of some banks can be attributed to the wider local knowledge their managers usually possess, which puts them in a better position to exercise flexibility and, as some banks suggested, to their information about their account-holders' income and status.

9.77. We received few direct complaints from borrowers although there were numbers from surveyors who had lost business. Some borrowers may already have been aware of the lenders' attitudes and arranged their affairs accordingly; others may have been able to take advantage of the more flexible attitude of, for example, some banks. However, it seems reasonable to assume that most borrowers have no complaint about their inability to choose the valuer and thus do not find the different levels of restriction operated by lenders a practical constraint. As noted, we found no evidence that the quality of valuation was currently affected.

### Use of in-house valuers

9.78. One aspect of selection of valuers by lenders is the use of in-house or subsidiary valuers. When the 1986 Act was passed most valuations were carried out by independent professionals and the increasing use of in-house valuers or valuers in a subsidiary company is one of the biggest changes in recent years in the arrangements for valuations. This use of in-house valuers was criticized primarily on grounds of potential conflicts of interest, particularly where the lender was involved in the sale of the property through an estate agent or other subsidiary. Conflicts of interest are considered in more detail in the following section (paragraphs 9.102 to 9.105). We note, however, the RICS view that it is difficult to draw a distinction between the potential conflicts of interest faced by in-house or associated valuers and those faced by panel valuers. We are not satisfied that potential conflicts of interest have in practice led to major problems in this area. Some external valuers also, however, criticized the quality of work of in-house valuers. As already stated in paragraph 9.73, we do not believe that their work is generally inadequate.

9.79. We have therefore not found evidence that the extent to which such staff are used leads to lower standards of service to borrowers nor that their use significantly increases the risks of any potential conflicts of interest arising. Those lenders we questioned follow the CML advice to inform borrowers that in-house or subsidiary valuers may be used; we have not found any evidence that this is a matter which concerns any significant number of borrowers. We consider that a lender should be free to employ in-house valuers or valuers in subsidiary companies where this seems to it an efficient way of conducting business and likely to assist in the control of standards of valuation.

9.80. We have identified an anomaly whereby valuations done in-house or by subsidiaries are not subject to VAT (see paragraph 9.59). We asked lenders whether in this situation it was feasible for the benefit to be passed on to borrowers. Lenders responded that when the charge is collected from borrowers it will usually not be known whether the valuation will be carried out in-house. Lenders assured us that the VAT position was not a factor in allocating individual instructions and suggested that a two-tier structure of fees would itself tend to create a bias against using panel valuers.

9.81. On the evidence available to us this difference in VAT treatment of valuations does not result in excess profits to lenders (see paragraph 9.53). While it may not influence the allocation of individual instructions, it does provide a general incentive to the maintenance of in-house valuation teams.

---

[1]For the purposes of this chapter we group Abbey National with the building societies (see paragraphs 3.11 and 9.2).

It arises, however, from the requirements of EC law and will apply equally to the provision of other services that the lender has a choice between buying-in or providing in-house, for example legal advice. We do not see it as an issue that can be tackled in isolation in the context of this inquiry.

*Charges to borrowers*

9.82. We considered whether, if borrowers had a greater say in the choice of valuer and were able to negotiate fees directly, they might secure lower prices. As stated earlier (see paragraph 9.51), the survey we carried out of fees quoted by independent valuers suggested that these varied widely but that the majority were slightly below the scale fees charged by the seven largest lenders and unlikely to be significantly below those set by lenders taken as a whole. The majority of the seven largest lenders' valuation work is at present carried out in-house and even if borrowers had greater influence on choice it is likely that most of these would continue to accept an in-house valuation, bearing in mind that were the valuation negligent the borrower would then have direct recourse against the lender. Of those prepared to shop around some probably would benefit from lower prices but the admittedly limited evidence before us does not suggest that the benefit would be significant. Any such benefits would probably be offset to some extent by lenders' charges for checking the valuations provided.

9.83. Lenders are likely also to have a stronger bargaining position on fees than borrowers, and in practice most lenders set their fees without discussion with valuers. The incentive to keep charges down may be weaker for a lender who has a high proportion of in-house work and may see this as an additional source of earnings but, provided competition is fully effective, sufficient incentives will exist to keep charges down. Although the largest lenders' profits on in-house valuations taken as a whole at present appear healthy, their returns overall on valuations are modest. We do not consider that these financial results could be relied on to support the view that charges for valuations are excessive.

9.84. We then considered the effect on prices to borrowers of the lenders' use of national fee scales. As discussed in paragraph 9.66, such fee scales cannot hope to mirror at all accurately either the resource cost of the individual valuation or variations in costs between different regions. There are, however, advantages to the borrower in knowing the fee he will have to pay at an early stage in the mortgage transaction. Regional scales could be established at some administrative cost to lenders; they would remove part, but not all, of existing cross-subsidy between borrowers and there is no reason to think the average fee would fall. The greater part of the largest lenders' valuation work is carried out in-house or through subsidiaries; to negotiate individual fees on a work or time basis would create considerable additional costs for these larger lending organizations. As long as lenders choose valuers it is not reasonable to expect them to abandon the negotiation of fees for panel valuers to the borrower. When account is taken of higher cost of administration for lenders it is difficult to be certain whether the general level of fees would fall except perhaps in depressed market conditions of the kind recently experienced. On balance we do not think there is evidence that as a result of the present system of national fee scales prices generally are higher than they would otherwise be.

9.85. We also considered whether the lenders' use of national scales for paying panel valuers disadvantaged borrowers. The effects on price are a direct reflection of the effects of the parallel scales for borrowers which we have already considered. The main concern must be that the use of such scales, combined with restricted panels, increases the difficulty for a new valuer in gaining entry to the panel, even if competent in all respects. In a more competitive situation such a valuer would be able to seek business by offering his services for a lower fee. In itself the fee scale does not formally preclude this action but lenders told us that they had received no such approaches and a number made clear that they would be suspicious of the motives for such an approach. Awareness of this attitude may itself discourage valuers from attempting to compete on price. There may be some loss of opportunities for recently qualified surveyors to enter through this route but, given the alternative opportunities for entry through existing panel firms and lenders' own organizations, we do not think borrowers will be disadvantaged in this respect by the continuation of lenders' national scales.

## *Effects of selection on individual borrowers*

9.86. We now consider the second more specific borrower interest identified in paragraph 9.71. The present situation disadvantages those borrowers who for good reasons wish their chosen surveyor to be instructed for the valuation, and in particular those who have already commissioned an SSY or HBR from a surveyor who would be prepared to quote for a combined report. As noted in paragraph 9.77, we received few direct complaints from borrowers but there were a number, purportedly on their behalf, from surveyors who had wished to act for them. It is difficult to estimate what proportion this reflects of the considerable numbers of borrowers who commission such reports, but who are themselves, as pointed out in paragraph 9.49, a minority of borrowers who might benefit from them.

9.87. We have set out above the benefits which arise from lenders' control of valuations, in fulfilling their prudential responsibilities, maintaining the quality of valuations and guarding against fraud and negligence. We consider that the benefits these provide for depositors, borrowers themselves and the public interest generally outweigh the disadvantages to particular borrowers outlined above that result from these controls. However, we recognize that for some of these borrowers the disadvantages may be serious. We therefore considered carefully whether some way could be found to introduce changes to lenders' present arrangements which would remove or lessen the disadvantages, while retaining the lenders' ultimate responsibility for selection. We had in mind that, were such changes feasible, we would need to consider whether the present arrangements were against the public interest to the extent that they did not incorporate these changes. We looked at a number of possibilities.

9.88. It was suggested to us at one stage that the RICS should co-operate with lenders in widening the numbers of acceptable valuers by drawing up a list of approved valuers selected by peer group review. It seems likely, however, that valuers could only reasonably be excluded from such a list on clear evidence of incompetence, and it would still be necessary for lenders in the light of their prudential responsibilities to approve the selection. The RICS itself acknowledged that in present circumstances it would be difficult for it to select valuers in this way to establish a wider but still restricted panel.

9.89. Moreover, even if large numbers of additional valuers were approved by lenders the total of valuations they commissioned would not thereby be increased; it would be spread more widely, with each valuer probably doing a smaller number of valuations for each lender, thus losing the advantages of a steady flow of instructions from the individual lender to the panellist. We noted in this context the RICS comment that it would normally expect a valuer to carry out sufficient volume of work to establish experience and meet the client's particular requirements. We did not therefore consider that this approach ought to be pursued.

9.90. Another possibility we examined was to require lenders to accept valuations from surveyors who were on the panels of other lenders. It may seem at first sight unreasonable for a major lender to refuse to accept a valuer acceptable to another reputable lender whose vetting procedures appear equally stringent. A lender may, however, have justifiable doubts about the vetting procedures of some other lenders and it is not easy to see how a line could be drawn between the acceptable and the unacceptable.

9.91. We next considered whether, in a case where a borrower has already selected a surveyor to carry out an HBR or SSY for him, the lender should be required to consider the suitability of that surveyor to provide the valuation required against its usual standards (ie professional qualifications, local knowledge, professional indemnity insurance). Such a procedure was recommended to its members in 1979 by the BSA in its Circular No 2274 (see paragraph 4.22) but does not now appear to be generally followed. While some lenders continue to do so others will only consider a valuer who is already on their panel. The BSC in its draft Prudential Note on Lending (currently under discussion) advises lenders to make thorough checks if a borrower asks a society to use a valuer not on the panel and to be especially wary if the borrower provides a completed valuation. Clearly these are safeguards all lenders should consider.

9.92. We recognize that vetting a borrower's chosen surveyor would involve some administrative costs to the lender. Building societies already operate a system in relation to property insurance, where the borrower may secure his own insurance cover but the society has to be satisfied that the terms of the cover are adequate and that the insurer is generally acceptable and may levy a charge to meet the costs of scrutinizing the insurance offered. The costs of verifying the standing of an individual surveyor might well be higher than those involved in assessing an insurance company. Moreover, while the lender might be required to consider the borrowers' nomination the ultimate responsibility for selection would still have to remain with the lender. It would be difficult to lay down guidance on when scrutiny should lead to acceptance without curtailing this responsibility and raising some issues of liability.

9.93. We also considered whether the problem might be dealt with by requiring lenders to cease charging borrowers for valuations and to meet the costs of valuations as part of their general overheads. This would leave the borrower free to make whatever arrangements he wished for his own survey or valuation advice. The current practice of lenders requiring borrowers to pay for the valuation commissioned by the lender arose from the situation where this was seen as a fee for professional services which the lender passed directly to an independent surveyor. If the borrower no longer pays, the costs of valuation will still have to be met, either as an administrative charge to the borrower or absorbed into the lender's general administrative costs and recouped as it thought fit. In the latter case new borrowers would be receiving a cross-subsidy at the expense of existing borrowers or depositors. A significant proportion, perhaps 20 per cent, of all valuations are not followed by a completed mortgage transaction and it would be unfair for these costs to be borne either by other borrowers, existing borrowers or depositors. We recognize that the costs have to be borne at some point in the business and that, as we discuss later, it would be unreasonable to prevent lenders charging administration fees to borrowers to cover the costs of an application. It seems unlikely therefore that the change would have any practical benefit.

9.94. The limitations which lenders place on acceptance of valuations carried out earlier on a property are a particular aspect of the selection of valuers which may disadvantage individual borrowers. Again it seems to us impossible to lay down general rules for the circumstances in which lenders should accept such valuations provided for other lenders, or the time within which they should be regarded as valid.

9.95. The best guarantee that lenders will take a reasonable approach to borrowers' requests lies in active competition in this aspect of the lending market. Lenders' approaches to valuation arrangements vary and some are prepared to be a good deal more flexible than others in accepting a borrower's nomination. Borrowers seriously concerned by the issue and not satisfied by the response from their initial choice of lender have the opportunity to seek a competitive mortgage package from another lender. Those who have already commissioned a survey and are concerned about additional costs or who wish an earlier valuation to be accepted may, for example, find some of the lending banks, who place more reliance on the judgment of their local managers, more willing to accommodate them.

## Conclusions on effects of selection on borrowers

9.96. We have identified in paragraph 9.87 the clear advantages of the prudential and other controls exercised by lenders to ensure the quality of the valuation provided, which we recognize require that lenders retain ultimate control over the choice of valuer. We have not found that the present arrangements for selection, combined with the use of fee scales, result in higher prices for valuations for borrowers generally. They do, however, directly disadvantage the minority of borrowers who wish to exercise their own choice of surveyor to provide an HBR or SSY, by requiring them either to pay for a separate valuation as well, or to abandon their initial choice of surveyor. We consider that the benefits that lenders' controls provide for depositors, for borrowers themselves, and for the public interest generally, outweigh the disadvantages that may result for these borrowers. As explained in paragraph 9.87, we have examined various ways in which these disadvantages might be overcome but consider that it would be neither practicable nor desirable to attempt to remove the disadvantages we have identified by regulating lenders' arrangements. We have reached the view that it is in fact not feasible to combine such regulation with the principle of ultimate discretion for the lender.

9.97. We conclude therefore that the lenders' refusal to accept valuations from any competent valuer, the use of panels of selected valuers, and the use of set national scales for charging borrowers and paying valuers are all steps taken by lenders to maintain the complex monopoly situation. We further conclude, however, that for the reasons set out above they are not facts which operate or may be expected to operate against the public interest.

9.98. Our consideration of the issues set out above has, however, suggested specific ways in which lenders could themselves go some way to meet borrowers' interests without prejudicing their prudential control. We suggest that the CML should examine the BSA Circular No 2274 (see paragraph 9.91) and consider reissuing a revised version under its name, to take account of subsequent changes, including advice on prudential safeguards and the introduction of HBRs. It would also be helpful if those lenders which operate panels of valuers were to indicate, in their initial discussions with borrowers, that only certain valuers are acceptable to that individual lender to carry out its valuation and therefore able to provide a joint SSY or HBR and valuation. The borrower who wishes to commission an HBR or SSY can then take this information into account in selecting the surveyor to carry out the work.

## Associated issues

9.99. We considered two related aspects of selection which were drawn to our attention but which did not arise directly in the preceding assessment: first, the importance of reciprocity in the selection of panel valuers and allocation of business to them, and secondly, the problem of conflicts of interest.

### Reciprocity

9.100. The application of reciprocity by some lenders results in some well-qualified valuers failing to get business, but this would only be a matter of general concern if those who received the business were less well qualified and were providing a lower standard of service. The RICS has accepted in discussions with the CML that, other things being equal, the availability of reciprocal business may be used to direct business between equally qualified and competent valuers. There have been criticisms from other surveyors of the work of surveyors used by lenders and in particular that such surveyors have been valuing out of area and were thus ill-informed about the local housing market; these criticisms related primarily to in-house and subsidiary valuers. There is no firm evidence that lenders have been employing less competent or poorly-qualified valuers in order to acquire reciprocal business. Rather the situation appears to be one where the decline in total instructions has led some lenders to be more selective within the pool of qualified and competent valuers.

9.101. We conclude that the use of reciprocity by lenders as a factor in selecting panel valuers is a step taken to maintain the complex monopoly situation, but we further conclude that it is not a fact which operates or may be expected to operate against the public interest.

### Conflicts of interest

9.102. The RICS drew our attention to its concerns over the conflicts of interest that arose from lenders' ability now to combine mortgage lending with other activities, in particular the ownership of estate agencies and numbers of surveyors, and in this context registered its concerns about the position of in-house valuers. There is clearly potential for conflicts of interest to arise. We take the lenders' argument about their overriding interest in a sound valuation. However, the most likely effect that might be expected from pressure on a valuer, from an estate agent wanting to make a sale or a branch manager hoping to make a loan, is a modest shading of a valuation within an acceptable range of opinion rather than a seriously defective estimate. Given the existence of mortgage indemnity insurance, this is unlikely to undermine the lender's interest. It may, however, involve significant extra expense for the borrower and may also harm the vendor's interest. We received evidence of a limited number of cases where valuations appeared to have been influenced. However, this is an extremely difficult area to test, given that valuations are ultimately a matter of judgment, and even significant variations between different valuations of the same property have been regarded in court cases as not necessarily open to challenge. We are not satisfied that this potential conflict of interest has in practice led to major problems which would affect our conclusions. Nor is it apparent that a valuer employed in-house or by a subsidiary is substantially more vulnerable to pressure arising from a conflict of interest within his organization than is a panel valuer to the pressure arising from his reliance on the lender for a steady flow of work.

9.103. The RICS was, however, concerned about pressures on all valuers, including independents, and thought that the potential adverse effects were exacerbated by borrowers' ignorance of the issues and their apparent confusion over the extent to which they could rely for their own purposes on the lenders' valuations. The RICS criticized the lenders' practice of requiring borrowers to pay for the valuation when the mortgage application is made as contributing to borrowers' confusion over the purpose of the valuation report and thus indirectly discouraging them from commissioning their own HBRs or SSYs, which it would be in their interest to obtain.

9.104. The RICS therefore urged two changes to achieve greater transparency and choice for borrowers. First, it suggested that the borrower should not only be informed whether an in-house or independent valuer was to be used by the lender but be given a say in the choice between them. On the suggestion that borrowers should be given a say in the decision on whether an in-house or independent valuer was to be used, we have already set out in paragraph 9.79 our view that lenders should be free to use in-house or subsidiary valuers where they wish to do so. We consider that they should be capable of identifying situations where these valuers might be thought open to such conflicts and taking steps to avoid them. Moreover to establish such a right for borrowers would not be consistent with the principle of lender control which we have earlier recognized.

9.105. Secondly, the RICS also urged that to increase his awareness the borrower should no longer be required to pay for the valuation. The lender should do so and to clarify the position further should no longer disclose the valuation report to the borrower, who would then be left under no misapprehension as to the ownership of the report and encouraged to seek his own professional advice. We have already discussed in paragraph 9.93 the proposal that borrowers should not pay for the valuation and the reasons that persuaded us not to adopt it. Moreover, even if the borrower were no longer to be required to pay for the valuation, we do not think that lenders would wish to 'turn back the clock' by withholding the valuation report from a borrower; or that, if they were to do so, this would in practice lessen the borrower's reliance on the report. Given the tenor of the court decisions referred to earlier (see paragraph 9.14), withholding the report would not appear likely to affect the duty of care thereby established. At the time when reports were not disclosed only a minority of borrowers took out independent advice and, even if the report were not disclosed, the borrower would normally infer that a valuation adequate for mortgage purposes guaranteed that the property was sound, since he would still have to be informed of major defects which affected the size of mortgage or retentions. We would not see merit in arrangements which would deprive borrowers of information they at present receive and influence them towards further expenditure, without clearer evidence that the majority who at present manage without independent advice are suffering harm. We therefore do not regard this as a practicable proposal, nor do we see that it would bring clear benefits for borrowers. However, we think that lenders should continue to make clear in their literature the distinction between their valuation and independent advice and to encourage borrowers to consider the options available by offering a choice of acceptable professionals.

## Scotland

9.106. We have borne in mind throughout our consideration of valuer selection the different legal framework for house purchase in Scotland from that in the rest of the UK and the different arrangements that have developed there for providing mortgages. In particular we noted the widespread use of intermediaries to handle the buying transaction, including the arranging of the mortgage and in the commissioning of the valuation. We concluded, however, that none of these differences affected our findings, which apply to the whole UK.

## Administration charges to borrowers

9.107. In recent years many lenders have begun to levy, or have increased, administration charges to meet part at least of their costs in arranging mortgages. These are sometimes charged separately. The usual practice, however, among building societies is to collect the charge from the borrower with the valuation fee. Information given to borrowers about the composition of the sum collected from them at that stage varies widely. Some lenders, including the two largest, Halifax Building Society and Abbey National, make clear in their literature that an administration fee is charged and state the amount. Others, however, state that there is an administration fee levied but do not disclose its amount. There are a number of lenders who do not disclose the existence of the charge nor its amount. Finally, some lenders make a deduction from the valuation fee passed to external valuers to cover their adminstration costs. Both these last practices leave the borrower under the incorrect impression that the up-front charge he pays is solely for carrying out the valuation.

## Conclusions on administration charges

9.108. We see no grounds for objecting in principle to administration charges. In a competitive situation it is for the lender to decide how to recoup his costs, and if he decides to do so at least in part by up-front charges, this is a factor that the borrower can take into account in selecting his preferred source of mortgage funds. Some lenders suggested that all that concerned the borrower and all that needs therefore to be disclosed to him is the total of up-front charges. We consider, however, that the borrower will attach importance to the nature of the charges. We were told, for example, by one of the largest lenders that while borrowers recognize the need to pay valuation charges, which many still see as a professional fee passed on by the lender, there is greater consumer resistance to paying administration charges; this severely limits the proportion of lenders' costs that can be recouped in this way. This indicates that the borrower should have this information as one of the elements which may affect his final choice of mortgage package. The borrower is more likely to examine critically the reasons for, and the size of, any administration charge levied and to look at the alternatives offered by other lenders particularly since, if the information is made available, he will find that many lenders make no such charge. If the information on the existence and amount of administration charges is not made available to him he is prevented from making these assessments. There is also a danger that a borrower who pays a substantial charge labelled as a valuation fee, of which only part is passed on to the surveyor, may assume that he is getting a fuller report than is in fact the case or may make distorted comparisons with other lenders' valuation fees. There is a further advantage in a separate identification of the level of valuation fee, since it is only through transparency of the fees actually being charged for those professional services that changes in their levels and those of administration charges can be monitored.

9.109. All borrowers need to have clear information on this, as on other aspects of the mortgage package, if they are to make fully informed choices in connection with what is probably the largest single financial commitment undertaken by most individuals. As we have pointed out earlier, we expect competition in the mortgage market to provide the best protection for consumers against any disadvantages of the present valuation arrangements. But if such competition is to work effectively, as we have already noted in paragraph 9.39, the consumer must have full information on the up-front charges he will have to meet and the breakdown of these between valuation and administration charges. Not disclosing such information distorts competition and increases the likelihood that borrowers will not select the best mortgage offer for their needs.

9.110. We find, therefore, that the practice by some lenders (see Appendix 9.1 for the lenders involved) of not disclosing the existence and amount of administration charges levied with the valuation fee is a step taken to exploit the complex monopoly situation and a fact which operates and may be expected to operate against the public interest with the adverse effects set out above in paragraphs 9.108 and 9.109.

9.111. We have not identified any action or omission attributable to the existence of the complex monopoly situation.

154

# Recommendation

9.112. We are required by section 54(3) of the Act to consider what action (if any) should be taken for the purpose of remedying or preventing the adverse effects we have identified and may, if we think fit, make recommendations as to such action.

9.113. We recommend that in order to remedy the adverse effects identified above all lenders should be required, where reference is made to a fee to be paid by the borrower in connection with the provision of a valuation in any promotional material, including that made available in response to initial enquiries from prospective borrowers and in their mortgage application forms, to specify separately and clearly the amount of any fee relating to the acquisition of the valuation and any other administration charge made in connection with this valuation fee. The amount of the valuation fee to be specified should be the fee that would be paid by the lender to an external valuer carrying out the valuation.

9.114. Our recommendation relates only to the need for greater information to be provided in relation to valuation and administration charges. In our discussion of the mortgage lending market in paragraph 9.8 we have drawn attention to some difficulties for borrowers arising from the presentation of some of the information they need. The main problem is that of shortcomings in the APR (see paragraph 9.6). While this rate should in principle provide a clear indication to the borrower of the cost of credit and of the relative competitiveness of different lenders, the way it is currently calculated, taking account of recent court rulings, means that it is no longer useful for that purpose. We suggest that the application to mortgage lending of the Regulations made under the Consumer Credit Act 1974, which set out the rules for calculating APRs, should be reviewed, in particular the arrangements for calculating APR on fixed-rate mortgages and for quoting truncated rates.

9.115. We have concluded above that, with the exception of some lenders' practice of failing to disclose administration charges levied with or within valuation fees, lenders' practices in commissioning and charging for valuations do not operate against the public interest. We have recognized that it is not possible to combine freedom for borrowers to select valuers with the lenders' ultimate responsibility for the valuation, which is in the interests of borrowers, lenders and depositors alike. Control must therefore remain with the lenders. We have, however, drawn attention to the position of borrowers for whom the lack of choice creates difficulties and can lead to extra expense, concerns about whose problems led to the present inquiry. We have made two suggestions in paragraph 9.98 designed to help these borrowers and we hope that lenders will give careful consideration to these.

9.116. We have also pointed out that some lenders are able, for various reasons, to be more flexible in their willingness to meet borrower wishes on selection, and we would expect in a competitive situation that such lenders would find it in their interests to make their attitude on valuations known to such borrowers. It is for the borrower who is concerned about the choice of valuer to shop around to find the lender who offers the best package to meet his needs, taking account of any special concerns he may have about the valuation. We would expect implementation of our recommendations for greater transparency of charges to help him to do so.

D G GOYDER *(Chairman)*

C M BLIGHT

R O DAVIES

D J MORRIS

A ROBINSON

A J NIEDUSZYNSKI *(Secretary)*

4 February 1994

# Glossary

In this report the expressions and abbreviations listed below have the meanings given here. They may have other meanings in other contexts. For the sake of simplicity only, the masculine pronoun has been used throughout the report in referring to borrowers, valuers and other persons. In every case the feminine pronoun would be equally applicable.

| | |
|---|---|
| **Accrued interest** | The amount of interest on a **mortgage** loan which arises in the period between receipt of the amount of the loan by the **borrower** and the date of the first regular interest payment due on it. |
| **Administration charge** | The charge to a **borrower** by a **lender** for the administration of a **mortgage** application. It may include a proportion of the **lender**'s costs in processing the **mortgage valuation**. |
| **APR** | Annual Percentage Rate. The annual cost of financial charges for credit expressed, in a property transaction, as the interest on the total of the **mortgage** loan and certain other charges (including the **valuation fee** and the **administration charge**) but excluding life insurance premiums attached to **endowment mortgages** or **mortgage** protection policy fees attached to **repayment mortgages**. |
| **Arrangement fee** | Fee charged to a **borrower** by a **lender** for arranging a **fixed-rate mortgage**, to meet the costs incurred by a **lender** in securing finance from the wholesale money markets. |
| **Borrower** | A person who borrows money from a **lender** on **mortgage**; includes prospective borrowers. |
| **Broker** | See **intermediary.** |
| **BSA** | Building Societies Association. |
| **BSC** | Building Societies Commission. |
| **Building society** | A mutual institution, regulated under the Building Societies Act 1986, established for the purpose of lending money on the security of freehold or leasehold property; largely financed by money obtained from the members' retail savings accounts; but also able to borrow in the wholesale money markets and to provide other financial and property services. |
| **Centralized lender** | Lending organization which does not operate via a network of branches. |
| **CML** | Council of Mortgage Lenders. |
| **Complex monopoly** | At least 25 per cent of goods or services of any description supplied in the UK (or in a defined part of it) is supplied by or to (in the case of services, by or for) persons or companies who are members of a group (not being an interconnected group of companies) who, whether voluntarily or not, by agreement or otherwise, conduct their respective affairs in such a way as to prevent, restrict or distort competition in connection with the production or supply of such goods or the supply of such services; the goods or services concerned need not necessarily be supplied by or to (or for) every member of such a group. See further paragraph 9.42. |

| | |
|---|---|
| **Conveyancing** | Engaging in the legal process of transferring the ownership of a property from the vendor to the purchaser. |
| **Endowment mortgage** | A **mortgage** loan which will be repaid through the proceeds of a maturing life insurance policy. The **loan** is discharged on the maturity of the policy. The interest (on the full value of the **loan**) is paid at prescribed intervals during the period of the **loan**. |
| **Estate agent** | A person normally acting on behalf of a vendor in the sale of residential property. May also act as an **intermediary**. |
| **First-time buyer** | A **borrower** buying a property for the first time. |
| **Fixed-rate mortgage** | A **mortgage** on which the **nominal interest rate** is fixed for a specified period. |
| **HBR** | See **homebuyer's report.** |
| **Homebuyer's report** | A report on the condition of a property (houses and flats) which a **borrower** may commission from a **surveyor**, normally following guidelines promulgated by the **RICS** and which often includes a **valuation** of the property. The report is similar but less detailed than a **structural survey**. |
| **Indemnity insurance** | See **professional indemnity insurance** and **mortgage indemnity insurance.** |
| **Interest rate** | The proportion of a sum of money that, over a specified period of time, is paid by the **borrower** to the **lender** as the consideration for its **loan**. See **nominal interest rate, APR, fixed-rate mortgage** and **variable rate mortgage**. |
| **Intermediary** | An adviser on the provision of retail **mortgage** products who introduces **borrowers** to **lenders**. He may act independently (in which case he may charge the **borrower** a fee) or he may act on behalf of a **lender**, who may pay him a commission. Usually he will earn commission from the sale of insurance products. |
| **Introducer** | See **intermediary.** |
| **ISVA** | Incorporated Society of Valuers and Auctioneers. |
| **Lender** | An organization which lends money to a **borrower** on a **mortgage** to purchase a property or for the purposes of remortgaging an existing property. |
| **Loan** | See **mortgage.** |
| **Loan:value ratio** | The ratio of **mortgage** debt to the estimated current value of a property. |
| **MIG** | **Mortgage** indemnity guarantee. See **mortgage indemnity insurance.** |
| **MIRAS** | **Mortgage Interest** Relief at Source. The administrative arrangement for implementing **mortgage interest** tax relief. |
| **Mortgage** | A **loan** made under the terms of a legal agreement which includes a pledge of the **borrower**'s ownership of the property to the **lender** as collateral security. |

| | |
|---|---|
| **Mortgage indemnity fee** | See **mortgage indemnity insurance.** |
| **Mortgage indemnity insurance** | Insurance policy covering the **lender** which it may require a **borrower** to pay for on high **loan:value ratio** loans. In the event of the sale of the property not being sufficient to repay the **loan**, the insurance company will pay part or all of the difference. |
| **Mortgage loan** | See **mortgage.** |
| **Mortgage valuation** | See **valuation.** |
| **Negative equity** | The amount by which the **mortgage** on a property exceeds the property's market value. |
| **Nominal interest rate** | The annual amount of **interest** due expressed as a percentage of the **loan** outstanding. |
| **Panel** | A list of **valuer**s approved by a **lender** (but not in its direct employ) for the purposes of undertaking **valuations.** |
| **Professional indemnity insurance** | Insurance paid for by a **valuer** to cover claims for compensation arising from professional negligence. |
| **Rate of interest** | See **interest rate.** |
| **Remortgage** | A **loan** against the security of residential property which the **borrower** already owns. |
| **Repayment mortgage** | Mortgage on which periodic payments (usually monthly) cover **interest** and **loan** repayment. |
| **Repossession** | Action by the **lender** to take ownership and control of a property on which the **borrower** has defaulted on his **mortgage loan** repayments. |
| **RICS** | Royal Institution of Chartered Surveyors. |
| **Scale fee** | A set of charges for **valuation** services related to different house price bands. |
| **Societies** | See **building societies.** |
| **SSY** | See **structural survey.** |
| **Structural survey** | Report commissioned by a **borrower** from a **surveyor** on the condition of a property and which often includes a **valuation** of the property. More detailed than a **homebuyer's report.** |
| **Surveyor** | A member of the **RICS/ISVA** who may undertake **mortgage valuations, HBRs, SSYs** and other survey work. |
| **Transparency** | The degree to which individual charges made by the **lender** are advertised or made known to **borrowers.** |
| **'Up-front' payments** | The initial payment made by a **borrower** prior to completion of the **mortgage** including **valuation fees** and any **administration charge.** |

| | |
|---|---|
| **Valuation** | The assessment of the open market value of a property, used by a **lender** to determine the level of security against which a **mortgage loan** is granted. |
| **Valuation fee** | The fee charged by a **lender** to a **borrower** for the cost of a **valuation**. |
| **Valuer** | A person who undertakes **mortgage valuations**. Most **valuers** are qualified as **surveyors,** and members of the **RICS/ISVA**. |
| **Variable rate mortgage** | **Mortgage loan** on which the **nominal interest rate** may be varied. |

## Conduct of the inquiry

1. On 6 May 1993 the OFT sent the MMC the following reference:

The Director General of Fair Trading, in exercise of his powers under section 47(1) and (2), 49(1) and 50(1) of the Fair Trading Act 1973 ('the Act'), hereby refers to the Monopolies and Mergers Commission the matter of the existence or possible existence of a monopoly situation in relation to the supply in the United Kingdom of services consisting of the lending of money on the security of any residential property.

The Commission shall investigate and report on the question whether a monopoly situation exists in relation to such supply and, if so:

   *(a)* by virtue of which provisions of sections 6 to 8 of the Act that monopoly situation is to be taken to exist;

   *(b)* in favour of what person or persons that monopoly situation exists;

   *(c)* whether any steps (by way of uncompetitive practices or otherwise) are being taken by that person or those persons for the purpose of exploiting or maintaining the monopoly situation and, if so, by what uncompetitive practices or in what other way;

   *(d)* whether any action or omission on the part of that person or those persons is attributable to the existence of the monopoly situation and, if so, what action or omission and in what way it is so attributable; and

   *(e)* whether any facts found by the Commission in pursuance of their investigations under the preceding provisions of this paragraph operate, or may be expected to operate, against the public interest.

The Commission shall, in investigating and reporting upon this reference, limit consideration to agreements and practices relating to the making or procuring of mortgage valuations and the making of charges, including administration or other charges, to borrowers in connection with such valuations.

In this reference:

   'mortgage valuation' means a valuation (whether or not contained in a report or survey) of residential property undertaken in connection with an application for a secured loan.

The Commission shall report on this reference within a period ending on 5 February 1994.

*(Signed)* BRYAN CARSBERG
*Director General of Fair Trading*

6 May 1993

2. The questions in the reference are answered in the following paragraphs of the report:

whether a monopoly situation exists: paragraph 9.40;

   *(a)*   paragraph 9.40;

   *(b)*   paragraph 9.41;

   *(c)*   paragraph 9.110;

*(d)*    paragraph 9.111; and

*(e)*    paragraphs 9.97, 9.101 and 9.110.

3. The composition of the group of members responsible for the inquiry and report is indicated in the list of members in the preface.

4. Notices inviting interested parties to submit evidence to the MMC were placed in: *Daily Mail*, *The Daily Telegraph*, *Estates Gazette* and *Law Society Gazette*.

5. Written and oral evidence was provided by the CML, building societies, banks, other mortgage lenders and by professional bodies representing surveyors, valuers and architects. Evidence was also received from individual firms of surveyors and valuers; from estate agents and their representative association; from regulatory bodies, The Law Society, the Metropolitan and Strathclyde Police Fraud Squads, the Consumers' Association and members of the public.

6. During the course of our inquiry members and staff of the MMC visited Abbey National's Mortgage Centre at Coventry. Members of staff also visited a number of other mortgage lenders.

7. In September 1993 and at various later dates, on the basis of the information made available to us in response to questionnaires, we informed certain building societies, banks and other mortgage lenders of our provisional conclusion that a complex monopoly situation, as defined in section 6(1)*(c)* and (2) of the Fair Trading Act 1973, existed in their favour. All of these parties were advised of the issues which we might have to consider when assessing the effects of the complex monopoly situation on the public interest and were invited to give their views.

8. We held two hearings with the CML and one each with Abbey National, Barclays, C&G, Halifax, Lloyds, Nationwide, TMC and Woolwich. The RICS and the ISVA each attended two hearings; the ISA and a firm of independent surveyors each attended one hearing. We also held hearings in Scotland with representatives of the RICS, the BSA Committee for Scotland, the Royal Incorporation of Architects in Scotland, and The Law Society of Scotland.

9. Some of the evidence we received during our inquiry was of a commercially confidential nature and our report contains only such information as we consider necessary for a proper understanding of our conclusions.

10. We wish to record our appreciation of all those who submitted evidence in writing, responded to our information requests, attended formal hearings or meetings with the MMC or otherwise helped with our inquiry.

APPENDIX 3.1
*(referred to in paragraph 3.5)*

## Numbers of mortgage loans in arrears and residential properties repossessed, 1985 to 1992

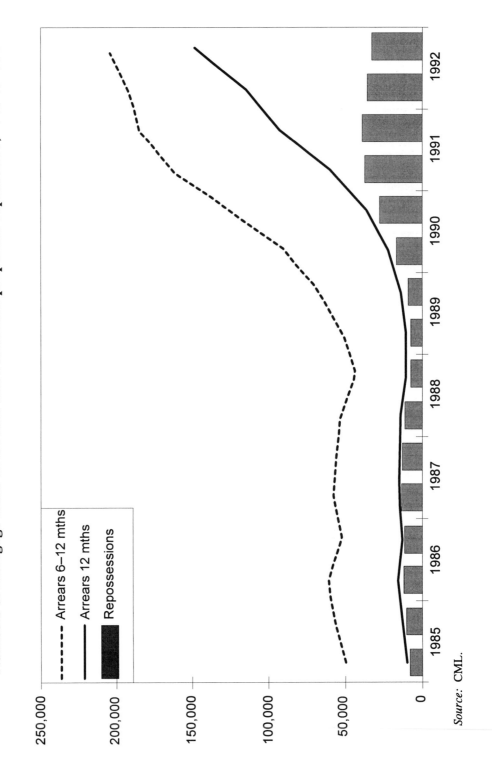

*Source:* CML.

*(referred to in paragraph 3.10)*

# Estate agencies owned by mortgage lenders and others

| *Estate agency* | *No of offices (end of 1992)* | *Change (no of offices) 1991* | *Profit/(loss) £m* | |
|---|---|---|---|---|
| | | | *1991* | *1992* |
| Halifax Property Services | 550 | -30 | [ | |
| Royal Life Estates | 517 | -50 | | |
| Hambro Countrywide | 473 | -7 | | |
| Black Horse Agencies (Lloyds) | 393 | -4 | *Figures* | |
| GA Property Services | 390 | -50 | *omitted.* | |
| Cornerstone (Abbey National) | 355 | -39 | *See note* | |
| Nationwide Estate Agents | 303 | -69 | *on page iv.* | |
| Legal & General | 264 | -26 | | |
| Woolwich Property Services | 257 | -55 | | |
| Connell (Scottish Widows) | 172 | -3 | | ] |
| Total | 3,674 | -333 | (126.1) | (142.4) |

*Source:* A mortgage lender.

# Mergers between building societies, 1980 to 1993

| Year | Acquiring society | Society taken over |
|------|-------------------|--------------------|
| 1980 | Northern Rock | Lancastrian |
|      |  | Walker & Byker Industrial Permanent |
|      | South of England (to form London & South of England) | London Goldhawk |
|      | Grainger (to form Newcastle) | Newcastle upon Tyne |
|      | Anglia | Oakleaf |
|      | City & Metropolitan | Premier Permanent |
|      | Ramsbury | St Martins le Grand Permanent Benefit |
|      | Bradford & Bingley | Spread Eagle |
|      | Peterborough | Stamford |
|      | Britannia | Stoke-on-Trent |
|      | Cheshire | Summers |
|      | North of England | Tyne |
| | | |
| 1981 | Britannia | Alfreton |
|      | Sunderland & Shields | Anchor |
|      | Cheshire | Ashton Stamford |
|      |  | Sandbach |
|      | Dunfermline | Edinburgh & Paisley |
|      | Bradford & Bingley | Hyde |
|      | Market Harborough | Kettering Permanent Benefit |
|      | London & South of England | Kingston |
|      | Midshires | Margam |
|      |  | Pontardulais |
|      | London Grosvenor | Official & General |
|      | Paddington | Peckham Permanent |
|      | Northern Rock | Pioneer |
|      |  | Stockport & County Permanent |
|      | Eastbourne Mutual | Rye Benefit |
|      | Country | Westminster |
|      | Huddersfield & Bradford (to form Yorkshire) | West Yorkshire |
| | | |
| 1982 | Cheshire | Accrington Savings |
|      |  | Leigh Permanent |
|      |  | Wigan |
|      | Darlington | Advance |
|      | Midshires | Banner |
|      |  | Liverpool |
|      | Bridgewater (to form Birmingham & Bridgewater) | Birmingham |
|      | Northern Rock | Blyth & Morpeth |
|      |  | Kilmarnock |
|      |  | Shields & Washington |
|      | Provincial | Burnley |
|      | Metrogas | City & District Permanent |
|      |  | Queen Victoria Street |
|      | Britannia | Denton |
|      |  | Driffield |
|      |  | Over Darwen |
|      |  | Wellington (Somerset) and District |
|      | Eastbourne Mutual | Dorking |
|      | Bradford & Bingley | Hearts of Oak & Enfield |
|      |  | Saddleworth |
|      |  | Swansea Park Permanent |
|      |  | Target |
|      | Skipton | Otley |
|      | Scottish | Strathclyde |
|      | Mid-Sussex | Sydenham |

| Year | Acquiring society | Society taken over |
|------|-------------------|--------------------|
| 1983 | London & South of England (to form Anglia) | Anglia |
|      | Britannia | Colne |
|      |  | Welsh Economic |
|      | Coventry Economic (to form Coventry) | Coventry Provident |
|      | Woolwich | Grangemouth |
|      | Sunderland & Shields | Hadrian |
|      |  | Shields Commercial |
|      | Bradford & Bingley | Horsham |
|      |  | Housing and General |
|      |  | Padiham |
|      |  | Stockport Mersey |
|      |  | United Provinces |
|      | Nottingham | London Commercial |
|      | Northern Rock | Musselburgh |
|      | Ridgeway (to form North Wilts Ridgeway) | North Wilts Equitable |
|      | Hinckley (to form Hinckley and Rugby) | Rugby Provident |
|      | Midshires | Severn |
|      | Mercantile | Tynemouth Victoria |
| 1984 | Scottish | Banffshire |
|      |  | Permanent Scottish |
|      | Leicester | Boston & Skirbeck |
|      | Bradford & Bingley | Clapham Permanent |
|      |  | Dover & Folkestone |
|      |  | Glamorgan |
|      | C&G | Cotswold |
|      | Anglia | Country |
|      | Midshires | Ealing & Acton |
|      | Chatham Reliance | Kent & Canterbury Permanent Benefit |
|      | Woolwich | London Grosvenor |
|      |  | New Cross |
|      | Chelsea | Marble Arch |
| 1985 | Leicester (to form A&L) | Alliance |
|      | Peterborough | Argyle |
|      | Stroud | Bristol Economic |
|      | Sun | British |
|      |  | Economic |
|      |  | Enterprise |
|      |  | Old England |
|      | Principality | Chatham |
|      | Sussex Mutual | Citizens Regency |
|      | Bradford & Bingley | Forresters |
|      |  | Hibernian |
|      |  | Merseyside |
|      | Northern Rock | Hartlepool & District |
|      |  | Manchester Unity of Odd Fellows |
|      |  | South Shields Sun Permanent |
|      | N&P | Haslemere |
|      | Scottish | Huntly |
|      | Woolwich | North Kent |
|      | Sunderland & Shields | South Durham |
|      | C&G | Waltham Abbey |
|      | Ramsbury | Western Counties |
| 1986 | Woolwich | Property Owners |
|      | West of England | Bideford |
|      | Peterborough (to form Norwich & Peterborough) | Norwich |
|      | Midshires | Metrogas |
|      | Midshires (to form Birmingham Midshires) | Birmingham & Bridgwater |
|      | Birmingham Midshires | King Edward |
|      | Middleton (to form Lancastrian) | Tyldesley |
|      | Universal | North East Globe |
|      | Sunderland & Shields (to form North of England) | North of England |
|      | Britannia | Blackheath |
|      | Herne Bay (to form Kent Reliance) | Chatham Reliance |
|      | Sussex County | Mitcham and Metropolian |
|      | Bradford & Bingley | Stanley |

| Year | Acquiring society | Society taken over |
|---|---|---|
| 1987 | West of England | Paddington |
|  | C&G | Cardiff |
|  |  | London Permanent |
|  |  | Colchester |
|  | Bradford & Bingley | Chilterns |
|  | Anglia (to form Nationwide Anglia) | Nationwide |
|  | Nationwide Anglia | City of Derry |
|  | Birmingham Midshires | Harrow |
|  |  | Hemel Hempstead |
|  |  | Civil Service |
|  | Cheshunt | Thrift |
|  | Northern Rock | Wishaw Investment |
|  |  | United Kingdom |
|  | Stroud (to form Stroud & Swindon) | Swindon Permanent |
| 1988 | C&G | Bolton |
|  |  | Essex Equitable |
|  | Cheshunt | Aid to Thrift |
|  | Chelsea | City of London |
|  | Woolwich | Gateway |
|  | West of England | North Wilts Ridgeway |
|  | Heart of England | Rowley Regis |
|  |  | Kidderminster Equitable |
| 1989 | Wessex (to form Portman Wessex) | Portman |
|  | West of England (to form Regency & West of England) | Regency |
|  | Saffron Walden & Essex | Herts & Essex |
|  | C&G | Bury St Edmunds |
| 1990 | Bradford & Bingley | Louth Mablethorpe & Sutton |
|  |  | Sheffield |
|  | C&G | Walthamstow |
|  |  | Peckham |
|  |  | Guardian |
|  |  | Bedford |
|  | Sussex County (to form Southdown) | Eastbourne Mutual |
|  | Regency & West of England (to form Portman) | Portman Wessex |
|  | Stroud & Swindon | Frome Selwood Permanent |
| 1991 | Bristol & West | Cheshnut |
|  | Britannia | Mornington |
|  | C&G | Bedford Crown |
|  |  | Portsmouth |
|  | Bradford & Bingley | Leamington Spa |
|  |  | Hampshire |
|  |  | Hendon |
| 1992 | Yorkshire | The Haywards Heath |
|  | C&G | Mid-Sussex |
|  | Northern Rock | Lancastrian |
|  | Woolwich | Town & Country |
|  | Leeds Permanent | Southdown |
| 1993 | Northern Rock | Surrey |
|  | Bradford & Bingley | Bexhill-on-Sea |
|  | C&G | Heart of England |
|  | Portman | St Pancras |

Total number of mergers completed in 1980 to 1993 (year-end) = 170, of which:

| | |
|---|---|
| Bradford & Bingley | 25 |
| C&G | 16 |
| Northern Rock | 15 |
| Birmingham Midshires | 12 |
| Britannia | <u>10</u> |
| Total | <u>78</u> |

# Overall value of the market for mortgage valuations and other residential valuations, HBRs and SSYs

1. A significant proportion of valuations for mortgage purposes are made either as part of HBRs or SSYs, and we have not found it possible to separate out amounts attributable to valuation from within these. However, we have made an estimate of the overall size of the residential valuation and surveying market, putting together information concerning lenders' own in-house teams, their subsidiary valuation companies, and external surveyors and valuers, most of whom will be included on one or more lender's panels of valuers. Our estimate is based on information received directly from lenders, and on the results of our sample survey of surveyors and valuers. Besides valuations and surveys carried out in anticipation of purchasing residential property, the overall market for residential valuations and surveys includes work in connection with remortgages, probate, capital gains tax, divorce settlements, housing association work, council tax valuations, and investment valuations.

2. The NOP survey (described in Appendix 4.4) provided information on numbers of panel instructions received in the course of a year, the proportions of residential work by value coming from panel instructions, turnover of residential survey and valuation work, and types of instructions received.

3. The overall value of the valuation and survey market is estimated at about £330 million in 1992, as shown in the following table. Apart from the figures in the first row of the table, the other elements of the table are estimated as explained in the following two paragraphs, in order to arrive at the broad orders of magnitude involved.

TABLE 1 **Estimated overall value of mortgage valuations and other valuations/HBR/SSY market, 1992**

*£ million*

|  | *Value of mortgage valuation and other valuations/ HBRs/SSYs carried out by:* | | | |
| --- | --- | --- | --- | --- |
|  | *In-house staff* | *Subs/ panel firms* | *Non-panel firms* | *Total* |
| *In-house/panel work* | | | | |
| –Top seven lenders* | 37 | 53 | - | 90 |
| –Other lenders | 10 | 73 | - | 83 |
| Total in-house/panel work | 47 | 126 | - | 173 |
| Independent commissions | - | 131 | 25 | 156 |
| Total | 47 | 257 | 25 | 329 |

*Source:* MMC estimates based on data from lenders and NOP estimates (grossed).

---

*Excluding Barclays, which uses only external valuers; valuations for Barclays are included in the estimates for independent commissions.

*Note:* Totals may include a small element of double counting, eg where a subsidiary carries out work on behalf of a lender which is not its own parent, and the commission has passed through the accounts of both.

4. Figures for the top seven lenders are derived from those in paragraphs 4.20 to 4.31. The aggregate for other lenders' in-house staff is based on information supplied by lenders. The remaining element of work carried out for other lenders is imputed, by scaling up valuation and survey work carried out for applicants for loans with the top seven, using the implied scaling factor in Table 3.5.

5. In the NOP survey, the results suggested that, on average, just under half of the combined work of those on panels came as a result of panel membership, suggesting, in conjunction with the figures in the top half of the table, the figure of £131 million shown for independent work for this group. On the basis of the figures given in the NOP survey for turnover of non-panel firms, it is estimated that in the industry as a whole, non-panel firms had a turnover of approximately £25 million in 1992.

# RICS/ISVA guidance notes on mortgage valuations

**GUIDANCE NOTES FOR VALUERS ON THE VALUATION AND INSPECTION OF RESIDENTIAL PROPERTY FOR MORTGAGE PURPOSES ON BEHALF OF BUILDING SOCIETIES, BANKS AND OTHER LENDERS.**

These Notes are for the guidance of valuers and apply to inspections carried out on or after 1 June 1992 and, in respect of such inspections, supersede previous published guidance. The Council of Mortgage Lenders and the Building Societies Association were consulted during the production of these notes.

### 1. The Valuer's Roles

1.1 The roles of the Valuer, who must have knowledge of and experience in the valuation of the residential property in the particular locality, are:

1.1.1 to advise the lender as to the open market value (not a forced sale valuation) (see section 4.4) at the date of inspection;

1.1.2 to advise the Lender as to the nature of the property (see section 4) and any factors likely materially to affect its value;

1.1.3 if required by the Lender, to provide an assessment of the estimated current reinstatement cost in its present form (unless otherwise stated) for insurance purposes including garage, outbuildings, site clearance and professional fees, excluding VAT (except on fees).

1.2 The Valuer should not make a recommendation as to the amount or percentage of mortgage advance or as to the length of the mortgage term. Nor is it the Valuer's responsibility to give advice as to the suitability of the property 'for second mortgage purposes'.

### 2. The Valuer's Inspection

**Subject to the Valuer's judgement,** a visual inspection is undertaken of so much of the exterior and interior of the property as is accessible to the Valuer without undue difficulty. Accordingly it is to include all that part of the property which is visible whilst standing at ground level within the boundaries of the site and adjacent public/communal areas and whilst standing at the various floor levels, as follows:

2.1 *Main Building—External*

Roof coverings, chimneys, parapets, gutters, walls, windows, doors, pipes, wood or metalwork, paintwork, damp proof curses, air bricks and ground levels.

2.2 *Main Building—Internal*

2.2.1 Parts not readily accessible or visible are not inspected, and furniture and effects are not moved, nor floor coverings lifted.

2.2.2 Subject to reasonable accessibility, the roof space is inspected only to the extent visible from the access hatch, without entering it.

2.2.3 Ceilings, walls, load bearers and floor surfaces are inspected except where covered or obscured. Readings should be taken with a moisture meter for rising dampness.

2.2.4 Cellars are inspected to the extent that they are reasonably accessible, but under floor voids are *not* inspected.

2.3 *Services*

The Valuer is to identify whether or not there are gas, electricity, central heating, plumbing and drainage services. Testing of services is *not* undertaken.

2.4 *Outbuildings*

Garages and other buildings of substantial permanent construction, and any structure(s) attached to the dwelling are inspected.

2.5 *Site*

The inspection should include the general state of boundaries, structures, drives, paths, retaining wall and the proximity of trees only to the extent that they are likely materially to affect the property's value.

2.6 *Neighbouring properties*

The nature, use and apparent state of repair of neighbouring properties in the immediate vicinity considered only to the extent that they may materially affect the value of the subject property.

**2.7** *Flats, maisonettes or similar units forming part of larger building or group of related buildings*

The above provisions apply, but here 'Main Building' means the building containing the proposed security but not including other building physically attached to it.

**2.7.1** *Main Building—External:* The exterior of the proposed security and sufficient of the remainder of the Main Building to ascertain its general state of repair.

**2.7.2** *Main Building—Internal:* The interior of the proposed security, the communal entrance areas within the Main Building from which the proposed security takes access and the communal area on the floor(s) of the proposed security. The roof space will only be inspected (as defined in paragraph 2.2.2) where access is directly available from within the subject flat.

**2.7.3** *Outbuildings:* Garaging, car parking, other buildings (excluding sports complexes) of permanent construction and any other structures attached to the Main Building or which serve the proposed security.

**■**

### 3. The Valuer's Report

**3.1** Subject to covering the matters referred to in section 1 above, reporting should be confined strictly to answering questions raised by the Lender.

**3.2** If it is suspected that hidden defects exist which could have a material affect on the value of the property, the Valuer should so advise and recommend more extensive investigation by the intending Borrower prior to entering into a legal commitment to purchase or, in the case of a re-mortgage, as a pre-condition of the mortgage advance. It may be appropriate in exceptional circumstances to defer making a valuation until the results of the further investigations are known.

**3.3** If it is not reasonably possible to carry out any substantial part of the inspection (see section 2 above) this should be stated.

**3.4** Any obvious evidence of serious disrepair to the property or obvious potential hazard to it should be reported, as should any other matters likely materially to affect the value.

**3.5** Where the Valuer relies on information provided, this should be indicated in the Report as also should the source of that information.

**3.6** The Lender should be informed of the existence of any apparently recent significant alterations and extensions so as to alert the lender's legal adviser to any enquiries to be made.

**3.7** Where the proposed security is part of a building comprising flats or maisonettes, the Valuer's Report should identify any apparent deficiencies in the management and/or maintenance arrangements observed during the inspection which materially affect the value.

**3.8** Where the apparent sharing of drives, paths, or other areas might affect the value of the subject property, the Valuer should inform the Lender.

**3.9** The form of construction should be reported, and where non-traditional the Valuer should advise accordingly, stating the type of construction and the source of this information if it is not apparent from the inspection.

**3.10** Where the Valuer decides to report a necessity for works to be carried out to a property as a condition of any advance and the Valuer identifies the property as being:

**3.10.1** of architectural or historic interest, or listed as such; or

**3.10.2** in a conservation area; or

**3.10.3** of unusual construction

the Valuer should advise that a person with appropriate specialist knowledge be asked to give advice as to the appropriate works unless, exceptionally, the Valuer believes he/she is competent to give advice which if adopted would not be detrimental to the property's architectural or historic integrity, its future structural condition or conservation of the building fabric.

**3.11** In the case of new properties or conversions where the Valuer is obliged to base the valuation upon drawings and a specification, this fact should be stated in the Report.

**■**

### 4. The Valuation

**4.1** Unless it is made apparent by an express statement in the Report the Valuer will have made the following assumptions and will have been under no duty to have verified these assumptions;

**4.1.1** that vacant possession is provided;

**4.1.2** that planning permission and statutory approvals for the buildings and for their use, including any extensions or alterations, have been obtained;

4.1.3 that no deleterious or hazardous materials or techniques have been used;

4.1.4 that the property is not subject to any unusual or especially onerous restrictions, encumbrances or outgoings and that good title can be shown;

4.1.5 that the property and its value are unaffected by any matters which would be revealed by inspection of the Contaminated Uses Land Register or by a Local Search (or their equivalent in Scotland and Northern Ireland) and replies to the usual enquiries, or by a Statutory Notice and that neither the property, nor its condition, nor its use, nor its intended use, is or will be unlawful;

4.1.6 that an inspection of those parts which have not been inspected or a survey inspection would not reveal material defects or cause the Valuer to alter the valuation materially;

4.1.7 that the property is connected to main services which are available on normal terms;

4.1.8 that sewers, main services and the roads giving access to the property have been adopted;

4.1.9 that in the case of a new property the construction of which has not been completed, the construction will be satisfactorily completed;

4.1.10 that in the case of a newly constructed property, the builder is a registered member of the NHBC or equivalent and has registered the subject property in accordance with the scheme concerned; and

4.1.11 that where the proposed security is part of a building comprising flats or maisonettes, unless instructed or otherwise aware to the contrary, the cost of repairs and maintenance to the building and grounds are shared proportionately between all the flats and maisonettes forming part of the block, and that there are no onerous liabilities outstanding.

4.2 Among the relevant factors to be taken into account in the valuation are:

4.2.1 the tenure of the interest to be offered as security, and if known the terms of any tenancies to which that interest is subject;

4.2.2 the age, type, accommodation, siting, amenities, fixtures and features of the property and other significant environmental factors within the locality; and

4.2.3 the apparent general state of and liability for repair, the construction and apparent major defects; liability to subsidence, flooding, and/or other risks. (Particular care is needed with non-traditional construction).

4.3 Unless otherwise instructed any development value is to be excluded from the open market valuation and the Valuer will not include any element of value attributable to furnishings, removable fittings and sales incentives of any description when arriving at an opinion of the value. Portable and temporary structures are to be excluded also.

4.4 The definition of 'open market value' is the best price at which the sale of an interest in the property might reasonably be expected to have been completed unconditionally for cash consideration at the date of the valuation assuming:

4.4.1 a willing seller;

4.4.2 that, prior to the date of valuation, there had been a reasonable period (having regard to the nature of the property and the state of the market) for the proper marketing of the interest, for the agreement of price and terms and for the completion of the sale;

4.4.3 that the state of the market, level of values and other circumstances were, on any earlier assumed date of exchange of contracts, the same as on the date of valuation; and

4.4.4 that no account is taken of any additional bid by a purchaser with a special interest.

5. **Valuation for Insurance Purposes**

In assessing the current reinstatement cost (see paragraph 1.1.3) the Valuer should have regard to the ABI/BCIS House Rebuilding Cost Index.

6. **The Valuer's Record of Inspection and Valuation**

6.1 The Valuer is advised to make and retain legible notes and to his/her findings and, particularly, the limits of the inspection and the circumstances under which it was carried out.

170

6.2 The Valuer is advised to keep a record of the comparable transactions and/or valuations to which he/she has had regard in arriving at his/her valuation.

## 7. The Variation of Instructions

All mortgage valuations should be in accordance with these Guidance Notes unless variations are notified to the Valuer in writing.

## MODEL CONDITIONS OF ENGAGEMENT BETWEEN THE LENDER AND THE VALUER

1. The Valuer will carry out for the Lender's current fee an inspection of the proposed security, and report, in accordance with the current RICS/ISVA Guidance Notes for Valuers on the valuation and inspection of residential property for mortgage purposes on behalf of building societies, banks and other lenders, subject to any variations specified by the Lender in the issue of instructions.

2. The purpose of the report and valuation for mortgage is to enable the Lending Institution to assess the security offered by the property for the proposed loan and, where applicable, to enable the Directors to fulfil the requirements of Section 13 of the Building Societies Act 1986.

3. The report and valuation will be presented on the lender's prescribed form or other type of form as may be agreed.

4. Before the Valuer proceeds, the Lender will take all reasonable steps to inform the Borrower as to the limitations of the inspection report and valuation, and will suggest that the Borrower commissions a more detailed inspection and Report before entering into a legal commitment.

5. All disputes arising out of this agreement shall be finally settled under English Law and the parties irrevocably submit to the jurisdiction of the English Courts.

# An example of a mortgage valuation, provided by Halifax

| Branch | Manchester | Branch ref. | MRA | Roll No. | A/ |
|---|---|---|---|---|---|
| Names(s) of applicant(s) | | | | Date | 25.5.93 |
| Property address | | | Manchester | Postcode | |

| | House | Bungalow | Converted flat | Purpose-built Flat | Other |
|---|---|---|---|---|---|
| **104** | 0 | 1 X | 2 | 3 | 4 |

If OTHER give details_____

Is a garden included?

| | Yes | No | Communal | | If more than 1 acre |
|---|---|---|---|---|---|
| **108** | 0 X | 1 | 0 | **109** | acres |

| | Semi Detached | Detached | End Terraced | Mid Terraced | Other |
|---|---|---|---|---|---|
| **105** | 0 X | 1 | 2 | 2 | 3 |

If OTHER give details_____

If a FLAT/MAISONETTE, number of storeys in the block **106**     Which floor in the block?

Are there any business premises in the block?

| | | Yes | No |
|---|---|---|---|
| If YES, See General observations | **107** | 1 yes | 0 |

CONVEYANCER to verify details of tenure in his report on title.

| Tenure | | Freehold | Leasehold | Feudal |
|---|---|---|---|---|
| | **115** | 0 | 1 X | 2 |
| Chief rent or feu duty pa | **116** | £ | | p |
| If LEASEHOLD, Term | **117** | | | 999 yrs |
| Terms starts from | **118** | | | 1935 |
| Ground rent pa | | | | |
| Term unexpired | **119** | £ | | p |
| | | | | 941 yrs |

Can Ground rent be increased?

| | | No | Yes | Not known |
|---|---|---|---|---|
| Service charge pa | **120** | 0 | 1 | 0 |
| | | | £ | p |

Construction

Walls     Brick Cavity

Roof     Hipped design with clay tiles

| Approximate age of property | **717** | 58 years |
|---|---|---|

| Estimated road charge liability | **718** | £ Nil |
|---|---|---|

| Approximate gross external floor area | **163** | 78 m² |
|---|---|---|

| Accomodation | Number of Floors | Habitable Rooms | | Bedrooms | | Living Rooms | | Kitchens | Bathrooms | | Separate WCs | | Garages | | Garage Spaces | | Outbuildings |
|---|---|---|---|---|---|---|---|---|---|---|---|---|---|---|---|---|---|
| | 2 | **150** | 6 | **154** | 3 | **151** | 2 | 1 | **152** | 1 | **153** | - | **155** | 2 | **156** | - | - |

Other Rooms     N/A

| | Gas | Electric | Water | Drainage | Central Heating | | None | Full | Part | | | Type | 1 Gas |
|---|---|---|---|---|---|---|---|---|---|---|---|---|---|
| | yes | yes | yes | yes | | **158** | 0 X | 1 | 2 | | **162** | | 2 Electric / 3 Oil / 4 Solid Fuel / 5 Other |

GENERAL OBSERVATIONS (with Essential Repairs numbered)

A semi detached dwelling house located within an area comprising of similar style residential properties, close to the embankment of the M602. The house is conveniently located for all local amenities, with Monton centre approximately ten minutes walk away.

Action on the following items is considered essential:—

1. Dampness is evident to parts of the ground floor walls. Timbers in contact with damp walls may also be affected by underlying rot. Instruct a specialist firm to investigate the cause and full extent of these faults and to carry out appropriate remedial work and allied repairs.

GENERAL OBSERVATIONS (continued)

2. Dated light switches were noted throughout the property. Instruct a competent electrician (preferably NICEIC registered) to make a thorough examination and to carry out any work considered necessary.

The applicant should be advised to obtain his own estimates and reports on the above before a legal commitment to purchase is made.

There is evidence the property has suffered some movement, with misalignment to internal door heads and floor levels. The movement appears longstanding with no evidence of recent or continuing movement.

A number of other items were noted which include repointing to brickwork, replacing the odd broken roofing tile, overhauling of external timbers and extensive repair to garage structures.

The property is of an age where recent research has shown that corrosion to wall ties cannot be completely discounted and it is often not readily apparent. The need for replacement of wall ties may therefore be anticipated as part of a future maintenance programme.

A hissing sound could be heard from the plumbing system. We would recommend that this be checked by a competent plumber. We would also recommend that the gas appliances be tested by a competent CORGI registered fitter in order to confirm their safety.

We were unable to gain access to the loft void area, the access hatch having been sealed. We would, therefore, recommend that access be created and that the timbers within the loft be inspected by a competent roofing contractor.

| | | | | | |
|---|---|---|---|---|---|
| Valuations: Present Condition | **719** | £  39,000 | Date of valuation | **726** | 2 5 0 5 9 3 |
| Valuations:(Essential repairs/ construction completed) | **719** | £  41,000 | Recommended insurance cover (Essential repairs/construction completed) | **720** | £ 58,000 |

I/We* certify that I/we* are not disqualified under Section 13 of the Building Societies Act 1986 from making this report.
I/We* further certify that the property is suitable for a mortgage advance. (*Delete as appropriate.)

This report was carried out by an independent valuer instructed by Halifax Building Society.

| | No | Yes |
|---|---|---|
| | | X |

| | | |
|---|---|---|
| Signed | | |
| Valuer's Name & Qualifications | | |
| Name of Company | Colleys Professional Services | |
| Valuer's Number | | |

Valuer's Charge £

VAT           £_____

Total          £  100.00

| | | | |
|---|---|---|---|
| **716** | **1** | 803649 | 9 |

*Source:* Halifax.

# An example of an HBR, provided by Nationwide

This Report is given on the terms set out in the Conditions of Engagement. Your attention is drawn particularly to Clauses 4,5,6,7 and 8 which define the scope and limits of the Report. The inspection is to provide a Report on the general state of repair of the property described below. It is not a Structural Survey but a Report by a surveyor, who will be a Chartered Surveyor or an Incorporated Valuer, on those matters expressly set out in this Report, together with valuation advice. This Report will not detail defects of no structural significance or of a minor nature.

You are advised to show a copy of this Report to your legal adviser who should find it to be of considerable help.

**Any enquiry concerning this Report must be addressed to the surveyor (see the last page of the Report) and NOT to Nationwide Building Society which does not receive a copy.**

**The information set out below must be read in conjunction with the notes in Appendix 'A' attached which are referred to within the report. These form an integral part of the Report, as do any Other Appendices which may be referred to.**

Key to abbreviations:-

LH—Left Hand ⎫
⎬ when viewed from the front of the property
RH—Right Hand ⎭

1. **Name and Address of Client**

   Mr D A & Mrs B
   　　Clifton Road　Wokingham　Berkshire　RG11

2. **Address of Property Inspected**

   　　　Furlong Crescent　Bishopstone　Aylesbury　Bucks　HP17

3. **Date of Inspection**

   Wednesday 28 April 1993

4. **Weather**

   Dull and overcast following a mixed period of weather including some heavy rain.

5. **Tenure and a note of Tenancies** (if Any)

   Freehold with the benefit of vacant possession assumed.
   No tenancies as premises were vacant at time of inspection.

6. **Personal Community Charge, per person** (oral enquiry only)

   Council Tax now operative from April and you should ascertain the level of charge from the Local Authority.

7. **Description** 　　　　　　　　　　　　　(See notes at the rear of the report)

   a) Detached bungalow originally constructed approximately 1965 although date is not verified.

   b) None. In popular residential village just outside Stone to the west of Aylesbury and with no immediate local facilities but generally good access to major roads.

   c) *Ground Floor* - Entrance hall with inner hallway, living room, kitchen, bathroom (bath, wc wash hand basin), two bedrooms.

   　　*Externally* 　- Attached large garage with workshop. Covered side passageway and gardener's wc. Gardens front and rear.

**STRUCTURE** (See notes at the rear of the report)

**8.   Chimney Stacks, Flashings and Soakers**     (as observed from the ground)

Single flue chimney stack constructed of brickwork with open pot at high level and with lead flashings at the roof line.

Brickwork and pointing considered to be satisfactory although there is some very slight weathering to the pointing. No immediate repairs are considered necessary.

From inspection within roof void face of chimney stack noted to be rendered. I noted no indications of any leaks around the flashings and although there was some slight dampness to the rendering this is to be expected and remedial work is not considered necessary. This dampness will dry out if the flue is used more often and it may be advisable to consider providing a cowl over the top of the external chimney pot.

**9.   Roofs—Exterior**     (See notes at the rear of the report)

Double pitched roof with gable facing the road finished with interlocking concrete pantiles and with roof perimeter finished with softwood barge and fascia boards.

The line of the ridge and the lie of the tiles to the pitches on either side is considered to be satisfactory and the verge pointing is acceptable although some slight attention may be required to the front right hand corner at lower level.

*Roof Spaces*     (See notes at the rear of the report)

Timber framework to the roof of a style and construction typical of the period and considered to be acceptable.

The underside of the tiles is lined with roofing felt which was noted to be in satisfactory condition.

The roof void is insulated and also contains the cold water storage tank.

**10.   Parapets, Parapet Gutters, Valley Gutters**

(See notes at the rear of the report)

None.

## 11. Gutters, Downpipes, Gullies where visible
(See notes at the rear of the report)

Pvc guttering draining to pvc downpipes directly into the ground and the whole appears to be satisfactorily fixed with the exception of a small section to the rear of the garage/workshop where there is evidence of a leak at one of the joints and local attention will be required.

There is also a downpipe to the right hand side at the front of the garage but this serves no guttering, the garage roof appearing to drain onto the wall of the adjacent property. Some making good is likely to be required as far as this aspect is concerned.

Guttering otherwise to the main part of the property appears to be acceptable but as it was not raining at the time of inspection I cannot comment upon the efficiency of the system. You should examine the guttering during some heavy rainfall and should any repairs be identified then they should be dealt with as soon as possible.

## 12. Main Walls
(See notes at the rear of the report)

The main walls are of fair face brickwork and of cavity two leaf construction with the front elevation featuring a reconstituted stone finished as random squared rubble.

There is some general cracking evident to this stonework on the front elevation but cracks in similar positions were not noted internally. I consider that it is likely that these cracks have resulted from movement of the lintel over the window openings on this front elevation, possibly from some slight deflection and, possibly, also from differential thermal expansion of the lintel as against the stonework.

As far as the remainder of the property is concerned I noted no indications of settlement, heave or other structural movement although, of course, I can give no guarantee that such future movement will not occur.

There is some slight deflection of the lintel over the rear left hand bedroom window and this has resulted in a slight drop of the brickwork with cracking along the bedding joint. This is not considered to be a serious defect.

I noted no evidence to suggest that there has been any cavity wall tie failure although I would point out that the ties themselves are set within the cavity and not available for inspection.

## 13. Damp-proof Course and Sub-Floor Ventilation
(See notes at the rear of the report)

A bituminous felt damp-proof course is provided and this is located at low level around the perimeter of the property.

Ideally there should be at least two courses difference between this damp-proof course and the ground level although in the instance of this bungalow this gap is generally one, or one and a half courses.

Tests taken internally with an electric moisture meter, however, showed no readings and I do not consider that there is any immediate necessity for external ground levels to be lowered.

There is no sub-floor ventilation as the ground floor is made of solid construction.

## 14. External Joinery including Window and Door Frames
(See notes at the rear of the report)

Gloss painted softwood external joinery including timberwork to the roof perimeters and to main windows and doors.

There is some general decay to the barge boards and fascia boards both on the front elevation, particular on the right hand side, and also to the rear elevation where the fascia is decayed adjacent to the downpipe to the rear left hand corner.

There is also some substantial decay to the front window of the main living room and there is some softening of the timber to the right hand side of the living room.

The large folding door to the garage was not operative at the time of inspection and some of the timberwork, again at low level, was beginning to decay.

Tests with a moisture meter showed some readings within the timberwork but this is to be expected taking into account the age of the property and the fact that there had, up until recently, been some fairly heavy rainfall.

## 15. Exterior Decorations & Paintwork    (See notes at the rear of the report)

External redecoration will be required, particularly to windows on the rear elevation where there is some substantial dirt and green staining both to windows and to the brickwork at low level.

## INTERNALLY

## 16. Ceilings, Walls and Partitions      (See notes at the rear of the report)

Ceilings are of plasterboard with a flat finish. There are several cracks evident but these are at joints between the boards and are to be expected. These cracks can be dealt with and covered over on redecoration.

Internal walls are of solid construction generally considered to be acceptable.

There is some very light cracking particularly under windows but these considered to be shrinkage cracks possibly helped by the slight lateral pressure exerted by the lintel and frames above.

There is also some very minor cracking above door heads but this is as a result of slight movement from the door frames as and when the doors are closed.

Tiling, where applied, is reasonably satisfactory although there is some slight cracking of tiles around the window in the kitchen.

## 17. Fireplaces, Flues and Chimney Breasts
(See notes at the rear of the report)

There is a feature tiled fireplace within the front reception room and this has the benefit of an open grate.

At the time of inspection the flue was noted to be reasonably clean but nevertheless should you wish to use this fireplace the flue ought to be swept not only to remove any soot that may be there but also to ensure that there are no blockages from birds nests etc.

There was an electric fire in place at the time of inspection and this may be indicative of the fact that this flue has not been used for some time.

As a result the flue, whilst ventilated, would not have been heated and this situation would not have provided any drying conditions for the chimney stack within the roof void.

Tests with the moisture meter at the top of the chimney breast showed no readings or indications of damp penetration.

## 18. Floors
(See notes at the rear of the report)

Solid floor generally carpeted.

There is the benefit of a plastic tiled finish.

I noted no indications of any settlement of the floor slab nor of any problems caused by sulphate attack although floor coverings do inhibit an inspection for this purpose.

## 19. Dampness
(See notes at the rear of the report)

Other than to the chimney stack within the roof void and externally to window frames no readings of any significance were noted internally to the premises. I therefore assume that the property is dry at least in those areas tested.

## 20. Internal Joinery, including Doors, Staircases and Built-in Fitments
(See notes at the rear of the report)

Gloss painted internal joinery with some flush doors provided to openings although there is full length glass fitted to the living room and the inner hallway.

I consider that glass in these positions is potentially dangerous particularly if young children are present and your attention is drawn to this hazard.

Built-in fittings are considered to be acceptable although those to the kitchen are rather basic and commensurate with the original construction and it is likely that you may wish to improve the standard of them.

### 21. Internal Decorations  (see notes at the rear of the report)

Internal decorative condition is slightly tired although clean and tidy and general attention particularly to bring into personal taste will be required with just some making good where there are present markings and fadings on wall surfaces.

Ceilings will need attention where there are the cracks between the boards.

### 22. Cellars and Vaults  (General comments only)

None.

### 23. Woodworm, Dry Rot and other Timber Defects
(See notes at the rear of the report)

I noted no woodworm within the property although there were several areas not available for inspection.

I noted no conditions which I consider to be conducive to the development of dry rot or other timber defects.

### 24. Thermal Insulations  (See notes at the rear of the report)

Some insulation provided by glass fibre quilt laid between the ceilings joists in the roof void and there is some secondary double glazing applied although this is of a fairly basic quality particularly on those windows to the rear and you may well find some difficulty in sliding the glass panes. Improvements in insulation, particularly to the roof void, would be substantially beneficial but it will be essential to couple this with the provision of ventilation to help prevent any condensation occurring. There is evidence of some condensation with some of the stored effects being damp and mould stained.

## SERVICES

### 25. Electricity

Mains electricity is provided, the fittings generally being commensurate with the age of the property.

Whilst I noted no immediately obvious signs which would suggest that a test of the system ought to be made you may well find that it in fact does not quite comply with current regulations and some improvements may well be necessary.

### 26. Gas  (If connected)

No gas connected.

**27. Cold Water, Plumbing and Sanitary Fittings**

Mains cold water is provided and the service was turned off and drained down at the time of inspection.

I was not able to find a stop cock isolating the service within the property and I understand that, in fact, it had been turned off via the external valve.

There should in fact be an internal stop cock, this should be located and overhauled if required. If there is not one present then ideally one should be provided so that the cold water supply can be turned off quickly in an emergency.

The main supply pipe was noted to be of galvanised steel leading to a cement fibre storage tank within the roof void. The down side of the plumbing being in copper with joints generally dry, where seen.

The tank was noted to be reasonably clean.

Sanitary fittings are satisfactory although, again, slightly dated but do require some cleaning as both wc pan and bath were substantially stained.


**28. Hot Water and Heating**                    (See notes at the rear of the report)

Hot water is provided by an immersion heater set in the lagged tank in the airing cupboard off the kitchen.

The lagging requires improving but the tank itself seems to be in satisfactory condition and there is the benefit of off peak electrical supply for the heating provision.

As the supply was drained down at the time of inspection the various appliances could not be tested.

There is no central heating as such to the property although there are a number of electric night storage heaters provided.

There are two radiators located in the bedroom areas and these no doubt run off the domestic hot water system.


**29. Underground Drainage**                    (See notes at the rear of the report)

Foul—Mains drainage is provided. There is access to the underground section of the system to the left hand side of the property. The cover to the chamber was lifted from which it was noted that the channel and chamber itself were clean and free of debris and evidence of any past blockages.

Surface Water—In the absence of any accessible manholes I assume the surface water is to soakaways although this has not been verified.

## GENERAL

### 30. Garage(s) and Outbuilding(s) (See notes at the rear of the report)

There is a substantial garage attached to one side of the property with access to the house being through the garage door.

While this does help to provide some thermal insulation it is a slight untidy means of access.

The garage itself is built of both brickwork and blockwork, with the blockwork along the right hand boundary being slightly damp stained and this is probably due to the lack of an adequate gutter.

The garage is partially covered with an asbestos sheet roof and partially pvc on a timber frame. This latter section towards the front no doubt having been added at a later stage.

The folding doors to the front require some attention, as previously mentioned, and some minor attention also required to the rear personal door where this binds within the frame.

As previously mentioned the guttering to the rear of the garage requires some general attention.

There are no other permanent outbuildings.

### 31. The Site (See notes at the rear of the report)

Rectangular site, the boundaries generally well defined and for the most part laid to lawn with a number of shrubs around the perimeter and it is to be noted that there is a small pond within the front garden.

The rear garden is marked by a hedge lying slightly within the rear boundary between which there is the possibility of a ditch and this should be further investigated.

Other than general maintenance there are no immediate or essential repairs or attention required.

### 32. Building Regulations, Town Planning, Roads, Statutory, Mining, Environmental Matters and Services (See notes at the rear of the report)

I noted no contravention of the Building Regulations which, in my opinion, would have an adverse effect upon the value of the property. I am not aware of any adverse proposals of the Local Authority or other Statutory Bodies in the immediate vicinity although no particular enquiries have been made.

You must nevertheless instruct your solicitors to undertake the usual searches in this regard.

### 33. Summary and Recommendations  (See notes at the rear of the report)

Detached bungalow in a pleasant situation overlooking open fields to the rear and with a south west facing frontage.

The orientation of the property has led to some deterioration particuarly of external timberwork to the front elevation although there are other areas requiring attention.

The garage area has been substantially extended and to the left hand side there is a covered passage way leading to a gardener's wc providing useful additions to the basic accommodation.

The bungalow is very much as originally constructed with original fittings and finishes generally applied.

No serious or substantial repairs are considered likely to be necessary but you will need to overhaul external timberwork including attention to the garage with guttering and to update the internal fittings, paying particular attention to the stop cock and bathroom fittings and you may find it necessary to improve the electrical system. This may fall short on earthing requirements and also on the number of power points which you might find necessary.

### 34. Valuation  (See notes at the rear of the report)

The proposed sale price of £75,500 is considered to be satisfactory.

### 35  Limitations

In making the Report, the following assumptions have been made:

(a) that no deleterious or hazardous materials or techniques have been used and that it is impracticable to comment on the state of any wall ties;
(b) that the property is not subject to any unusual or especially onerous restrictions, encumbrances or outgoings and that good title can be shown;
(c) that the property and its value are unaffected by any matters which would be revealed by a Local Search (or Search in Scotland) and Replies to the Usual Enquiries, or by any Statutory Notice, and that neither the property, nor its condition, nor its use, nor its intended use, is or will be unlawful;
(d) that inspection of those parts which have not been inspected would neither reveal material defects nor cause the Surveyor to alter the valuation materially.
The Surveyor will be under no duty to verify these assumptions.

Signature

Surveyor _____ [ _____ ] _____ FRICS/ARICS (Chartered Surveyor) : FSVA/ASVA (Incorporated Valuer)*

Firm        Nationwide Surveyors

Address     17 Temple Street

            Aylesbury   Bucks   HP20 2RK        Telephone   0296 398296

Dated this   5 May 1993

*Delete as appropriate

The attached report is prepared under the following headings and the related notes must be included as an integral part of it. The report will merely state 'see related notes—Appendix A attached.'

1 **Name and Address of Client**

2 **Address of Property Inspected**

3 **Date of Inspection**

4 **Weather**

5 **Tenure and a note of Tenancies (if any)**

6 **Personal Community Charge, per person**
(oral enquiry only)

7 **Description**
(a) Type and age of Property

(b) Unusual factors regarding location
(ie remote, steep hill, liability to flooding, etc)

(c) Accommodation
(Brief description including garage(s) and outbuilding(s))

**Structure**
(The exterior has been inspected from ground level only)

8 **Chimney Stacks, Flashings and Soakers**
(As observed from the ground)

9 **Roofs-Exterior**
(Roof slopes or flat areas which cannot be seen have been specifically excluded although attention has been drawn to their presence)

**Roof Spaces**
(Internal roof voids have only been inspcted where there are access hatches which are reasonably accessible. If this is not possible the Surveyor has indicated. The presence of thermal insulation will limit the extent of inspection.)

10 **Parapets, Parapet Gutters, Valley Gutters**
(A positive statement is made of unseen areas)

11 **Gutters, Downpipes, Gullies where visible**
(Unless it was raining at the time of inspection it might not be possible to state whether of not the rainwater fittings are watertight or properly aligned)

12 **Main Walls**
(Inspected only from ground level, and the foundations have not been exposed for examination. Mention will be made of any indications of settlement, heave, or structure movement. In the case of timber framed or system built houses it may be impossible to confirm the constructional detail)

13 **Damp-Proof Course and Sub-floor Ventilation**
(Comment will be made as to whether apparent and effective)

14 **External joinery including Window and Door Frames**
(These have been examined as far as possible)

15 **Exterior Decorations and Paintwork**
(The general condition only has been noted)

**Internally**

16 **Ceilings, Walls and Partitions**
(These have been inspected from floor level but furniture and wall hangings have not been moved)

17 **Fireplaces, Flues and Chimney Breasts**
(Normally flues to open fireplaces should be swept prior to occupation. It is not possible to indicate the condition of flues or the presence of the flue liners. No assumption has been made as to the practicality of using the chimneys)

18 **Floors**
(The surface of all floors not covered with fixed coverings has been inspected as far as practicable. Fixed floorboards have not been lifted. NB: Fixed coverings will not be lifted but the Surveyor will, where possible, lift accessible corners sufficiently to identify the nature of the finish beneath. Ths surface areas of solid floor construction will be inspected as for timber floors)

19 **Dampness**
(Damp meter readings have been made where appropriate and possible to the external and internal walls, floors, etc, without moving heavy furniture fixtures and fittings)

20 **Internal Joinery - including Doors, Staircases and built-in Fitments**
(General comment only)

21 **Internal Decorations**
(General comment only: It should be noted that decorations to walls are likely to be marked and faded when pictures and furniture have been removed)

22 **Cellars and Vaults**
(General comments only)

23 **Woodworm, Dry Rot and other Timber Defects**
(Defects revealed by the examination of the structure, but excluding those areas of the building which were covered, unexposed or not readily accessible)

24 **Thermal Insulation**
(An overall comment only is made in connection with visible areas, but it may not be possible to verify information given or the condition of the material)

**Services**
(These have only been inspected visually where they were accessible and tests have not been applied. Standards and adequacy of installations can only be ascertained as a result of a test by an appropriate specialist. A general comment only is made at Nos 25 to 29 inclusive)

25 **Electricity**

26 **Gas**
(If connected)

27 **Cold water, Plumbing and Sanitary Fittings**

28 **Hot Water and Heating**
(Other than balanced flue outlets internal heating appliances normally require a flue liner, but a visual inspection does not always reveal that one has been fitted)

29 **Underground Drainage**
(a) Foul
(b) Surface Water
(Inspection covers have only been raised where visible and possible)

**General**

30 **Garage(s) and Outbuilding(s)**
(Comments are restricted to important defects only. Other buildings, swimming pools, tennis courts, etc are excluded)

31 **The Site**
(General reference is made and only significant defects in boundary fences, walls, retaining walls, paths and drives are reported. Reference to flooding, tree roots, and other potential hazards is included where applicable)

32 **Building Regulations Town Planning, Roads, Statutory, Mining, Environmental Matters and Services**
(General comment where appropriate - no enquiries have been made as these are the responsibility of your legal adviser)

33 **Summary and Recommendations**
(The more important defects are reiterated with a note as to whether these defects are normally found in property of this type and age)

34 **Valuation**
(The surveyor will report on the open market value of the property at the date of inspection, taking into account its repair and condition but excluding carpets, curtains and other sales inducements)

35 **Limitations**

## Survey of surveyors by NOP Corporate and Financial

1. A survey of surveyors was carried out in September 1993 by NOP on behalf of the MMC. A description of the survey and a summary of results of the survey is given below.

### Research objectives

2. The main purpose of the study was to understand the agreements and practices in the making or procuring of mortgage valuations, and the making of charges for such valuations, from the viewpoint of the surveyors and valuers themselves.

3. The key objectives of the research were as follows:

— to collect information on the extent of the market accounted for by surveyors on lenders' approved lists or panels or via a parent or associated company;

— to provide details of fees and fee scales used: independent versus lenders' commissions; and of different types of commissions undertaken; and

— to obtain a measure of the proportion of valuation and surveying business accounted for by residential work.

4. Within this framework, the following subsidiary issues were also covered:

— issues associated with panel membership including rules governing membership of lenders' approved lists/panels, conditions of membership, ease of access to panels, and whether reciprocity is a consideration; and

— proportion of residential business sourced by lenders' panels versus independent commissions.

### Research method

5. A total of 886 interviews were conducted amongst the target market in the UK, ie England, Scotland, Wales and Northern Ireland.

6. All interviewing was conducted by NOP Corporate & Financial's in-house computer-assisted telephone interviewing (CATI) centre.

7. The sample consisted of 'surveyors who currently carry out, or have carried out within the last year, surveys/valuations connected with purchases or prospective purchases or remortgages of residential property'.

8. The views of all types of residential surveyor were established, with the exception of those surveyors and valuers who are directly employed by, and work exclusively for, the parent organization. In these cases, the survey was considered not to be relevant, since all of the business of such companies would be closed to competition and they would not be 'competing' from day to day in the market.

9. This exception aside, the sample was drawn to provide adequate representation of the views of surveyors who fall into each of the different types of organization, ie sole practitioners, partnerships and limited companies. On the assumption that virtually all relevant firms would be included, *The Business Data Base (Yellow Pages)* was used as a sampling frame.

10. All respondents were screened upon initial contact in order to ensure that they carried out business relevant to the survey, and that they were of sufficient seniority to qualify for the sample, and that their company fitted the conditions of the brief, as described above. Given the detailed nature of some of the information being sought during the course of interview, only surveyors and valuers who are currently involved in the provision of valuations and surveys were interviewed.

11. In order to ensure that a representative sample of the relevant catchment of surveyors was achieved, quota controls were imposed on:

— geographical region (eight regions within England, Scotland, Wales and Northern Ireland); and

— company size (small, medium and large as classified by *The Business Data Base*).

12. Quotas were set in accordance with existing proportions within the total *Yellow Pages* classification. A comparison of numbers of interviews obtained with quotas by size of establishment and region is shown in Tables 1 and 2.

TABLE 1  **Number of employees**

|  | Quota | Number interviewed |
|---|---|---|
| 1–5 | 584 | 651 |
| 6–10 | 130 | 145 |
| 11–49 | 75 | 81 |
| 50+ | 11 | 9 |
| Total | 800 | 886 |

*Source:* NOP Survey.

TABLE 2  **Geographical region**

|  | Quota | Number interviewed | % |
|---|---|---|---|
| London | 188 | 166 | 19 |
| South-East | 180 | 212 | 24 |
| South-West | 73 | 86 | 10 |
| Wales | 39 | 51 | 6 |
| Midlands | 127 | 137 | 15 |
| North | 130 | 150 | 17 |
| Scotland | 56 | 75 | 8 |
| Northern Ireland | 7 | 9 | 1 |
| Total | 800 | 886 | 100 |

*Source:* NOP Survey.

13. As can be seen from the above tables, three-quarters of those businesses interviewed had up to five employees and 43 per cent were based in London and the South-East.

14. Interviews were conducted on a 'per establishment' base, that is, only one respondent was contacted per site.

## Project findings

### Market structure

15. A high proportion of surveyors interviewed (86 per cent) represented a sole practice business or were in a partnership. Only one in ten was a limited company. The business breakdown can be seen in Table 3.

185

TABLE 3  **Market structure**

|  | Total sample |
|---|---|
|  | % |
| *Type of business* | |
| Base | (886) |
| Sole practice | 44 |
| Partnership | 42 |
| Limited company | 13 |
| Other | 1 |

*Source:* NOP Survey.

16. Typically the number of branches of the company fell into single figures with nearly six out of ten businesses offering surveying/valuation services having just one branch. However, 29 per cent of limited companies had more than 50 branches. This can be seen in Table 4. Those belonging to a limited company were far more likely to be a subsidiary, part of the same company or group, or otherwise associated with another company than those in a sole practice or partnership. They also had a far larger number of branches on average.

TABLE 4  **Number of branches**

| | | | | per cent |
|---|---|---|---|---|
| | Total sample | Sole practice | Partnership | Limited company |
| Base | (886) | (394) | (370) | (112) |
| 1–5 | 85 | 100 | 87 | 36 |
| 6–10 | 5 | - | 8 | 9 |
| 11–50 | 6 | - | 5 | 26 |
| 50+ | 4 | - | - | 29 |
| Mean | 10.1 | 1.2 | 3.1 | 58.7 |

*Source:* NOP Survey.

17. The total value (in pounds sterling) of valuation and surveying business for both residential and non-residential commissions within the latest year for which they had information available varied enormously. For some companies this value was below £10,000, whilst others peaked at £500,000. However, the average was just over £112,000 per annum. This is detailed in Table 5. As might be expected, the value of valuation and surveying business increased with company size. Partnerships and limited companies had significantly higher average annual turnovers of around £154,000 and £166,000 respectively than sole practitioners at about £60,000.

18. Turnover was higher among panel members at about £116,000 per annum than non-panel members at £97,000 per annum.

19. The geographical region with the highest average value of business was Scotland with 19 per cent of valuation and surveying turnover falling into the £150,000 to £500,000 range, compared against 8 per cent nationally.

20. This reflects a different mix of business sizes with 19 per cent of respondents from Scotland working in offices of more than ten employees as against an average of 9 per cent across the whole of the UK.

TABLE 5   **Total annual valuation and surveying work for residential and non-residential commissions**

|  | % of businesses |
|---|---|
| Up to £10,000 | 10 |
| £10,001–£25,000 | 11 |
| £25,001–£50,000 | 18 |
| £50,001–£100,000 | 18 |
| £100,001–£150,000 | 8 |
| £150,001–£500,001 | 8 |
| £500,000 + | 3 |
| DK/NS | 24 |
|  |  |
| Mean (£) | 112,170 |
| Base | 886 |

*Source:* NOP Survey.

21. Amongst those interviewed, only one in five was associated with another financial institution or property agency. Of those associated, over two-thirds were with estate agents. The tendency to be associated rose with turnover and number of employees.

TABLE 6   **Whether business is a subsidiary, part of the same company or group or associated with other businesses**

|  |  |  | per cent |  |
|---|---|---|---|---|
|  |  | Type of business |  |  |
|  | Total | Sole practice | Partnership | Limited company |
| Not associated | 82 | 92 | 86 | 36 |
| Associated with estate agent | 12 | 6 | 13 | 33 |
| Associated with other companies |  |  |  |  |
| Mortgage lender | 4 | 1 | 1 | 26 |
| Other financial institutions | 3 | 1 | 1 | 18 |
| Other companies | 2 | 2 | 1 | 10 |

Base: 886

*Source:* NOP Survey.

22. Respondents were asked whether they carried out HBRs, full SSYs, including or excluding valuations, and mortgage valuations on their own. Results of their replies are shown in Table 7.

TABLE 7   **Type of residential survey work conducted**

|  |  |  | per cent |  |
|---|---|---|---|---|
|  |  | Type of business |  |  |
|  | Total | Sole practice | Partnership | Limited company |
| Mortgage valuations on their own | 87 | 82 | 82 | 86 |
| HBR | 90 | 87 | 91 | 93 |
| Full SSYs including/ excluding valuations | 83 | 82 | 82 | 93 |

Base: All respondents (886)

*Source:* NOP Survey.

23. Limited companies were more active in all areas than sole practitioners and partnerships. More panel members conducted HBRs (94 per cent) than non-panel members (68 per cent); the same was true for mortgage valuations on their own; 97 per cent of panel members carried these out, compared with only 43 per cent of non-panel members. Activities in all areas rose with turnover.

## Lenders panels and approved lists

### Membership of panels/lists

24. A very high proportion, over 80 per cent, of those interviewed stated that they were on a lender's panel or approved list. This was particularly true amongst partnerships and limited companies, where nine out of ten respondents' companies were on a panel/list.

25. Although two-thirds of surveyors were on up to ten panels or lists the average of 18 per surveyor was a little higher due to 49 respondents (7 per cent) claiming to be on over 50 panels/lists. Those on the most panels/lists tended to be limited companies and those with more employees.

TABLE 8 **Membership of panels**

|  | Numbers of lenders' panels of which a member | Number of lenders' panels regularly do business with |
|---|---|---|
| 1–20 | 63 | 81 |
| 11–20 | 16 | 10 |
| 20+ | 20 | 7 |
| DK/NS | 1 | 3 |
| Average number of panels | 18.4 | 9.2 |

Base: 725

*Source:* NOP Survey.

26. On average, residential work commissioned via a panel/list or via a parent or associated company represented 41 per cent of the total residential work conducted. Those companies on panels or lists, however, receive half their work via this route, on average. Proportions of residential work commissioned via a panel/list tended to rise with turnovers and number of employees.

TABLE 9 **Proportion of residential work commissioned via membership of a panel or list or via a parent or associated company**

|  | Proportion of residential work | per cent 886 respondents |
|---|---|---|
| 0 |  | 19 |
| 1–10 |  | 13 |
| 11–25 | 11 |  |
| 26–50 | 18 |  |
| 51–75 | 17 |  |
| 76–100 | 19 |  |
| DK/NS |  | 5 |
| Mean | 41 |  |

*Source:* NOP Survey.

27. Limited companies (59.8 per cent) and companies with over 50 employees (61.6 per cent) acquired the highest proportion of their residential work from this source.

28. In terms of the actual volume of residential work received via panels/lists, 43 per cent of respondents' companies estimated that they had received 200 or more instructions a year. Table 10 shows that limited companies received the greatest number of instructions (1,034) on average during a year. The figure also increased with turnover from an average of 63 instructions at the bottom end of the scale (companies with an annual turnover of up to £10,000) to 2,860 instructions received by companies with an annual turnover of £550,000 and above.

TABLE 10 **Number of instructions received for residential work via a lenders' panel or approved list within last year**

|  | | | | per cent |
| --- | --- | --- | --- | --- |
|  | Total | Sole practice | Partnership | Limited company |
| 1–50 | 28 | 42 | 22 | 9 |
| 51–200 | 28 | 34 | 28 | 11 |
| 201–500 | 21 | 19 | 23 | 22 |
| 500+ | 22 | 4 | 24 | 58 |
| DK/NS | 2 | 1 | 3 | 1 |
| Mean number of instructions | 448 | 175 | 4,760 | 1,034 |

Base: 725

*Source:* NOP Survey.

29. Residential instructions commissioned via a panel/list and which were mortgage valuations on their own typically represented two-thirds of the total number of instructions received. This tended to be the case for all business types and sizes.

30. The majority of businesses recognized that over the last 12 months the proportion of residential work commissioned via a panel/list had decreased. Only 16 per cent stated that this proportion had increased within the last year. This can be seen in Table 11. Limited companies and surveyors with higher turnovers felt that the proportion of instructions from this source had increased to a greater extent compared with other categories.

TABLE 11 **Proportion of instructions from panels/lists compared with previous 12 months**

|  | Total |
| --- | --- |
| More | 16 |
| Same | 19 |
| Less | 62 |
| DK/NS | 3 |

Base: 725

*Source:* NOP Survey.

## New business leads

31. The majority of surveyors who are on lenders' panels or approved lists said that they do not provide new business instructions to the lenders with whom they are on a panel. In fact, only a quarter of those interviewed said that they provided new business leads to a lender with whom they were on a panel/list. Of these, 80 per cent provided up to ten new contacts in a single year.

32. Even though three-quarters of respondents on panels/lists said that they were not under any obligation to provided new business introductions to the lenders with whom they were on a panel or list, over half said that they were aware of other lenders where the provision of such introductions was expected in order to obtain valuation work.

33. When asked how many lenders with such requirements they were aware of, the average figure quoted was 14.

34. Amongst those surveyors on panels providing new business introductions to lenders (185 respondents in total), only half (89 respondents) considered the provision of new business contacts to be a condition for inclusion on the panels or approved lists on which they featured.

35. However, three-quarters of this latter sub-group (68 respondents) said that they had experienced a reduction in the number of instructions received in the last year as a result of not being able to provide new business introductions.

36. On average up to five instructions from lenders had been lost in the last year due to failure to provide new business leads.

## 'Lost' residential survey work

37. Many surveyors had experienced loss of survey work from clients who were prepared to select them, but were unable to since the surveyor was not included on an appropriate panel or list.

38. Although 16 per cent of surveyors reported no lost work during last year, over 50 per cent said that they had lost up to 25 lender instructions within the same time period.

39. Limited companies appear to be twice as likely to lose business in this way when compared with sole practices. Panel members said that on average they had lost 45 instructions from not being on the appropriate panel, whereas non-panel members said that they had lost, on average, 12 instructions. (See Table 12 for further details on survey work lost due to not being on appropriate panel/list.)

TABLE 12  **Number of instances over last year when survey work lost due to not being on appropriate panel/list**

| | | Type of business | | per cent |
| | Total | Sole practice | Other partnership | Limited company |
| --- | --- | --- | --- | --- |
| None | 16 | 12 | 17 | 29 |
| 1–25 | 53 | 61 | 47 | 46 |
| 26–50 | 15 | 12 | 18 | 15 |
| 51–100 | 6 | 6 | 6 | 4 |
| 101–200 | 3 | 3 | 5 | 1 |
| 200+ | 2 | 2 | 3 | 1 |
| DK/NS | 4 | 4 | 4 | 4 |
| Average instructions lost | 39 | 28 | 45 | 62 |
| Base: | 886 | 394 | 370 | 112 |

*Source:* NOP Survey.

## Fees and fee scales for residential surveying work

40. Amongst those surveyors interviewed, the majority had a set list of charges for independent non-panel mortgage valuation work, one-third did not have a fixed fee whilst just under 10 per cent did not conduct independent mortgage valuation work. The term 'independent' work refers, in this context, to work which is commissioned with surveyors independently and not through membership of a panel or list or via a parent or associated company.

41. The average fees for independent mortgage valuation work are detailed in Table 13.

42. Approximately one-third of surveyors rigidly followed their set fee scale for independent work, whilst the remaining two-thirds used their fee scales as a basis for negotiation of charges. No clear pattern about attitudes to charging relating to business type and size of company emerged.

TABLE 13  **Average fees at particular property value levels**

£

| Property value £ | Average surveyors' charge with set fees policy (inc VAT) | Average surveyors' charge without set fees policy (inc VAT) |
|---|---|---|
| 25,000 | 86 | 88 |
| 50,000 | 99 | 107 |
| 75,000 | 119 | 126 |
| 100,000 | 136 | 151 |

Base: 725

*Source:* NOP Survey.

It can be seen that a slightly higher charge is made on average by surveyors not using their own set fee scale.

43.  Table 14 shows the extent to which quotations varied among those with set fee policies, at particular property values. By comparing the distributions of fee quotations in this table with the averages (means) in Table 13, it can be seen that the distributions are skewed with more than half of the businesses with set fee policies quoting figures significantly below the average.  ·

44.  Amongst those surveyors who were willing to negotiate their fees for residential valuation works, just under two-thirds gave up to a 10 per cent reduction in their costs. Fee reductions of more than 25 per cent were exceptionally rare. This can be seen in Table 15.

TABLE 14  Distribution of charges for those with set fee policy at specified property values

| Fee £ | At property value of £25,000 | | | At property value of £50,000 | | | At property value of £75,000 | | | At property value of £100,000 | | |
|---|---|---|---|---|---|---|---|---|---|---|---|---|
| | Number of surveyors with fees in range | % | Cumulative % | Number of surveyors with fees in range | % | Cumulative % | Number of surveyors with fees in range | % | Cumulative % | Number of surveyors with fees in range | % | Cumulative % |
| Up to 50 | 14 | 2.7 | 2.7 | 1 | 0.2 | 0.2 | - | 0.0 | 0.0 | - | 0.0 | 0.0 |
| 51–75 | 199 | 38.3 | 41.0 | 66 | 12.7 | 12.9 | 17 | 3.3 | 3.3 | 3 | 0.6 | 0.6 |
| 76–80 | 49 | 9.4 | 50.4 | 48 | 9.2 | 22.1 | 11 | 2.1 | 5.4 | - | 0.0 | 0.6 |
| 81–85 | 40 | 7.7 | 58.1 | 61 | 11.7 | 33.8 | 14 | 2.7 | 8.1 | 3 | 0.6 | 1.2 |
| 86–90 | 61 | 11.7 | 69.8 | 110 | 21.2 | 55.0 | 45 | 8.7 | 16.7 | 11 | 2.1 | 3.3 |
| 91–95 | 13 | 2.5 | 72.3 | 39 | 7.5 | 62.5 | 32 | 6.2 | 22.9 | 10 | 1.9 | 5.2 |
| 96–100 | 26 | 5.0 | 77.3 | 59 | 11.3 | 73.8 | 71 | 13.7 | 36.5 | 31 | 6.0 | 11.2 |
| 101–105 | 3 | 0.6 | 77.9 | 12 | 2.3 | 76.2 | 36 | 6.9 | 43.5 | 8 | 1.5 | 12.7 |
| 106–110 | 4 | 0.8 | 78.7 | 13 | 2.5 | 78.7 | 72 | 13.8 | 57.3 | 24 | 4.6 | 17.3 |
| 111–115 | 4 | 0.8 | 79.4 | 6 | 1.2 | 79.8 | 18 | 3.5 | 60.8 | 28 | 5.4 | 22.7 |
| 116–120 | 15 | 2.9 | 82.3 | 27 | 5.2 | 85.0 | 64 | 12.3 | 73.1 | 96 | 18.5 | 41.2 |
| 121–125 | 6 | 1.2 | 83.5 | 11 | 2.1 | 87.1 | 27 | 5.2 | 78.3 | 40 | 7.7 | 48.8 |
| 126–130 | 2 | 0.4 | 83.8 | 4 | 0.8 | 87.9 | 15 | 2.9 | 81.2 | 76 | 14.6 | 63.5 |
| 131–135 | 1 | 0.2 | 84.0 | 2 | 0.4 | 88.3 | 6 | 1.2 | 82.3 | 22 | 4.2 | 67.7 |
| 136–140 | - | 0.0 | 84.0 | 2 | 0.4 | 88.7 | 8 | 1.5 | 83.8 | 20 | 3.8 | 71.5 |
| 141–145 | 2 | 0.4 | 84.4 | 7 | 1.3 | 90.0 | 7 | 1.3 | 85.2 | 24 | 4.6 | 76.2 |
| 146–150 | 2 | 0.4 | 84.8 | 8 | 1.5 | 91.5 | 13 | 2.5 | 87.7 | 25 | 4.8 | 81.0 |
| 151–200 | 8 | 1.5 | 86.3 | 8 | 1.5 | 93.1 | 25 | 4.8 | 92.5 | 53 | 10.2 | 91.2 |
| Over 200 | 8 | 1.5 | 87.9 | 13 | 2.5 | 95.6 | 19 | 3.7 | 96.2 | 29 | 5.6 | 96.7 |
| Not stated | 63 | 12.1 | 100.0 | 23 | 4.4 | 100.0 | 20 | 3.8 | 100.0 | 17 | 3.3 | 100.0 |
| Total | 520 | 100.0 | 100.0 | 520 | 100.0 | 100.0 | 520 | 100.0 | 100.0 | 520 | 100.0 | 100.0 |

*Source:* NOP Survey.

192

## TABLE 15  Average fee reduction

% reduction in valuation work fees

Type of business

| | Total of respondents | Sole practice | Partnership | Limited company |
|---|---|---|---|---|
| 1–10 | 63 | 61 | 63 | 66 |
| 11–20 | 17 | 19 | 18 | 11 |
| 21–25 | 4 | 5 | 4 | 4 |
| 25+ | 2 | 1 | 3 | 2 |
| Increased rather than decreased | 7 | 7 | 6 | 9 |
| DK/NS | 7 | 8 | 6 | 8 |

Base: 337

*Source:* NOP Survey.


## Comparison of fees for independent commission and commissions via panels/lists

45. We collected 1,920 observations of panel-related work and 2,448 observations of independent work, each based on the last three commissions of respondents to the survey. The percentage of surveyors in each fee range is shown in Table 16.

## TABLE 16  Comparison of fees for independent work and via a panel/list

| Fee | % panel/list | % independent |
|---|---|---|
| £1–£75 | 17 | 7 |
| £76–£100 | 30 | 12 |
| £101–£150 | 23 | 12 |
| £151–£200 | 8 | 12 |
| £201–£500 | 20 | 50 |
| £500+ | 2 | 9 |
| Mean | 154 | 313 |
| Base | 1,920 | 2,296 |

*Source:* NOP Survey.

*Note:* Average fees tended to increase with turnover for both panel and independent sources.


## Comparison of lenders' panels/lists commissions versus independent commissions

46. On analysis of the types of commission conducted by surveyors it can be readily seen, as shown in Table 17, that approximately two-thirds of commissions via a panel/list are mortgage valuation on their own compared with only 16 to 19 per cent for independent commissions.

TABLE 17 **Types of commission**

| | Panel/list % | Independent commission % |
|---|---|---|
| House Buyers Report including valuation | 12 | 25 |
| House Buyers Report excluding valuation | * | 5 |
| Flat Buyers Report including valuation | 1 | 3 |
| Flat Buyers Report excluding valuation | * | 1 |
| Full SSY including valuation | 4 | 12 |
| Full SSY excluding valuation | 1 | 15 |
| Mortgage Valuation on its own | 68 | 17 |
| Other valuation | 8 | 13 |
| Other | 5 | 8 |
| Base | 1,985 | 2,448 |

*Source:* NOP Survey.

*Less than 0.5 per cent.

47. Table 18 details the type of commissions conducted by surveyors by property type, both through panel/lists and independent commissions.

TABLE 18 **Comparison of property type—panel commissions verses independent commissions**

| | Via panel/list % | Independent commission % |
|---|---|---|
| Detached house | 28 | 34 |
| Semi-detached house | 28 | 24 |
| Terraced/town house | 25 | 18 |
| Purpose-built flat | 8 | 7 |
| Converted flat/bedsitter | 5 | 4 |
| Other | 7 | 12 |
| Base | 1,983 | 2,448 |

*Source:* NOP Survey.

48. Table 19 shows that work commissioned independently includes a higher proportion of properties in the higher value ranges than panel/list commissioned work.

TABLE 19 **Comparison of property values between independent commissions and work via panels/lists**

Value of property

| | Via panel/list % | Independent commission % |
|---|---|---|
| Up to £25,000 | 3 | 2 |
| £25,00–£150,000 | 32 | 23 |
| £50,001–£75,000 | 29 | 26 |
| £75,001–£100,000 | 14 | 16 |
| More than £100,000 | 22 | 32 |
| Base | 1,927 | 2,296 |

*Source:* NOP Survey.

| Proportion of valuation and surveying which is residential % | Percentage of firms % |
|---|---|
| Up to 25 | 15 |
| 26–50 | 14 |
| 51–75 | 19 |
| 76–90 | 27 |
| 91–100 | 21 |
| DK/NS | 4 |

Base 886

*Source:* NOP Survey.

49. As Table 20 shows, the proportion of valuation and surveying business accounted for by residential work varied considerably across all firms in the survey. The average for the 886 respondents was 67 per cent. The proportion of residential work tended to be lower the larger the total amount of valuation and surveying work carried out by the firm.

50. When analysed by business type the highest proportion of residential survey work occurred within limited companies (71 per cent).

## Summary

51. The main findings of the NOP survey may be summarized as follows:

— 886 surveyors were interviewed, of whom 44 per cent were sole practitioners; 42 per cent were in partnerships and the remaining 13 per cent worked for a limited company.

— Typically, companies averaged ten branches with annual turnovers for valuation and surveying work ranging from under £10,000 to more than £0.5 million.

— Four-fifths of those interviewed belonged to one or more lender's panels or approved lists. Respondents were, on average, members of 18 different panels or lists. However, in the course of the last year, commissions were rarely derived from more than ten different panels or lists.

— Work commissioned via a panel or list typically represented two-fifths of the total residential work conducted; for 'associated'[1] companies, however, this proportion increases to three-fifths.

— On average a company on panels or lists will receive 450 instructions for residential work during a year. The range extended from sole practitioners averaging 175 to limited companies averaging 1,030 per annum. Nearly two-thirds of respondents, however, claimed that the number of instructions received via panels/lists had decreased during the last year.

— 26 per cent of respondents said that they passed on new business leads to lenders with whom they were on a panel.

— 80 per cent of the sample interviewed said that they had lost residential survey work on the grounds of not being included on an appropriate panel or list. The range of responses to this question extended from 86 per cent of sole practitioners down to 67 per cent of limited companies saying that they had lost work on this condition.

— Two-thirds of the work commissioned via a panel or list consisted of mortgage valuations alone.

---

[1]Respondents working for companies which were either a subsidiary, part of the same company or otherwise associated by ownership with an estate agent, a mortgage lender, any other financial institutions or any other company.

195

## Abbey National leaflet on valuation services

### THE FACTS ABOUT VALUATION SERVICES

Whichever mortgage you choose, you and Abbey National will need certain information about the home you want to buy.

### VALUATION FOR MORTGAGE PURPOSES

Before we can lend on a property, at least a Valuation for Mortgage Purposes must be carried out. This valuation report is designed specifically for Abbey National and is required so that we can decide if the property is a suitable security for the loan you require. Although you will receive a copy of the report, you should not rely on it for the purpose of deciding whether or not to purchase the property. The valuation is based on limited inspection and is neither a structural survey nor a condition report. Defects which a more detailed inspection should reveal may not be discovered or commented upon.

You are advised to consider (with your legal advisor) the merits of a more detailed report. Abbey National offers two options.

### 1. REPORT ON CONDITION AND VALUATION
- This report offers you specific advice based on a more detailed inspection than that made for a Valuation for Mortgage Purposes.
- The report gives you general information on the state of repair and condition of the property. However, it will not include areas which are not easily accessible, eg floor covered by fitted carpets or parts of the roof which can't be seen.
- If the valuer notices major defects he will give you an opinion about their cause, and recommend an appropriate course of action.
- The valuer will give you an opinion about the current market value of the property, and the prospects of selling it in the future.
- The report is also used by Abbey National to decide whether your property is suitable security for the loan you want.
- If you have this report you won't have to pay for a Valuation for Mortgage Purposes.
- The conditions of engagement and limitations are given in the report and at the end of this factsheet.

### 2. STRUCTURAL SURVEY REPORT AND VALUATION FOR MORTGAGE PURPOSES

This service consists of two documents:
1. A Structural Survey based on a detailed and lengthy examination of the property.

2. A Valuation for Mortgage Purposes.

The Structural Survey will be a detailed and lengthy examination of the property tailored to your requirements and can include tests of drains and services. It is particularly useful for purchasers of older properties or those proposing extensions or alterations. The fee for a structural survey (which generally will reflect factors such as age, size and type of property) is additional to the fee for the Valuation for Mortgage Purposes and will be agreed between you and the valuer.

Whichever valuation service you choose, it will be carried out by a qualified surveyor/valuer either employed by Abbey National or a firm on its approved panel (at Abbey National's sole discretion).

### RE-INSPECTION
Sometimes Abbey National will retain part or all of a mortgage advance until outstanding works recommended by the valuer are completed.

In this case, the valuer may have to make a re-inspection, to advise Abbey National on whether to release the money. If a re-inspection is necessary for the release of a retention, the valuer will only be concerned with the work specified in the original valuation report.*
It is the applicant's responsibility to ensure that the work has been properly completed, and meets all the correct standards.

The minimum fee for re-inspection is £50.

*This will not apply when the re-inspection is of a newly built property.

## VALUATION SERVICES—WHAT YOU SHOULD EXPECT TO PAY

How much you pay for your valuation depends on the purchase price of the property as well as the type of valuation you want.

| PURCHASE PRICE NOT EXCEEDING* £ | VALUATION FOR MORTGAGE PURPOSES £ | REPORT ON CONDITION AND VALUATION £ |
| --- | --- | --- |
| 50,000 | 140.00 | 260.00 |
| 100,000 | 175.00 | 335.00 |
| 150,000 | 215.00 | 395.00 |
| 200,000 | 250.00 | 450.00 |
| 250,000 | 285.00 | 510.00 |
| 300,000 | 320.00 | 570.00 |
| Over 300,000 | On Application | On Application |

*Where the purchase price is a concessionary or reduced figure for example, when purchasing your council home, the fee will be based on the valuation.

Valuation fees as shown in this Factsheet are payable when you apply for a mortgage and include a mortgage set up fee of £50.

If you decide to have a Structural Survey, Abbey National will collect a fee only for the Valuation for Mortgage Purposes and the valuer will negotiate with you a separate fee for the Structural Survey.

### MORE HELP AND ADVICE?

The Factsheet gives only a brief description of Valuation Services. One of our Abbey National Personal Financial Advisors will talk you through all the different types of valuations at your mortgage interview.

---

### REPORT ON CONDITION & VALUATION

#### CONDITIONS OF ENGAGEMENT AND LIMITATIONS

These terms will apply between you and the Surveyor, Abbey National's responsibility is only to obtain the Report on your behalf.

1. The report gives an opinion on the property and advice generally on condition and marketability.
2. The report is for your own use and also will be used by Abbey National. However, no responsibility will be accepted in relation to other persons seeing the report who rely upon it at their own risk.
3. The surveyor inspects and investigates in whatever way is appropriate and possible in his or her professional judgement, bearing in mind the agreed limitations of the inspection. The rest of these notes explain what this means.
4. To provide an opinion on the condition of the property, the surveyor inspects as much of the surface areas as reasonably possible. The surveyor is not obliged to raise the floorboards and coverings or to inspect or report upon those areas of the property that are covered, unexposed or inaccessible. This would exclude the roof space (if there is no suitable roof hatch) and the outer surfaces of the roof (if they cannot be readily seen). Where practicable ladders will be used to inspect areas up to 10 feet/3 metres above ground level which are otherwise inaccessible.
5. The surveyor advises whether the price for the property is reasonable, taking into account the repair and condition of the property and market conditions generally. The report does not express an opinion about, or advice upon, the condition of the uninspected parts. You should not take it as an implied representation or statement about such parts.
6. The surveyor relies upon information contained in the inspection instruction about tenure, tenancies and other relevant matters. When information is taken from other sources these sources are recorded in the report.
7. The surveyor does not carry out a structural survey or inspect woodwork and other parts of the structure which are covered, unexposed, or inaccessible, and therefore, is unable to report on the condition of any such part of the property.
8. The surveyor only makes visual inspection and does not comment on the adequacy, safety or efficiency of the services (including the heating system). Services and appliances are not tested and the surveyor is not responsible for arranging for tests. The surveyor does not inspect chimney flues and therefore cannot comment on their condition or adequacy.
9. The surveyor does not comment on the compliance or otherwise with Public Utility Company requirements or regulations.
10. Only significant defects to boundary fences, walls, retaining walls, paths and drives will be reported. The surveyor will only comment on trees likely to affect the property.
11. The surveyor relies on personal knowledge to comment on Building Regulations, Town Planning, etc. Your solicitor should subsequently advise of any adverse comments arising from local searches.
12. In relation to purpose-built and converted flats/maisonettes, only the unit is reported upon. General comment will be made on common parts and services.

13. Individual and communal swimming pools, tennis courts, jetties and other shared amenities are excluded from this inspection and report other than in regard to 'Marketability' in Section 39 of the report. Only those main outbuildings (as determined by the surveyor) as detailed in Section 32(a) are included within the scope of this report. Comments on defects will be restricted to those of a significant nature.

14. In making the report, the following assumptions are made:

    (a) that no high alumina cement, concrete or calcium chloride additive or other deleterious material was used in the construction of the property.

    (b) that the property is not subject to any unusual or especially onerous restrictions, encumberances or outgoings and that good title can be shown.

    (c) that the property and its value are unaffected by any matters which would be revealed by a Local Search and Replies to the Usual Enquiries, or by any Statutory Notice and that neither the property, nor its condition, nor its use, nor its intended use, is or will be unlawful.

    (d) that inspection of those parts which have not been inspected would neither reveal significant defects nor cause the surveyor to alter materially the valuation.

## APPENDIX 4.6

*(referred to in paragraphs 4.21, 5.9, 5.14 and 9.40)*

## The practices of selected mortgage lenders with regard to valuations

| Lender | 1 | 2 | 3 | 4 | 5 | 6 | 7 | 8 | 9 | 10 | 11 | 12 | 13 | 14 | 15 | 16 | 17 | 18 | 19 | 20 | 21 |
|---|---|---|---|---|---|---|---|---|---|---|---|---|---|---|---|---|---|---|---|---|---|
| Halifax | Y | Y | Y | Y | Y | N | 36 | 35 | 29 | 0 | Y | Y | Y | Y | Y | Y | Y | Y | Y | N | N |
| Abbey National | Y | Y | Y | Y | Y | Y | 69 | 8 | 23 | 0 | Y | Y | Y | Y | Y | Y | Y | Y | Y | N | N |
| Nationwide | Y | Y | Y | Y | Y | N | 0 | 95 | 5 | 0 | Y | Y | N | Y | N | Y | N | Y | Y | N | N |
| Barclays | Y | Y | Y | Y | N | N | 0 | 0 | 0 | 100 | Y | Y | N | N/A | N/A | N/A | N/A | Y | Y | N | N |
| Woolwich | Y | Y | Y | Y | Y | N | 0 | 86 | 14 | 0 | Y | Y | N | N | N | N | N/A | Y | Y | N | N |
| Leeds | Y | Y | Y | Y | Y | N | 64 | 4 | 32 | 0 | Y | Y | N | N/A | N/A | N/A | N/A | Y | Y | N | N |
| C&G | Y | Y | Y | Y | Y | Y | 37 | 0 | 63 | 0 | Y | Y | N | Y | Y | N | N/A | Y | Y | N | N |
| N&P | Y | Y | N | N | Y | N | 30 | 0 | 70 | 0 | Y | Y | Y | Y | Y | N | N/A | Y | Y | N | N |
| NatWest* | Y | Y | Y | Y | Y | N | 0 | 0 | 99 | 1 | N | Y | N | N/A | N/A | N | N/A | Y | Y | N | N |
| Bank of Scotland:* of which | | | | | | | | | | | | | | | | | | | | | |
| Branches exc Berwick-upon-Tweed | N | N | N | N | N | N | 0 | 0 | 0 | 100 | N | N | N | - | - | - | - | Y | Y | N | N |
| Berwick-upon-Tweed | - | - | N | N | Y | N | 0 | 0 | 100 | 0 | N | Y | N | - | - | - | - | Y | Y | N | N |
| Centrebank | Y | Y | N | N | Y | N | 0 | 0 | 100 | 0 | N | Y | Y | N | N | N | N | Y | Y | N | N |
| A&L | Y | Y | Y | N | Y | Y | 60 | 2 | 38 | 0 | N | Y | Y | Y | Y | Y | N | Y | Y | N | N |
| TSB* | Y | Y | Y | N | Y | N | 0 | 15 | 85 | 0 | Y | Y | Y | N/A | N/A | N/A | N/A | Y | Y | N | N |
| Britannia | Y | Y | Y | N | Y | Y | 0 | 10 | 89 | 1 | Y | Y | Y | Y | Y | Y | Y | Y | Y | N | N |
| Bristol & West | Y | Y | Y | N | Y | Y | 0 | 40 | 60 | 0 | Y | Y | Y | N | N | Y | Y | Y | Y | N | N |
| Lloyds* | N | N | N | N | N | N/A | 0 | 41 | 0 | 59 | Y | Y | Y | N/A | N/A | N/A | N/A | Y | Y | N | N |
| Bank of Ireland Home Mortgages† | Y | Y | Y | N | Y | Y | 1 | 0 | 99 | 0 | Y | Y | Y | Y | Y | Y | N/A | Y | Y | N | N |
| BNP Mortgages† | Y | Y | Y | N | Y | Y | 0 | 0 | 100 | 0 | Y | Y | Y | N/A | N/A | N/A | N/A | Y | Y | N | N |
| Bradford & Bingley | Y | Y | Y | N | Y | Y | 65 | 0 | 34 | 1 | Y | Y | Y | Y | Y | Y | Y | Y | Y | N | N |
| Buckinghamshire | N | Y | Y | N | Y | N | 0 | 0 | - | - | Y | Y | Y | Y | Y | Y | Y | N | Y | N | N |
| Citibank* | N | N | N | N | N | N/A | 0 | 0 | 100 | 0 | N | N | N | N | N | N | N | Y | N | N | N |
| Clydesdale* | N | N | N | N | N | Y | 0 | 0 | 0 | 100 | N | N | N | N | N | N | N | Y | Y | N | N |
| Cumberland | N | N | N | N | Y | Y | 0 | 0 | 100 | 0 | Y | Y | N | N | N | N | N | Y | Y | N | N |
| Dunfermline | N | Y | N | N | Y | Y | 1 | 0 | 98 | 1 | Y | Y | N | N | N | Y | N | Y | Y | N | N |
| First National Bank* | Y | Y | Y | N | Y | Y | 0 | 0 | 100 | 0 | Y | Y | Y | N/A | N/A | N/A | Y | Y | Y | N | N |
| Household Mortgage Corporation† | Y | Y | Y | N | Y | Y | 0 | 0 | 100 | 0 | Y | Y | Y | Y | Y | Y | Y | Y | Y | N | N |
| Kent Reliance | Y | Y | Y | N | Y | Y | 0 | 0 | 99 | 1 | Y | Y | Y | N | N | Y | Y | Y | Y | N | N |
| Mercantile | Y | Y | Y | N | Y | N | 0 | 0 | 90 | 10 | Y | Y | Y | Y | Y | N | N | N | N | N | N |
| Midland* | Y | Y | N/A | N/A | Y | Y | 0 | 0 | 25 | 75 | Y | N | N/A | N | N | N/A | N/A | Y | N | N | N |
| National Home Loans Corporation† | Y | Y | N/A | N/A | Y | Y | No lending | | | | Y | Y | N/A | Y | Y | N/A | Y | Y | Y | N | N |
| Northern Rock | Y | Y | Y | N | Y | N | 20 | 0 | 80 | 0 | Y | Y | Y | Y | Y | Y | Y | Y | Y | N | N |
| Royal Bank of Scotland* | N | N | N | N | Y | N | 0 | 0 | 0 | 100 | N | N | N | N/A | N/A | N/A | N/A | Y | Y | N | N |
| Scottish Building Society | N | N | N | N | N | N | 0 | 0 | 90 | 10 | Y | N | N | N/A | N/A | N/A | N/A | N | N | N | N |
| The Ecology | Y | Y | Y | Y | N | N | 0 | 0 | 100 | 0 | Y | N | Y | N | Y | Y | Y | Y | Y | N | N |
| The Mortgage Corporation† | Y | Y | Y | N | Y | Y | 0 | 0 | 100 | 0 | Y | N | N | N | N | Y | Y | N | N | N | N |
| Tipton & Coseley | Y | Y | Y | N | Y | N | 0 | 0 | 79 | 21 | N | N | N | N/A | N/A | N/A | N/A | Y | Y | N | N |

| | 1 | 2 | 3 | 4 | 5 | 6 | 7 | 8 | 9 | 10 | 11 | 12 | 13 | 14 | 15 | 16 | 17 | 18 | 19 | 20 | 21 |
|---|---|---|---|---|---|---|---|---|---|---|---|---|---|---|---|---|---|---|---|---|---|
| UCB Home Loans Corporation | Y | Y | Y | Y | Y | N | 0 | 0 | 100 | 0 | Y | Y | Y | Y | Y | N | N/A | Y | Y | N | N |
| Ulster Bank* | Y | Y | Y | Y | Y | N | 0 | 0 | 95 | 5 | Y | N | N | N/A | N/A | N/A | N/A | Y | Y | N | N |
| West Bromwich | Y | Y | Y | Y | Y | N | 40 | 0 | 58 | 2 | Y | Y | Y | Y | N | Y | Y | Y | Y | Y | N |
| Yorkshire | Y | Y | N | N | Y | N | 45 | 0 | 54 | 1 | Y | Y | Y | Y | Y | N | N/A | Y | Y | N | N |
| Yorkshire Bank* | N | N | N | N | N | N | Branch managers | | | | Y | Y | Y | N | Y | Y | Y | Y | Y | N | N |

*Source:* Mortgage lenders.

---

*Bank.
†Centralized lender.
N/A=not applicable.
*Note:* The table shows the 15 largest lenders in order of market share and the other lenders in alphabetical order.

*Key:*

*Note:* This key describes the practices in summary form. The full questionnaire to which lenders responded is attached to this appendix and the practices of the seven largest lenders are described more fully in Chapters 4 and 5.

1. Select valuer to provide mortgage valuation.
2. Restrict borrower's ability to choose valuer for mortgage valuation.
3. Restrict borrower's choice of valuer for HBRs to contain a valuation which is acceptable to the lender.
4. Restrict borrower's choice of valuer for SSYs to contain a valuation which is acceptable to the lender.
5. Have own surveyors/panel of surveyors/surveyors regularly used.
6. Size of panel/surveyors regularly used reduced over last five years.
7. Percentage of 1992 valuations carried out in-house.
8. Percentage of 1992 valuations carried out by subsidiary companies.
9. Percentage of 1992 valuations carried out by panel valuers.
10. Percentage of 1992 valuations carried out by non-panel valuers.
11. Set national valuation fee scales for borrowers.
12. Set national valuation fee scales for valuers.
13. Include administration charge in fee collected from borrowers.
14. Administration charge identified.
15. Amount of administration charge identified.
16. Fee contains elements unrelated to mortgage valuation.
17. Borrowers told that fee contains elements unrelated to mortgage valuation.
18. Require borrower to pay a valuation fee.
19. Require borrower to pay a valuation fee at the outset of the proposed transaction.
20. Expect valuers on panel/valuers regularly used to introduce business.
21. Expect valuers who receive instructions to introduce business.

*Sample base:*

(a) 27 largest lenders.

(b) 5 centralized lenders (ie Bank of Ireland Home Mortgages, BNP Mortgages, Household Mortgage Corporation, National Home Loans Corporation and The Mortgage Corporation).

(c) 2 large lenders who are not members of the CML (ie Clydesdale Bank and Yorkshire Bank).

(d) 1 in 10 sample of remaining building society members of the CML, ranked by size.

(e) 1 in 10 sample of other members of the CML, not size related.

*Notes:*

1. BNP Mortgages: only where value of property exceeds £250,000.
1. Royal Bank of Scotland: valuer approved by branch managers. Central operations use a panel.
1,2 TSB: will consider any request from a mortgage applicant who wishes to be involved in the selection process.
2,5. Midland: introduce borrowers to Direct Valuations Ltd who organize a valuation service but are not part of the Midland Group.
2. Clydesdale: surveyor must be fully qualified and acceptable to lender.
2,3,4. Cumberland: professional indemnity cover of £500,000.
2,3,4. Lloyds: suitable qualified surveyor (RICS or ISVA) and conflicts of interest avoided.
2,3,4. Buckinghamshire: taken from the RICS yearbook providing has adequate professional indemnity cover.
3,4. Midland: any suitably qualified surveyor, eg RICS etc.
3,4 West Bromwich: applicant offered a choice of three panel valuers.
3,4 TSB: qualified surveyor with adequate professional indemnity cover.
3,4. NatWest branches: due to small amount of traditional mortgage lending.
4. Yorkshire BS: suitably qualified surveyor with adequate professional indemnity cover and circumstances known by chief valuation surveyor.
5. Royal Bank of Scotland: panel of valuers relates only to the Central operations.
5. The Ecology BS: use qualified surveyor (RICS or ISVA) with professional indemnity cover.
6. Lloyds: uses surveyors in associated company, but does not have a panel.
7. Britannia: expects in-house valuers to complete 50 to 60 per cent of its valuations in 1993 in England and Wales.
7. Yorkshire BS: possible that additional in-house surveyors may be recruited.
7-9 Woolwich: percentages based on 1993.
9. TSB: 100 per cent in Scotland.
9,10 Buckinghamshire: usual local surveyors. 10 per cent of business is local whilst 90 per cent is from a wider area.
10. Bristol & West: small number in remote areas and simultaneous SSYs and mortgage valuations.
11. Midland: Direct Valuations Ltd does.
11,12 Royal Bank of Scotland: national scales used by Central operations. Branches negotiate on an individual basis.
11,12 Ulster Bank: employs a fee scale in its local area of operation.
13. Leeds: 10 per cent of the fee is retained when work carried out by a panel member.
13. Centrebank: 12.5 per cent of the valuation fee is retained.
13. First National Bank, BNP Mortgages, The Ecology BS, The Mortgage Corporation: has an administration fee but seems to be separate from mortgage valuation.
13. Lloyds: surveys carried out by Black Horse Agency (BHA); a commission is retained by the branch.
13. Royal Bank of Scotland: arrangement fees chargeable on fixed interest and high loan:value products.
14,15 N&P: borrower advised at interview.
14,15 Bradford & Bingley: readily available, but cannot be guaranteed given to every applicant.
18. Yorkshire Bank: charge a mortgage establishment fee of £150.
18. Berwick-upon-Tweed: agreed between customer/introducer and surveyor.
18. Clydesdale, NatWest Home Loans, Midland: fee paid to surveyor.
19. TSB: fee collected in advance of valuation for new customers.
20. Lloyds: BHA introduces business.
20. TSB: not a prime factor, may influence the final choice of valuer, subject to borrower's agreement.

# SHORTENED LENDERS QUESTIONNAIRE

*PLEASE CIRCLE THE APPROPRIATE ANSWER*

**Detailed answers can be attached as Annexes**

Q.1.    Does your organisation have its own valuation and surveying arms for the residential property market (in-house and/or staff in associated companies)?    **YES/NO**

If **YES**, please give their names.

. . . . . . . . . . . . . . . . . . . . . . . . . . . . . . . . . . . . . . . . . . . . . . . . . . . . . . . . . .

. . . . . . . . . . . . . . . . . . . . . . . . . . . . . . . . . . . . . . . . . . . . . . . . . . . . . . . . . .

. . . . . . . . . . . . . . . . . . . . . . . . . . . . . . . . . . . . . . . . . . . . . . . . . . . . . . . . . .

Q.2.    Please give the approximate number and value of valuations carried on on your behalf in 1992 (where value is that paid by the borrower).

Number        _____

Value         _____

Q.3.    *(a)*    Please give the number of surveyors you employed in-house (for the purpose of valuations)

_____

*(b)*    Please give the number of surveyors employed in your associated companies (for the purpose of valuations)        _____

Q.4.    What is the approximate proportions of your valuations in 1992 that were carried out by:

your in-house staff                    _____

staff in your associated companies          _____

your panel or surveyors regularly used by you      _____

non-panel                        _____

Q.5.    *(a)*    Have the above proportions changed since the beginning of 1988?    **YES/NO**

*(b)*    Please indicate the broad changes.

. . . . . . . . . . . . . . . . . . . . . . . . . . . . . . . . . . . . . . . . . . . . . . . . . . . . . . . . . .

. . . . . . . . . . . . . . . . . . . . . . . . . . . . . . . . . . . . . . . . . . . . . . . . . . . . . . . . . .

. . . . . . . . . . . . . . . . . . . . . . . . . . . . . . . . . . . . . . . . . . . . . . . . . . . . . . . . . .

*(c)*    You may comment if you wish.

. . . . . . . . . . . . . . . . . . . . . . . . . . . . . . . . . . . . . . . . . . . . . . . . . . . . . . . . . .

. . . . . . . . . . . . . . . . . . . . . . . . . . . . . . . . . . . . . . . . . . . . . . . . . . . . . . . . . .

. . . . . . . . . . . . . . . . . . . . . . . . . . . . . . . . . . . . . . . . . . . . . . . . . . . . . . . . . .

Q.6.   (a)   Are the above proportions likely to change in the immediate future?   **YES/NO**

(b)   Please indicate the likely broad changes.

. . . . . . . . . . . . . . . . . . . . . . . . . . . . . . . . . . . . . . . . . . . . . . . . . . . . . . . .

. . . . . . . . . . . . . . . . . . . . . . . . . . . . . . . . . . . . . . . . . . . . . . . . . . . . . . . .

. . . . . . . . . . . . . . . . . . . . . . . . . . . . . . . . . . . . . . . . . . . . . . . . . . . . . . . .

(c)   You may comment if you wish.

. . . . . . . . . . . . . . . . . . . . . . . . . . . . . . . . . . . . . . . . . . . . . . . . . . . . . . . .

. . . . . . . . . . . . . . . . . . . . . . . . . . . . . . . . . . . . . . . . . . . . . . . . . . . . . . . .

. . . . . . . . . . . . . . . . . . . . . . . . . . . . . . . . . . . . . . . . . . . . . . . . . . . . . . . .

Q.7.   (a)   Do you use a panel of surveyors for valuation work?   **YES/NO**

(b)   If **YES**, give approximate number of firms on your panel   _____

Q.8.   (a)   Do you use a selected group of surveyors for valuation work?   **YES/NO**

(b)   If **YES**, give approximate number of firms you use.

Q.9.   If **NO** to Q.7(a) and Q.8(a), how do you determine the surveyors to carry out your work?

. . . . . . . . . . . . . . . . . . . . . . . . . . . . . . . . . . . . . . . . . . . . . . . . . . . . . . . .

. . . . . . . . . . . . . . . . . . . . . . . . . . . . . . . . . . . . . . . . . . . . . . . . . . . . . . . .

. . . . . . . . . . . . . . . . . . . . . . . . . . . . . . . . . . . . . . . . . . . . . . . . . . . . . . . .

Q.10.   (a)   Do you expect the surveyors on your panel or regularly used by you to introduce business to you?   **YES/NO**

(b)   Do you expect surveyors who receive valuation instructions from you to introduce business to you?   **YES/NO**

Q.11.   Have you reduced the panel or selected group of surveyors you use within the last five years?
**YES/NO**

If **YES**, please explain the criteria used and scale of reduction.

. . . . . . . . . . . . . . . . . . . . . . . . . . . . . . . . . . . . . . . . . . . . . . . . . . . . . . . .

. . . . . . . . . . . . . . . . . . . . . . . . . . . . . . . . . . . . . . . . . . . . . . . . . . . . . . . .

. . . . . . . . . . . . . . . . . . . . . . . . . . . . . . . . . . . . . . . . . . . . . . . . . . . . . . . .

Q.12.   Do you charge borrowers for valuations done?   **YES/NO**

Q.13.   Do you employ a national scale of charges to borrowers?   **YES/NO**

If **NO**, please explain how charges are set?

. . . . . . . . . . . . . . . . . . . . . . . . . . . . . . . . . . . . . . . . . . . . . . . . . . . . . . . .

. . . . . . . . . . . . . . . . . . . . . . . . . . . . . . . . . . . . . . . . . . . . . . . . . . . . . . . .

. . . . . . . . . . . . . . . . . . . . . . . . . . . . . . . . . . . . . . . . . . . . . . . . . . . . . . . .

If **YES**, please provide existing scale showing their start date.

203

Q.14.　Is the charge collected from the borrower the same as the fee paid to the surveyor?
**YES/NO**

If **NO**, please give details of the purpose and size of the deductions.

. . . . . . . . . . . . . . . . . . . . . . . . . . . . . . . . . . . . . . . . . . . . . . . . . . . . . . . . . . . . .

. . . . . . . . . . . . . . . . . . . . . . . . . . . . . . . . . . . . . . . . . . . . . . . . . . . . . . . . . . . . .

. . . . . . . . . . . . . . . . . . . . . . . . . . . . . . . . . . . . . . . . . . . . . . . . . . . . . . . . . . . . .

Q.15.　Do you also collect an administration fee from borrowers at the same time as you collect the valuation charge?　**YES/NO**

If **YES**, please provide existing fees showing their start date.

If **YES**, do these charges cover costs other than those associated with the valuation?

If **NO**, please describe how you cover the costs of handling the mortgage application.

. . . . . . . . . . . . . . . . . . . . . . . . . . . . . . . . . . . . . . . . . . . . . . . . . . . . . . . . . . . . .

. . . . . . . . . . . . . . . . . . . . . . . . . . . . . . . . . . . . . . . . . . . . . . . . . . . . . . . . . . . . .

. . . . . . . . . . . . . . . . . . . . . . . . . . . . . . . . . . . . . . . . . . . . . . . . . . . . . . . . . . . . .

Q.16.　Do you have a national scale of valuation fees paid to surveyors?　**YES/NO**

If **NO**, please explain how fees are determined.

. . . . . . . . . . . . . . . . . . . . . . . . . . . . . . . . . . . . . . . . . . . . . . . . . . . . . . . . . . . . .

. . . . . . . . . . . . . . . . . . . . . . . . . . . . . . . . . . . . . . . . . . . . . . . . . . . . . . . . . . . . .

. . . . . . . . . . . . . . . . . . . . . . . . . . . . . . . . . . . . . . . . . . . . . . . . . . . . . . . . . . . . .

If **YES**, please provide your existing scale showing its start date.

Q.17.　Are the fees paid to surveyors contractually negotiated with the surveyors?　**YES/NO**

If **YES**, please describe the process.

. . . . . . . . . . . . . . . . . . . . . . . . . . . . . . . . . . . . . . . . . . . . . . . . . . . . . . . . . . . . .

. . . . . . . . . . . . . . . . . . . . . . . . . . . . . . . . . . . . . . . . . . . . . . . . . . . . . . . . . . . . .

. . . . . . . . . . . . . . . . . . . . . . . . . . . . . . . . . . . . . . . . . . . . . . . . . . . . . . . . . . . . .

Q.18.　Do you ever refund (in part or in full) valuation fees to borrowers?　**YES/NO**

If **YES**, please explain in what circumstances and whether full or partial.

. . . . . . . . . . . . . . . . . . . . . . . . . . . . . . . . . . . . . . . . . . . . . . . . . . . . . . . . . . . . .

. . . . . . . . . . . . . . . . . . . . . . . . . . . . . . . . . . . . . . . . . . . . . . . . . . . . . . . . . . . . .

. . . . . . . . . . . . . . . . . . . . . . . . . . . . . . . . . . . . . . . . . . . . . . . . . . . . . . . . . . . . .

Q.19.  Do you insist on nominating the particular surveyor to be used for a valuation? **YES/NO**

If **NO**, please explain how the valuer is selected and give the approximate proportion of valuations where you do not insist on nominating the surveyor.

. . . . . . . . . . . . . . . . . . . . . . . . . . . . . . . . . . . . . . . . . . . . . . . . . . . . . . . . . . . . . . . . . .

. . . . . . . . . . . . . . . . . . . . . . . . . . . . . . . . . . . . . . . . . . . . . . . . . . . . . . . . . . . . . . . . . .

. . . . . . . . . . . . . . . . . . . . . . . . . . . . . . . . . . . . . . . . . . . . . . . . . . . . . . . . . . . . . . . . . .

Approximate proportion                                                                    _____

Q.20.  Do you allow the borrower any choice of surveyor when he opts to have a housebuyer report which includes a mortgage valuation acceptable to you?          **YES/NO**

If **YES**, please describe the circumstances under which you allow the borrower a choice and state how frequently you allow such a choice.

. . . . . . . . . . . . . . . . . . . . . . . . . . . . . . . . . . . . . . . . . . . . . . . . . . . . . . . . . . . . . . . . . .

. . . . . . . . . . . . . . . . . . . . . . . . . . . . . . . . . . . . . . . . . . . . . . . . . . . . . . . . . . . . . . . . . .

. . . . . . . . . . . . . . . . . . . . . . . . . . . . . . . . . . . . . . . . . . . . . . . . . . . . . . . . . . . . . . . . . .

Q.21.  Do you allow the borrower any choice of surveyor when he opts to have a structural survey including a mortgage valuation acceptable to you?          **YES/NO**

If **YES**, please describe the circumstances under which you allow the borrower a choice and state how frequently you allow such a choice.

. . . . . . . . . . . . . . . . . . . . . . . . . . . . . . . . . . . . . . . . . . . . . . . . . . . . . . . . . . . . . . . . . .

. . . . . . . . . . . . . . . . . . . . . . . . . . . . . . . . . . . . . . . . . . . . . . . . . . . . . . . . . . . . . . . . . .

. . . . . . . . . . . . . . . . . . . . . . . . . . . . . . . . . . . . . . . . . . . . . . . . . . . . . . . . . . . . . . . . . .

Q.22.  Do you ever accept a valuation contained in a housebuyer's report or structural survey which was carried out *before* the borrower approached you?          **YES/NO**

If **YES**, please describe the circumstances under which you would accept such a valuation and state how frequently you accept them.

. . . . . . . . . . . . . . . . . . . . . . . . . . . . . . . . . . . . . . . . . . . . . . . . . . . . . . . . . . . . . . . . . .

. . . . . . . . . . . . . . . . . . . . . . . . . . . . . . . . . . . . . . . . . . . . . . . . . . . . . . . . . . . . . . . . . .

. . . . . . . . . . . . . . . . . . . . . . . . . . . . . . . . . . . . . . . . . . . . . . . . . . . . . . . . . . . . . . . . . .

Q.23.  Do you ever accept a valuation contained in a housebuyer's report or structural survey where the borrower has decided upon the surveyor he/she wants to use but where the valuation has *not* been carried out before the borrower approached you?          **YES/NO**

If **YES**, please describe the circumstances under which you would accept such a valuation and state how frequently you accept them.

. . . . . . . . . . . . . . . . . . . . . . . . . . . . . . . . . . . . . . . . . . . . . . . . . . . . . . . . . . . . . . . . . .

. . . . . . . . . . . . . . . . . . . . . . . . . . . . . . . . . . . . . . . . . . . . . . . . . . . . . . . . . . . . . . . . . .

. . . . . . . . . . . . . . . . . . . . . . . . . . . . . . . . . . . . . . . . . . . . . . . . . . . . . . . . . . . . . . . . . .

Q.24. When considering a mortgage application do you make the borrower aware of any relationship between you and the surveyor that it is proposed is used for the mortgage valuation or more detailed survey? **YES/NO**

If **YES**, please describe how.

Q.25. Do you reveal to the borrower when an in-house surveyor is to be used and when a panel surveyor is to be used? **YES/NO**

Q.26. When considering a mortgage application do you make the borrower aware of the options of a housebuyer report or structural survey? **YES/NO**

If **YES**, please describe (you may enclose any relevant literature).

. . . . . . . . . . . . . . . . . . . . . . . . . . . . . . . . . . . . . . . . . . . . . . . . . . . . . . . . . . . . . . . . . . .

. . . . . . . . . . . . . . . . . . . . . . . . . . . . . . . . . . . . . . . . . . . . . . . . . . . . . . . . . . . . . . . . . . .

. . . . . . . . . . . . . . . . . . . . . . . . . . . . . . . . . . . . . . . . . . . . . . . . . . . . . . . . . . . . . . . . . . .

Q.27. When considering a mortgage application do you fully disclose to the borrower the nature and amount of any valuation charge and administration fee? **YES/NO**

If **YES**, please describe (you may enclose any relevant literature).

. . . . . . . . . . . . . . . . . . . . . . . . . . . . . . . . . . . . . . . . . . . . . . . . . . . . . . . . . . . . . . . . . . .

. . . . . . . . . . . . . . . . . . . . . . . . . . . . . . . . . . . . . . . . . . . . . . . . . . . . . . . . . . . . . . . . . . .

. . . . . . . . . . . . . . . . . . . . . . . . . . . . . . . . . . . . . . . . . . . . . . . . . . . . . . . . . . . . . . . . . . .

Q.28. Are there any other observations relevant to this inquiry on valuation services that you would like to offer?

. . . . . . . . . . . . . . . . . . . . . . . . . . . . . . . . . . . . . . . . . . . . . . . . . . . . . . . . . . . . . . . . . . .

. . . . . . . . . . . . . . . . . . . . . . . . . . . . . . . . . . . . . . . . . . . . . . . . . . . . . . . . . . . . . . . . . . .

. . . . . . . . . . . . . . . . . . . . . . . . . . . . . . . . . . . . . . . . . . . . . . . . . . . . . . . . . . . . . . . . . . .

*(referred to in paragraphs 4.21, 5.9 and 5.14)*

## The practices of other mortgage lenders with regard to valuations

|  | | | | | | Question | | | | | | | |
|---|---|---|---|---|---|---|---|---|---|---|---|---|---|
| Lender | 1 | 2 | 3 | 4 | 5 | 6 | 7 | 8 | 9 | 10 | 11 | 12 | 13 |
| AIB Bank plc | Y | N | N/A | Y | N | | Y | N | Y | N | N | N/A | Y |
| Allchurches Mortgage Company Ltd | Y | N | N/A | Y | Y | | Y | Y | Y | N | N | N/A | Y |
| Allied Dunbar Mortgages Ltd | Y | N | N/A | Y | Y | | Y | Y | Y | Y | Y | N | Y |
| Associates Capital Corporation Ltd | Y | N | N/A | Y | N | | N | N/A | N/A | Y | Y | N | Y |
| Banque Paribas (London Branch) | Y | N | N/A | Y | Y | | Y | Y | Y | N | N | N/A | Y |
| Barnsley Building Society | Y | Y | Y | Y | Y | | Y | Y | Y | Y | N | N | Y |
| Bath Investment & Building Society | Y | N | N/A | Y | Y | | Y | Y | Y | Y | N | Y | Y |
| Beverley Building Society | Y | N | N/A | N | Y | | Y | Y | Y | N | N | N/A | Y |
| Birmingham Midshires Building Society | Y | Y | Y | Y | Y | | Y | Y | Y | Y | N | Y | Y |
| Cambridge Building Society | Y | N | N/A | Y | Y | | Y | Y | Y | N | N | N/A | Y |
| Capital Home Loans Ltd | Y | N | N/A | Y | - | | Y | Y | Y | N | Y | N | Y |
| Chelsea Building Society | Y | Y | Y | Y | Y | | Y | Y | Y | Y | N | N | Y |
| Chesham Building Society | Y | N | N/A | N | Y | | Y | Y | N | N | N | N/A | N |
| Cheshire Building Society | Y | Y | Y | Y | N | | Y | Y | Y | Y | Y | N | Y |
| The Chorley & District Building Society | Y | N | N/A | Y | Y | | Y | Y | Y | Y | Y | N | Y |
| City & Metropolitan Building Society | Y | N | N/A | Y | Y | | Y | Y | Y | N | Y | Y | Y |
| Clay Cross Benefit Building Society | Y | N | N/A | Y | N | | Y | Y | Y | Y | N | N | Y |
| The Colonial Mutual Life Assurance Society Ltd | Y | N | N/A | N | Y | | Y | Y | Y | N | N | N/A | Y |
| Confederation Bank Ltd | Y | N | N/A | Y | Y | | Y | Y | Y | Y | Y | Y | Y |
| Co-operative Insurance Society Ltd | Y | N | N/A | Y | N | | Y | Y | Y | N | N | N/A | Y |
| Coutts Finance Co | Y | N | N/A | Y | Y | | Y | N | Y | N | Y | Y | Y |
| Coventry Building Society | Y | N | N/A | Y | Y | | Y | Y | Y | Y | Y | N | Y |
| Credit Agricole Personal Finance plc | Y | N | N/A | Y | Y | | Y | Y | Y | N | N | N/A | Y |
| Credit Lyonnais | Y | N | N/A | Y | N | | Y | Y | Y | Y | N | N | Y |
| Darlington Building Society | Y | Y | Y | N | Y | | Y | Y | N | Y | N | Y | N |
| Derbyshire Building Society | Y | Y | Y | Y | - | | Y | Y | Y | Y | N | Y | Y |
| Dudley Building Society | Y | N | N/A | Y | Y | | Y | Y | Y | Y | N | Y | Y |
| Framework Homeloans | Y | N | N/A | Y | N | | Y | Y | Y | N | N | N/A | Y |
| Furness Building Society | Y | Y | - | Y | Y | | Y | Y | Y | N | Y | Y | Y |
| Gainsborough Building Society | Y | N | N/A | N | Y | | Y | Y | Y | N | N | N/A | Y |
| Greenwich Building Society | Y | N | N/A | Y | Y | | Y | Y | Y | N | Y | Y | Y |
| Hanley Economic Building Society | Y | N | N/A | Y | N | | Y | Y | Y | N | N | N/A | Y |
| Harpenden Building Society | Y | N | N/A | Y | Y | | Y | Y | Y | Y | Y | Y | Y |
| HFC Bank plc | Y | N | N/A | Y | N | | Y | Y | Y | N | N | Y | Y |
| Hinckley & Rugby Building Society | Y | N | N/A | Y | Y | | Y | Y | Y | N | Y | N | Y |
| Holmesdale Building Society | Y | N | N/A | Y | Y | | Y | Y | Y | Y | Y | Y | Y |
| Ilkeston Permanent Building Society | Y | Y | Y | N | Y | | Y | Y | Y | N | Y | N | N |
| Ipswich Building Society | Y | N | N/A | Y | N | | Y | Y | Y | N | Y | N | Y |
| Irish Permanent Building Society | Y | N | N/A | Y | N | | Y | Y | Y | N | N | N/A | Y |
| Kleinwort Benson Private Bank | Y | N | N/A | Y | N | | Y | Y | Y | N | N | N/A | Y |
| Lambeth Building Society | Y | N | N/A | N | Y | | Y | Y | Y | N | Y | Y | Y |
| Leeds & Holbeck Building Society | Y | Y | Y | Y | Y | | Y | Y | Y | N | N | Y | Y |
| Leek United Building Society | Y | N | N/A | Y | Y | | Y | Y | N | N | Y | N | N |
| Legal & General Mortgage Services Ltd | Y | N | N/A | Y | N | | Y | Y | Y | N | N | N/A | Y |
| Lloyds Bowmaker Finance Ltd | Y | Y | Y | Y | Y | | N | N/A | N/A | N | N | N/A | Y |
| London & Manchester (Mortgages) Ltd | Y | N | N/A | Y | N | | Y | Y | Y | N | N | N/A | Y |
| Londonderry Provident Building Society | Y | N | N/A | N | Y | | Y | Y | Y | Y | N | N | Y |
| Loughborough Building Society | Y | N | N/A | Y | Y | | Y | Y | Y | Y | N | N | Y |
| Manchester Building Society | Y | N | N/A | Y | - | | Y | Y | Y | Y | Y | Y | Y |

| Lender | 1 | 2 | 3 | 4 | 5 | 6 | 7 | 8 | 9 | 10 | 11 | 12 | 13 |
|---|---|---|---|---|---|---|---|---|---|---|---|---|---|
| The Mansfield Building Society | Y | N | N/A | Y | Y | | Y | Y | Y | N | N | N/A | Y |
| Market Harborough Building Society | Y | N | N/A | - | Y | | Y | Y | Y | N | Y | N | N |
| Marsden Building Society | Y | Y | Y | Y | - | | Y | Y | Y | Y | Y | N | Y |
| Melton Mowbray Building Society | Y | N | N/A | Y | Y | | Y | Y | Y | N | Y | N | Y |
| Monmouthshire Building Society | Y | N | N/A | N | Y | | Y | Y | Y | Y | N | N | Y |
| The Mortgage Business plc | Y | N | N/A | Y | N | | Y | Y | Y | N | Y | N | Y |
| Mortgage Services Ltd | Y | Y | N | Y | - | | Y | Y | Y | - | - | - | Y |
| Mortgage Trust Ltd | Y | N | N | Y | N | | Y | Y | Y | Y | Y | Y | Y |
| National Counties Building Society | Y | Y | Y | Y | N | | Y | Y | Y | N | N | N/A | Y |
| National Mutual Life Assurance Society | Y | N | N/A | N | Y | | Y | Y | Y | N | N | N/A | Y |
| Newbury Building Society | Y | Y | Y | Y | Y | | Y | Y | Y | N | Y | Y | Y |
| Newcastle Building Society | Y | Y | Y | Y | Y | | Y | Y | Y | N | Y | Y | Y |
| North of England Building Society | Y | Y | Y | Y | Y | | Y | Y | Y | N | Y | Y | Y |
| Norwich & Peterborough Building Society | Y | Y | Y | Y | N | | Y | Y | Y | Y | N | Y | Y |
| Nottingham Building Society | Y | Y | N | Y | N | | Y | Y | Y | Y | Y | N | Y |
| Nottingham Imperial Building Society | Y | Y | Y | N | N | | Y | Y | N | N | Y | N | N |
| Penrith Building Society | Y | N | N/A | N | Y | | Y | Y | N | N | N | N/A | N |
| Portman Building Society | Y | Y | Y | Y | Y | | Y | Y | Y | N | Y | Y | Y |
| Principality Building Society | Y | Y | Y | Y | N | | Y | Y | Y | Y | N | N | Y |
| Progressive Building Society | Y | Y | N | Y | Y | | Y | Y | N | Y | N | N | N |
| Royal London Homebuy Ltd | Y | N | N/A | Y | Y | | Y | Y | Y | N | N | N/A | Y |
| Saffron Walden Herts & Essex Building Society | Y | N | N/A | Y | N | | Y | Y | Y | N | N | N/A | Y |
| Scarborough Building Society | Y | N | N/A | Y | Y | | Y | Y | Y | N | Y | Y | Y |
| Shepshed Building Society | Y | N | N/A | N | Y | | Y | Y | Y | N | N | N/A | Y |
| Skipton Building Society | Y | N | N/A | Y | N | | Y | Y | Y | N | Y | N | Y |
| The Stafford Railway Building Society | Y | N | N/A | N | Y | | Y | N | Y | N | N | N/A | Y |
| Staffordshire Building Society | Y | N | N/A | Y | Y | | Y | Y | Y | Y | N | Y | Y |
| The Standard Building Society | Y | N | N/A | Y | Y | | Y | Y | Y | N | Y | N | Y |
| Stroud & Swindon Building Society | Y | Y | Y | Y | Y | | Y | Y | Y | N | Y | Y | Y |
| Sun Life Assurance Society plc | Y | N | N/A | Y | N | | Y | Y | Y | Y | N | N | Y |
| Sun Life of Canada Home Loans Ltd | Y | N | N/A | Y | N | | Y | Y | Y | Y | N | N | Y |
| Swansea Building Society | Y | N | N/A | N | Y | | Y | Y | N | N | Y | N | N |
| Teachers' Building Society | Y | N | N/A | N | Y | | Y | Y | Y | N | N | N/A | Y |
| Tynemouth Building Society | Y | N | N/A | Y | Y | | Y | Y | N | Y | N | N | N |
| The United Bank of Kuwait plc | Y | N | N/A | Y | N | | Y | Y | Y | N | Y | Y | Y |
| United Friendly Insurance plc | Y | N | N/A | Y | N | | Y | Y | Y | N | N | N/A | Y |
| Universal Building Society | Y | N | N/A | Y | Y | | Y | Y | Y | N | Y | Y | Y |
| Vernon Building Society | Y | N | N/A | Y | Y | | Y | Y | Y | N | Y | Y | Y |
| Wesleyan Home Loans Ltd | Y | N | N/A | Y | Y | | Y | Y | Y | N | N | N/A | Y |
| West Cumbria Building Society | Y | N | N/A | Y | Y | | Y | Y | N | N | N | N/A | N |
| Western Trust & Savings Ltd | Y | N | N/A | Y | N | | Y | Y | Y | Y | N | N | Y |

*Key:*

1. Do you lend money on the security of residential property?
2. Do you or an associated company employ staff to carry out valuations of residential property for mortgage purposes?
3. If so, do you give them priority in carrying out valuations for you?
4. Do you use a 'panel' or other selected group of surveyors?
5. Do you accept mortgage valuations from any valuer you regard as competent?
6. This question sought information on how lenders assess competence (and cannot be summarised in this form for the purposes of the table).
7. Do you require the prospective borrower to pay for a mortgage valuation?
8. If so, do you require the borrower to do so before he or she is granted a mortgage?
9. Do you have a set National scale of fees charged to borrowers for valuations?
10. Does your charge to the borrower contain an administrative charge for arranging the valuation?
11. Does your charge to the borrower contain charges for other services than arranging the valuation?
12. Are these charges separately identified to the borrower?
13. Do you have a set National scale of fees you pay to external valuers for residential mortgage valuations?

*Source:* MMC.

*Notes:*

1. Q9 and Q13: the following lenders employ a fee scale in their local area of operation:

    Chesham Building Society
    Darlington Building Society
    Ilkeston Permanent Building Society
    Leek United Building Society
    Nottingham Imperial Building Society
    Progressive Building Society
    Swansea Building Society
    Tynemouth Building Society
    West Cumbria Building Society

2. Q5: the following lenders qualify their acceptance of non-panel valuers in one of the following ways: either in regard to circumstances, eg by not accepting an already prepared valuation or nomination by borrower, or considering each case on its merits; or the criteria for acceptance are more than general requirements of RICS/ISVA qualification, experience, local knowledge and professional indemnity cover, eg that they have to be formally accepted to the panel or that there must be a minimum of two partners in the firm:

    Banque Paribas
    Birmingham Midshires Building Society
    Cambridge Building Society
    Capital Home Loans
    Chelsea Building Society
    The Chorley & District Building Society
    City & Metropolitan Building Society
    Confederation Bank Ltd
    Coutts Finance Co
    Credit Agricole Personal Finance plc
    Derbyshire Building Society
    Greenwich Building Society
    Harpenden Building Society
    Holmesdale Building Society
    Ilkeston Permanent Building Society
    Lloyds Bowmaker Finance Ltd
    Manchester Building Society
    Marsden Building Society
    Melton Mowbray Building Society
    National Mutual Life Assurance Society
    Newcastle Building Society
    Newbury Building Society
    Penrith Building Society
    Portman Building Society
    Progressive Building Society
    Royal London Homebuy Ltd
    The Standard Building Society
    Stroud & Swindon Building Society
    Universal Building Society

## BSA Circular No 2274

8th June 1979

### SIMULTANEOUS STRUCTURAL SURVEY AND VALUATION PROCEDURE

#### Introduction

1. It is already not unknown for a structural survey and a building society valuation of a property offered as security to be carried out simultaneously by one person who is acceptable for the relevant purpose both to the applicant for the mortgage and to the society. The object of such a combined exercise is of course to save expense to the applicant who wants a structural survey because in many cases there will be only one visit to the property instead of two.

2. The possibility of such a combined exercise is perhaps not so well known as it might be and the Office of Fair Trading is very keen that this facility should be generally available to applicants and that applicants should be made aware of this. The Office has expressed concern to the Council at the possibility that some societies may refuse to accede to requests by applicants, for arrangements to be made for such a combined exercise.

3. The term 'structural survey' is used in this Circular to denote both a full structural survey and a survey (as distinct from a building society valuation) which is rather less than a full structural one.

#### Recommendation of the Council

4. After a full consideration of all facets of this matter and a full discussion of them with the Office the Council now recommends that—

    *(a)*    a society should be willing to consider making appropriate arrangements on receiving a request from an applicant that the valuer who will carry out the valuation for the society should carry out a structural survey for the applicant, and

    *(b)*    a society should be willing to consider, subject to the right of refusal, having a valuation carried out by the surveyor from whom the applicant wishes to commission a structural survey.

#### Comments on Recommendation *(a)*

5. The difficulty here is of course that the valuer normally employed by the society may not be competent to do a structural survey or, if he is competent, he may not be willing to do such a survey for reasons which societies will readily appreciate. In these circumstances the Council is asking societies to be ready to consider making other arrangements for the valuation, subject naturally to meeting the overriding obligation of their directors to comply with section 25 of the Building Societies Act 1962. Where the society agrees to its valuer being used for a structural survey it will no doubt bear in mind the possibility that it may be accepting a measure of responsibility for the competence of the valuer in carrying out any aspect of his work, be it the structural survey or of course the valuation which is taken for the society's use. Accordingly, the society may wish to consider whether it should state in writing that it cannot accept any responsibility.

6. As a society's valuation is a much less involved document than a purchaser's structural survey it is essential for the surveyor to ascertain at the outset what the purchaser requires and for the purchaser to know what the surveyor can give him for whatever amount the purchaser is prepared to pay. Consequently, the surveyor must see or speak to the purchaser personally and agree what shall be

done—the scope of the structural survey required by the applicant is not the concern of the society. (The Association understands that the Royal Institution of Chartered Surveyors strongly advises its members who intend to carry out a structural survey to agree with purchasers, before they carry out the work, the terms on which they are accepting instructions and to confirm these in writing as soon as reasonably practicable.) In their dialogue the purchaser and the surveyor will fix the fee (including attendant costs) for the structural survey (there being no scale of fees for structural surveys) and payment will in due course be made direct. The recommended scale of charges for valuation services is set out in Appendix I to Circular No. 1833 and any reduction stemming from the combined exercise will be in the structural survey element of the total fee.

7. As regards structural surveys for applicants being carried out by staff valuers, a society will have to consider, even where the staff valuer has the necessary experience, whether, in the light of his terms of employment and that society's general policy, it wishes its staff to undertake work for third parties which may involve the society or its staff in liability for negligence.

**Comments on Recommendation (b)**

8. If the applicant wishes to use a surveyor of his own and wants the society therefore to use this surveyor for its valuation, the Council asks the society to consider the case on its merits. Doubtless, the society will do its best to agree but, if after careful consideration it comes to the conclusion that the surveyor so suggested does not measure up to the requirements of section 25 either generally or in respect of the particular property in contemplation or indeed because he is in any other way a person who is not able to meet the society's requirements, it will have no option but to decline him. The Office appreciates that because of section 25 the society must have the last word on this matter, hence the reference to the right of refusal in the recommendation.

9. The Office also appreciates that, if the surveyor proffered by the applicant is not known to the society, checking of his suitability to perform the valuation, however quickly this is carried out, must cause some delay which may result in the applicant losing the house. It seems to the Council that, if delay may occur while enquiries are made and a decision is taken, the society should at least bear in mind the need to warn the applicant thereof. This is particularly important in Scotland where the bids have to be in by a certain day. A structural survey will in any event take longer than a valuation.

**General**

10. Under the combined procedure the surveyor completes the:society's valuation report form in the normal way and a structural survey report for the applicant. Neither party is entitled to see the other's document. The surveyor is liable to each party for any negligent error in or omission from that party's document which results in loss.

11. In view of the Office of Fair Trading's concern, societies are asked to consider mentioning in their mortgage prospectuses that, if an applicant wants a structural survey (as defined in paragraph 3 above) on his own behalf and lets the society know before its own valuation is arranged, it may be possible for the society to arrange for the valuer who carries out the valuation for the society to do the structural survey for the applicant. If mention is made, the society may wish to emphasise that, if there is to be a possibility of a reduced charge for the combined procedure, the applicant should inform the society of his intention before it arranges the valuation and he should negotiate the structural survey element of the reduced charge with the valuer direct. The prospectus may also with advantage then state (in order that the applicant appreciates beforehand the expense involved) that a simultaneous structural survey and valuation is going to cost the applicant considerably more than a valuation on behalf of the society and will almost certainly take longer to complete.

12. The recommendations made in this Circular are not restrictive. There is no question therefore of its being registrable under the Restrictive Trade Practices Act 1976 but because of its interest in this matter the Office has seen the text, as have the Royal Institution of Chartered Surveyors, the Royal Institute of British Architects and the Incorporated Society of valuers and Auctioneers. The Office of Fair Trading will be issuing a Press Statement about the subject-matter of this Circular when the Circular has been in societies' hands for sufficient time for them to assimilate it.

## CML guidance on conflicts of interest

### Introduction

1. This part of section C follows on from the conclusion by the CML Executive Committee that members should be advised to inform prospective borrowers (where relevant) that the mortgage valuation might be carried out by an employed staff valuer, a valuer employed by a subsidiary company, or by an independent panel valuer. Such notice need only be given where there is a possibility that a staff valuer or a valuer employed by a subsidiary may value a property that is being sold through an estate agency subsidiary of the lending institution. This is the outcome of discussions between the CML, the Royal Institution of Chartered Surveyors (RICS) and the Incorporated Society of valuers and Auctioneers (ISVA). The guidance is relevant to all members and, briefly:

— outlines the discussions which took place between the BSA (later the CML) the RICS and the ISVA;

— explains why the outcome is considered acceptable by all sides;

— suggests that members should if applicable incorporate an appropriate notice in the mortgage documentation.

### Background

2. The BSA first met the RICS and ISVA in June 1989 to discuss possible conflicts of interests. The RICS/ISVA held a view that there was potential for a perceived conflict of interest where a lending institution owned an estate agency subsidiary and the property was sold through the agency and was valued by a valuer employed by the parent body that owned the agency. The issue related initially to building societies but it was clear that it could also affect other lending institutions. Their concern was that a valuer could come under pressure from the selling agency or lending institution to be less than objective in his submitted report.

3. The secretariat has always been clear in its view that, in law, there was no conflict. In 1989 the BSA Legal Advisory Panel confirmed this view. It was emphasized, for example, that section 13(2) of the Building societies Act 1986 did not prevent a staff valuer, nor a valuer employed by an estate agency subsidiary, from valuing a property being sold through the agency of another subsidiary company within the same group (see Brief No 47 in the BSA Practice Manual).

4. Whilst supporting this view of the law affecting building societies, the RICS and the ISVA perceived the potential for an ethical professional conflict existing beyond the law, and affecting all lenders, where there were circumstances similar to those outlined above.

### Subsequent developments

5. Discussions continued between the CML and the RICS/ISVA during 1990 and a number of proposals for dealing with the matter were considered. None, however, was felt to be wholly satisfactory. In September 1990 the RICS informed the CML that it was considering a number of alternatives, one of which would have involved altering its rules to prohibit its members from acting where there was a perceived conflict of interest. This alternative caused concern to the CML but, following further discussions, it was agreed that this would have presented difficulties for staff valuers in lending institutions or employed by subsidiaries because, if they remained members of the RICS, they would no longer be able to act in all the circumstances required by their contracts of employment.

6. After further discussion the RICS Working Party which was considering this issue agreed that a prohibition was not appropriate and that it would be sufficient to progress by way of disclosure which would satisfactorily address the situation from the RICS/ISVA and consumer perspectives without being unnecessarily onerous for lenders. This proposal was considered by the CML Executive committee at its September 1990 meeting, when it resolved that members should be advised that they should give prospective borrowers the information outlined in paragraph 1 above. The CML Valuation Panel was fully involved throughout this process.

7. The RICS Working Party therefore recommended to the General Council of the RICS that such disclosure was an appropriate means of dealing with the perceived conflict of interest. This would allow prospective borrowers to make an informed decision as to whether they wished to continue with the application for mortgage finance through a lender that was connected with the vendor's agent and the valuer. The recommendation received the General Council's approval on 29 April 1991. RICS rule changes will be required as a result of other aspects of the Working Party's report. It is understood that these will be put to the RICS membership in April 1992. The ISVA has been fully aware of developments and agrees with the RICS decision regarding the giving of notices.

8. The recommendation underlines the importance of preserving and respecting lenders' absolute discretion as to which valuer should be instructed and it was against this background that the discussions took place.

## The conclusion

9. Accordingly, the CML suggestion is that each member informs mortgage applicants, where relevant, that it might use any one of a staff valuer, a subsidiary valuer or a panel valuer in order to value the property. No exact form of wording was agreed with the RICS/ISVA but it is suggested that it might be along the following lines: 'The valuation may be carried out by a valuer employed by [the lender], a valuer from a subsidiary company of [the lender], or by an independent panel valuer not connected with [the lender].' Such notice would of course be irrelevant where the institution has no in-house estate agency, as the perceived conflict cannot exist. Further, the wording of the notice may need to be modified where necessary eg if the lender uses only employed valuers and independent panel valuers, but not valuers from a subsidiary.

10. The phrase would be included in the lender's mortgage documentation. There was no specific agreement as to where in the documentation it should be located; that would be for each lender to decide. The positioning of the phrase is at the discretion of each member. The mortgage application form may be considered the most suitable vehicle or perhaps the valuation and survey literature. However, it is advised that prominence be given to the notice—ie it should not be a 'small prints' exercise. It is not intended that any change of mortgage lending practice should be necessitated as a result of the operation of this procedure.

## Extract from the CML Mortgage fraud manual

Date:  August 1989

Subject:  TYPES OF FRAUD

---

**Introduction**

1.       Although it would be difficult to produce a comprehensive list of ways to perpetrate fraud or criminal deception in the mortgage area, the following list refers to the most prevalent types—

(a)  The mortgage applicant himself giving a false income on the mortgage application form to increase the size of the mortgage. This will enable him to buy a property which he could not otherwise afford, or to obtain a loan for which he would not otherwise qualify.

(b)  Stating that the property will be used for owner-occupation when the applicant's real intention is to let it (it is likely that some breach of the MIRAS provisions will be involved in such cases—see section D).

(c)  Falsification of personal details, particularly relating to income, by introducers on behalf of their clients to obtain mortgages which they would not otherwise be granted.

(d)  False valuation of properties by valuers to obtain, for example, a higher mortgage than is necessary to purchase the property, or where there is collusion between the valuer and purchaser to defraud the owner.

(e)  Fraud by professionals can involve introducers, solicitors, licensed conveyancers, valuers and accountants, either individually or in collusion. Mortgages may be obtained for applicants who do not exist, or on properties which do not exist. Alternatively, a number of mortgages may be obtained from different lenders on the same property at the same time.

(f)  Forged deeds—falsifying the deeds of a property could enable the fraudster to sell it to a number of different buyers at the same time.

(g)  Staff fraud—a member of staff processes the fraudulent mortgage application(s) with full knowledge and participation in the deception.

The main characteristic of each of these types of fraud are considered in the following paragraphs.

**Status Fraud**

2.       This may be committed on the applicant's own initiative, if he is able to provide a forged reference in support of the stated income, but can also involve the deceitful collusion of his employer. In cases where a reference is forged by the individual acting alone, the applicant might not work for the employer stated or, if he does, his income would be inflated. An applicant may misrepresent his credit status, eg by not giving information on a County Court judgment against him, or that he has previously been evicted, or that he is or has been bankrupt, or that he has an existing mortgage or other loan. Assuming that the mortgage valuation is valid and a charge is validly executed

on the property to protect the lender's security, the only person who may suffer is the applicant if he takes on a commitment which he subsequently finds difficult to meet. Lenders would be unlikely to suffer a financial loss, even if mortgage arrears subsequently accrued, if the security can be realised by possession and sale of the property (depending on the accuracy of the valuation, the position of the property in the country and the state of the housing market).

**Unauthorised Letting**

3.      The most usual method of committing the most serious type of this particular fraud is for a number of properties to be purchased by the same person with mortgage advances from different lenders. The applicant may use his own name in each case or, alternatively, adopt one or more assumed names. Obviously, the employer's reference would normally be forged but there would be no need for a dishonest solicitor or valuer to assist in the fraud if different solicitors and lenders are employed in each case. The normal practice would be for the owner to let properties purchased, typically to students or homeless persons whom the local authority is obliged to rehouse, and the rent would be used to make the monthly mortgage payments. The fraudster would pocket the difference between mortgage repayments and the rent received from the tenants (or from the local authority on their behalf) each month. If the mortgage application states that the purchaser will occupy the property as his only or main residence, and the loan has been included within MIRAS, this will amount to a breach of the MIRAS provisions (see Section D). Lenders which suspect that there has been a MIRAS fraud must notify the Inland Revenue. From lenders' financial point of view, as it is often a feature of this type of case that the mortgage repayments are made with scrupulous regularity, they may not suffer any financial loss (and if arrears did accrue, they should still be able to obtain possession of the property to realise their security). However, if a lender writes to the occupants to notify them that it is aware there has been an unauthorised letting, but fails to seek possession, a court might construe this as a waiver of any rights under the mortgage to take possession if proceedings are subsequently taken.

**Introducers and Applicants acting together**

4.      A variation of the status fraud highlighted in paragraph 2 above can be committed where an introducer eg a mortgage broker, instigates the fraud, by encouraging the applicant to give false details on the application form, and arranges the mortgage on his behalf. The introducer may benefit by charging the applicant a substantial fee for his advice, for processing the application, or even for forging references. He may also receive commission from the mortgage lender in respect of the mortgage arranged through it, and commission on any endowment policy. The introducers are helped by the ease with which blank P60 forms and company notepaper can be obtained or falsified. The lender has been notified of cases where the introducer has encouraged an applicant to purchase a number of properties in the same way, through different lenders, and so the unauthorised letting fraud referred to in paragraph 3 may also be involved.

**Valuation Frauds**

5.      The simple example of this type of fraud is where the property is over-valued to obtain a larger mortgage than would otherwise have been granted and the funds not needed to purchase the property are divided between the valuer and the fraudster.

6.      A fraud may also be committed in connection with an under-valuation of the property. This would normally be arranged by an estate agent who would fix the price for the property and introduce the purchaser, who would be acting in collusion with the agent. Once the purchase was completed, the usual practice is to arrange a quick re-sale of the property at its proper valuation. A lender would not normally be adversely affected by such a fraud, if it provided a mortgage to the purchaser, as it would have the security of a charge on the property. The financial loser would be the original seller who would have sold the property at too low a price as a result of the fraud by the estate agent.

7.      Another variation of the valuation fraud is where the valuation report is itself a forgery. This is designed to either benefit a vendor who is defrauding a purchaser and the lender or

a purchaser/owner who is defrauding the lender. The forged report could give false details of the valuation, of the age and condition of the property, or of the occupancy, all of which would mislead a lender's assessment of the property as a mortgage security. Clearly the valuation fraud could cause considerable loss to the secured lender. It is unlikely to be detected by the solicitor.

**Frauds by Professionals**

8.      This type of fraud, in its different guises, is particularly serious as it can lead to the highest financial losses for mortgage lenders. Where a mortgage is obtained in the name of a non-existent borrower, the lender may obtain redress eg rights of subrogation. Alternatively, if the solicitor or licensed conveyancer commits fraud or is dishonest, compensation may be obtained by making a claim against the Law Society's or the Council for Licensed Conveyancers' Compensation Funds. However, this redress is discretionary. Compensation from the Law Society's Compensation Fund is not available as of right and to succeed a claimant must always in addition to fraud or dishonesty prove 'loss or hardships' (see Section 36 of the Solicitors Act 1974). Under Rule 4 of the Council for Licensed Conveyancers Compensation Fund Rules 1987, a grant may be given out of that compensation fund for the purpose of relieving or mitigating a loss suffered in consequence of fraud or dishonesty. Where there are multiple applications and loans on the same property, involving the same solicitor or licensed conveyancer acting in all transactions, it is likely that all of the mortgage lenders involved will lose financially. It is this type of fraud which has been the main subject of press speculation and substantial police investigations.

9.      A variation on the 'professionals' fraud theme can arise where a dishonest conveyancer arranges a number of completions on one day, or over a short period of time, on properties which have been properly valued but on behalf of applicants who do not exist and/or who may not have entered into a contract to purchase. In a case highlighted in the past, a solicitor who committed this type of fraud cleared the proceeds of the advance cheques through his account and left the country with the proceeds before the fraud was discovered. A further variation, which involves the collusion of estate agent, solicitor and purchaser, is to overstate the house purchase price in the mortgage application form so that the purchaser is granted a larger mortgage loan than he would otherwise obtain from the lender. The difference between the actual price of the property and the amount of the loan could be used to enable the purchaser to pay his costs in connection with the transaction or for some other purpose.

10.     Other professional fraud can arise where a solicitor/licensed conveyancer acts for both the vendor and purchaser and the desire to please the vendor client leads to a lack of attention to the interests of the purchaser and/or his mortgagee. Ordinarily, to act on behalf of both vendor and purchaser could give rise to a conflict of interest and would be contrary to the Solicitors' Practice Rules. However, Rule 6(2) sets out exceptions to this general principle, and it is in respect of these cases that the possibility of fraud may arise. Fraud can also arise where a solicitor/conveyancer is allowed to act for the society if he/she is personally interested in the conveyance either as vendor or purchaser.

**Forged Deeds**

11.     Forged deeds could cause substantial loss to lenders where a number of mortgages on the same property are obtained at the same time from different lenders. The main danger area at present is in respect of unregistered land. However, the Police are particularly concerned that this type of fraud may become more prevalent in the future for registered land if the Land Registry is opened to the public, as provided for in the Land Registration Act 1988. This Act is not yet in force, but it is proposed that it should be implemented in the next two years.

**Staff Fraud**

12.     Each of the frauds set out in paragraphs 2 to 11 above can be more easily carried out, and can be potentially more damaging to the lenders involved in both money and public relations terms, if a member of staff is a party to the fraud and processes the fraudulent applications.

**An example of a leaflet detailing valuation and administration charges: Halifax**

## HALIFAX HOME BUYING SERVICE

## VALUATION SCHEMES AND FEES

After you have applied for a Halifax mortgage for the property you wish to buy the Society has a legal requirement to have the property valued, to find out if it represents adequate security for a loan.

You are strongly recommended to have your own survey in order to obtain the information you need to help you decide whether you should purchase it.

As well as the basic valuation there are two different valuation and survey reports—one more detailed than the other—for you to choose from.

The valuation may be carried out by a valuer who is employed directly by the Society or one of its subsidiary companies. Alternatively, it may be carried out by a member of our extensive panel of independent valuers and surveyors around the UK.

It is important that you study carefully any notes or conditions accompanying the report you select, as they will explain how it was prepared and any limitations.

### FLATS AND MAISONETTES

If the property is a flat or maisonette the valuation and inspection schemes described in this leaflet still apply. However, you should bear in mind that the valuer probably won't be able to inspect the whole of the building so his report will be limited to the flat or maisonette you wish to buy. Where possible, comment will be made on the general condition of the main fabric of the whole building. Incidentally, provision is usually made for each flat owner to pay a share of the maintenance and repair of the building and any common parts of the block. You should ask your solicitor to obtain this information so you know what obligations and provisions are contained in the lease or title deeds. The valuer will also need this information to complete a reasonable report, otherwise he will have to make assumptions

### SCHEME 1

### REPORT AND VALUATION FOR MORTGAGE ASSESSMENT

This is a basic report for the Society's use which meets the legal requirements and a copy will be sent to you. The report enables us to decide if the property you wish to buy is suitable security for a mortgage.

The valuer carries out a visual inspection of as much of the exterior and interior of the property as is easily accessible. This includes the parts of the property which are visible while standing at ground level within the boundaries of the site and on adjacent public areas, and while standing at the various floor levels.

It is possible that there are defects in the property which are not reported but which a more detailed inspection would reveal. This means that the report may not make you aware of defects which could affect your decision to buy. You are, therefore, strongly recommended to obtain a more comprehensive report. Two alternative schemes are described in this leaflet.

| FEES—SCHEME 1 | |
|---|---|
| Purchase price not exceeding £ | Fee £ |
| 50,000 | 125 |
| 100,000 | 165 |
| 150,000 | 195 |
| 200,000 | 225 |
| 250,000 | 255 |
| 300,000 | 285 |
| 350,000 | 315 |
| 400,000 | 345 |
| 450,000 | 375 |
| 500,000 | 405 |
| Over 500,000 | By arrangement |

No additional VAT is included.
A £25 administration charge is included with the fee.
The valuation fees for Scheme 1 reports will be based on the valuation figure if the purchase price is discounted.

## SCHEME 2

### REPORT AND VALUATION FOR MORTGAGE ASSESSMENT AND FOR HOME BUYERS

This scheme combines a valuation report for the sole use of the Society with a survey report for the home buyer. The inspection is less comprehensive than a structural survey (Scheme 3), but should give you a general opinion of the quality and condition of the fabric of the property.

The valuation report is used to enable the Society to decide if the property you wish to purchase is suitable security for a mortgage.

The survey report covers those parts of the property which are readily visible and accessible, including the roof space if there is easy access by the roof-hatch, however, the underfloor area will not be inspected. The surveyor will list all visible and major defects and will advise you of defects he suspects may exist in those areas which have not been inspected. The report may contain either recommendations for further investigation to be carried out or suggested courses of action in respect of the defects. Please note that minor or cosmetic defects won't necessarily be listed by the surveyor.

Overall, the report and valuation will be based on the standard report used by either the Royal Institution of Chartered Surveyors, the Incorporated Society of Valuers and Auctioneers or the Royal Institute of British Architects. It will be subject to the standard conditions of engagement issued by those organisations which you should receive from your surveyor.

| Fees—Scheme 2 | |
|---|---|
| Purchase price not exceeding £ | Fee £ |
| 50,000 | 250 |
| 100,000 | 330 |
| 150,000 | 380 |
| 200,000 | 430 |
| 250,000 | 480 |
| 300,000 | 530 |
| 350,000 | 580 |
| 400,000 | 630 |
| 450,000 | 680 |
| 500,000 | 730 |
| Over 500,000 | By arrangement |

VAT is included if appropriate.
A £25 administration charge is included with the fee.
The valuation fees for Scheme 2 reports will be based on the valuation figure if the purchase price is discounted.

## SCHEME 3

### STRUCTURAL SURVEY REPORT

This report is based on a very detailed examination of the property and is essentially a technical inspection and report. The structural survey provides a comprehensive report on the condition of the property, describing in detail any structural or other defects.

A valuation isn't normally included, however, it may be possible for the structural survey report to be combined with Scheme 1. In this way you may be able to save some money—as long as the valuer knows that you require a structural survey before he visits the property.

The Society will let you know which valuer it will instruct to carry out the valuation, so that you can contact him to discuss your requirements and the scope and extent of the survey.

## FEES — SCHEME 3

Fees vary according to age, size and type of property, which is why it is essential for the Society's valuer to know at the outset what you require, and equally, for you to know what service he can provide, and the fees he will charge. When you make arrangements for a structural survey to be carried out, be sure to discuss the fees for the survey report before agreeing any terms of engagement.

# The distribution of the number of mortgage loans in the UK by house price bands, 1992

TABLE 1   **Distribution of mortgage loans by house price bands, 1992**

*Percentage of total number of loans granted*

*(a) Loans by building societies*

| Price band | All buyers | First time buyers | Former owner occupiers |
|---|---|---|---|
| Under £25,000 | 8 | 13 | 2 |
| £25,000–£29,999 | 6 | 9 | 2 |
| £30,000–£39,999 | 16 | 23 | 9 |
| £40,000–£49,999 | 19 | 22 | 16 |
| £50,000–£59,999 | 15 | 14 | 16 |
| £60,000–£69,999 | 10 | 8 | 13 |
| £70,000–£79,999 | 7 | 4 | 10 |
| £80,000–£99,999 | 8 | 4 | 13 |
| £100,000–£124,999 | 4 | 1 | 8 |
| £125,000–£149,999 | 3 | 1 | 5 |
| £150,000–£199,999 | 2 | 1 | 4 |
| £200,000 and over | 1 | - | 3 |
| Total | 100 | 100 | 100 |

*(b) Loans by high street banks*

| Price band | Percentage of total number of loans approved |
|---|---|
| Under £15,000 | 4 |
| £15,000–£19,999 | 2 |
| £20,000–£29,999 | 9 |
| £30,000–£39,999 | 16 |
| £40,000–£49,999 | 17 |
| £50,000–£59,999 | 13 |
| £60,000–£69,999 | 10 |
| £70,000–£79,999 | 7 |
| £80,000 and over | 22 |
| Total | 100 |

*Source:* CML and DoE sample survey.

TABLE 2  Regional distribution of mortgage loans by building societies by house price bands, 1992

*Percentage of number of loans granted per region*

| Region | Under £25,000 | £25,000–£29,999 | £30,000–£39,999 | £40,000–£49,999 | £50,000–£59,999 | £60,000–£69,999 | £70,000–£79,999 | £80,000–£99,999 | £100,000–£124,999 | £125,000 and over |
|---|---|---|---|---|---|---|---|---|---|---|
| Northern | 14 | 10 | 20 | 18 | 14 | 9 | 5 | 5 | 3 | 2 |
| Yorks & Humber | 7 | 9 | 22 | 22 | 14 | 9 | 5 | 7 | 2 | 3 |
| East Midlands | 5 | 7 | 23 | 23 | 14 | 7 | 6 | 6 | 4 | 4 |
| East Anglia | 5 | 6 | 19 | 24 | 16 | 9 | 6 | 6 | 4 | 5 |
| Greater London | 3 | 2 | 5 | 12 | 17 | 15 | 13 | 14 | 8 | 11 |
| South-East | 3 | 3 | 11 | 17 | 17 | 13 | 9 | 11 | 6 | 11 |
| South-West | 4 | 4 | 14 | 25 | 17 | 11 | 7 | 8 | 4 | 6 |
| West Midlands | 6 | 4 | 17 | 25 | 14 | 10 | 7 | 7 | 4 | 5 |
| North-West | 8 | 7 | 21 | 20 | 14 | 9 | 5 | 6 | 3 | 6 |
| Wales | 10 | 8 | 24 | 23 | 12 | 7 | 5 | 6 | 3 | 3 |
| Scotland | 26 | 6 | 15 | 14 | 10 | 7 | 7 | 7 | 3 | 4 |
| Northern Ireland | 27 | 13 | 28 | 12 | 7 | 5 | 3 | 3 | 1 | 1 |
| UK | 8 | 6 | 16 | 19 | 15 | 10 | 7 | 8 | 4 | 7 |

*Source:*  CML and DoE sample survey.

221

## Financial results of the seven largest lenders[1]

### Halifax

1. Set out in Table 1 are the summarized results of Halifax. Halifax transfers all its income in respect of valuations not carried out in-house to its subsidiary or to its external valuers. Thus all its direct surplus on valuations is made on in-house activity. As a percentage of its total income Halifax reported a drop from [ * ] to [ * ] per cent from 1990 to 1991 and since then a consistent recovery to [ * ] per cent in 1993 (estimated).

2. Halifax charges an administration fee in addition to its scale fee for mortgage valuations. The administration fee is used, it told us, as a contribution towards the general expenses of Halifax in the processing of mortgage applications.

TABLE 1   **Halifax: all residential valuations, 1990 to 1993**

|  | 1990 | 1991 | 1992 | 1993 estimated |
|---|---|---|---|---|
| | | | | £'000 |
| *Income* | | | | |
| In-house | [ | | | |
| By subsidiary | | *Figures omitted.* | | |
| By external valuers | | *See note on page iv.* | | ] |
| Total | 24,082 | 27,988 | 28,115 | [ |
| | | | | * |
| Administration fees | 939 | 3,101 | 4,327 | ] |
| *Surplus/(deficit)* | | | | |
| In-house | [ | | | |
| By subsidiary | | *Figures omitted.* | | |
| By external valuers | | *See note on page iv.* | | |
| Total | | | | ] |
| | | | | *per cent* |
| *Surplus/(deficit) as a percentage of income received* | | | | |
| In-house | [ | | | |
| By subsidiary | | *Figures omitted.* | | |
| By external valuers | | *See note on page iv.* | | |
| Total | | | | ] |

*Source:* Halifax.

3. Table 2 sets out further details of Halifax's in-house activity. This shows that although Halifax made relatively large surpluses on mortgage valuations, these were, to an extent, offset by deficits on HBRs. Halifax told us that the reason for the deficits was that about four times as many man-hours were devoted to producing an HBR than in producing a mortgage valuation only. This extra expense outweighed the fact that the average income for an HBR was twice that of a mortgage valuation only.

[1]The bases used to present the information summarized in this appendix are set out in paragraph 5.33.

*Figures omitted. See note on page iv.

TABLE 2   **Halifax: results of residential valuations carried out in-house, 1990 to 1993**

| | 1990 | 1991 | 1992 | 1993 estimated |
|---|---|---|---|---|
| | | | | £'000 |
| *Income* | | | | |
| Mortgage valuations | [ | | | |
| HBRs | | | | |
| Other | | | | |
| Total | | | | |
| | | *Figures omitted.* | | |
| | | *See note on page iv.* | | |
| *Surplus/(deficit)* | | | | |
| Mortgage valuations | | | | |
| HBRs | | | | |
| Other | | | | |
| Total | | | | ] |
| | | | | per cent |
| *Surplus/(deficit) as a percentage of income received* | | | | |
| Mortgage valuations | [ | | | |
| HBRs | | *Figures omitted.* | | |
| Other | | *See note on page iv.* | | |
| Total | | | | ] |

Source: Halifax.

4. Turning to Halifax's subsidiary company, within its income from third parties it was not able to separate out panel fee income from its valuation income from other sources. These two sources of income are shown together in Table 3. Like Halifax itself, the subsidiary firm made surpluses on mortgage valuations and deficits on HBRs. Again we were told that this was because of the higher manpower requirements for HBRs than for mortgage valuations only. The surplus on mortgage valuations undertaken for Halifax as a percentage of income received from Halifax was in the range of about [ * ] to [ * ] per cent over the review period. Overall the percentage surplus was in the range of about [*] to [ * ] per cent.

TABLE 3   **Halifax subsidiary company: results for all residential valuations, 1990 to 1993**

| | 1990 | 1991 | 1992 | 1993 estimated |
|---|---|---|---|---|
| | | | | £'000 |
| *Income in respect of work undertaken:* | | | | |
| For owning lender: | | | | |
| Mortgage valuations | [ | | | |
| HBRs | | | | |
| Other valuations | | | | |
| Total | | | | |
| For others | | | | |
| Total | | | | |
| *Surplus/(deficit)* | | *Figures omitted.* | | |
| For owning lender: | | *See note on page iv.* | | |
| Mortgage valuations | | | | |
| HBRs | | | | |
| Other valuations | | | | |
| Total | | | | |
| For others | | | | |
| Total | | | | ] |
| | | | | per cent |
| *Surplus/(deficit) as a percentage of income received* | | | | |
| For owning lender: | | | | |
| Mortgage valuations | [ | | | |
| HBRs | | | | |
| Other valuations | | | | |
| Total | | *Figures omitted.* | | |
| | | *See note on page iv.* | | |
| For others | | | | |
| Total | | | | ] |

Source: Halifax.

*Figures omitted. See note on page iv.

## Abbey National

5. Set out in Table 4 are the results of Abbey National, and in Table 5 its subsidiary valuation company (Cornerstone) which was sold in August 1993. Abbey National also stated that for substantial intervals throughout the period under review a special 'Mortgage Movers' promotion was in existence. In 1992 up to [ * ] per cent of Abbey National's lending was conducted under the 'Mortgage Movers' promotion. Under this promotion borrowers first paid Abbey National's initial fees but the bulk of these fees were refunded to borrowers when the mortgage was completed. The effect of the promotion was to lower the up-front fees (including valuation fees) for those borrowers taking advantage of the promotion. While the initial fees and valuation costs are reflected in the figures reported to us the promotion costs borne through Abbey National's marketing budget are not included. Abbey National observed that, in its view, excluding the benefits offered to borrowers through the 'Mortgage Movers' promotion from our figures would make the analysis incomplete.

6. Over the period 1990 to 1993 the profitability (measured as surplus as a percentage of income) of residential mortgage valuation activities of Abbey National increased from [ * ] to [ * ] per cent in 1992 (actual) and to [ * ] per cent in 1993 (estimated). The in-house activities were the main contributors to this figure and showed profitability percentages increasing from [ * ] per cent in 1990 to an estimated [ * ] per cent in 1993. Abbey National charges borrowers an administration fee together with the fee solely in respect of mortgage valuations. It explained that the income from administration fees was used to defray the general expenses of processing borrowers' applications and was not an additional fee in respect of valuations. It thought that viewing the surpluses and deficits on mortgage valuations alone without taking into account the administration fees charged and the related costs of processing applications was misleading.

TABLE 4   **Abbey National: results from all residential valuations, 1990 to 1993**

£'000

| | 1990 | 1991 | 1992 | 1993 estimated |
|---|---|---|---|---|
| *Income* | | | | |
| In-house | [ | | | |
| By subsidiary | | Figures omitted. | | |
| By external valuers | | See note on page iv. | | ] |
| Total | 18,070 | 17,312 | 16,231 | [ |
| Administration fees | 3,060 | 3,450 | 4,692 | ] |
| | | | | |
| *Surplus/(deficit)* | | | | |
| In-house | [ | | | |
| By subsidiary | | Figures omitted. | | |
| By external valuers | | See note on page iv. | | |
| Total | | | | ] |

per cent

| | | | | |
|---|---|---|---|---|
| *Surplus/(deficit) as a percentage of income received* | | | | |
| In-house | [ | | | |
| By subsidiary | | Figures omitted. | | |
| By external valuers | | See note on page iv. | | |
| Total | | | | ] |

*Source:* Abbey National.

7. Abbey National passed over to its subsidiary company all the valuation income it received for the valuations undertaken by the subsidiary. Accordingly, it made no surplus or deficit on that part of its activities. However, the subsidiary consistently made a deficit on this business from 1990 to 1992 as it did in all its activities in residential mortgage valuation with substantial deficits (around [ * ] per cent of income) in 1992. Abbey National sold its Cornerstone subsidiary in August 1993.

*Figures omitted. See note on page iv.

224

TABLE 5  Abbey National subsidiary company: results for all residential valuations, 1990 to 1993

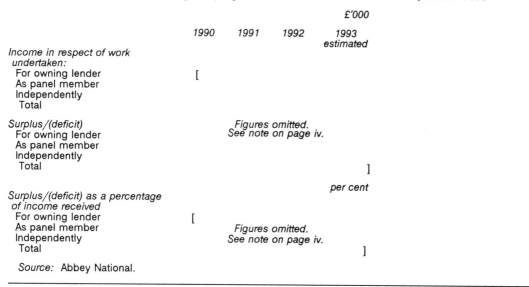

TABLE 5  Abbey National subsidiary company: results for all residential valuations, 1990 to 1993

£'000

|  | 1990 | 1991 | 1992 | 1993 estimated |
|---|---|---|---|---|
| *Income in respect of work undertaken:* |  |  |  |  |
| For owning lender | [ |  |  |  |
| As panel member |  |  |  |  |
| Independently |  |  |  |  |
| Total |  |  |  |  |
| *Surplus/(deficit)* |  | *Figures omitted.* |  |  |
| For owning lender |  | *See note on page iv.* |  |  |
| As panel member |  |  |  |  |
| Independently |  |  |  |  |
| Total |  |  |  | ] |

per cent

| *Surplus/(deficit) as a percentage of income received* |  |  |  |  |
|---|---|---|---|---|
| For owning lender | [ |  |  |  |
| As panel member |  | *Figures omitted.* |  |  |
| Independently |  | *See note on page iv.* |  |  |
| Total |  |  |  | ] |

*Source:* Abbey National.

## Nationwide

8.  Set out in Table 6 are the results for Nationwide from 1990 to 1993. Because of limitations on the information available prior to 1992 Nationwide found it difficult to identify and allocate its own costs to the valuations undertaken by its subsidiary company and external valuers for 1990 and 1991. The society therefore reported that it made neither a surplus nor deficit on these valuations. Nationwide reorganized its valuation operations substantially in 1992 when it transferred all its mortgage valuation activity to its subsidiary, Nationwide Surveyors. [

*Details omitted. See note on page iv.*

]

9.  In addition to a valuation fee Nationwide charges an administration fee to potential borrowers and transfers the total amount (the valuation fee and the administration fee) to Nationwide Surveyors. Nationwide Surveyors then decides whether the mortgage valuation is to be undertaken by its own staff or by an external valuer. External valuers are paid the valuation fee only.

TABLE 6  Nationwide: results from all residential valuations, 1990 to 1993

£'000

|  | 1990 | 1991 | 1992 | 1993 estimated |
|---|---|---|---|---|
| *Income* |  |  |  |  |
| In-house | [ | *Figures omitted.* |  |  |
| By subsidiary |  | *See note on page iv.* |  |  |
| By external valuers |  |  |  | ] |
| Total | 11,663 | 12,680 | 6,967 | [  * |
| Administration fees | 5,479 | 5,957 | 2,449 | ] |
| *Surplus/(deficit)* |  |  |  |  |
| In-house | [ |  |  |  |
| By subsidiary |  | *Figures omitted.* |  |  |
| By external valuers |  | *See note on page iv.* |  |  |
| Total |  |  |  | ] |

per cent

| *Surplus/(deficit) as a percentage of income received* |  |  |  |  |
|---|---|---|---|---|
| In-house | [ |  |  |  |
| By subsidiary |  | *Figures omitted.* |  |  |
| By external valuers |  | *See note on page iv.* |  |  |
| Total |  |  |  | ] |

*Source:* Nationwide.

*Figures omitted. See note on page iv.

10. The results for Nationwide Surveyors are set out in Table 7. For both 1992 (actual) and 1993 (estimated) mortgage valuations for Nationwide were more profitable than HBRs. [

*Details omitted. See note on page iv.*

] This contrasts with Nationwide Surveyors' outside work, the surplus on which is estimated to increase from around [ * ] per cent in 1992 to [ * ] per cent in 1993.

TABLE 7   **Nationwide subsidiary company: results of all valuations, 1992 and 1993**

£'000

| | 1990 | 1991 | 1992 | 1993 estimated |
|---|---|---|---|---|
| *Income in respect of work undertaken:* | | | | |
| For owning lender: | | | | |
| Mortgage valuations | [ | | | |
| HBRs | | | | |
| Total | | | | |
| As panel member | | | | |
| Independently | | | | |
| Total | | | | |
| | | | | |
| *Surplus/(deficit)* | | *Figures omitted.* | | |
| For owning lender: | | *See note on page iv.* | | |
| Mortgage valuations | | | | |
| HBRs | | | | |
| Total | | | | |
| As panel member | | | | |
| Independently | | | | |
| Total | | | | ] |

per cent

| | 1990 | 1991 | 1992 | 1993 estimated |
|---|---|---|---|---|
| *Surplus/(deficit) as a percentage of income received* | | | | |
| For owning lender: | | | | |
| Mortgage valuations | [ | | | |
| HBRs | | | | |
| Total | | *Figures omitted.* | | |
| As panel member | | *See note on page iv.* | | |
| Independently | | | | |
| Total | | | | ] |

*Source:* Nationwide.

# Barclays

11. Barclays uses only external valuers for its valuation work. Barclays pays over all the income it collects to its external valuers and as shown in Table 8 neither surplus nor deficit arises from these activities. However, these results are struck without making any allowance for the administrative costs incurred by Barclays in obtaining the valuations.

TABLE 8   **Barclays: results of all residential valuations, 1990 to 1993**

£'000

| | 1990 | 1991 | 1992 | 1993 estimated |
|---|---|---|---|---|
| Income | 2,103 | 3,405 | 5,104 | [ * ] |
| Surplus/(deficit) | [ | * | | ] |

*Source:* Barclays.

*Figures omitted. See note on page iv.

226

## Woolwich

12. From 1993 onwards Woolwich concentrated all its mortgage valuation activity in its subsidiary which trades as Ekins. Woolwich told us that it does not charge an administration fee to its prospective borrowers and pays over all amounts it receives for valuations to its subsidiary. Before 1993 when the society used third party valuers, it paid over to them directly all amounts received from borrowers except for HBRs where the society retained £10. From 1993 onwards the society paid all receipts to its subsidiary. If the valuation is undertaken by an external valuer the subsidiary in turn pays over the amounts received from the society less £25 (in the case of mortgage valuations) or £50 (in the case of HBRs).

13. Table 9 sets out the results of Woolwich for its mortgage valuation activities from 1990 to 1993. Woolwich estimates that the retentions prior to 1992 in respect of panel mortgage valuations were sufficient to cover any costs of the society relating to these valuations. 1992 was the only year in which the society reported a surplus (of [ * ] per cent) on its in-house valuation activities. This surplus produced an overall surplus of [ * ] per cent.

TABLE 9  **Woolwich: results of all residential valuations, 1990 to 1993**

£'000

|  | 1990 | 1991 | 1992 | 1993 estimated |
|---|---|---|---|---|
| *Income* |  |  |  |  |
| In-house | [ |  |  |  |
| By subsidiary |  | *Figures omitted.* |  |  |
| By external valuer |  | *See note on page iv.* |  | ] |
| Total | 11,011 | 8,123 | 9,235 | [ * ] |
| Administration fees* | N/A | N/A | N/A |  |
|  |  |  |  |  |
| *Surplus/(deficit)* |  |  |  |  |
| In-house | [ |  |  |  |
| By subsidiary |  | *Figures omitted.* |  |  |
| By external valuer |  | *See note on page iv.* |  |  |
| Total |  |  |  | ] |

per cent

|  | 1990 | 1991 | 1992 | 1993 estimated |
|---|---|---|---|---|
| *Surplus/(deficit) as a percentage of income received* |  |  |  |  |
| In-house | [ |  |  |  |
| By subsidiary |  | *Figures omitted.* |  |  |
| By external valuer |  | *See note on page iv.* |  |  |
| Total |  |  |  | ] |

*Source:* Woolwich.

*These are not identified separately on an accounting basis. Estimates of amounts retained (by calendar year) can be found in Table 3.7.

14. The estimated results for Ekins for 1993 are set out in Table 10. The table shows that the subsidiary made a surplus in mortgage valuations only undertaken for its parent but that it suffered a small deficit in respect of HBRs. A similar pattern of surplus and deficit arises in the subsidiary's activities as an external valuer for other lenders.

*Figures omitted. See note on page iv.

227

TABLE 10  **Woolwich subsidiary company: results of all residential valuations, 1990 to 1993**

£'000

| | 1990 | 1991 | 1992 | 1993 estimated |
|---|---|---|---|---|
| *Income in respect of work undertaken:* | | | | |
| For owning lender: | | | | |
| Mortgage valuations | N/A | N/A | N/A | [ |
| HBRs | N/A | N/A | N/A | |
| Other | N/A | N/A | N/A | |
| Total | N/A | N/A | N/A | |
| Other | N/A | N/A | N/A | |
| Total | N/A | N/A | N/A | |
| | | | | |
| *Surplus/(deficit)* | | | | * |
| For owning lender: | | | | |
| Mortgage valuations | N/A | N/A | N/A | |
| HBRs | N/A | N/A | N/A | |
| Other | N/A | N/A | N/A | |
| Total | N/A | N/A | N/A | |
| Other | N/A | N/A | N/A | |
| Total | N/A | N/A | N/A | ] |

per cent

| | 1990 | 1991 | 1992 | 1993 estimated |
|---|---|---|---|---|
| *Surplus/(deficit) as a percentage of income received* | | | | |
| For owning lender: | | | | |
| Mortgage valuations | N/A | N/A | N/A | [ |
| HBRs | N/A | N/A | N/A | |
| Other | N/A | N/A | N/A | * |
| Total | N/A | N/A | N/A | |
| Other | N/A | N/A | N/A | |
| Total | N/A | N/A | N/A | ] |

*Source:* Woolwich.

# Leeds

15. Leeds was not able to give us a breakdown of valuations by type of valuation but estimated that about 89 per cent of valuations were mortgage valuations, 10 per cent were HBRs and about 1 per cent were SSYs. For its allocation of costs the society assumed that the man-hours required to carry out HBRs in comparison with those required for valuations alone were proportional to the fees charged, ie that about twice as much time was required for an HBR as for a mortgage valuation. As a consequence, the surpluses and deficits as a percentage of income for each type of valuation tended to be the same. In Table 11 are set out the results for the society in the UK for the review period.

16. Leeds transfers all the income it receives in respect of mortgage valuations to its subsidiary when the subsidiary performs the valuation. In the case of external valuers the society transfers 90 per cent of such income to the external valuer. Leeds states that it does not charge an administration fee to potential borrowers. Because of the costs of control and administration of the valuation activities allocated internally at Leeds it reported deficits for those valuations not performed in-house. In 1990 it reported a deficit on in-house valuations but this was followed by surpluses in subsequent years. These surpluses on in-house work produced an overall surplus on all valuations from 1991 onwards.

*Figures omitted. See note on page iv.

TABLE 11  **Leeds: results of all residential valuations, 1990 to 1993**

<table>
<tr><td></td><td></td><td></td><td></td><td>£'000</td></tr>
<tr><td></td><td>1990</td><td>1991</td><td>1992</td><td>1993<br>estimated</td></tr>
<tr><td>*Income*</td><td></td><td></td><td></td><td></td></tr>
<tr><td>In-house</td><td>[</td><td colspan="2">Figures omitted.</td><td></td></tr>
<tr><td>By subsidiary</td><td></td><td colspan="2">See note on page iv.</td><td></td></tr>
<tr><td>By external valuer</td><td></td><td></td><td></td><td>]</td></tr>
<tr><td>Total</td><td>7,181</td><td>10,804</td><td>10,166</td><td>[   *   ]</td></tr>
<tr><td>Administration fees*</td><td>N/A</td><td>N/A</td><td>N/A</td><td></td></tr>
<tr><td colspan="5"></td></tr>
<tr><td>*Surplus/(deficit)*</td><td></td><td></td><td></td><td></td></tr>
<tr><td>In-house</td><td>[</td><td></td><td></td><td></td></tr>
<tr><td>By subsidiary</td><td></td><td colspan="2">Figures omitted.</td><td></td></tr>
<tr><td>By external valuer</td><td></td><td colspan="2">See note on page iv.</td><td></td></tr>
<tr><td>Total</td><td></td><td></td><td></td><td>]</td></tr>
<tr><td colspan="5" align="right">per cent</td></tr>
<tr><td>*Surplus/(deficit) as a percentage<br>of income received*</td><td></td><td></td><td></td><td></td></tr>
<tr><td>In-house</td><td>[</td><td></td><td></td><td></td></tr>
<tr><td>By subsidiary</td><td></td><td colspan="2">Figures omitted.</td><td></td></tr>
<tr><td>By external valuer</td><td></td><td colspan="2">See note on page iv.</td><td></td></tr>
<tr><td>Total</td><td></td><td></td><td></td><td>]</td></tr>
</table>

*Source:* Leeds.

*These are not identified separately on an accounting basis. Estimates of amounts retained (by calendar year) can be found in Table 3.7

17. The results of the Leeds valuing subsidiary, PLUK, are set out in Table 12. Because of the method of allocating costs to the various types of activity, the surplus or deficit as a percentage of income is the same in each year for each activity. However, returns on work undertaken were highest in 1991 (actual) at [*] per cent and lowest in 1993 where the estimated deficit is [ * ] per cent.

TABLE 12  **Leeds subsidiary company: results of all residential valuations, 1990 to 1993**

<table>
<tr><td></td><td></td><td></td><td></td><td>£'000</td></tr>
<tr><td></td><td>1990</td><td>1991</td><td>1992</td><td>1993<br>estimated</td></tr>
<tr><td>*Income in respect of work<br>undertaken:*</td><td></td><td></td><td></td><td></td></tr>
<tr><td>For owning lender:</td><td></td><td></td><td></td><td></td></tr>
<tr><td>Mortgage valuations</td><td>[</td><td></td><td></td><td></td></tr>
<tr><td>HBRs</td><td></td><td></td><td></td><td></td></tr>
<tr><td>Total</td><td></td><td></td><td></td><td></td></tr>
<tr><td>Other</td><td></td><td></td><td></td><td></td></tr>
<tr><td>Total</td><td></td><td></td><td></td><td></td></tr>
<tr><td></td><td></td><td colspan="2">Figures omitted.</td><td></td></tr>
<tr><td>*Surplus/(deficit)*</td><td></td><td colspan="2">See note on page iv.</td><td></td></tr>
<tr><td>For owning lender:</td><td></td><td></td><td></td><td></td></tr>
<tr><td>Mortgage valuations</td><td></td><td></td><td></td><td></td></tr>
<tr><td>HBRs</td><td></td><td></td><td></td><td></td></tr>
<tr><td>Total</td><td></td><td></td><td></td><td></td></tr>
<tr><td>Other</td><td></td><td></td><td></td><td></td></tr>
<tr><td>Total</td><td></td><td></td><td></td><td>]</td></tr>
<tr><td colspan="5" align="right">per cent</td></tr>
<tr><td>*Surplus/(deficit) as a percentage<br>of income received*</td><td></td><td></td><td></td><td></td></tr>
<tr><td>For owning lender:</td><td></td><td></td><td></td><td></td></tr>
<tr><td>Mortgage valuations</td><td></td><td></td><td></td><td></td></tr>
<tr><td>HBRs</td><td></td><td></td><td></td><td></td></tr>
<tr><td>Total</td><td>[</td><td></td><td>*</td><td>]</td></tr>
<tr><td>Other</td><td></td><td></td><td></td><td></td></tr>
<tr><td>Total</td><td></td><td></td><td></td><td></td></tr>
</table>

*Source:* Leeds.

*Figures omitted. See note on page iv.

229

# C&G

18. At the end of 1991 C&G disposed of its subsidiary valuation company and could not provide us with information concerning its mortgage valuation activities for the years 1990 and 1991. Accordingly, set out in Table 13 are the results of C&G alone in respect of residential mortgage valuations.

19. The surplus as a percentage of income received in respect of all mortgage valuations undertaken in-house is substantial and has been maintained over the review period in the range between [ * ] and [ * ] per cent. This is substantially higher than the other lenders. C&G had some difficulty in allocating overhead costs to its mortgage valuation activities and this may account for this substantial surplus. It charges valuation and administration fees to potential borrowers. It told us that the income from administration fees is used to defray the general expenses of processing mortgage applications and is not income in respect of valuations.

**TABLE 13   C&G: results of all residential valuations, 1990 to 1993**

£'000

| | 1990 | 1991 | 1992 | 1993 estimated |
|---|---|---|---|---|
| **Income** | | | | |
| In-house | [ | *Figures omitted.* | | |
| By subsidiary | | *See note on page iv.* | | |
| By external valuer | | | | ] |
| Total | 8,000 | 10,000 | 9,970 | [ |
| Administration fees | 4,879 | 6,517 | 6,361 | * ] |
| | | | | |
| **Surplus/(deficit)** | | | | |
| In-house | [ | | | |
| By subsidiary | | *Figures omitted.* | | |
| By external valuer | | *See note on page iv.* | | |
| Total | | | | ] |

per cent

| | | | | |
|---|---|---|---|---|
| **Surplus/(deficit) as a percentage of income received** | | | | |
| In-house | [ | | | |
| By subsidiary | | *Figures omitted.* | | |
| By external valuer | | *See note on page iv.* | | |
| Total | | | | ] |

*Source:* C&G.

---

*Figures omitted. See note on page iv.

## Metropolitan and City Police Company Fraud Squad recommended code of lending practice

## Code of practice

*(a)*    All questions on the application forms to be answered and if not applicable to be marked so no blank spaces to be left. A standard format of questions by all lenders even though all lenders will wish to retain their own style of application forms.

*(b)*    Date of birth of the applicant to be required with proof, such as a passport, birth certificate, marriage certificate or driving licence.

*(c)*    Details of present and previous addresses. Present address ought to be verifiable by virtue of the electoral roll. Check out landlords, it may be an accommodation address.

*(d)*    Inland Revenue P60 forms should be not accepted on their own as proof of income, wage slips ought to be supplied by the applicant.

*(e)*    A certificate as to who actually completed the form, if the form was submitted as part of a package application by the broker, the name of the broker and a certificate to the effect that they have checked the details and they are true and correct to the best of the brokers knowledge. Make it a condition that the solicitor sees the application form and certifies accordingly. Do not accept 'broker introduced' surveys. Survey instructions should be separate.

*(f)*    A requirement that all mortgages past and present, county court judgements and any previous repossessions should be entered on the form.

*(g)*    Direct mandate repayments to be required, if this is refused, the reasons to be given for that refusal with the application form.

*(h)*    Employment references ought to be on the paper of the employer's company or firm, not on a proforma supplied by the lenders. Check with the author to ensure that the applicant has not written his own.

*(i)*    Employers should be asked to give their employees' tax references and tax office.

*(j)*    The lenders ought to try and verify that the employer exists by reasonably simple checks in business directories or directory enquiries. Beware of off-shore companies.

*(k)*    With regard to self employed applicants. Ensure that their accounts exist and are registered. Ask the applicant for their copy of the Inland Revenue agreed assessment of Schedule D. Tax.

*(l)*    Only panel solicitors or licensed conveyancers should be used by the lender. Demand that the solicitor sees the client and application form. Demand to be informed of sub-sales.

*(m)*    Any new candidates for the panels for new solicitors or new conveyancers for attachment to the panels ought to be strictly checked with the Law Society and telephone directory. The local manager should visit their offices with a request to see their practice certificate in the case of solicitors or their licence in the case of licensed conveyancers.

*(n)*    Use a panel valuer. If the valuer is operating out of his area seek a second person.

At present, due to the different approaches adopted by police forces around the country, lenders cannot be sure whether particular cases or mortgage fraud will be investigated or not. The Metropolitan and City Police Company Fraud Squad has drawn up a 'Code of Lending Practice' which identifies criteria which the Metropolitan and City Police have suggested that lenders might comply with when processing mortgage applications. Failure to comply with the criteria on particular cases, will make it unlikely that any complaints of fraud in those cases will be investigated by the Metropolitan and City Police in the future. The Code has also been adopted by the West Yorkshire Police Force and it seems likely that other forces will follow. While it remains entirely a matter for lenders to decide whether or not to follow the police advice, failure to do so could limit the likelihood of future fraud complaints being investigated.

## List of complex monopolists identified

This list has been compiled on the basis of information provided by lenders as set out in Appendices 4.6 and 4.7 together with additional information provided by the seven largest lenders.

| *Lenders* | *a* | *c* | *d* | *e* |
|---|:---:|:---:|:---:|:---:|
| | | *Practices* | | |
| Abbey National plc | ✓ | ✓ | ✓ | - |
| AIB Bank | ✓ | ✓ | ✓ | - |
| Allchurches Mortgage Company Ltd | - | ✓ | ✓ | - |
| Alliance & Leicester Building Society | ✓ | ✓ | ✓ | ✓ |
| Allied Dunbar Mortgages Ltd | - | ✓ | ✓ | ✓ |
| Associates Capital Corporation Ltd | ✓ | - | ✓ | ✓ |
| Bank of Ireland Home Mortgages Ltd | ✓ | ✓ | ✓ | - |
| Bank of Scotland: | | | | |
|   Branches | - | - | - | - |
|   Centrebank | - | ✓ | ✓ | ✓ |
| Banque Paribas (London Branch) | ✓ | ✓ | ✓ | - |
| Barclays Bank plc | ✓ | ✓ | ✓ | - |
| Barnsley Building Society | - | ✓ | ✓ | ✓ |
| Bath Investment & Building Society | - | ✓ | ✓ | - |
| Beverley Building Society | - | ✓ | ✓ | - |
| Birmingham Midshires Building Society | ✓ | ✓ | ✓ | - |
| BNP Mortgages Ltd | ✓ | ✓ | ✓ | - |
| Bradford & Bingley Building Society | ✓ | ✓ | ✓ | - |
| Bristol & West Building Society | ✓ | ✓ | ✓ | ✓ |
| Britannia Building Society | ✓ | ✓ | ✓ | - |
| Buckinghamshire Building Society | ✓ | ✓ | ✓ | - |
| Cambridge Building Society | ✓ | ✓ | ✓ | - |
| Capital Homes Loans Ltd | ✓ | ✓ | ✓ | ✓ |
| Chelsea Building Society | ✓ | ✓ | ✓ | ✓ |
| Cheltenham & Gloucester Building Society | ✓ | ✓ | ✓ | - |
| Chesham Building Society | - | ✓ | ✓ | - |
| Cheshire Building Society | ✓ | ✓ | ✓ | ✓ |
| Chorley & District Building Society, The | ✓ | ✓ | ✓ | ✓ |
| Citibank Trust Ltd | ✓ | ✓ | ✓ | - |
| City & Metropolitan Building Society | ✓ | ✓ | ✓ | - |
| Clay Cross Benefit Building Society | ✓ | ✓ | ✓ | ✓ |
| Colonial Mutual Life Assurance Society Ltd, The | - | ✓ | ✓ | - |
| Confederation Bank Ltd | ✓ | ✓ | ✓ | - |
| Co-operative Insurance Society Ltd | ✓ | ✓ | ✓ | - |
| Coutts Finance Co | ✓ | ✓ | ✓ | - |
| Coventry Building Society | - | ✓ | ✓ | ✓ |
| Credit Agricole Personal Finance plc | ✓ | ✓ | ✓ | - |
| Credit Lyonnais | ✓ | ✓ | ✓ | ✓ |
| Cumberland Building Society | - | ✓ | ✓ | - |
| Darlington Building Society | - | ✓ | ✓ | - |
| Derbyshire Building Society | ✓ | ✓ | ✓ | - |
| Dudley Building Society | - | ✓ | ✓ | - |
| Dunfermline Building Society | ✓ | ✓ | ✓ | - |
| Ecology Building Society, The | ✓ | ✓ | ✓ | - |
| First National Bank plc | - | ✓ | ✓ | - |
| Framework Homeloans Ltd | ✓ | ✓ | ✓ | - |

| Lenders | Practices | | | |
|---|---|---|---|---|
| | a | c | d | e |
| Furness Building Society | - | ✓ | ✓ | - |
| Gainsborough Building Society | - | ✓ | ✓ | - |
| Greenwich Building Society | ✓ | ✓ | ✓ | - |
| Halifax Building Society | ✓ | ✓ | ✓ | - |
| Hanley Economic Building Society | ✓ | ✓ | ✓ | - |
| Harpenden Building Society | ✓ | ✓ | ✓ | - |
| HFC Bank plc | ✓ | ✓ | ✓ | - |
| Hinckley & Rugby Building Society | - | ✓ | ✓ | ✓ |
| Holmesdale Building Society | ✓ | ✓ | ✓ | - |
| Household Mortgage Corporation plc | ✓ | ✓ | ✓ | ✓ |
| Ilkeston Permanent Building Society | ✓ | ✓ | ✓ | ✓ |
| Ipswich Building Society | ✓ | ✓ | ✓ | ✓ |
| Irish Permanent Building Society | ✓ | ✓ | ✓ | - |
| Kent Reliance Building Society | ✓ | ✓ | ✓ | ✓ |
| Kleinwort Benson Private Bank | ✓ | ✓ | ✓ | - |
| Lambeth Building Society | - | ✓ | ✓ | - |
| Leeds & Holbeck Building Society | - | ✓ | ✓ | - |
| Leeds Permanent Building Society | ✓ | ✓ | ✓ | - |
| Leek United Building Society | - | ✓ | ✓ | ✓ |
| Legal & General Mortgage Services Ltd | ✓ | ✓ | ✓ | - |
| Lloyds Bank plc | - | ✓ | ✓ | - |
| Lloyds Bowmaker Finance Ltd | ✓ | - | ✓ | - |
| London & Manchester (Mortgages) Ltd | ✓ | ✓ | ✓ | - |
| Londonderry Provident Building Society | - | ✓ | ✓ | ✓ |
| Loughborough Building Society | - | ✓ | ✓ | ✓ |
| Manchester Building Society | ✓ | ✓ | ✓ | - |
| Mansfield Building Society, The | - | ✓ | ✓ | - |
| Market Harborough Building Society | - | ✓ | - | ✓ |
| Marsden Building Society | ✓ | ✓ | ✓ | ✓ |
| Melton Mowbray Building Society | ✓ | ✓ | ✓ | ✓ |
| Mercantile Building Society | ✓ | ✓ | ✓ | - |
| Midland Bank plc | - | ✓ | - | - |
| Monmouthshire Building Society | - | ✓ | ✓ | ✓ |
| Mortgage Business plc, The | ✓ | ✓ | ✓ | ✓ |
| Mortgage Corporation Group Ltd, The | ✓ | ✓ | ✓ | - |
| Mortgage Services Ltd | ✓ | ✓ | ✓ | - |
| Mortgage Trust Ltd | ✓ | ✓ | ✓ | - |
| National & Provincial Building Society | ✓ | ✓ | ✓ | - |
| National Counties Building Society | ✓ | ✓ | ✓ | - |
| National Home Loans Corporation plc, The | ✓ | ✓ | ✓ | - |
| National Mutual Life Assurance Society | ✓ | ✓ | ✓ | - |
| National Westminster Bank plc | ✓ | - | ✓ | - |
| Nationwide Building Society | ✓ | ✓ | ✓ | ✓ |
| Newbury Building Society | ✓ | ✓ | ✓ | - |
| Newcastle Building Society | ✓ | ✓ | ✓ | - |
| North of England Building Society | - | ✓ | ✓ | - |
| Northern Rock Building Society | ✓ | ✓ | ✓ | - |
| Norwich & Peterborough Building Society | ✓ | ✓ | ✓ | - |
| Nottingham Building Society | ✓ | ✓ | ✓ | ✓ |
| Nottingham Imperial Building Society | ✓ | ✓ | ✓ | ✓ |
| Penrith Building Society | ✓ | - | - | - |
| Portman Building Society | ✓ | ✓ | ✓ | - |
| Principality Building Society | ✓ | ✓ | ✓ | ✓ |
| Progressive Building Society | ✓ | ✓ | ✓ | ✓ |
| Royal Bank of Scotland plc, The | ✓ | ✓ | ✓ | - |
| Royal London Homebuy Ltd | ✓ | ✓ | ✓ | - |

| Lenders | Practices | | | |
|---|---|---|---|---|
| | a | c | d | e |
| Saffron Walden Herts & Essex Building Society | ✓ | ✓ | ✓ | - |
| Scarborough Building Society | - | ✓ | ✓ | - |
| Scottish Building Society | - | ✓ | ✓ | - |
| Shepshed Building Society | - | ✓ | ✓ | - |
| Skipton Building Society | ✓ | ✓ | ✓ | ✓ |
| Stafford Railway Building Society, The | - | ✓ | ✓ | - |
| Staffordshire Building Society | - | ✓ | ✓ | - |
| Standard Building Society, The | ✓ | ✓ | ✓ | ✓ |
| Stroud & Swindon Building Society | ✓ | ✓ | ✓ | - |
| Sun Life Assurance Society plc | ✓ | ✓ | ✓ | ✓ |
| Sun Life of Canada Home Loans Ltd | ✓ | ✓ | ✓ | ✓ |
| Swansea Building Society | - | ✓ | ✓ | ✓ |
| Teachers' Building Society | - | ✓ | ✓ | - |
| Tipton & Coseley Building Society | ✓ | - | - | - |
| TSB Bank plc | ✓ | - | - | - |
| Tynemouth Building Society | - | ✓ | ✓ | ✓ |
| UCB Home Loans Corporation Ltd | ✓ | ✓ | ✓ | - |
| Ulster Bank Ltd | ✓ | ✓ | ✓ | - |
| United Bank of Kuwait plc, The | ✓ | ✓ | ✓ | - |
| United Friendly Insurance plc | ✓ | ✓ | ✓ | - |
| Universal Building Society | ✓ | ✓ | ✓ | - |
| Vernon Building Society | - | ✓ | ✓ | - |
| Wesleyan Home Loans Ltd | - | ✓ | ✓ | - |
| West Bromwich Building Society | ✓ | ✓ | - | ✓ |
| West Cumbria Building Society | - | ✓ | ✓ | - |
| Western Trust & Savings Ltd | ✓ | ✓ | ✓ | ✓ |
| Woolwich Building Society | ✓ | ✓ | ✓ | ✓ |
| Yorkshire Bank Home Loans Ltd | - | ✓ | - | - |
| Yorkshire Building Society | ✓ | ✓ | ✓ | - |

Key:

✓ indicates that the lender engages in the practice specified.

a = refusing to accept valuations by any competent valuer;

c = requiring the prospective borrower to pay a set fee for the valuation based on a national scale established by the lender;

d = paying external valuers a set fee based on a national scale established by the lender;

e = requiring borrowers to pay fees in connection with valuation services which do not separately identify any administrative charges levied in connection with or incorporated in the fee.

Notes:

1. Practice b was removed during the course of the inquiry—see paragraph 9.35.

2. Practices c and d interpret national scales as those applied by lenders to mortgage transactions within their normal area of operation—see paragraph 9.37.

# Index

Printed in the United Kingdom for HMSO
Dd 509883   4/94   C15   51-1278   (3840)